H4S

Food & Nutrition

Anita Tull

Oxford University Press

Oxford University Press, Great Clarendon Street, Oxford OX2 6DP

Oxford New York

Athens Auckland Bangkok Bogota Buenos Aires
Calcutta Cape Town Chennai Dar es Salaam
Delhi Florence Hong Kong Istanbul Karachi
Kuala Lumpur Madrid Melbourne Mexico City
Mumbai Nairobi Paris São Paulo Singapore
Taipei Tokyo Toronto Warsaw

and associated companies in
Berlin Ibadan

Oxford is a trade mark of Oxford University Press

© Oxford University Press 1996
First published   1983
Second edition   1987
Third edition   1996
Reprinted   1997, 1998, 1999, 2000
ISBN 0 19 832766 8 (Student's edition)
ISBN 0 19 832768 4 (Bookshop edition)

A CIP catalogue record for this book is available from
the British Library.

Typeset and illustrated by Pentacor PLC,
High Wycombe, Bucks
Printed and bound in Spain by
Gráficas Estella, S. A.

Acknowledgements

*The publishers would like to thank the following for permission
to reproduce their photographs:*

p. 8 Chubb, p. 13 C James Webb, p. 14 Science Photo
Library/Dr Marazzi, p. 16 C James Webb, p. 17 TALC
(left), SPL/St Mary's Hospital Medical School (right), p.
20 SPL/Biophoto Associates, p. 22 SPL/Prof. Motta, p.
25 National Medical Slide Bank (right), p. 43 Tropix, p.
45 Telegraph Colour Library (bottom), pp. 46 & 47 Sally
& Richard Greenhill, p. 49 Ace Photo Agency (left),
TALC (right), p. 57 Tropix, p. 58 Telegraph Colour
Library, p. 61 Bubbles, p. 66 Ace, p. 71 Anthony Blake
(top), Sally & Richard Greenhill (bottom), p. 78
Telegraph Colour Library, p. 80 Robert Harding, p. 88
Anthony Blake (right), p. 89 Telegraph Colour Library
(top), Tropix (bottom), pp. 100 & 101 National Dairy
Council, p. 102 Ace, p. 107 National Dairy Council, p.
112 Telegraph Colour Library (bottom left & right), p.
117 Meat and Livestock Commission, p. 123 Robert
Harding, pp. 127 & 137 Telegraph Colour Library, p.
164 Canned Food Information Centre, p. 169 Birds Eye
Walls, p. 181 Kenwood, p. 183 Anthony Blake, p. 185
Brannen Thermometers, p. 188 Kenwood, p. 189
London Fire Brigade, p. 190 Anthony Blake (left),
Robert Harding (right), p. 196 Zanussi, pp. 213, 214,
215, 225 Anthony Blake, p. 245 Addis, p. 246 Anthony
Blake, p. 248 Tricity Bendix, p. 249 Anthony Blake, pp.
255 & 256 Kenwood, p. 259 Prestige, p. 260 Salters, p.
266 Nat West Stream Line, p. 269 SHOUT!

Special thanks to J Sainsbury plc; Tesco Stores Ltd; the
Domestic Fowl Trust.

Additional photographs by Martin Sookias.

Pie chart on p. 74 reproduced by permission of The
Food Magazine, published by the Food Commission.
Graphs on pp. 148 & 149 from *Social Trends 25*, 1995,
Office for National Statistics. Crown Copyright 1995.
Reproduced by permission of the Controller of HMSO
and the Office for National Statistics.
Diagrams on p. 192 (bottom) reproduced by permission
of Panasonic Consumer Electronics UK.
Graphs and charts on pp. 234, 273, 275 reproduced by
permission of the Consumers' Association. *Which?* is
published by the Consumers' Association and is available
only on subscription. For details write to *Which?*,
Freepost, Hertford SG14 1YB, UK.

Preface

This book is designed to provide a comprehensive text for students working towards GCSE examinations in food and nutrition. It will also be a valuable resource for students on GCSE courses in food technology, and on related GNVQ courses.

The text has been fully revised to include the latest dietary guidelines, up-to-date information on diet and health, and current legislation on the safe supply of food. The impact of food technology on choice and availability of food is covered, and a new chapter looks at providing food for different needs. Scientific aspects of the subject are emphasized so that students can understand the value of food, and the principles behind its production, storage, preparation, and use. Practical food preparation, hygiene and safety, kitchen equipment, and consumer protection are also covered.

The book is divided into five chapters. At the end of each section within a chapter there are short revision questions, arranged in order of difficulty, for use in class or for private study. Each chapter ends with a series of more structured questions and activities that require investigation and individual or group study. The clearly illustrated, full colour text also includes experimental work to form a link between the practical and theoretical aspects of food science.

Contents

5 The kitchen

Index

❶ Nutrition

Diet and health

Food is vital to life. It can be defined as any solid or liquid substance which, when taken by the body, provides it with the necessary materials to enable it to grow, to replace worn-out and damaged parts, and to function normally.

The human body is like a complex piece of machinery in that it is prone to faults and weaknesses it if is poorly maintained. This can happen if too little or too much food is eaten, or if the daily food intake is in any way unbalanced.

One way of ensuring that health and fitness are maintained, when food is plentiful, is to have an understanding of food and its effects on the body and to use this knowledge wisely.

What is nutrition?

Food, like other substances, is composed of different chemical elements, arranged in a variety of ways to form **molecules**. These molecules collectively give individual foods their flavour, colour, and texture, and affect their reaction to heat and their digestion.

The body uses some of the molecules in food to function correctly and to stay healthy. These are the **nutrients**. There are many different nutrients, and each has its own function in the body. Each nutrient is vital to life, and the health of an individual will suffer if any one nutrient is in short supply.

The study of nutrients and their relationship with food and living things is called **nutrition**.

Most foods contain more than one nutrient, so are of use to the body in several ways. Some foods, such as sugar, contain only one nutrient, and are of limited use to the body. However, no single food provides *all* the nutrients required by the body in sufficient quantities, so a variety of foods must be eaten.

The terms used in the study of nutrition include the following.

Diet means the food that a person normally eats every day. There are also special diets, e.g. slimming diets, low-fat diets.

Malnutrition means an incorrect or unbalanced intake of nutrients.

Under-nutrition means an insufficient total intake of nutrients.

Balanced diet means a diet that provides the correct amount of nutrients for the needs of an individual.

Metabolism

The human body is a complex living structure composed of millions of individual units called **cells**. Cells are grouped into systems containing various **tissues** and **organs**, each performing special functions.

Within the body, chemical reactions and changes are continually taking place. These enable the body to carry out all the necessary functions and processes, as well as to grow and to replace damaged and worn-out body cells. This complex collection of chemical reactions is called **metabolism**.

Energy is required for all metabolic reactions, and the body must remain healthy if it is to be efficient. This is mainly achieved by the intake of nutrients in food. Humans, like all living things, must have a regular supply.

The nutrients

There are five main groups of nutrients:

protein
fat
carbohydrate
vitamins
minerals

Each group has several members, which each have their own chemical names.

Macronutrients are needed by the body in relatively large amounts. They include protein, fat, carbohydrate, and the mineral elements sodium, calcium, potassium, phosphorus, and magnesium.

Micronutrients are needed by the body in smaller amounts. They include vitamins, essential fatty acids, and trace elements (the minerals iron, zinc, copper, iodine, selenium, chromium, and cobalt).

Water can also be called a nutrient, as it is vital to life.

Some foods contain **dietary fibre** or **non-starch polysaccharide (NSP)**, which is not strictly a nutrient, but is still of importance to the body. It will be discussed separately.

Dietary reference values

The Department of Health has compiled charts showing people's requirements for energy and nutrients. The figures in the charts are given the general name dietary reference values (DRVs). People's need for nutrients varies throughout their life. For example, the needs of a 5-year-old boy are different from those of a pregnant woman. DRVs are therefore given for particular groups of the population. They are not meant to be specific targets for individuals.

Two particular DRVs are important:

estimated average requirement (EAR) and
reference nutrient intake (RNI).

The RNI is the amount of a nutrient required to meet the daily needs of 97% of each group in the population. In this book, we use RNIs.

People who are ill, undernourished, or have a particular medical condition may have different needs for certain nutrients.

For energy requirements an average figure is given because people vary greatly in how much energy they use every day. If the figure was set too high some people would become obese if they were to eat food with the recommended energy value each day.

Protein

Functions

Our bodies are composed of millions of cells which are constantly being replaced and repaired. As the body grows, new cells are added.

Each cell contains a substance called **protoplasm**, which contains (amongst other things) protein. Protein is vital for the **growth**, **repair**, and **maintenance** of the body.

Protein can also be used to provide the body with energy, once it has been used for its main functions of growth and repair.

Chemistry

There are many different proteins and they are all complex molecules which contain these elements:

oxygen (O)   carbon (C)
hydrogen (H)   nitrogen (N)

and sometimes:

sulphur (S)   phosphorus (P)

The protein molecules are made up of small units joined together like links in a chain. These units are called **amino-acids**.

At least 22 different amino-acids are known to occur naturally, and each has its own chemical name. Different proteins are made when different numbers and types of amino-acids

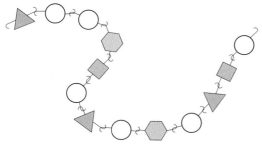

A protein chain. Each different shape represents a different amino acid.

These foods are good sources of animal protein.

combine. An enormous number of different proteins can be made from 22 amino-acids. (Think how many words can be made from the 26 letters of the alphabet.)

Sources

Of these 22 amino-acids:

ten are **indispensable** (**essential**) for growth and repair in **children**.

eight are **indispensable** for repair and maintenance in **adults**.

This means that they must be obtained from foods containing protein in the diet, as they cannot be made in the body.

Proteins that contain all the **indispensable amino-acids** (IAAs) in sufficient quantity are said to be of **high biological value** (HBV). They are sometimes also called **complete** proteins.

HBV proteins are found mainly in animal foods:

meat, cheese, fish, milk, eggs

Proteins that lack one or more of the IAAs are said to be of **low biological value** (LBV). They are sometimes also called **incomplete** proteins.

LBV proteins are found mainly in plant foods:

cereals, e.g. wheat, rice, oats

pulses, e.g. peas, beans, lentils

some nuts

vegetables (a little)

quorn mycoprotein (see p. 130)

There are two exceptions to this:

soya beans (plant) contain HBV protein

gelatine (animal) contains LBV protein

LBV protein foods are not inferior to HBV protein foods. Indeed, if a combination of LBV foods is eaten together, e.g. beans on toast (wheat), or lentil soup with bread, then the IAAs which are limited in one are provided by the other. In this way, proteins complement each other to provide a sufficient supply of IAAs.

Animal protein foods are expensive to produce, and recently there have been attempts to manufacture alternative protein-rich foods from, for example, soya beans. This is discussed in greater detail on pp. 129–30).

Protein names

Each protein has its own chemical name.

Protein name	Where found
Collagen	meat, fish (connective tissue)
Myosin	meat, fish (muscle tissue)
Elastin	meat (muscle fibres)
Caseinogen	milk, cheese
Lactalbumin	milk
Lactoglobulin	milk
Ovalbumin	egg white
Mucin	egg white
Lipovitellin	egg yolk
Gluten (glutenin)	wheat
Gliadin	wheat
Zein	maize
Hordenin	barley

Protein requirements

Everyone needs some protein in their daily diet, even when they have stopped growing, but at certain times of our lives these needs increase. For example:

Babies and children require a lot of protein as they are growing rapidly.

Adolescents require protein for their rapid spurt of growth.

Pregnant women require more than normal to cater for the growing baby.

Nursing mothers require more than normal for milk production during breast-feeding (lactation).

Protein is required at all other times for body maintenance, repair, and the growth of hair, nails, and skin.

RNIs for protein

Age	Grams per day
Children	
0–3 months	12.5
4–6 months	12.7
7–9 months	13.7
10–12 months	14.9
1–3 years	14.5
4–6 years	19.7
7–10 years	28.3
Males	
11–14 years	42.1
15–18 years	55.2
19–50 years	55.5
50+ years	53.3
Females	
11–14 years	41.2
15–18 years	45.4
19–50 years	45.0
50+ years	46.5
Pregnant	51.0
Lactating	56.0

Deficiency

Protein deficiency is rare in the UK, but in poor countries it may contribute to the symptoms associated with famine (see p. 43).

Effect of heat

When proteins are heated, their chemical structure is **denatured** (changed). This is a permanent alteration and cannot be reversed. As heating continues, proteins **coagulate** (set), and generally become less soluble. If overheated, they become less digestible. The effect of heat on specific proteins is shown below.

Meat
Dry or moist heat

Collagen and elastin molecules start to coagulate at 60°C, contracting as they do so, and causing the meat to shrink. Under 100°C, coagulation is slow; over 100°C, coagulation is rapid and the protein becomes hard and less digestible. In the presence of moisture, collagen is converted into the protein gelatin, which is soluble.

Milk
Boiling or baking

Lactalbumin and lactoglobulin coagulate gradually as milk is heated, and form a 'skin' on the surface.

Cheese
Dry heat

Protein coagulates rapidly to a rubbery texture and finally to a crisp and less digestible state.

Egg white
Dry or moist heat

At 60°C coagulation starts when ovalbumin denatures into a solid, and continues until the whole white is solid and opaque.

Egg yolk
Dry or moist heat

Proteins start to denature at 70°C, and continue to do so until the yolk becomes dry and hard.

Wheat
Dry heat

Gluten starts to coagulate at 80°C, and continues to do so until the heating ends. In this way it helps to form the structure of cakes, bread, and other baked wheat products, during baking (see pp. 87–8).

Denaturation of protein is also brought about by:

Mechanical agitation, as in the whipping of egg white, which causes ovalbumin to set partially.

Acids and alcohol, as in the marinading of meat in vinegar, wine, etc., and the clotting of caesinogen in the stomach, which is aided by acid.

Revision questions

1 What are the functions of protein?
2 What chemical elements make up proteins?
3 What is an amino-acid?
4 What is an indispensable amino-acid?
5 How many indispensable amino-acids do
   a adults require?
   b children require?
6 Explain why the following have a high requirement for protein:
   a children
   b pregnant women
   c adolescents
7 What are high biological value proteins and in which foods are they mainly found?
8 What are low biological value proteins and in which foods are they mainly found?
9 How can LBV protein foods be made more valuable to the body?
10 Name two proteins found in
   a meat
   b milk
   c egg
   d cereals
11 Describe the effect of heat on meat, egg, and milk proteins.
12 What is denaturation?

Fat

Functions

1 Provides a convenient and concentrated source of energy, supplying more energy than the same weight of carbohydrate or protein (see p. 29).
2 Surrounds and protects certain vital organs, e.g. kidneys, glands.
3 Forms an insulating layer (adipose tissue) beneath the skin to help preserve body heat and protect the skeleton and organs.
4 Forms part of the structure of cell membranes throughout the body, especially in the brain.
5 Provides a source of the fat-soluble vitamins A, D, E, and K.
6 Provides a reserve of energy for long–term storage, which can be used if energy intake is restricted.
7 Provides texture and flavour in food and helps to make it palatable.
8 Foods containing fat provide a feeling of fullness (satiety) after a meal, as fat digestion is slow.

Chemistry

Fats and oils have the same basic chemical structure, but their physical appearances differ at normal room temperature.

Fats are **solid** at room temperature.

Oils are **liquid** at room temperature.

In this section the word 'fat' refers to both fats and oils. Sometimes the word 'lipid' is used to describe a fat. This is a scientific term for all types of fats and oils, not all of which are edible. If the word lipid appears on a food label, it is referring to fat.

Fats are composed of the elements:

carbon
oxygen
hydrogen

These elements make up molecules of glycerol and fatty acids, which combine to form fat molecules in the following way:

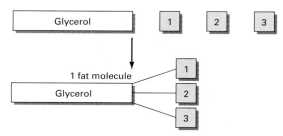

1 unit of glycerol + 3 fatty acids

The scientific name for this fat molecule is a triglycerol (sometimes called a triglyceride).

At least 40 different fatty acids are known, each with its own chemical name. They may be either **saturated** or **unsaturated**, according to the way in which their carbon and hydrogen atoms are arranged.

Saturated fatty acids

All the carbon atoms are **saturated** with hydrogen atoms and cannot accept any more:

$$\cdots C - C - C \cdots$$

Examples	*Found mainly in:*
Butyric acid	milk, butter
Palmitic acid	animal fats
Lauric acid	dairy foods, coconut oil
Stearic acid	beef fat

Fats that are solid at room temperature are mostly made up of saturated fatty acids.

Unsaturated fatty acids

Some of the carbon atoms are joined to others by a **double bond** and so are not completely saturated with hydrogen atoms. They could therefore accept more hydrogen atoms:

$$\cdots C - C - C = C - C \cdots$$

Monounsaturated fatty acids have one double bond in the molecule, e.g. oleic acid, found in most animal and plant fats and oils, especially olive oil.

Polyunsaturated fatty acids have more than one double bond in the molecule, e.g. linoleic acid and linolenic acid, both found mainly in vegetable oils. Unsaturated fatty acids occur mainly in oils.

Unsaturated fatty acids may be either **cis** or **trans**, depending on how the atoms are arranged at the double bonds. Cis fatty acids are thought to be better for us than trans fatty acids.

Different combinations of fatty acids combine with glycerol to form a wide variety of fat molecules.

Sources

Most fats contain a mixture of saturated and unsaturated fatty acids, but in widely varying proportions. This affects the hardness of the fat. Fats and oils are obtained from both plants and animals.

These foods are high in fat.

Fat is present in food either as visible or invisible fat.

Visible fat is easy to detect in food:
fat on meat
butter, margarine, lard, suet
cooking fats and oils

Invisible fat is a constituent part of food, and is difficult to detect:
lean meat – fat within muscle (marbling)
egg yolk
flesh of oily fish
nuts, seeds, fruits
prepared foods, e.g. pastry, cakes, biscuits
fried foods, e.g. fritters, croquettes

Animal sources

Meat Lard, bacon fat (pigs) Suet (cattle) Visible and invisible fat	Solid fats, containing mostly saturated fatty acids.
Dairy produce Fat in milk and milk products (butter, cream, cheese) Egg yolk	A mixture of unsaturated and short-chain saturated fatty acids, as oils.
Fish Fish-liver oils (cod, halibut) Oily fish (tuna, herring, salmon, pilchard, etc.)	Oils, containing mostly unsaturated fatty acids.

Plant sources

Seeds Cotton, maize, sesame, olive, soya, sunflower, rapeseed, etc. *Nuts and pulses* Brazil, peanut, etc. *Kernels* Palm etc.	Oils, containing mostly polyunsaturated fatty acids.
Fruits Avocado pear (oil in flesh)	Mostly mono-unsaturated fatty acids.

Requirements

The body can adapt most fatty acids in food to suit its requirements. However, there are some fatty acids that the body needs but cannot make itself. These are called **essential fatty acids (EFAs)**.

Linoleic acid and linolenic acid are essential fatty acids which are found mainly in plant oils. They are needed for the brain development of babies. Humans make special essential fatty acids from linolenic and linoleic acids in breast milk. This is one of the reasons why human breast milk is best for babies.

Oily fish (e.g. herrings, sardines, mackerel) contain EFAs called **omega 6** and **omega 3**. Omega 3 EFAs may help lower the blood cholesterol and help prevent blood clots. For this reason it is recommended that people eat two portions of oily fish per week. Some oily fish products now mention omega 3 on their labels.

Dietary reference values for fat

The figures below show the maximum percentage of total daily intake of energy that should come from fat, for adults, to help prevent heart disease and obesity.

Saturated fatty acids	no more than 11% of energy intake
Polyunsaturated fatty acids	no more than 6% of energy intake
Monounsaturated fatty acids	no more than 12% of energy intake
Trans fatty acids	no more than 2% of energy intake
Total fatty acids	no more than 30% of energy intake
Total fat	no more than 35% of energy intake

Fat-soluble vitamins A, D, E, and K must also be provided by food containing fat.

A fat-free diet is not only difficult to prepare but also very unpalatable. The amount of fat that people eat varies greatly according to individual taste and according to traditional methods of food preparation in different societies. In the UK, our total fat consumption has risen steadily since the beginning of this century (except during food rationing in the Second World War), and currently, fat provides an average of 35–45% of our total energy requirements. For total energy requirement figures, see p. 32.

There have also been major changes in the types of fat that we eat. We eat more invisible fat today, in the form of crisps, snacks, cakes, and biscuits, and more fat from plant sources, as oils and margarine.

This increase in fat consumption has led to concern for our health, as it has been linked to a variety of diseases including obesity (see p. 47) and heart disease (see p. 45).

Food manufacturers have responded to the advice that people should reduce the total amount of fat they eat. A variety of low- and reduced-fat food products are available, including items such as biscuits, creams, cheeses, milk, sausages, margarines, and prepared main meals (see p. 33 for more information).

When fat catches fire, it burns rapidly.

These foods are low in fat.

Effect of heat

When heated, solid fats melt to become liquid oils. As heating continues, the oil becomes thinner, and begins to bubble. At very high temperatures, the fat molecules begin to decompose into glycerol and fatty acids. A blue haze can be seen, then smoke, and soon after this, the fat ignites and burns rapidly.

Fried foods readily absorb fat and this increases their energy value (see p. 33).

Fat-soluble vitamins are not affected by heat.

Revision questions

1. What are the functions of fat in the body?
2. What is the difference between fats and oils?
3. What chemical elements make up fats?
4. How are fat molecules composed?
5. Name four plant and four animal sources of fat.
6. What is the difference between visible and invisible fat?
7. Name three saturated and three unsaturated fatty acids.
8. Why is an excessive intake of fat undesirable?
9. What factors are associated with coronary heart disease?
10. Describe the effect of heat on fat.
11. What are essential fatty acids?
12. How does breastfeeding help to make sure that babies get EFAs in their diet?

Carbohydrate

Functions

The body requires a source of **energy** in order to function. Carbohydrate is an important source of energy and it acts as a 'protein sparer', so that protein can be used for its primary functions rather than as a source of energy (see p. 2).

Chemistry

There are several types of carbohydrate, but they all contain three elements:

carbon

oxygen

hydrogen

Oxygen and hydrogen are present in the same proportion as in water (H_2O), hence the term 'hydrate'.

Sources

Carbohydrates are produced mainly by plants during the process of **photosynthesis**, in which the following reaction occurs:

carbon dioxide + water
(CO_2)   (H_2O)

ENERGY FROM
SUNLIGHT

carbohydrate + oxygen
(O_2)

The carbohydrate produced by the plants is stored for future use.

Classification of carbohydrates

Monosaccharides

These are sometimes called **simple sugars**, as they are the common base units from which other carbohydrates are built, and they are chemically sugars. They are soluble in water and of varying sweetness.

There are three main monosaccharides.

Fructose

Fructose is sometimes called 'fruit sugar', because it is found predominantly in fruits, plant juices, and honey.

Glucose

Glucose is the form of carbohydrate that the body uses for energy, and all other carbohydrates are converted into glucose during digestion. The glucose is then circulated around the bloodstream to the body cells.

Glucose is found in ripe fruits and some vegetables, e.g. onions, beetroot. It is also available commercially in powdered, liquid, or tablet form. It provides a fast source of energy and is often taken by athletes for this reason.

Galactose

Galactose is found in the milk of mammals, where it forms part of the milk sugar, lactose.

Disaccharides

These are sometimes called **double sugars**, as they are composed of two monosaccharide units joined together. They are soluble in water.

There are three main disaccharides.

Sucrose

Sucrose is formed from one unit of **glucose** and one unit of **fructose**:

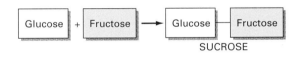

SUCROSE

Sucrose is most commonly used in cookery, and is obtained by refining sugar cane or beet. It is also present in some fruits and vegetables.

Lactose

Lactose is formed from one unit of **glucose** and one unit of **galactose**:

LACTOSE

Lactose is found in the milk of mammals, to supply the infant with a source of energy. It is not as sweet as sucrose.

Maltose

Maltose is formed from two units of **glucose**:

It is sometimes called 'malt sugar', and is found in cereals such as barley, where it is formed during germination.

During digestion, disaccharides are broken down to glucose and other monosaccharides before being absorbed into the bloodstream.

Sugars are also classified as follows:

Intrinsic sugars are those that form part of the cell structure of plants, e.g. in fruit.

Extrinsic sugars are not part of the cell structure of plants. They include **non-milk extrinsic sugars** (**NMES**) (e.g. refined sugar, extracted sugars in honey and fruit juice, sugars added to foods) and **milk sugars** (mostly lactose, found naturally in milk and milk products).

Polysaccharides

These are formed from a varying number of monosaccharide units – the prefix 'poly' means 'many'. They are usually insoluble in cold water and are tasteless.

There are five main polysaccharides.

Starch

Starch is formed from many **glucose** units joined together like links in a chain:

It is formed during photosynthesis in plants as

a chief food reserve, in particular in root vegetables, cereals, and pulses.

During digestion, the chains of glucose units are broken down into smaller chains, then into disaccharides, and finally into single glucose units, which are absorbed into the blood.

Dextrin

Dextrin is formed when foods containing starch, e.g. bread, are baked or toasted. The dextrin forms part of the crust on such foods and is more soluble than starch.

Cellulose

Cellulose is formed by plants from **glucose** units joined together in such a way that a strong, structural material is produced. The plants uses this for support in stems, leaves, husks of seeds, and bark. It is found in virtually all foods of plant origin. Despite being composed of glucose, it cannot be digested by humans, but it is of great value to the body as dietary fibre, NSP (see p. 26).

Pectin

Pectin is a complex polysaccharide formed by some plants, e.g. plums, apples, in their fruits and roots. It forms gels in water and is responsible for setting jam (see p. 171). It can be commercially extracted for this purpose.

Glycogen

Glycogen is formed after digestion in humans and other animals. To ensure that the body has a reserve of energy that can be quickly used, some glucose is converted into glycogen for temporary storage in the liver and muscles. When energy is required, it is converted to glucose.

Non-starch polysaccharides (NSP)

Non-starch polysaccharides include cellulose, pectin, and gums such as carrageenan, gum arabic, and locust bean gum. They make up what we know as dietary fibre. They are not digested by micro-organisms in the large intestine, and are very important in removing waste from the digestive system (see pp. 26–8).

Carbohydrate requirements

Carbohydrate should be used in preference to protein as an energy supplier, so that protein can be used for body growth and repair. Protein- and carbohydrate-rich foods are usually eaten together for this reason, e.g. meat and potatoes, bread and cheese.

If someone eats more carbohydrate than the body requires, the excess is converted into fat and stored under the skin. This is one of the major causes of obesity (see pp. 46–7). Eating too many carbohydrate-based snack and convenience foods, e.g. sweets, chocolate, instant meals, and puddings,

These foods are rich in carbohydrates.

may lead to an excess intake of energy from carbohydrate, so these foods should be eaten in moderation.

For total energy requirement figures see p. 32.

Effect of heat on carbohydrate

Sugar
Dry heat
Sugar first melts, then caramelizes, and finally burns, leaving a black residue.
Wet heat
Sugar first dissolves, then becomes a syrup which caramelizes, and finally burns when the water has evaporated.

Starch
Dry heat
Starch changes to dextrin.
Wet heat
Starch grains first soften, then absorb water and swell, causing some to rupture. The starch then dissolves to form a paste.

Revision questions

1 Why does the body require carbohydrate?
2 What chemical elements make up carbohydrates?
3 What happens if too much carbohydrate is eaten?
4 Name three monosaccharides and give their sources.
5 Name three disaccharides, describe their composition, and give their sources.
6 Name four polysaccharides, describe their composition, and give their sources.
7 What is photosynthesis and why is it important?
8 Explain, with examples, the difference between intrinsic and extrinsic sugars.
9 What is NSP?
10 Describe the effects of heat on sugar and starch.

Food tests

It is possible to test different foods for the presence of protein, fat, and carbohydrate by using special chemical solutions. Such experiments should only be carried out in a laboratory. Wear protective clothing and goggles, do not eat the food, and wash your hands thoroughly afterwards.

Test for protein
The **Biuret test** is used. Make the food to be tested as liquid as possible (e.g. milk, egg white, cheese liquidized with water), and place in a test tube. Add an equal volume of 2 molar sodium hydroxide plus 1 drop of 0.1 molar copper(II) sulphate solution.

A mauve colour develops if protein is present.

Test for fat
Ethanol is used. Place the food to be tested, e.g. cooking oil, egg yolk, finely grated cheese, crushed nut, in a clean, dry test tube with some ethanol (2 drops of oil to 5 cm^3 of ethanol). Shake thoroughly to dissolve the fat, then pour the solution into another test tube containing a little water.

A cloudy white emulsion indicates the presence of fat.

Tests for carbohydrate
Test for starch
Iodine solution is used. Heat the food to be tested, e.g. starch powder, potato, flour, ground rice, in water and boil to cook the starch. When cool, add a few drops of iodine solution.

A dark blue colour means starch is present.

Test for glucose

Benedict's solution is used. Boil the food to be tested, e.g. glucose syrup, banana, in a test tube with a little of the Benedict's solution. Take care as it may boil out of the tube.

If glucose is present, the mixture will change from clear blue to opaque green, then to yellow, then to brick red.

Vitamins

Vitamins are a group of chemical substances, most of which have been identified during this century as vital to the body. At first, scientists labelled each with a letter, but once their chemical composition was discovered, they were all given names. However, the letter classification is still in use.

The body requires only small amounts of each vitamin, but as it cannot make most of them itself, they must be supplied by food. In general, vitamins are required to regulate the maintenance and growth of the body, and to control metabolic reactions in cells.

A diet lacking in one or more vitamins will result in specific **deficiency diseases**. Many of these occur in poor countries.

Vitamins can be classified according to the substances in which they dissolve. There are two groups:

1   **Fat-soluble vitamins**: vitamins A, D, E, and K.
2   **Water-soluble vitamins**: vitamin C and the vitamin-B complex.

Fat-soluble vitamins

Retinol (vitamin A)

Functions

1   Required to make a substance called **visual purple**, which is formed in the retina of the eye to enable it to see in dim light.
2   Required to keep the **mucous membranes** in the throat and the digestive,

bronchial, and excretory systems moist and free from infection.

3   Required for the maintenance and health of the skin.
4   Required for the normal growth of children, particularly the bones and teeth.

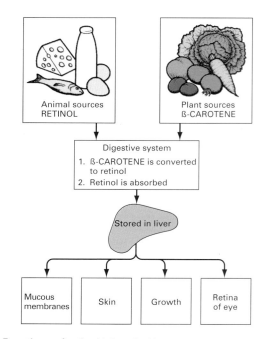

Functions of retinol (vitamin A)

Sources

Vitamin A is found as **retinol** in animal foods, particularly:

milk, cheese, eggs (yolk), butter
oily fish, e.g. herring, pilchard, sardine
liver, kidney, cod- and halibut-liver oil

Vitamin A is found as beta(β)-carotene in plant foods, especially:

carrots, spinach, watercress, apricots, parsley, cabbage, tomatoes, prunes

It gives plants their orange/yellow colour, although in green vegetables, the colour is masked by green chlorophyll. In the body, β-carotene is converted to retinol. Two parts of β-carotene are required to form one part of retinol.

β-Carotene is used as a food colouring in many different foods, and has the number E160(a) (see p.143).

It may offer protection against heart disease (see p. 45) and some cancers.

Requirements

As vitamin A is fat-soluble, it can be stored in the body, mainly in the liver, so a daily supply is not always necessary.

RNIs for vitamin A	
Age	**µg per day**
Children	
0–12 months	350
1–3 years	400
4–6 years	400
7–10 years	500
Males	
11–14 years	600
15–50+ years	700
Females	
11–50+ years	600
Pregnant	700
Lactating	950

One microgram (µg) is one millionth of a gram.

Too much vitamin A in the diet is poisonous, as it is stored in the body, and can seriously affect skin and joints, especially in children.

Pregnant women are advised not to eat liver, because it contains very high amounts of retinol which could lead to damage and defects in the unborn baby. β-Carotene does not cause harm in this way, so it is advisable for pregnant women to eat plenty of fresh fruit and vegetables, in order to receive the extra vitamin A that they need.

Special requirements

Children need plenty for growth and development.

People who cannot digest and absorb fat well may need a vitamin A injection to overcome this.

Deficiency

1   The retina ceases to make visual purple, and vision in dim light is impaired, leading to **night blindness**. In severe cases the structure of the eye deteriorates and eventually ruptures, causing total blindness.

2   The skin and mucous membranes become dry and infected, and resistance to disease is reduced.

3   Growth of children is retarded.
    This occurs frequently in poor countries, such as India, where the diet is deficient in vitamin A and the liver does not build up a store of the vitamin. During pregnancy, many women develop a deficiency, as the growing baby takes any vitamin A that is available. Many babies develop a deficiency soon after birth as they do not receive an adequate supply from food. Every year, many children go blind as a result.

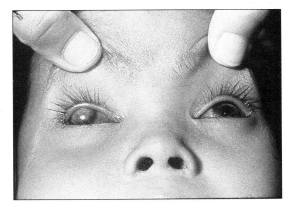

A deficiency of retinol (vitamin A) can cause blindness.

Stability in food preparation

Retinol and β-carotene are both insoluble in water, and are unaffected by normal temperatures and methods of food preparation.

Cholecalciferol (vitamin D)

Functions

Required for the proper formation of bones and teeth, which contain large amounts of the minerals **calcium** and **phosphorus**. Vitamin D helps to promote the absorption of these minerals. After digestion, they are absorbed from the small intestine into the blood, which takes them to the bones and teeth.

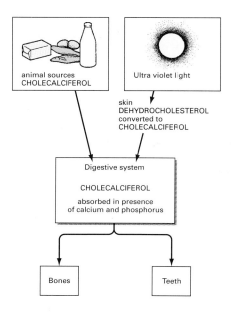

Functions of cholecalciferol (vitamin D)

Sources

Cholecalciferol is found in good supply in:
    liver
    fish–liver oils
    oily fish, e.g. herring, pilchard, sardine
It is found in smaller amounts in:
    egg yolk
    margarine (added by law)
    milk and dairy products (variable supply)
Sunlight is also an important source. When the body is exposed to the ultra-violet rays of the sun, a substance under the skin (dehydrocholesterol) is converted to cholecalciferol, which is stored in the liver, to be used as required. This accounts for the variable supply of vitamin D in dairy foods, as it depends on the dairy animal's exposure to the sun.

Requirements

Vitamin D is fat soluble and can be stored in the body. Most people make enough vitamin D from the action of sunlight on their skin, so no RNIs are given for school-age children, adolescents, and adults. Only people who do not get enough sunlight – because they are housebound or totally cover their body as part of a religious custom – are likely to be deficient.

RNIs for vitamin D

Age	µg per day
Children	
0–6 months	8.5
7 months – 3 years	7.0
Pregnant women	10.0
Lactating women	10.0
65+ years	10.0

Too much vitamin D in the diet can be dangerous as it results in an excess absorption of calcium into the blood. The extra calcium is deposited in the lungs and kidneys and can cause death.

Deficiency

1. Absorption of calcium and phosphorus from the small intestine is reduced, so that there is insufficient to maintain the strength of the teeth and bones. These become weak, and the bones of the legs may bend under the weight of the body. The ends of the limb bones become enlarged and the skull becomes fragile. This disease is called **rickets**, and mainly affects children.
2. An adult form of rickets known as **osteomalacia** may occur, particularly in the elderly, and can result in serious fractures after even a minor fall.
3. Growth of children is retarded.

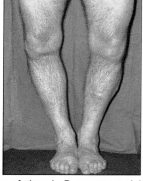

A deficiency of vitamin D can cause rickets in children and osteomalacia in adults.

Stability in food preparation

Vitamin D is unaffected by normal cooking temperatures and processes, and does not dissolve in water.

Tocopherol (vitamin E)

Functions

Vitamin E is a very effective antioxidant, and protects polyunsaturated fatty acids from damage by free radicals, especially in cell membranes in the body. Research shows that this can help protect against heart disease (see p. 45). It also has other functions in the body which are still being researched.

Vitamin E is widely used in the food industry as an antioxidant to stop fats becoming rancid (see p. 92).

Sources

Vitamin E is found in small quantities in many plants, especially:

    lettuce, grasses
    peanuts, seeds
    wheatgerm oil
    vegetable oils, especially sunflower seed oil

It is also found in milk and milk products and in egg yolk.

These foods are rich in vitamin E.

Deficiency

Deficiency of vitamin E is rare, but premature babies and people who cannot absorb fat may show signs of an increased breakdown of red blood cells, muscle tissue damage, and swelling of adipose (fatty) tissue.

Vitamin K

Several substances with similar functions are known to exist in this group, so there is more than one vitamin K.

Functions

Vitamin K assists in the production of coagulation factors in the blood, to enable it to clot properly after an injury.

Sources

Vitamin K is widely distributed in foods, especially in leafy vegetables such as spinach. Bacteria that are normally present in the intestinal tract also produce a useful supply of the vitamin, which the body is able to use.

Deficiency

A deficiency is rare, but as a precaution, babies are given vitamin K immediately after they are born, so that their blood will clot if they are injured.

Revision questions

1 List the functions of vitamins A and D.
2 List the sources of retinol.
3 List the sources of β-carotene.
4 List the food sources of vitamin D.
5 Why is margarine a good source of vitamins A and D?
6 What are the symptoms of a deficiency of vitamins A and D?
7 Why are babies prone to vitamin A deficiency in poor countries?
8 What is the link between vitamin D and the minerals calcium and phosphorus?
9 Why is milk produced in summer richer in vitamins A and D than winter milk?
10 How does ultra-violet light help the body to make vitamin D?
11 Why is too much vitamin D dangerous?
12 What are the functions of vitamins E and K?
13 List the main sources of vitamins E and K.
14 What is the link between β-carotene, vitamin E, and coronary heart disease?

Water-soluble vitamins

Vitamin-B complex

At one time it was thought that vitamin B was a single compound, but further research revealed that it is made up of at least 13 substances, which is why it is called the vitamin-B complex. The main vitamins in the complex are described here.

Sources

The main food sources of the vitamin-B complex are:

cereals, especially wholegrain cereals
cereal products, e.g. bread, flour
yeast and yeast extracts, beer
wheatgerm
all meat, especially pork, ham, bacon
liver, kidney, heart
eggs
fish roe
milk

These foods are rich in B vitamins.

Thiamin (vitamin B₁)

Functions

1   Involved in the complex series of metabolic reactions that release **energy** from carbohydrate.
2   Required for the normal **growth** of children and for general health.
3   Required for the function and maintenance of the **nerves**.

Requirements

Thiamin cannot be stored by the body, so a daily supply is necessary for all age groups (see p. 18).

(see p. 18)

Requirements increase during pregnancy and lactation, and during periods of increased metabolism, e.g. muscular activity, and some illnesses. People in very active jobs are therefore likely to need more thiamin.

Bacteria that are normally present in the intestinal tract are able to make some thiamin in humans and other mammals. However, this is only a small contribution to the daily intake.

Deficiency

A deficiency of thiamin may occur for several reasons, including:

alcoholism
some digestive disorders
pregnancy, due to loss of appetite, vomiting

A deficiency may cause:

1   Depression, irritability, difficulty in concentration, defective memory, anxiety.
2   Growth retarded in children.
3   Nerves become inflamed and painful (neuritis), muscles become weak, reflexes are reduced.
4   Severe deficiency leads to the disease **beri-beri**.

A patient with beri-beri becomes exhausted and loses weight; muscles become weak, especially in the legs; ankles and wrists drop. Fluid may be retained in the tissues, causing swelling.

Stability in food preparation

Thiamin is very soluble in water, and some is destroyed by the high temperatures used in cooking.

Riboflavin (vitamin B₂)

Functions

1 Essential for normal growth.
2 Required for the release of energy from food, especially amino-acids and fat, by **oxidation**.

Requirements

Riboflavin can be stored in small amounts in the liver, spleen, and kidneys, but a daily supply is required by all age groups.

Bacteria normally present in the intestine can produce some riboflavin, but not enough to meet all the body's needs.

Deficiency

A deficiency of riboflavin can result in:

1 Failure to grow.
2 Skin lesions, dermatitis (skin disorder), and conjunctivitis (disorder of the outer membrane of the eye).
3 Tongue may swell, mouth and lips become sore.

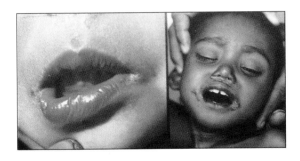

Stability in food preparation

Riboflavin is soluble in water, and is destroyed if heated in the presence of an alkali (e.g. bicarbonate of soda). Exposure to light also destroys the vitamin. This is why foods such as milk should be stored in the dark.

Nicotinic acid (niacin)

Functions

Like the other B vitamins, nicotinic acid is an important factor in the release of energy from food, especially carbohydrate, by oxidation.

Sources

Apart from the food sources listed on p. 16, nicotinic acid can be made in the body from the amino-acid **tryptophan** (in protein). Foods such as egg and milk, which are poor sources of nicotinic acid, contain tryptophan and are therefore useful to the body in this way.

Some foods contain nicotinic acid in a form that is unavailable to the body. This is true of the cereal **maize**, and in areas of the world where maize is the staple food, nicotinic acid deficiency is a major problem. However, in Mexico, where maize is the staple food, it is the custom to treat it with limewater before making the maize into tortillas. The limewater releases the nicotinic acid from the maize, so that a deficiency is unlikely.

Requirements

Nicotinic acid is required every day, and more is needed during pregnancy and lactation.

Deficiency

Nicotinic acid results in the disease **pellagra**, which has these symptoms:

1 **Dermatitis**, especially on the skin that is exposed to the sun.
2 **Dementia**, loss of memory, confusion, depression.
3 **Diarrhoea**, abdominal discomfort, loss of appetite, loose and frequent stools.

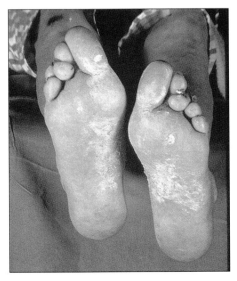

The symptoms of pellagra include dermatitis.

RNIs for the vitamin B complex

Age	Thiamin mg/day	Riboflavin mg/day	Nicotinic acid mg/day	Folate µg/day	Cobalamin µg/day
Children					
0–6 months	0.2	0.4	3	50	0.3
7–12 months	0.3	0.4	5	50	0.4
1–3 years	0.5	0.6	8	70	0.5
4–6 years	0.7	0.8	11	100	0.8
7–10 years	0.7	1.0	12	150	1.0
Males					
11–14 years	0.9	1.2	15	200	1.2
15–50+ years	1.0	1.3	17	200	1.5
Females					
11–14 years	0.7	1.1	12	200	1.2
15–50+ years	0.8	1.1	13	200	1.5
Pregnant	0.9	1.4	13	300	*
Lactating	1.0	1.6	15	260	+0.5µg/day

* No increase when pregnant

Stability in food preparation

Nicotinic acid is readily soluble in water, but is resistant to heat, oxidation, and alkali. It is the most stable vitamin in the B complex in normal cooking processes.

Folate

Functions

1 Essential for normal growth.
2 Essential for the formation of red blood cells (erythrocytes).
3 Required for the release of energy from food, especially amino-acids.
4 Important for the production of the nucleic acids RNA and DNA.

Requirements

A daily supply of folate is required (see table). The requirement increases in pregnancy.

Deficiency

A deficiency of folate may result in:
1 Failure to grow properly.
2 Megaloblastic anaemia, where the red blood cells become enlarged (megalo-) and cannot give up their oxygen properly to the body cells.
3 A lack of folate in early pregnancy may lead to a condition called spina bifida in the baby, which causes permanent disability. Women are advised to eat foods with a good folate content, and take supplements before becoming pregnant and in the first 12 weeks of pregnancy.

Sources

Folate is found in potatoes, spinach, green leafy vegetables, Brussels sprouts, green beans, peas, okra, bananas, grapefruit, oranges, yeast extract, bread, cereals, pulses, and dairy products.

Stability in food preparation

Folate is soluble in water and destroyed by prolonged cooking.

Cobalamin (vitamin B$_{12}$)

Functions

Cobalamin is required for the metabolism of amino-acids as well as other enzyme systems throughout the body.

Requirements

Cobalamin is produced in the intestines by bacteria, and is only found in useful amounts in animal foods. Vegans, who eat no animal foods, may have an insufficient intake. Requirements are higher during lactation.

Deficiency

A deficiency of cobalamin results in megaloblastic anaemia. This may occur in patients with dietary disorders or in old age.

Ascorbic acid (vitamin C)

Functions

1 Required to make connective tissue which binds the body cells together.
2 Assists the absorption of the mineral iron from the small intestine during digestion.
3 Assists in the building of strong bones and teeth.
4 Required for the production of blood and the walls of blood vessels.
5 Required for the building and maintenance of the skin and linings of the digestive system.
6 Assists vitamin E in its role as an antioxidant in the prevention of coronary heart disease (see p. 45).

Sources

Vitamin C is found mainly in fresh fruits and vegetables.

Rich sources
   rosehips, blackcurrants, green peppers, kiwi fruit

Good sources
   citrus fruits – oranges, grapefruits, lemons
   strawberries
   cabbage, spinach
   Brussels sprouts, broccoli

Reasonable sources
   bean sprouts, peas
   potatoes – these make a real contribution to supplies of vitamin C in the UK because we eat potatoes in large quantities.
The amount present in food varies according to the time of year, stage and place of growth, variety of plant, and degree of ripeness.

These foods are rich in ascorbic acid (vitamin C).

Requirements

Although it is a water-soluble vitamin, ascorbic acid has been shown to be stored in the body, mainly in the liver and adrenal glands, and throughout the body fluids and tissues. A healthy man has up to 1.5 g of ascorbic acid stored in this way, of which about 45 mg are used per day. Symptoms of scurvy (see below) appear when this store drops to below 300 mg, which takes about three months on a diet completely devoid of vitamin C. A daily supply of vitamin C keeps the store 'topped up', but it is not a vital requirement.

RNIs for vitamin C	
Age	**mg/day**
Children	
0–1 year	25
1–10 years	30
Adolescents	
11–14 years	35
15–18 years	40
Adults	
18–75+ years	40
Pregnant women	50
Lactating women	70

Deficiency

Prolonged deficiency may lead to:

1   Connective tissue not made or maintained correctly.
2   Walls of blood vessels weaken and break in places. Blood escapes and appears as small red spots (haemorrhages) under the skin.
3   General weakness, irritability, pain in muscles and joints, loss of weight, fatigue.
4   Gums bleed, teeth loosen.

A severe deficiency leads to the disease **scurvy**, which was common years ago among sailors on long sea voyages, where fresh fruit and vegetables were not available. The symptoms, in addition to the above, include:

5   Cuts and wounds fail to heal properly.
6   Scar tissue may weaken and break open.
7   Anaemia, because iron is not absorbed properly without vitamin C.

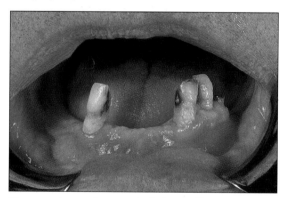

The symptoms of scurvy include swollen gums and loose teeth.

It is rare to see true cases of scurvy in the UK, but some elderly people or people on low incomes are slightly deficient and may show some of the symptoms.

Stability in food preparation

Vitamin C is very quickly and easily destroyed by:

1   Heat – dry or moist.
2   Exposure to air – this leads to the oxidation of ascorbic acid into a form which is useless to the body.
3   The presence of an alkali, such as bicarbonate of soda, which causes vitamin C to be oxidized.
4   Water – vitamin C dissolves in water, so cooking methods which use the minimum amount of water should be chosen.

To prevent the loss of vitamin C, foods should be cooked and served as quickly as possible.

Revision questions

1   Name the vitamins in the B group.
2   List the functions and food sources of three of the B vitamins.
3   Why do people who are very active require plenty of thiamin?
4   What are the symptoms of beri-beri and how is it caused?
5   What are the symptoms of a deficiency of riboflavin?
6   What are the symptoms of pellagra, and how is it caused?
7   Why is folate important in pregnancy?
8   What effects do cooking processes have on the main B vitamins?
9   What are the functions of vitamin C?
10   What is the connection between vitamin C and iron?
11   List the main sources of vitamin C.
12   What factors affect the amount of vitamin C present in food?
13   What are the symptoms of a deficiency of vitamin C, and what is the name of the disease associated with it?
14   What effect does preparation and cooking of food have on vitamin C?

Mineral elements

Apart from carbon, hydrogen, and oxygen (the main elements that make up protein, fat, and carbohydrate), the body requires at least 20 other elements for a variety of reasons. These are called mineral elements and they are required for:

1 Body building.
2 Control of body processes, e.g. transmission of nerve impulses.
3 Essential parts of body fluids.

Some mineral elements are required in relatively large amounts. These include:

calcium (Ca)
iron (Fe)
phosphorus (P)
potassium (K)
sulphur (S)
chlorine (Cl)
sodium (Na)
magnesium (Mg)

Others are required in minute amounts and are known as **trace elements**:

iodine (I)
copper (Cu)
manganese (Mn)
fluorine (F)
cobalt (Co)
nickel (Ni)
zinc (Zn)
chromium (Cr)
selenium (Se)

Most trace elements are supplied by a wide variety of foods, and the body is unlikely to be deficient in them. Only the mineral elements of greatest importance are included here.

Calcium

Functions

1 With phosphorus, it combines to make **calcium phosphate**, which is the chief material that gives hardness and strength to **bones** and **teeth**.
2 Required for part of the complex mechanism which causes blood to **clot** after an injury.
3 Required for the correct functioning of **muscles and nerves**.
4 Required for maintenance of bones and teeth once formed.

Sources

Calcium is found in good supply in:

milk
cheese
bread (added to white flour by law)
bones of canned fish
hard water

It is also found in green vegetables, but it may be unavailable to the body, because cellulose (which the body cannot digest) affects calcium absorption. It is also found in whole grain cereals, but there it may combine with a substance called **phytic acid** which makes it unavailable to the body.

Requirements

The absorption of calcium (and phosphorus) and the mineralization of bones and teeth is controlled by vitamin D. The body must have a sufficient supply of all three in order to function properly.

RNIs for calcium	
Age	**mg/day**
Children	
0–6 months	525
7–12 months	525
1–3 years	350
4–6 years	450
7–10 years	550
Males	
11–18 years	1000
19–50 years	700
50+ years	700
Females	
11–18 years	800
19–50 years	700
50+ years	700
Pregnant	700
Lactating	1250

Humans have a constant need for calcium throughout their lives. While new bone is made, existing bone is taken away, so that in young children the whole skeleton is replaced over 2 years. In adults, this process takes between 7 and 10 years. Research shows that regular exercise stimulates new bone production. Even when the skeleton stops growing (in the late teens), the need for calcium to make the bones strong continues.

Around the age of 30, calcium starts to be lost and is not replaced. This process speeds up in women at the menopause, and hormone replacement therapy (HRT) may help to slow it down. Eventually, the continual loss of bone mass can lead to **osteoporosis**, which means that the bones become weak, brittle, and break easily. Women are most at risk from osteoporosis, but it can also affect men.

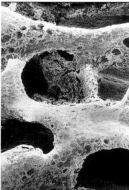

The bone of a person suffering from osteoporosis (right) is much weaker and more brittle than normal bone (left).

Deficiency

1 Children – bones and teeth are not mineralized properly, and are improperly formed. The leg bones may bend under the weight of the body as in rickets (see p. 14), although this is not due to a deficiency of calcium alone.
2 Adults – strength of bones and teeth is not maintained, possibly resulting in **osteomalacia** (adult rickets).
3 Muscles and nerves do not function correctly, which may result in a condition called **tetany**, where the muscles contract rigidly and the patient has convulsions.

Too much calcium in the body is dangerous, as it will be deposited in organs such as the kidneys, and this can be fatal. The effects of this were demonstrated after the Second World War, when extra vitamin D was given in cod-liver oil, to safeguard against rickets. People who took too much vitamin D absorbed calcium in excessive amounts, which resulted in several deaths.

Phosphorus

Functions
Phosphorus works in conjunction with calcium and therefore has the same functions. In addition, it is essential for the production of energy in the body.

Sources
Phosphorus is present as **phosphate** in all plant and animal cells, and is therefore present in all natural foods. It forms part of many proteins, and is often used as an additive in manufactured foods.

Requirements
A normal diet will supply sufficient phosphorus for all age groups.

Deficiency
A deficiency of phosphorus is not known to occur in humans.

Iron

Functions
Iron is a component of haemoglobin, the substance which gives red blood cells their colour. Haemoglobin is required to transport oxygen around the body to every cell, for the production of energy and the maintenance of all cell functions.

Sources
Good sources
 liver, kidney, corned beef, cocoa, plain chocolate, watercress
Reasonable sources
 white bread (added by law), curry powder, treacle, dried fruit, pulses, wholegrain cereals, green leafy vegetables

Absorption of iron

Iron in its ferrous form is easier to absorb than in its ferric form. Iron from plant foods, e.g. grains, leafy vegetables, and soya protein may be made more difficult to absorb by the presence of phytic acid (see p. 86). Ascorbic acid (vitamin C) significantly increases iron absorption, especially from plant foods, as it changes the iron from the ferric to the ferrous form.

Egg yolk is a good source of iron, but the iron is poorly absorbed by humans. Egg yolk should not be relied on as the main source of iron in the diet, and foods containing vitamin C should be eaten with it whenever possible.

Requirements

Red blood cells die after about six weeks, and must be replaced. This process is continually occurring in the body. As the blood cells are removed from the body, some of the iron is saved. However, some iron is lost, and must be replaced by a daily food supply.

These foods are good sources of iron.

RNIs for iron	
Age	**mg/day**
Children	
0–3 months	1.7
4–6 months	4.3
7–12 months	7.8
1–3 years	6.9
4–6 years	6.1
7–10 years	8.7
Males	
11–18 years	11.3
19–50+ years	8.7
Females	
11–50 years	14.8*
50+ years	8.7
Pregnant	14.8
Lactating	14.8

* This may not be enough if a woman loses a lot of blood during menstruation.

Absorption of iron is controlled in the small intestine. Normally, only a small percentage of the iron in the diet is absorbed, but if more is required (e.g. in pregnancy), then more is absorbed to meet these demands.

To ensure that iron is properly absorbed, foods containing iron should be eaten with foods containing vitamin C.

Special requirements

Babies are born with a supply of iron to last them up to four months, as milk contains very little iron. After this time they need to be given iron in the form of solid food or mineral drops.

Pregnant women Iron requirements increase in pregnancy to allow for the development of the growing baby's blood supply. The body usually adapts to meet these demands, but some women may require iron tablets.

Girls and women The regular menstrual loss of blood means that iron is lost and must be replaced. After the birth of a baby, iron supplies must be replaced.

Injuries and operations result in loss of blood and the iron must be replaced.

Deficiency

1 Haemoglobin is not made properly, so insufficient oxygen is carried around the body. This leads to fatigue, weakness, and a pale complexion. In severe cases this leads to the condition known as **iron deficiency anaemia**.

2 General health is affected, as cells cannot function properly

Sodium, chloride, and potassium

Functions

These are all required to maintain the correct concentration of the body fluids. Chloride is also required for the production of **hydrochloric acid** in the gastric juice of the stomach.

Sources

All three are usually eaten as sodium chloride or as potassium chloride in food.

They are also added as salt to foods, e.g.:

yeast extract   bacon
cheese   fish

They are found naturally in fish, meat, and many other foods.

Sodium in the form of sodium chloride (salt) is added to many manufactured foods, especially savoury snacks. It also forms part of monosodium glutamate (MSG) which is a flavour enhancer (see p. 143) used in many foods. Sodium bicarbonate and sodium nitrite are other commonly used additives. Food labels often give the sodium content.

Requirements

Everyone needs these elements. Sodium and chloride are especially necessary in hot climates where they are lost in sweat. Workers in heavy industry need them for the same reason. Excess intakes are excreted in the urine and sweat.

It is sometimes necessary to place a person on a **salt-restricted diet**, for certain medical conditions, e.g.:

heart, kidney, or liver disease
high blood pressure

This means that low-salt foods (e.g. natural cereals, fruit, unsalted butter) must be eaten, with small amounts of fresh meat and fish, and root vegetables. No salt many be added to food but alternative flavourings, e.g. herbs, spices, can be used as a substitute. Low-sodium table salt is also available.

Deficiency

Salt tablets are issued to some workers in hot climates (e.g. in civil engineering) if they are unused to long periods in such heat.

Cured meat, smoked fish, yeast extract, and crisps are high in salt; the other foods are low in salt.

Fluoride

Functions

Fluoride is important in strengthening teeth against decay. It is thought to combine with the protective enamel coating of the teeth, making them more resistant to attack by the acid produced by bacteria in the mouth.

Sources

Fluoride is found naturally in tea, sea-water fish, and in some parts of the country in water supplies.

Fluoridation of water supplies

In areas of the country where fluoride occurs naturally in the water supply, the number of children who need treatment for tooth decay is significantly lower than in other areas. Because

Fluoride is found in tea, sea-fish, and some water supplies, and is added to many toothpastes.

of this, it has been recommended that all water supplies should have fluoride added to them at a strength of 1 mg per litre, to reduce the number of children requiring dental treatment. There have, however, been problems in putting this into practice as many people object to having their water supply interfered with. As a result, only 10% of the population have fluoride added to their water supply.

Requirements

The strengthening effect that fluoride has on the teeth is only of value when the teeth are developing in children. Only minute quantities are required for this. Too much fluoride can be harmful, as it causes the teeth to become 'mottled' with dark brown spots.

Iodine

Functions

Iodine is required to make the hormone **thyroxine**, which is produced by the **thyroid gland** in the neck.

Thyroxine, along with other hormones, helps to control the rate of metabolism in the body.

Sources

Iodine is widely distributed in foods, but is found in good supply in:

    sea foods
    milk
    green vegetables, especially spinach
    fresh water (depending on area)
    iodized salt (added commercially)

These foods are rich in iodine.

Requirements

A minute quantity is required every day, and in our whole life 2.8 g is needed by the body.

Deficiency

A deficiency of iodine leads to a reduction in the amount of thyroxine produced by the thyroid gland. As a result the metabolism slows down, and the gland swells up. This swelling can be seen in the neck and is called a **goitre**.

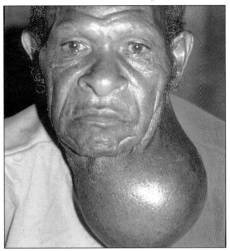

Iodine deficiency can cause goitre.

Revision questions

1 List five mineral elements needed in large amounts, and five trace elements.
2 List the functions and main sources of calcium, iron, sodium and chloride, iodine, and fluoride.
3 What is rickets, and what is its connection with vitamin D?
4 What is phytic acid, and what effect does it have on certain mineral elements?
5 What is tetany, and what causes it?
6 What is the function of haemoglobin, and which mineral element is connected with it?
7 Why do women, babies, and people recovering from injuries require extra iron?
8 Why is it necessary to take salt tablets in hot climates?
9 Why is it recommended that water supplies should be fluoridated?
10 What is a goitre and how is it caused?
11 What is osteoporosis and what are its effects on the body?

Water

Functions

1 Water is vital to life – 70% of the human body is water.
2 Required for all body fluids, e.g. digestive juices, mucus, saliva, blood, lymph, sweat, and urine.
3 Required as part of many metabolic reactions.
4 Keeps linings of mucous membranes, digestive tract, and bronchial tubes moist.
5 Some nutrients need to dissolve in water for proper absorption.
6 Lubricates joints and membranes.

Sources

Many foods contain water, and some, such as fruits and vegetables, are composed mainly of water. In addition to the water that is taken in food and as liquids, some water is produced during the many metabolic reactions of the body.

Tap water is safe to drink in most developed countries where it is treated to kill harmful bacteria.

In some areas where large amounts of fertilizers are used on growing crops, nitrate levels in tap water can be high. The EU maximum limit for nitrate in tap water is 50 mg/litre.

Water softeners are installed in many homes in hard-water areas. Some of these work by replacing the calcium and magnesium in the water with sodium. The water from these softeners should not be drunk by people with high blood pressure and should not be used to mix baby feeds, as it contains high levels of sodium.

Bottled mineral waters (both still and carbonated) are often advertised as being healthy. There is no evidence that they are better for health than tap water, and they are much more expensive. However, health authorities recommend drinking bottled water when staying in developing countries where tap water may be contaminated with disease-giving bacteria.

Requirements

Water should be drunk every day, especially in hot weather when much is lost through sweating. Water is constantly lost in this way through the skin, and also from the lungs, kidneys, and bowels. A minimum of two to three litres per day is recommended.

Extra water is required:

1 During illness where a raised temperature results in increased sweating.
2 If vomiting or diarrhoea has occurred, both of which can cause **rapid dehydration**, especially in babies.
3 In lactation, when extra water is required for milk production.
4 After intense physical activity such as sport, especially at a high altitude.

Dietary fibre (NSP)

After food has been digested, absorbed, and metabolized, waste products are removed from the body by the process of **excretion**.

Liquid waste is processed by the **kidneys** and excreted as **urine**, and solid waste as **faeces**, from the large intestine.

The removal of waste products is vital as they are potentially harmful (toxic) to the body. Normally, urine is excreted regularly throughout the day, and faeces are excreted every day or so according to individual variation (which is quite normal).

The faeces are formed in the large intestine after the nutrients and some of the water have been absorbed following digestion. The solid residues pass along the intestine by the process of **peristalsis**, which involves regular muscular contractions of the intestinal wall. These push the residues along.

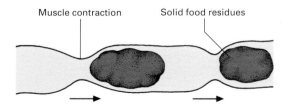

Muscle contraction   Solid food residues

The **faeces** finally collect in the rectum and are passed out through the anus (see p. 34). Usually the whole process takes place with minimum effort, providing the faeces are **bulky** and **soft**.

Non-starch polysaccharides or NSP (dietary fibre) are found in the cell walls of plants (see p. 10). They are not digested, but remain in the large intestine before passing out in the faeces. The main sources of NSP are:

wholegrain cereals (as **bran**), e.g. wheat, rice, oats, wholemeal bread, breakfast cereals, wholegrain pasta, crispbreads (bran can also be purchased separately)

fruits, especially skins of apples, plums

vegetables, especially leafy vegetables, celery, potato skins

Functions

Even though it is not digested, NSP is of great importance as it absorbs a lot of water, and binds other food residues to itself, ensuring that the faeces are soft and bulky and pass easily out of the body in the minimum time.

If the faeces are not removed quickly and regularly, several problems can arise, including:

Constipation

Many people suffer from constipation. The faeces become very hard and move slowly through the intestine, and a lot of effort is required to remove them. Abdominal discomfort and a general feeling of ill health accompany this condition.

People who suffer from constipation often resort to using laxatives, which irritate the intestine and cause it to expel the faeces unnaturally quickly. This is unwise as it can lead to dependence on laxatives, as the normal process will be stopped.

Diverticular disease

The extra strain put on the muscular walls of the intestine through constipation may lead to **diverticular disease**. This may develop if the faeces are small and hard (due to a lack of NSP and insufficient water), and the muscular walls of the intestine have to work harder to move them along. This causes increased pressure in the intestine and leads to pouches of the bowel lining being forced out through the intestine wall. If the pouches (called diverticula) become inflamed, this causes discomfort. Part of the treatment for this is to put the patient on a high-fibre diet.

(a) High-fibre diet – the soft, large faeces are moved along the intestine easily.

(b) Low-fibre diet – the small, hard faeces cannot be moved so easily, and extra effort is required to push them.

(c) This leads to the development of diverticula.

Haemorrhoids (piles) and hernias

These may be caused by the increased effort required to remove hard faeces in constipation sufferers.

Refined foods

It is often suggested that people today do not eat enough NSP, and that this is a major cause of many disorders of the intestinal tract, including those described above and bowel cancer.

Many foods eaten today are **refined**. This means that they are processed in food factories into a variety of products, and much of their NSP content is removed. Refined foods include:

white flour, white bread, white sugar

instant puddings and desserts

white (polished) rice

instant potato

Such foods are often blamed for the reduction in the amount of NSP eaten, as they are convenient to prepare, highly palatable, and relatively inexpensive.

Lack of exercise is also a major factor in causing intestinal disorders, as exercise helps to keep the intestine active.

Everyone should eat plenty of NSP to avoid constipation and its accompanying disorders. The regular consumption of wholegrain cereals, wholemeal bread, fruit, and vegetables, and an increase in exercise should prevent such problems. A reduction in the amount of refined foods eaten is also advisable, although they need not be avoided altogether.

These foods are high in NSP (dietary fibre).

Revision questions

1 Why is water vital to life?
2 Name five foods that have a high water content.
3 Apart from water taken in foods, how else does the body obtain it?
4 How is water lost from the body?
5 What is the recommended daily intake of water?
6 When does the body require extra water?
7 Why are vomiting and diarrhoea dangerous to babies and young children?
8 Why must the body remove waste products?
9 What is peristalsis?
10 Why is NSP important to the body?
11 List the main sources of NSP.
12 Why is constipation undesirable?
13 What is diverticular disease?
14 How do refined foods affect the removal of waste products?
15 Why is the continued use of laxatives undesirable?

Energy

Every function and process in the body requires a source of energy. All energy is supplied initially by food, and released for use in the body after digestion and absorption.

Use of energy in the body

Energy is used in various forms in the body:

Mechanical energy for the movement of muscles (voluntarily and involuntarily).

Chemical energy for all chemical and metabolic reactions.

Heat energy to maintain the body temperature.

Electrical energy for the transmission of nervous impulses.

One form of energy can be converted into another form in the body, but all energy is supplied initially by food.

Foods that supply energy

The three main nutrients, protein, fat, and carbohydrate, all supply energy. Of the three, fat provides the most concentrated source of energy, weight for weight, so the most energy-dense foods are:

fats (lard, butter, margarine, suet)
oils (vegetable, nut, animal)
fatty foods, e.g. egg yolk, cheese, cream, meat
sugar, cereals, cereal products, starchy vegetables.

These foods are good sources of energy.

Energy release in the body

Energy is released in a reaction between glucose and oxygen, which takes place in all body cells.

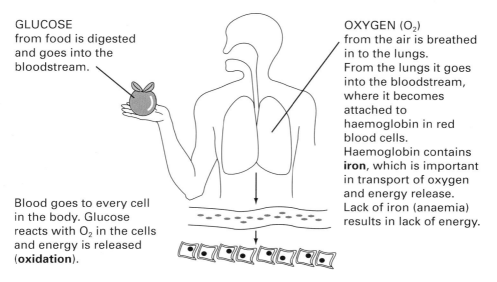

GLUCOSE from food is digested and goes into the bloodstream.

OXYGEN (O_2) from the air is breathed in to the lungs.
From the lungs it goes into the bloodstream, where it becomes attached to haemoglobin in red blood cells.
Haemoglobin contains **iron**, which is important in transport of oxygen and energy release.
Lack of iron (anaemia) results in lack of energy.

Blood goes to every cell in the body. Glucose reacts with O_2 in the cells and energy is released (**oxidation**).

The reaction produces **energy**, with **carbon dioxide** and **water** as by-products.

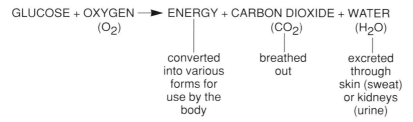

GLUCOSE + OXYGEN ⟶ ENERGY + CARBON DIOXIDE + WATER
(O_2)   (CO_2)   (H_2O)

converted into various forms for use by the body

breathed out

excreted through skin (sweat) or kidneys (urine)

The reactions that produce energy involve the **B vitamins** and **phosphorus**. **Iodine** is also important: it is part of the hormone thyroxine which controls the speed of energy release (metabolic rate).

Not all the glucose is converted to energy. Some is stored as glycogen (in the liver and muscles), and some as fat (in adipose tissue under the skin). Energy from glycogen can be released quickly (e.g. to run a race); energy stored as fat is released slowly (e.g. in time of famine).

Measurement of energy

Energy is measured in kilocalories (kcal) or kilojoules (kJ).

A kilocalorie (sometimes written as Calorie) is defined as: *the amount of heat energy that is required to raise the temperature of 1 kilogram of pure water by 1°C.*

1 kcal = 4.2 kJ (the joule is the metric unit of measurement for heat and energy).

The three main nutrients, protein, fat, and carbohydrate, can all supply the body with energy, and are therefore said to have a calorific value or energy value.

1 gram of pure **protein** has an energy value of 4 kcal or 17 kJ.

1 gram of pure **fat** has an energy value of 9 kcal or 38 kJ.

1 gram of pure **carbohydrate** has an energy value of 3.75 kcal (usually rounded up to 4 kcal) or 16 kJ.

Energy values of various food

Food	kcals/100g	kJ/100g
Apple	35	150
Apricot (dried)	180	750
Aubergine (raw)	15	60
Avocado pear	220	920
Bacon (streaky, grilled)	400	1670
Banana	80	330
Baked beans in tomato sauce	65	270
Beans (mung, cooked)	100	420
Beef (corned)	220	920
Beef (minced, stewed)	230	960
Biscuits (chocolate coated)	520	2180
Biscuits (cream crackers)	440	1840
Bread (white)	230	960
Bread (wholemeal)	220	920
Butter	750	3140
Cake (fruit)	330	1380
Carrots (raw)	25	100
Chapati (made with fat)	340	1420
Cheese (cheddar)	400	1670
Cheese (cottage)	100	420
Chicken (roasted)	150	630
Chocolate (milk)	530	2220
Coconut (desiccated)	600	2510
Cod (raw)	80	330
Cod (baked)	100	420
Cod (fried)	170	710
Egg (whole raw)	150	630
Honey	290	1210
Ice-cream	170	710
Lentils (boiled)	100	420
Lettuce	10	40
Margarine	730	3060
Matzos	380	1590
Milk (whole)	65	270
Milk (skimmed)	33	140
Milk (skimmed condensed)	270	1130
Peanut butter	620	2600
Potatoes (raw)	90	380
Potato crisps	530	2200
Rice (white boiled)	120	500
Tuna (canned in oil)	190	790
Tuna (canned in brine)	99	422
Sausages (pork grilled)	320	1340
Yam (boiled)	120	500

Fat supplies over twice as much energy as the same weight of protein or carbohydrate. Protein is normally only used as an energy supply once it has performed its primary functions of growth and repair, or if the diet is deficient in fat or carbohydrate.

Most foods are a mixture of these nutrients and so their energy values vary greatly. Energy value can be assessed by burning a carefully weighed portion of a particular food in a special piece of equipment called a **calorimeter**. The amount of heat energy produced is measured in kcal or kJ.

Energy requirements

The amount of energy used by the body is the **energy expenditure**. This varies widely from individual to individual, according to:

    age
    sex
    occupation
    physical activity
    state of body, e.g. pregnancy, illness

Age

Young children require more energy for their size than adults as they are growing rapidly and tend to be very active most of the time.

With increasing age, the need for energy decreases, partly due to a slowing down of the body and partly because of reduced physical activity.

Gender (sex)

Men tend to be larger overall in body size than women, so they have a higher metabolic rate and use more energy. This does not really apply to children.

Occupation and physical activity

The amount of energy people use depends on their occupation and their recreational activities. Occupations are classified according to how active they are as follows:

Sedentary: Office workers, clerical tasks, drivers, pilots, teachers, journalists, clergy, doctors, lawyers, architects, shop workers.

Moderately active: Light industry and assembly plants, railway workers, postmen and women, joiners, plumbers, bus conductors, farm workers, builders' labourers.

Very active: Coal miners, steel workers, dockers, forestry workers, army recruits, some farm workers, builders' labourers, unskilled labourers.

State of body

Pregnancy: Extra energy is required for the growth of the baby, and the adjustment of the mother's body to pregnancy.

Lactation: Extra energy is required for the production of milk, and some of this is laid down as fat stores during the pregnancy.

Illness: The metabolism of the body may be raised at times during an illness or fever, but at other times may be decreased due to a reduction in physical activity.

At least half of the energy released in the body is used for **basal metabolism** (resting metabolism). This is the amount of energy that is required to keep the body alive when it is at complete rest and warm. It is used to keep the heart, lungs, and digestive system moving, to maintain the nerve impulses to and from the brain, and for all the necessary chemical reactions in the body.

The rest of the energy is used by the **muscles** for physical work and to maintain **posture**. Energy expenditure for these purposes varies widely from person to person, but for an average-sized man aged about 30, energy expenditure for different activities is as follows:

Activity	kcals used per hour	kJ used per hour
Sleeping	70	294
Sitting	85	357
Standing	90	378
Playing tennis	350	1470
Playing football	480	2000
Cycling	400	1680
Walking slowly	185	777
Swimming	575	2415
Housework	200	840
Walking upstairs	1000	4200

If the energy intake in food exceeds the amount of energy expended by an individual, then the excess is stored in the body as fat. This is one of the major causes of obesity, but it does not account for those people who appear to be able to eat what they like without putting on weight. It is likely that differences in **metabolic rate** (i.e. the rate at which oxidation occurs), and the amount of heat produced during oxidation, account for this variation.

Dietary reference values for energy (average amounts, see p. 2)

Age	MJ/day	kcal/day
Males		
0–3 months	2.28	545
4–6 months	2.89	690
7–9 months	3.44	825
10–12 months	3.85	920
1–3 years	5.15	1230
4–6 years	7.16	1715
7–10 years	8.24	1970
11–14 years	9.27	2220
15–18 years	11.51	2755
19–50 years	10.60	2550
51–59 years	10.60	2550
60–64 years	9.93	2380
65–74 years	9.71	2330
75+ years	8.77	2100
Females		
0–3 months	2.16	515
4–6 months	2.69	645
7–9 months	3.20	765
10–12 months	3.61	865
1–3 years	4.86	1165
4–6 years	6.46	1545
7–10 years	7.28	1740
11–14 years	7.92	1845
15–18 years	8.83	2110
19–50 years	8.10	1940
51–59 years	8.00	1900
60–64 years	7.99	1900
65–74 years	7.96	1900
75+ years	7.61	1810
Pregnant (last 3 months)	+0.8	+200
Lactating	+1.9–2.0	+450–480

These low-energy foods are suitable for a weight-reducing diet.

Foods that have high energy values should be eaten in moderation by people who lead sedentary lives. Some foods, such as chocolates, sweets, crisps, and similar snacks, are particularly bad in this respect as they are **energy dense**, but contain very little else in the way of nutrients. Such foods are sometimes referred to as providing 'empty calories', because they are of little value to the body.

Weight reduction

To lose weight, a person must reduce the energy intake from food, so that the reserves of energy in body fat are used and weight is lost. An increase in physical activity also helps.

A weight-reducing diet involves calculating the day's energy intake and reducing it to a level at which energy reserves will be used up. Usually, an intake of 1000 kcal (4200 kJ) per day for women and 1500 kcal (6300 kJ) per day for men is prescribed. A reduction of 3500 kcal will cause about 0.5 kg of body fat to be lost. On 1000 kcals a day a woman could lose 1–1.5 kg a week. Charts showing the energy values of different foods can be used to help plan a weight-reducing diet. It is, however, important to take the advice of a doctor before attempting to lose weight as some diet sheets are misguided and nutritionally unsound.

Weight reduction is a gradual and fairly long-term process. The aim should be to change one's eating habits to prevent future weight gain.

Effect of cooking on energy values

The energy values of some foods can be increased considerably by adding fat. For example, a fried egg has an energy value almost double that of a boiled egg. (A boiled egg yields 80 kcal; a fried egg yields 150 kcal.) This is because most foods absorb a substantial amount of fat during frying. They absorb even more if they are placed in the fat before it has reached the correct cooking temperature.

Adding fat to a food, e.g. butter to mashed potato or sweetcorn, also increases the energy value.

This should be taken into account when planning meals, especially for someone who is on a weight-reducing diet.

Grilling foods such as chops and sausages is better than frying them, as some of the fat in the food will drain away, and reduce the energy value accordingly.

Low-energy sugar substitutes (which are very sweet but have little energy value) can be used to reduce the energy value of drinks and other dishes, e.g. custard, which are traditionally sweet.

Foods that contain a high proportion of water, e.g. fruits and vegetables, are low in energy value as water yields no energy. Such foods are useful in weight-reducing diets.

Many special foods and meal substitutes are produced with the intention of helping people on weight-reducing diets, but they are often expensive, and do not necessarily help to re-educate people's eating habits. It is better just to follow a diet that contains plenty of fruit and vegetables and a balanced amount of protein, fat, and carbohydrate.

Revision questions

1 Why does the body require energy?
2 What forms of energy does the body use?
3 How is energy measured?
4 How does the body store energy?
5 Why do people have different requirements for energy?
6 Why is it unwise to exceed daily energy requirements?
7 How many kilocalories do one gram of pure fat, protein, and carbohydrate each produce?
8 Why do the energy values of foods differ?
9 What effect does frying have on the energy value of foods?
10 What is the best way to lose weight?
11 How are sugar substitutes useful in weight-reducing diets?
12 Give the energy values for five different foods and say why they are different.
13 What is oxidation and where does it occur?
14 What is basal metabolism?
15 Which nutrients are involved with energy release in the body?

Digestion and absorption

When food has been eaten, it must be broken down in the body by the process of **digestion**, so that the molecules of which it is composed (in particular the nutrients) can be **absorbed** into the bloodstream. The whole process takes place in the **digestive system** (sometimes called the **alimentary canal**), which begins at the mouth and ends at the anus (see p. 34). It consists of various organs and tissues, each with special functions.

Digestion and absorption occur by both physical and chemical means.

Physical breakdown of food

Food must be small enough to swallow, and is first broken up (masticated) in the mouth by the action of the teeth and jaws. The muscular action of the stomach also reduces the size of the food particles.

Chemical breakdown of food

During digestion, a variety of chemicals or 'digestive juices' are produced. These contain **enzymes**, which speed up chemical reactions, and are found in all living matter. Each chemical reaction that occurs in living plants and animals has a **specific enzyme** to speed it up. This means that a particular enzyme can only work on one type of reaction. Consequently there are many enzymes.

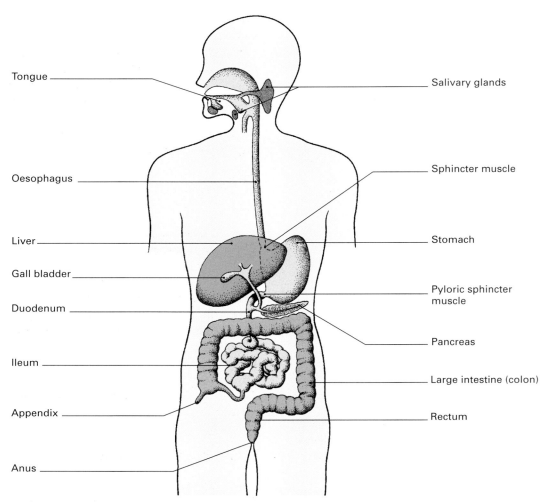

The human digestive system

The enzymes in digestion speed up the breakdown of food and the release of nutrients, and without them the process would be impossible. In the following equation, A stands for a food and B for a nutrient it contains.

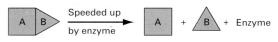

In order to enable food to move through the digestive system, mucus is produced. This lubricates the food and the membranes of the system, which enables the food to move easily. The muscular walls of the various parts of the system push the food along by means of regular contractions known as **peristalsis** (see p. 26).

Digestion at each stage of the digestive system

The physical and chemical breakdown of food at each stage will be discussed here, and the *enzymes* involved are shown in *italic*.

Mouth

Physical breakdown

Teeth tear, rip, and grind the food into pieces small enough to swallow.

Tongue pushes the food round the mouth and down the throat.

Salivary glands produce saliva to moisten food and make it easy to swallow.

Chemical breakdown
Protein None.

Fat None.

Carbohydrate *Salivary amylase* produced by the salivary glands converts some starch to maltose. Cooked starch is acted on more quickly than raw starch.

Oesophagus
Food is transported down to the stomach by peristalsis.

There is no physical or chemical breakdown here.

Stomach
Physical breakdown
Food enters the stomach via the sphincter muscle at the top. Strong muscular waves move the food around and help to break it down and mix it with gastric juices and mucus produced in the stomach. The broken-down food is referred to as **chyme**.

Chemical breakdown
Protein *Pepsin* starts the breakdown of protein into smaller chains of amino-acids called **peptides**.

Rennin clots milk so that *pepsin* can act on it more efficiently. More rennin is produced in young mammals whose diet consists solely of milk.

Fat None.

Carbohydrate Hydrochloric acid produced by the stomach stops the action of salivary amylase, and helps pepsin to work.

Food stays in the stomach for about four to five hours, and leaves in small amounts via the pyloric sphincter muscle.

Duodenum
Physical breakdown
None.

Chemical breakdown
The chyme is mixed with bile from the gall bladder and pancreatic juice from the pancreas. Bile neutralizes the acid and stops the action of pepsin.

Protein *Trypsinogen* (an inactive enzyme) produced by the pancreas mixes with *enterokinase* which activates trypsinogen to form *trypsin*.

Trypsin continues the breakdown of proteins to peptones.

Fat Bile emulsifies fats to disperse them in the liquid in small droplets, and *pancreatic lipase* breaks fat into soluble glycerol and insoluble fatty acids. The fatty acids react with the bile to become soluble.

Carbohydrate *Pancreatic amylase* breaks down undigested starch to maltose.

Ileum
Physical breakdown
None.

Chemical breakdown
The glands produce intestinal juice which contains a variety of enzymes.

Protein *Erepsin* converts peptones to amino-acids to complete protein digestion.

Fat Further broken down by *lipase*.

Carbohydrate *Maltase* breaks down maltose to glucose.

Invertase breaks down sucrose to glucose and fructose.

Lactase breaks down lactose to glucose and galactose.

Absorption of nutrients

Small intestine
The absorption of nutrients occurs in the small intestine, along its whole length. Alcohol is the only substance that can be absorbed elsewhere, usually in the stomach.

Food is passed along the small intestine slowly, taking about two to three hours to reach the large intestine. This allows plenty of time for absorption to take place. The walls of the intestine are lined with thousands of tiny finger-like projections called **villi**.

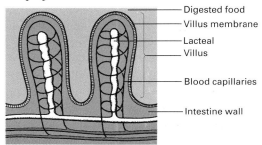

Labels: Digested food, Villus membrane, Lacteal, Villus, Blood capillaries, Intestine wall

Each villus is surrounded by a wall of single cells, through which the nutrients pass, to reach the centre. In the centre is the **lacteal** which is connected to the lymphatic system. The lacteal is surrounded by tiny **blood capillaries**, which are connected to larger blood vessels. Absorption of the various nutrients occurs as follows:

Monosaccharides, amino-acids, water-soluble vitamins, and **minerals** are all absorbed into the blood capillaries, where they dissolve in the blood, and are carried away to other parts of the body. Glucose is either used immediately for energy, or converted (along with other monosaccharides) to glycogen and stored in the liver and muscles.

Glycerol and **fatty acids** are absorbed into the lacteal where they recombine to form fats, which mix with the lymphatic fluid. They then pass round the body in the lymphatic system, and join the blood circulation as insoluble fat. They are converted to soluble fat in the liver.

The **fat-soluble vitamins** are absorbed with the fats, and are taken to the liver as well.

Large intestine (colon)

After the nutrients have been absorbed, the waste products and food residues pass into the large intestine, still in a liquid state. Water is absorbed along the large intestine, thus making the food residues (faeces) more solid. This may take up to 12 hours, and the faeces finally collect in the rectum, ready for excretion. The whole process is assisted by dietary fibre (NSP) in food (see pp. 26–8).

Digestion and cooking

Digestion is assisted by the cooking of foods to soften or tenderize them, e.g.:

meat – cooking breaks down tough connective tissue and makes the meat more digestible (see p. 118).

cheese – fat surrounding the protein melts, exposing the protein for digestion.

Cooking also renders some foods more solid so that the enzymes are able to act upon them more efficiently, e.g.:

eggs – cooking them lightly coagulates the protein, thus making them set so that they stay in the stomach for longer.

Revision questions

1. What is the purpose of digestion?
2. Draw and label the various organs of the digestive system.
3. What do enzymes do?
4. Why is mucus produced throughout the digestive system?
5. Copy out and complete the chart below, showing the digestion of the various nutrients:

Organ	Protein	Fat	Carbohydrate
Mouth			
Oesophagus			
Stomach			
Duodenum			
Ileum			
Colon			

Indicate which enzymes are involved in each case.

The nutrient content of foods

It is difficult to measure accurately the amounts of the different nutrients that people eat every day, and the amounts that are present in the food they consume.

The nutritional value of different foods is affected by:

1. The species or type of plant or animal.
2. Where and how they are grown or reared.
3. The effect of harvesting and slaughter.
4. The time taken to transport food.
5. The effect of processing the food in a factory.
6. The amount of wastage when preparing a food.
7. The effect of various processes and cooking practices in the kitchen.

The way food is prepared for consumption in the kitchen has an important effect on the nutritional content. Some processes and practices lead to a loss of nutrients, whilst others conserve or enhance the nutritional value of food.

Practices that lead to a loss of nutrients

Heating

1 Destroys some vitamin C, thiamin, and riboflavin.
2 With an alkali (as in the addition of bicarbonate of soda to green vegetables to preserve their colour), heating leads to the destruction of vitamin C and riboflavin.
3 Overheating protein leads to hardening and reduced digestibility.
4 Keeping food hot further destroys vitamin C, thiamin, and riboflavin.

Soaking

Leads to loss of vitamin C, thiamin, riboflavin, and nicotinic acid into the liquid.

Exposure to air

1 Leads to the oxidation of vitamin C in vegetables, fruit, and fruit juices.
2 Leads to the gradual deterioration of fat, and rancidity (see p. 92).

Exposure to light

Leads to the destruction of riboflavin and vitamin A.

Practices that conserve nutrients

Steaming

Water-soluble vitamins are retained more effectively as food does not come into direct contact with water.

Stews and gravy

Preparation of gravy from vegetable cooking water retains some water-soluble vitamins. Water-soluble vitamins are retained in liquid used in a stew.

Pressure cooking

Less destruction by heat as cooking time is reduced.

Vegetable preparation

1 Preparation just before cooking prevents the oxidation of vitamin C.
2 If vegetables are prepared some time before they are to be cooked, they can be stored in an air-tight plastic bag to prevent the oxidation of vitamin C.
3 Placing green vegetables into boiling water, for cooking without pre-soaking, reduces the loss of water-soluble vitamins by leaching.
4 Minimum cooking time reduces heat destruction of vitamin C, thiamin, and riboflavin.

Practices that enhance nutritional value

Combining foods

1 The combination of low biological value protein foods (e.g. bread with lentil soup, baked beans on toast) means that indispensable amino-acids lacking in one food, can be provided by the other.
2 The combination of vitamin C with foods containing iron enhances the absorption of iron from the small intestine.

Preparing food

1 The preparation of curry spices in iron pots leads to iron passing into the spices.
2 Grating cheese enables the fat to be more easily digested.
3 Homogenizing milk (see p. 101) reduces the size of the fat droplets, which enables them to be digested more easily.

Revision questions

1 Explain how
   a heating, **b** soaking, **c** exposure to air affect the nutrient content of foods.
2 Which cooking methods help to conserve water-soluble vitamins?
3 How should vegetables be stored, prepared, and cooked to retain vitamins?

Dietary guidelines

There has been much research over many years into the effect that food has on people's health, well being, and life expectancy. Governments in all countries have responsibility for nutrition and health in the population. In the UK the Departments responsible include:
Agriculture, Fisheries, and Food; Health; Social Security; Environment; Education and Employment; Trade and Industry.

Current dietary guidelines for people living in the UK are outlined in the document 'Eat Well'. This was produced as part of a report called 'The Health of the Nation'.

People with certain health conditions, e.g. high levels of blood cholesterol, heart disease, high blood pressure, diabetes, or chronic constipation may require more or less of the nutrient than the figures given in the guidelines, which are averages.

The dietary recommendations for a healthy lifestyle include:
Eat less sugar
Eat less fat
Eat more fibre and starchy foods
Eat less salty food
Drink less alcohol
Eat a variety of foods
Enjoy your food
Eat more fruit and vegetables
Eat the right amount to maintain a healthy weight

Eat less sugar

It is recommended that refined (extrinsic) sugars provide no more than 10% of total energy intake. This will help reduce cases of dental caries (see p. 48–50) and obesity.

Reducing sugar consumption

1 Avoid adding sugar to drinks, and choose soft drinks that have a reduced sugar content or contain sugar substitutes (see p. 97).
2 Include more naturally sweet foods, e.g. fruits, in meals, without adding more sucrose to them.
3 Use sugar-reduced products, such as fruit canned in fruit juice, jams, and other spreads, which are now available in many shops.
4 Gradually cut down the amount of sugar normally added to items such as custard, breakfast cereals, cakes, and biscuits.
5 Restrict the consumption of sweets and other sugar-containing snacks, so that they become a treat rather than a habit.

Eat less fat

It is recommended that total fat intake is no more than 35% of total energy intake (at present, the average is about 42%), which is 75 g per day for an average woman, and 100 g a day for an average man. Of this, no more than 11% of energy intake should come from saturated fats (at present it is about 16%) (see p. 7).

This will help reduce the risk of developing heart disease.

Reducing fat consumption

1 Use low-fat dairy products, e.g. yogurt (can be used as substitute for cream in many dishes), cheeses (e.g. cottage), skimmed and semi-skimmed milk in cooking and for normal consumption.
2 Make more use of poultry and white fish, both of which contain less fat than red meat.
3 Avoid fried foods, and grill or bake instead.
4 Make more use of low-fat spreads as a substitute for margarine and butter.
5 Become aware of the foods, such as sausages, cakes, biscuits, crisps, and pastries, that have a high 'hidden' fat content (i.e. fat which is not visible) and restrict the consumption of these.
6 Make more use of fat-reduced products, e.g. canned fish in brine, low-fat salad dressings.

Eat more fibre (NSP) and starchy foods

It is recommended that the intake of fibre is at least 30 g per day for an average adult. It can be obtained from vegetables, fruit, and wholegrain cereals. This will help to prevent the development of intestinal disorders (see p. 27).

Starchy foods are filling and help to reduce the need to eat between meals.

Increasing dietary fibre consumption

1 Make more use of wholegrain cereal products in cooking, e.g. wholemeal flour instead of white, wholegrain rice, and wholemeal pasta.
2 Eat wheatmeal or wholemeal bread instead of white bread.
3 Eat more fresh fruit and vegetables.
4 Choose breakfast cereals and snacks that are rich in fibre and, preferably, low in sugar.
5 Add a little bran to soups and casseroles.
6 Make more use of pulses (see p. 136), many of which are rich in dietary fibre.

Eat less salt

It is recommended that the intake of salt is no more than 6 g per day.

Reducing salt intake

1 Try alternative flavours to salt (e.g. spices and herbs) when cooking, or, if a salty flavour is required, make use of salt substitutes which contain less sodium (see p. 24).
2 Reduce the amount of salt added to cooked items, such as vegetables and soups, and the amount added to meals at the table.
3 Cut down on salty snack foods (e.g. roasted peanuts and crisps).
4 Reduce the number and amount of foods eaten, that have salt added as part of their processing, e.g. bacon, cheese, sausages, cooked meats, smoked fish, canned vegetables in brine.

Drink less alcohol

It is recommended that the amount of energy obtained from alcohol is no more than 4% per day. This would lower the risk of damage to the liver, and help prevent obesity.

Reducing alcohol consumption

1 Become aware of the alcohol content of different types of drinks.
2 Where possible, dilute alcoholic drinks with fruit juices, mineral waters, etc.
3 Make a positive effort to limit the number of alcoholic drinks taken at any one time.
4 Try some of the alcohol-reduced beverages that are now available.

Eat a variety of foods and enjoy your food

For many people who try to follow dietary guidelines, checking lists of ingredients and working out the amount of fat, sugar, fibre, etc. in their food is time-consuming and not always easy.

To help people follow a healthy lifestyle, there have been various attempts to explain the dietary guidelines in a clearer way. In 1994, the Health Education Authority (HEA), Department of Health, and the Ministry of Agriculture, Fisheries, and Food (MAFF) produced a National Food Guide. This shows the relative proportions of different groups of foods people should aim to eat, to encourage them to eat a variety.

The National Food Guide. We should aim to eat foods from all the different food groups, in the proportions shown on the plate.

Another idea to help promote healthy eating is the '5 a day' campaign. This aims to increase the consumption of fruit and vegetables, and follows research showing the link between anti-oxidants in fruit and vegetables and the prevention of heart disease (see p. 45). The aim is to encourage people to eat at least 400 g of fruit and vegetables a day, which works out at least 5 portions a day – fresh, frozen, or canned.

The '5 a day' campaign promotes healthy eating by encouraging people to eat more fruit and vegetables – at least five portions each day.

Eat the right amount to maintain a healthy weight

People are encouraged not to over eat, because of the risk of becoming obese. Energy-dense foods, i.e. those with a high fat or sugar content, should be eaten in small amounts. Cooking methods that add fat to foods, such as frying, should be avoided and substituted with grilling or baking.

Eating too little food can also have serious effects on health (see p. 43 and pp. 47–8).

Following the guidelines

To follow dietary guidelines successfully, people need to know which nutrients are found in particular foods. Food labels, advice leaflets from supermarkets and health centres, and books about food can be helpful.

Ideally, healthy eating should begin when a baby is weaned on to solid foods. This means encouraging the baby to eat a variety of foods, including fruit and vegetables, low-sugar foods, and wholegrain cereals. It is then easier to continue good eating habits into childhood and later life.

Nutritional labelling

Nutritional labelling is essential to help people follow the dietary goals. Guidelines for nutritional labelling are produced by the Ministry of Agriculture, Fisheries, and Food, and at present food manufacturers do not have to use them, unless they are making a nutritional claim for the food, e.g. it is low in fat. The guidelines say how the information should be presented:

1 The nutrient values must be shown per 100g of food.
2 If there is less than 100 g of food in the package, the amount of nutrients per portion must be shown.
3 Foods claiming to be a good source of a nutrient must have at least one-sixth of the RNI.

The European Union (EU) has also issued guidelines for labelling.

INGREDIENTS

BRAN ENRICHED WHEAT, SUGAR, HONEY, SALT, MALT FLAVOURING, VITAMIN C, IRON, NIACIN, VITAMIN B6, RIBOFLAVIN (B2), THIAMIN (B1), FOLIC ACID, VITAMIN D, VITAMIN B12.

NUTRITION INFORMATION

		Typical value per 100g	Per 30g Serving with 125ml of Semi-Skimmed Milk
ENERGY	kJ	1350	650 *
	kcal	320	160
PROTEIN	g	11	8
CARBOHYDRATE	g	64	26
(of which sugars)	g	(24)	(14)
(starch)	g	(40)	(12)
FAT	g	2.0	2.5 *
(of which saturates)	g	(0.4)	(1.5)
FIBRE	g	16	5
SODIUM	g	0.9	0.3
VITAMINS:		(%RDA)	(%RDA)
VITAMIN D	µg	4.2 (85)	1.3 (25)
VITAMIN C	mg	50 (85)	16.3 (25)
THIAMIN (B1)	mg	1.2 (85)	0.4 (30)
RIBOFLAVIN (B2)	mg	1.3 (85)	0.6 (40)
NIACIN	mg	15 (85)	4.6 (25)
VITAMIN B6	mg	1.7 (85)	0.6 (30)
FOLIC ACID	µg	167 (85)	60 (30)
VITAMIN B12	µg	0.85 (85)	0.75 (75)
IRON	mg	11.7 (85)	3.6 (25)

* For whole milk increase energy by 100kJ (25kcal) and fat by 3g.
* For skimmed milk reduce energy by 70kJ (20kcal) and fat by 2g.
Contribution provided by 125ml of semi-skimmed milk:- 250kJ (60kcal) of energy, 4g of protein, 6g of carbohydrates (sugars), 2g of fat.

Food labels help consumers to make healthy food choices.

Understanding and using the information

Some studies suggest that consumers find it difficult to interpret the information on labels, so many food retail companies have produced advisory leaflets and now use easy-to-recognize symbols on their products in response to this.

Confusion can occur when labels claim that a food is 'low in' or 'reduced' fat or sugar, or 'light'. A 'low-fat' sausage may have far more fat per 100 g than a 'low-fat' fromage frais. The consumer will not realize this unless they compare the fat contents of different foods.

The word 'light' (often written as Lite) does not have a legal definition, but is used to give the impression of being healthier, when in fact the foods may still contain a relatively high amount of fat or sugar.

'No added sugar' or 'sugar free' may mean that no sucrose has been added, but that the product still contains a high concentration of naturally occurring sugars, or that other sugars, e.g. glucose, have been added.

'Low calorie' by law means that the food must provide no more than 40 kcals per 100 g or 100 ml. 'Diet' does not have a legal definition, and 'reduced-calorie' means that the food must not provide more than 75% of the kcals in its usual equivalent.

Most people will not use nutrition labels to work out a detailed account of their daily nutrient intake. The value of nutrition labels is to help consumers compare different foods, and decide how much of each to eat in order to stay healthy.

Choice of food

People who are fortunate enough to have a choice of food to eat (i.e. people in most affluent countries) have the opportunity to choose a healthy and varied food intake, and to control their eating habits. How that choice is made, however, depends on several different factors, some of which may be more influential than health considerations.

Personal likes and dislikes

Most people enjoy food. However, we all choose certain foods more often than others. Reasons for avoiding particular foods may include:

1   Dislike of the flavour, appearance, or texture.
2   Disagreement with the way the food is produced, e.g. using crates for rearing calves to produce veal.
3   Dislike of the way that food is prepared or cooked.
4   Associating the food with feeling ill, e.g. because of an allergy or past food poisoning.

Food presentation

Food that is well prepared, well cooked, and attractively presented is more likely to be chosen and enjoyed.

Religious and moral beliefs

Religious beliefs are very important to many people, and some religions have specific rules about what should and should not be eaten. Some examples are listed on p. 70.

Customs, traditions, and festivals

Many occasions and ceremonies – e.g. funerals, marriages, religious festivals, harvests – are celebrated with feasts or fasts (not eating food for a specific amount of time), or special meals and foods only prepared at that time. Some examples are given on pp. 70–1.

Availability of food

Affluent countries such as the UK, USA, France, and Germany, have plenty of food to feed their populations. Such countries grow some of their own food and import (bring in) the rest from around the world. Some countries grow little food (and are too poor to import enough) for various reasons (see p. 77).

Variety of food

Many foods in the UK and other countries are imported from all around the world, making food choice even greater. People can travel abroad more easily, and try foods, which then may become available back at home. Recipe books, prepared dishes, and media coverage also encourage people to try new foods.

Foods from other countries are an increasingly popular part of our diet.

Cost of food

The price of food depends on many factors, including:

1 The cost of growing, harvesting/ slaughtering, storing, processing, distributing, packaging, advertising, and selling the food.

2 Seasonal variations in fresh foods, e.g. soft fruit is cheaper in the summer when it is most available.

3 Variations in the quality of a particular food, e.g. tougher cuts of meat that require more cooking are generally cheaper.

Food technology

Food technology has increased food choice in various ways, including:

1 Producing cheaper versions of basic foods, e.g. margarine instead of butter.

2 Producing new types of food from unusual sources, e.g. quorn from mycoprotein (see pp. 129–30).

3 Producing quick-to-prepare foods and ready-prepared meals.

4 Increasing food production by developing new agricultural practices, e.g. hormone injections to cattle to improve milk yield, genetic engineering to produce high-yield cereal plants.

5 Increasing the shelf-life of foods to avoid wastage and preserving the food in good condition.

6 Improving packaging to enable more foods to be easily eaten away from the home, e.g. ring-pull cans, plastic food trays.

Revision questions

1 List the dietary guidelines.
2 At what age should healthy eating begin?
3 Why is it important to eat plenty of fruit and vegetables?
4 Why is it important to reduce the amount of fat in the diet?
5 Why are nutrition labels useful when planning a healthy diet?
6 What influences affect food choice?
7 What affects the availability of food in poor countries?
8 What factors influence the price of food?

Nutritional disorders related to food shortages

It is a tragic fact that today, in an age of advanced technology and scientific knowledge, there are still many people in the world (see p. 77) whose health and quality of life suffer through lack of food, as a result of poverty, war, disaster, pollution, or other social and political factors.

When the choice of food is severely limited, as during a famine, illness and death on a large scale are the usual results. Famines in countries including Ethiopia and the Sudan have been brought to the public's attention, but they are by no means the only examples of famine.

Many people in such countries receive little and often no food for long periods of time for a variety of reasons (see p. 77), and as a result suffer from malnutrition and the effects of long-term starvation.

Children in particular suffer badly, as their requirements for nutrients are high. In such a situation, they may develop one of the following conditions.

In a refugee camp in Somalia, this child receives nutritionally enriched porridge and biscuits.

Marasmus

This name comes from the Greek word meaning 'wasting', and it mainly affects babies under one year old. The body adapts to the shortage of food by the wasting of muscles and the depletion of fat stores, so that energy is only supplied to vital organs, e.g. brain, heart. The child therefore becomes very thin and weak and the condition often results in death.

Kwashiorkor

At one time it was thought that this condition resulted from a lack of protein in the diet. It is now known to be a poor adaptation to famine (where total food intake is reduced) and results in these symptoms:

retarded growth
chronic diarrhoea and infections
deterioration of hair, skin, and nails
retention of fluid under the skin, causing
    swelling (called **oedema**)
poor digestion of food

In adults, starvation results in a variety of symptoms, including:

1 Wasting of body tissue, especially adipose tissue (see p. 5).
2 Wasting of muscles and organs, such as the heart and intestines, to a size where they are too small and weak to function properly.
3 Dryness of hair and skin.
4 Oedema in the limbs and on the face.
5 Personality changes, causing restlessness, indifference, hysteria, and severe moodiness.

The treatment of starving people is difficult, not only because of lack of money and political reasons. Infections such as gastroenteritis, cholera, and pneumonia often aggravate the plight of the starving and are the final cause of many deaths.

When digestion (see p. 33) is poor, due to changes in the intestines, small, frequent feeds of specially formulated food have to be given, and recovery may be very slow. Large numbers of volunteer helpers are needed to distribute food and assist medical teams, often in very difficult situations where roads are bad and transport is scarce.

Health disorders related to unwise food choice

It is unfortunate and disturbing that many people in affluent societies (such as the UK), who have enough to eat, suffer from health disorders that are the result of over-indulgence in food, or unwise choices of diet. An unbalanced diet, e.g. one containing too much fat or sugar, can result in a variety of nutritional disorders, including:

    heart disease
    obesity
    tooth decay and gum disease
    intestinal diseases

Heart disease

Heart disease is a major cause of death in the UK, the USA, and other Western countries. In England and Wales approximately 27% of all deaths are due to coronary heart disease (CHD). About 180,000 people die each year and a further 115,000 are treated in hospital because of CHD. Treatment costs around £500 million a year. CHD is the most common type of heart disease and can eventually lead to **heart attacks**.

What happens in heart disease

To work normally, the heart muscle needs a supply of oxygen from blood in the coronary arteries so that it can pump blood through vessels to all parts of the body.

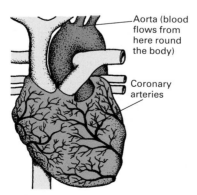

Aorta (blood flows from here round the body)

Coronary arteries

If one or more of the coronary arteries become blocked with fatty deposits (called atheromas), the blood carrying oxygen cannot reach the heart so easily.

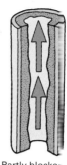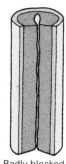

Normal artery: blood can flow through normally.

Partly blocked artery: blood flow is restricted.

Badly blocked artery: blood cannot flow through.

As a result, the heart muscle becomes partially starved of oxygen. This causes a temporary, severe, cramp-like pain across the chest, down the left arm, and around the neck. This is called **angina**. The pain is usually brought on by exercise, when the heart has to work harder, and it usually passes with rest and medication.

If there is a sudden and complete blockage in the arteries, caused by a blood clot (**thrombus**) in the artery, no blood will get through, and the person will suffer a heart attack. Doctors call a heart attack a **coronary thrombosis** (because of the blood clot) or a **myocardial infarction** (which means death of the heart muscle).

The patient will suffer severe pain lasting for several hours, and will feel sick and faint. In a heart attack, the heart muscle is badly damaged because it does not have enough oxygen, and afterwards it is weaker. Prompt treatment can limit the damage. If the heart stops beating during the attack, (a **cardiac arrest**), the patient will die unless emergency first aid is at hand.

Causes of heart disease

Heart disease is a major concern, and there has been much research into its causes and ways of preventing it.

It has become clear that there is no single cause of heart disease, but many **risk factors**. Usually CHD is brought on by more than one of these. Some of the risk factors can be prevented or reduced by changing habits or lifestyle, but some can not.

Risk factors that cannot be prevented:

1 **Being male** – more men than women have CHD, though it affects an increasing number of women.
2 **Increasing age**.
3 **Heredity** – heart disease often runs in families.

Risk factors that can be prevented or reduced:

1 **Smoking cigarettes** – increases the risk of CHD for both females and males.
2 **Choice of food** – eating less fat and more fruit and vegetables can help prevent CHD.
3 **Being overweight**.
4 **Lack of exercise** – regular exercise strengthens the heart muscle and makes it work more efficiently.
5 **Stress** – people who are impatient, ambitious, competitive, tense, and anxious seem more likely to suffer from CHD than those who are calmer, less worried, and more relaxed.
6 **High blood pressure** – makes the heart work harder and speeds up the blocking of arteries. The other risk factors listed above may cause high blood pressure.

All these risk factors are important, but in this book we will only look at choice of food.

Choice of food and heart disease

Research has shown that our diet, especially the amount and type of fat we eat, can increase the risk of CHD. Diets that are high in saturated fatty acids (see p. 6), may raise the level of **cholesterol** in the blood. High blood cholesterol levels are linked to the development of CHD.

Cholesterol is found in some foods, and is also made in the body by the liver, mainly from saturated fatty acids in food. If cholesterol is **oxidized** (picks up oxygen circulating in the blood), it can be deposited in the linings of the coronary arteries, which start to become blocked.

Antioxidants found naturally in foods, especially vitamin E, vitamin C, ß-carotene, and selenium (see pp. 15, 19, 12, and 21), help to stop cholesterol picking up oxygen, so that it is deposited less readily in the coronary arteries.

Choosing healthy foods like these can help to protect against heart disease.

(Artificial antioxidants, which are added to foods to preserve them (see p. 169), do not help the body in this way.)

Cholesterol is not made so readily by the liver if a person eats foods that contain poly-unsaturated fatty acids (PUFAs), and some monounsaturated fatty acids (see p. 6). For example, the PUFAs in oily fish (e.g. herring, sardine, mackerel, and pilchards), seem to reduce the amount of cholesterol made by the liver.

Research has shown that when oils are processed to make them into margarine and other cooking fats, the PUFAs in the oil may change to **trans fatty acids**. These may increase the amount of cholesterol made by the liver. Some margarine manufacturers have tried to reduce the amount of trans fatty acids formed during processing, so that they can promote the healthy image and benefits of using their products.

Exercise can be fun! Regular excercise also strengthens the heart and reduces the risk of CHD.

Prevention of heart disease should begin in early childhood. Research has shown that fatty streaks have appeared in the arteries of some children as young as 10 years old. To prevent later problems, parents should encourage their children to:

1   Eat a variety of foods.
2   Eat fresh fruit, vegetables, and salads.
3   Take exercise and be active, as this strengthens the heart and will be a good habit to continue in adult life.
4   Eat less high-fat food.
5   Eat less sweet food, as excess sugar is converted into fat in the body causing weight gain and therefore a strain on the heart.
6   Eat less salty food, as too much salt can lead to high blood pressure and therefore a strain on the heart.

Adults should also follow this advice. It can be hard to alter your eating habits and way of life, but it is worth the effort. CHD patients are usually given dietary advice and are encouraged to stop smoking and limit the amount of alcohol they drink.

Obesity

Obesity (excessive weight gain) is a very common and increasing nutritional disorder in affluent countries. It can be caused by hormonal disorders, but the major cause is eating more food than the body needs. The excess is stored as fat in the body.

Obesity is usually caused by eating more food than the body needs.

Years ago, it was considered desirable to be overweight, because it indicated that a person was wealthy and could afford to live richly. This idea has now changed, and obesity is known to be undesirable and unhealthy because:

1   Obese people are more prone to heart disease, chest infections, varicose veins, hernias, high blood pressure, diabetes, gall stones, osteoarthritis of the back, knees, and hips, and skin infections.
2   Extra body fat can cause complications during operations.
3   Unhappiness about being obese, and comments made by other people, may make an obese person turn to food for comfort, making their condition worse.

Losing weight

Many people feel that they need to lose weight and take action to do so. A great deal of money is spent on slimming aids and products, by people trying to lose weight quickly and with the minimum effort.

Some people who try to lose weight are not obese or even overweight. Girls and women in particular may feel under pressure to conform to the sort of 'ideal' body image they see in magazines and on television. However, they will find it difficult and unhealthy to maintain a body weight that is too low for them.

A person who is trying to lose weight should seek advice from a doctor or dietician, to agree a weight-reducing diet that suits them. Weight loss takes time and requires changes to a person's eating habits and way of life (e.g. taking more exercise). Will-power, determination, and an understanding of how food affects the body are needed.

The most effective and healthy way to reduce weight is to take in slightly less energy from food than the body needs each day. The body then makes up the difference by releasing the energy it has stored in fat. Gradually the stores of fat are reduced.

Depending on the weight, height, and age of the person, a diet providing 4200–6700 kJ (1000–1500 kcal) per day is usually recommended. The weight-reducing diet should include a good variety of foods to make it interesting, with plenty of fresh fruit, vegetables, and wholegrain cereals, and very little fatty or sugary food. High-protein foods and alcohol should also be limited.

Exercising uses more energy, which promotes weight loss, tones the muscles, and generally helps to make a person feel better.

Very low calorie diets are heavily advertised as a quick and easy way to lose weight. They usually consist of a flavoured drink, containing a variety of nutrients, to replace breakfast and the midday meal. A well-balanced, 'proper' meal is then eaten at the end of the day. This type of diet can cause problems because:

1 It does not encourage the dieter to change their eating habits at every meal or in the long term.
2 It often leads to loss of muscle instead of fat.
3 Once normal eating resumes, weight may be put back on quickly.
4 It can be expensive.

Many communities have weight-loss groups where people who want to lose weight can meet regularly, receive dietary advice and information, have their weight measured and monitored, and encourage each other to succeed in reaching their target weight.

These groups are often successful, and help many people who find it difficult to lose weight alone. Once the target weight is reached, people should stay in contact to try and maintain their new, healthier eating habits.

Eating disorders

Eating disorders have been widely reported and researched since the beginning of the 1980s. Most publicity has been given to **anorexia nervosa** and **bulimia nervosa**. These disorders have quite a lot in common, and a person may show symptoms of both.

Anorexia nervosa

This disorder affects mainly teenage girls and young women, and sometimes boys and young men. Many patients who receive treatment return to their normal weight after two to ten years, but may still have difficulty in eating normally. Some patients with anorexia eventually starve themselves to death.

Anorexia nervosa

A person with anorexia nervosa:

1 Refuses to eat enough to maintain their body weight for their age and height.
2 Believes and sees their body to be much bigger than it really is.
3 Has a real and great fear of becoming fat.
4 Develops dry skin, and brittle, dry hair on their cheeks, back of the neck, arms, and legs.
5 In females, menstruation (periods) stop, and may not return for years. This can lead to osteoporosis (see p. 22) and infertility (being unable to have children).
6 Has cold feet and hands, and possibly serious heart problems.
7 Has constipation.

Patients with anorexia nervosa control their body weight in one of two ways:

1 Eating very little, often no more than 200–300 kcals (840–1260 kJ) per day.
2 Eating food in varying amounts and then getting it out of their body, either by making themselves vomit (being sick) or by taking laxatives. The food leaves the body before it has been digested properly, and so does not give the body energy or nutrients.

Patients are often very fussy about food, but talk a lot about it and like to cook for other people. They often exercise vigorously so that they 'burn off' any energy they have taken from food.

Bulimia nervosa

Patients with bulimia nervosa have powerful urges to eat very large amounts of food, and then often make themselves sick or take laxatives to prevent gaining weight. Eating large amounts of food like this is called binge eating. It may happen several times a week and be alternated with periods of eating almost nothing.

Like anorexic patients, bulimic patients are often afraid of becoming fat and have a distorted image of what shape and size they are.

Bulimic patients often eat in private, hiding their problem away from other people. They may suffer:

1   Kidney problems and swelling of the tissue under the skin (oedema).
2   Muscle weakness, constipation, and headaches through losing potassium and chloride (see p. 24) when they vomit.
3   Sore throat, swollen salivary glands, and tiredness.
4   Severe dental problems caused by acid from the stomach coming in contact with the teeth when they vomit. The acid dissolves the tooth enamel (see p. 49).

Causes of eating disorders

There is no single cause of eating disorders. Many factors may lead to a person having an eating disorder, including:

1   Emotional shock or grief.
2   Stress over a period of time.
3   Fear of growing up.
4   An unhappy childhood.
5   Unhappiness about body size and shape.
6   Unhappy relationships within the family.
7   A need to have control over one's life.

People react very differently to these, so this list is only a guide.

Treatment

Treatment for eating disorders is usually long, and it is often not possible to say whether a patient has been cured.

Patients often return to normal weight and eat regularly, but tend to slip back into old habits of controlling what they eat if they come under pressure or are unhappy again. Special clinics dealing only with eating disorders have expert help at hand. Patients must want to be helped and co-operate with the treatment if it is to work.

Occasionally a patient is so weak that they are put into hospital against their will in order to try to save them. They have to stay in bed and are given food regularly in the hope that they will gradually put on weight.

Treatment often includes the whole family, to give them an understanding of the problem. Much patience and understanding is needed if the treatment is to have any chance of success.

Tooth decay and gum disease

Tooth decay and gum disease affect many people worldwide, especially in countries where people often eat foods containing added sugar.

Dental caries is the name given to tooth decay.
Periodontal disease is the name given to gum disease.

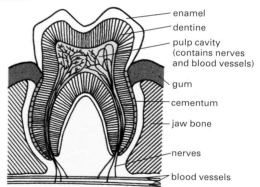

The diagram shows the structure of a tooth. The enamel covering the tooth is 96% minerals (mainly calcium, and phosphorus). Teeth form in the jaws long before they erupt (come through the gum), and must be looked after if they are to last, and chew food efficiently.

When food is eaten, a white, sticky substance called **plaque** builds up on the surface of the teeth, especially next to the gum. Plaque is mostly micro-organisms, plus some water and polysaccharides (see p. 10). When sugar is eaten, it is absorbed into the plaque, broken down by the micro-organisms, and turned into acid.

pH is a measure of acidity. Plaque normally has a pH of 6.8, but when sugar is eaten it can fall as low as pH 4.5 within seconds. Below pH 5.5, the mineral part of tooth enamel dissolves. It cannot be replaced, and leaves a weak spot, which gets larger and deeper until a cavity (hole) is made in the tooth (this is sometimes called 'acid attack'). If unchecked, the decay will continue until the whole tooth is affected and has to be removed.

1. Decay starts in enamel.

2. Decay affects dentine.

3. Decay reaches nerves.

4. Infection may cause abscess.

Eating a lot of sugary foods makes teeth more likely to decay. This is because the plaque pH stays low, as acid forms every time sugar is in the mouth. This is why it is sensible to avoid eating sweet foods between meals (see grazing, p. 53).

Plaque can be stained using special disclosing tablets (available from the chemist or dentist). This helps when cleaning the teeth, because you can see whether they are really clean after brushing.

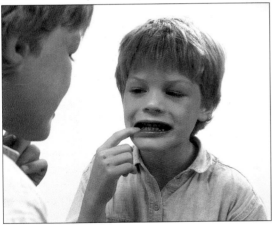
Plaque disclosing tablets show you where plaque has built up on your teeth.

Dental plaque also causes periodontal disease. This is where the gums become irritated and infected by micro-organisms in the plaque. The infection is called **gingivitis**. The gums swell, become inflamed and sore, and bleed easily. Eventually, the ligaments and bone that hold the teeth in place are destroyed and the teeth become loose and fall out. Bad breath (**halitosis**) is

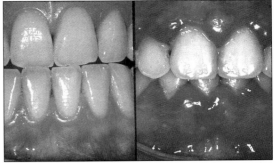
Look after your teeth (left) to avoid tooth decay and gum disease (right).

another symptom of periodontal disease. Teeth and gums can be kept healthy and look attractive by following these guidelines:

1 **Babies** – do not add sugar to bottle feeds or solid foods. Babies do not need it and will not notice that the food is not sweetened. Do not introduce babies to sweetened fruit juices and squashes too young. Encourage them to drink water between milk feeds. Do not give a sweetened dummy to suck as this can cause tooth decay even when the teeth have not erupted (come through).

2 **Children and teenagers** – limit their consumption of sweet drinks and sweet foods between meals. Have a special day of the week for eating sweets, preferably at the end of a meal, not between meals.

3 Study food labels. Many foods have sugar added, but give the chemical name, e.g. maltose, glucose, sucrose, fructose (see pp. 9–10). These too can cause tooth decay.

4 Look for low-sugar biscuits, soft drinks, and medicines. They often have artificial sweeteners added and will say so on the label.

5 Put less sugar into home-made foods. Many cakes, biscuits, and puddings can be made successfully with less sugar.

6 Avoid acidic drinks, especially concentrated fruit juices and carbonated (fizzy) sweet drinks, which can damage tooth enamel.

7 Brush the teeth at least twice a day using a brush which is the right size, and in good condition. Pay particular attention to the biting surfaces of the teeth, and the point where the teeth meet the gums. Do not brush too hard as this can damage the enamel.

8 Learn how to use dental floss to clean between teeth and round the back teeth.

9 When the second (permanent) teeth erupt, the molars can be **fissure sealed** by the dentist. This is a painless process where the fissures (tiny nooks and crannies) on the top surface of the molar teeth are filled with a white plastic which sets and prevents particles of food becoming trapped there, and reduces the risk of decay.

10 Use a fluoride toothpaste to strengthen the enamel of growing teeth (see p. 24). Toothpastes, mouthwashes, tablets, and drops containing fluoride can all be obtained from the chemist or dentist. Tablets and drops should only be given under the instructions of the dentist, as too much fluoride can damage tooth enamel.

11 Have regular dental check–ups, at least twice a year.

Revision questions

1 What effect does a shortage of food have on children and adults?
2 Which risk factors in heart disease can be prevented?
3 Why are saturated fatty acids linked to heart disease?
4 Why are vitamins C and E and ß-carotene important in the prevention of heart disease?
5 Why is obesity dangerous to health?
6 Why do very low calorie diets often cause problems to those who use them to try to lose weight?
7 What are the symptoms and eating habits of someone with anorexia nervosa?
8 How can dental caries be prevented?
9 What is periodontal disease?
10 What is 'acid attack'?
11 How can fluoride help to prevent dental caries?

Questions and activities

1 These three pie charts show the amounts of different nutrients eaten by British, Ugandan, and Japanese people:

a Which community eats the most fat and sugar?

b Which community eats the most starch and NSP?

c Which community eats the least protein?

d What are plantains?

e Japanese recipes often use stir-frying to cook vegetables and meat/fish. Why is this healthier than shallow and deep-fat frying?

f Which community is more likely to have the highest rates of heart disease and obesity? Why?

g Which community is likely to have low rates of constipation and diverticular disease? Why?

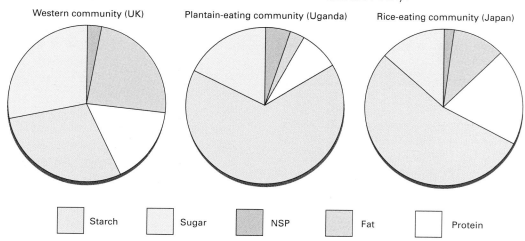

Western community (UK)　　Plantain-eating community (Uganda)　　Rice-eating community (Japan)

☐ Starch　☐ Sugar　☐ NSP　☐ Fat　☐ Protein

(Source: *Human nutrition and dietetics*. 9th edn, ed. Garrow and James. Churchill Livingston.)

2 The graph shows the DRVs for energy for males and females at different ages.

  a Which age group needs the most energy (males and females)?

  b Do energy needs increase or decrease from birth to 18 years? Why?

  c Why do energy needs decrease as people get older?

  d Do males or females have greater energy needs? Why?

  e What would happen if people ate more food but did not increase their activity?

  f What would happen if people did not eat enough food to match their energy needs?

  g In what situations might a person only get a small percentage of their daily energy needs? How would the body adapt?

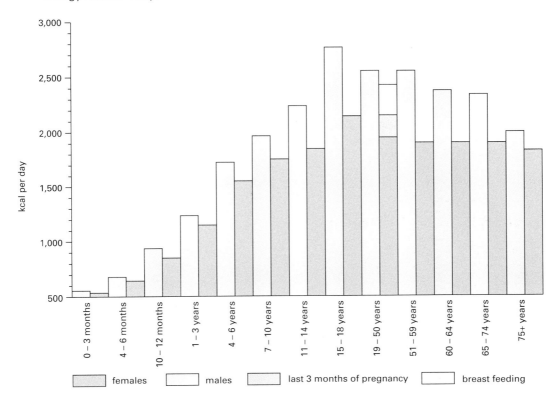

3 Study the main meal menu below:

> fried sausages and onions
> fried chips
> baked beans in tomato sauce
> white bread roll and butter
>
> jam tart
> custard

  a Which nutrients are found in largest amounts in this meal?

  b Is it a high or low energy meal? Why?

  c What is the latest healthy eating advice from the Government?

  d How could the menu be changed to suit this healthy eating advice?

4 People are advised to increase their intake of fresh fruit and vegetables to at least 5 portions a day.

  a Plan 3 meals for a family of 2 adults and 3 children and include at least 5 portions of fruit and vegetables.

  b Why are fruit and vegetables beneficial to health?

  c In what ways can a family with a low income follow this advice and provide healthy, satisfying meals?

5 Food labels provide consumers with information. Collect a variety of food labels (fresh and processed foods), and read them carefully.

  a What attracts you to some labels but not others?

  b Which labels are the easiest and which are the most difficult to read. Why?

  c How do you think the labels could be improved and who would benefit from these improvements?

  d What symbols are on the labels? What do they mean?

  e What information would someone with heart disease find useful? Why?

  f What information would someone on a weight-reducing diet find useful? Why?

  g What information would someone with high blood pressure find useful? Why?

6 **a** What type of nutrients are the following?

   ascorbic acid
   folate
   calcium
   iron

  b Name 3 good sources of each.

  c What is the connection of any of these nutrients to:

   pregnancy
   old age
   teenage girls and women
   the prevention of CHD?

7 What effect(s) do the following have in each case on the nutrients in the foods listed? How could the nutrients be preserved?

  a leaving milk in a bottle outside in sunlight for several hours

  b boiling cabbage for 20 minutes in a pan full of water

  c grilling a lamb chop until it is dry and hard

  d leaving a carton of fresh orange juice open for several days

Which groups of people in the UK today might need to take extra nutrients to maintain their health? Give reasons why this may be necessary.

8 Obesity is a major health hazard and affects many people. Make a study of the help that is available in the media (TV, radio, magazines, etc.) for people who are trying to reduce their weight. Investigate a variety of products (foods, drinks, exercise machines, etc.) that are sold to encourage people to slim. How are such products promoted? Criticize (constructively) such products, and suggest how they could be improved or what alternatives could be used by people trying to lose weight.

❷ Providing food for different needs

Meal planning

Food is a vital part of our lives and much of our time is spent in its preparation.

Everyone has different needs and requirements for food, according to:

    their age and sex

    their health condition

    their daily activity

    the climate in which they live

    their likes, dislikes, food customs and taboos

The preparation and consumption of food is also influenced by:

1   The interest and motivation of the person who is preparing the food.
2   The culinary abilities and skills of the food preparer.
3   The time and the facilities that are available for preparing food.
4   The foods that are available.
5   The income available to be spent on food.

Appetite and the desire to eat food are also affected by:

1   The colour, appearance, and presentation of the food.
2   The taste, smell, and texture of the food.
3   The surroundings and atmosphere in which the food is eaten.

Until fairly recently, meals were a very time-consuming part of family life. Long and elaborate preparation was often involved, and the whole family would sit down together to eat in a leisurely manner.

Food habits have changed to fit in with rapidly changing lifestyles. The increase in shift-working, more women going out to work, and television viewing at mealtimes have all contributed to a general reduction in the time spent preparing food and eating meals. One or more members of the family will often be absent at mealtimes.

There has been an increase in what nutritionists call 'grazing'. Grazing is when food is eaten in small quantities throughout the day, with or without main meals. Many food manufacturers produce 'snack' sized versions of their existing products (e.g. biscuits), which encourages people to graze. Grazing can lead to obesity and dental caries (see pp. 46 and 49).

Advances in kitchen technology, such as the introduction of freezers and microwave ovens, have helped to reduce the time spent on food preparation. The availability of convenience foods has also been important, and many ready-prepared dishes and main meals require only heating in an oven or microwave.

There is now a great variety of foods to choose from in the shops, thanks to advances in food production, technology, transport, and storage. In our multicultural society many foods are imported from overseas. Foreign restaurants and take-away food shops have also contributed to the change in eating habits.

Meals still have to be planned, however, and individual needs have to be considered. Few people work out a detailed weekly plan for their

Supermarkets now sell a wide range of ready-prepared dishes.

meals, and buy their food strictly according to that plan. But in some cases this long-term meal planning is necessary; in catering establishments such as canteens, hospital kitchens, restaurants, and hotels, it is vital.

Terminology associated with meal planning

Balanced meal

A balanced meal is one that provides all the nutrients an individual needs in suitable amounts throughout the day. It should also provide a balance of texture, flavour, colour, and variety of foods in order to be appetizing.

Diet

The word 'diet' refers to the food eaten by an individual every day. There are also special diets, e.g. low-fat diets, low-salt diets, diabetic diets.

Meals

Breakfast

The word means to break a fast, i.e. a period of time when food is not eaten (during sleep).

Lunch/dinner

There are regional differences in the meanings of these two words. Some people refer to the meal eaten at midday as dinner; others call it lunch and refer to the meal eaten in the evening as dinner.

In this section, the following words will be used to denote the main meals of the day:
  breakfast
  midday meal
  evening meal

Tea

Tea used to be served in many homes at about four o'clock in the afternoon, and usually consisted of a drink of tea with some form of cake or biscuit. It is less common now, but often children have tea when they arrive home from school.

High tea

The meal eaten at about six o'clock in the evening is sometimes called high tea. It usually consists of a cooked dish, with a drink and some form of cake or biscuit.

Supper

The last meal eaten before bedtime is usually called supper. This might be a full evening meal, or it might be a hot drink and biscuits.

Courses

The wood 'courses' refers to how a meal is divided up. A three-course meal consists of:
  1st course – starter/appetizer
  2nd course – main part of meal
  3rd course – sweet, or cheese and biscuits.

Following dietary guidelines

To achieve a healthy diet, the dietary guidelines set out in Chapter 1 (see p. 38) should be followed as closely as possible. Information about how different foods can be used in a healthy diet is available from various places, including:
  food labels (see pp. 40 and 81)
  supermarket information leaflets
  food advice centres (often supermarkets
    and large food companies have these)
  health visitors
  health centres
  child care clinics
  magazine articles and TV programmes
  computer databases

A mixture of foods every day makes meals more varied and interesting, and provides different nutrients. The next sections look at individual requirements for food.

Pregnant women

It is important that the diet of a pregnant woman is nutritionally sound, so that she produces a healthy baby, and at the same time maintains her own health. Even before pregnancy, it is vital that a woman of child-bearing age has a balanced diet so that she can cope with the demands of pregnancy.

There used to be a popular saying that a pregnant woman should 'eat for two'. In one sense this is true, but it does not mean that she should eat double her normal amount of food. This is not necessary, and it could lead to obesity. It does mean, however, that her diet should provide sufficient nutrients to cope with the demands of the growing baby (foetus) as well as the needs of her own body. The increased requirements for individual nutrients in pregnancy are shown in the tables of Reference Nutrient Intakes.

The foetus receives nutrients from the mother. The nutrients are carried from the mother's bloodstream through the **placenta** and **umbilical cord** into the baby's bloodstream

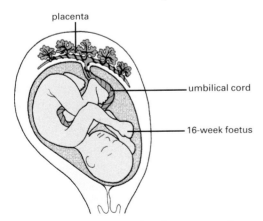

The mother's blood enters the placenta, carrying nutrients, and the blood from the foetus leaves, carrying waste products.

If the woman is healthy and has a good, mixed diet, then both she and the foetus will receive all the nutrients they need. However, if a particular nutrient is in short supply, the foetus may receive it and not the mother. This may happen if food is scarce or the mother has a poor diet, and it will affect the health of both mother and baby quite drastically.

Pregnant women can get dietary advice from the community midwife, doctor, and health visitor, who keep a careful check on the health of mother and baby. During early pregnancy a woman may feel sick (nauseous) or be sick at any time of the day or night. This can make eating well very difficult. The sickness often passes after 10–12 weeks, but can go on right through the pregnancy. If the mother is very unwell and not gaining weight she may be admitted to hospital and fed through an intravenous drip to ensure that she gets all the nutrients and energy that she needs.

All nutrients are important in pregnancy, but particularly the following:

Essential fatty acids (see p. 7)
These are needed by the foetus for brain growth and cell division.

Vitamin D (see p. 13)
A deficiency can lead to low birth weight and tetany in the baby, and to oesteomalacia in the mother.

This problem may occur in communities that live in areas where there is little sunlight, e.g. in northern countries, or have religious customs requiring the whole body to be covered with clothing.

Vitamin E (see p. 15)
Most vitamin E is transferred to the foetus in the last 10 weeks of pregnancy. If a baby is born prematurely, it may need a vitamin E supplement.

Vitamin K (see p. 15)
Vitamin K deficiency can lead to haemorrhaging (bleeding where the blood will not clot) in the first month after birth. Most newborn babies are given vitamin K, either by mouth or as an injection, to prevent this.

Folate (see p. 18)

Folate is required very early in pregnancy for the correct development of the brain and nervous system in the foetus.

A woman needs sufficient folate in her diet even before she becomes pregnant, or there may be problems in the pregnancy. Folate deficiency can lead to miscarriage (losing the developing foetus), slow growth, malformations in the foetus (e.g. spina bifida), or premature birth.

Vitamin B$_{12}$ (see p. 18)

A vegetarian mother may be deficient in vitamin B$_{12}$, and may need to take a supplement during pregnancy and while breastfeeding to ensure she has sufficient. The foetus stores vitamin B$_{12}$ so that it has enough for the first 6 months after birth.

Calcium (see p. 21)

The foetus needs a lot of calcium in the last few weeks of pregnancy, as the skeleton develops. If there is not enough calcium or vitamin D in the mother's diet, she may lose calcium from her skeleton, which can lead to weakened bones and teeth.

Iron (see p. 22)

The mother must have enough iron during pregnancy. It is needed to supply her own body and to provide the growing baby with a store of iron for the first few months after birth. Breast milk and cow's milk are both poor sources of iron, so this store is vital.

During pregnancy, the level of haemoglobin in the blood is checked regularly. If there is less than 10mg per dl, the mother is anaemic (see p. 23), and the doctor may prescribe iron tablets.

NSP (see p. 26)

Constipation can be a problem in pregnancy. If it is, women should increase the amount of fibre in their diet and take gentle exercise, e.g. walking and swimming.

Weight gain in pregnancy

A woman normally gains weight during pregnancy. How much she gains is influenced by her diet, age, level of activity, weight before pregnancy, and whether or not she smokes. The weight gained is approximately 62% water (including extra blood), 30% fat, and 8% protein. As the baby is breast-fed, the energy stored as fat is gradually used up.

Fasting during pregnancy

Some religious customs require people to fast for a certain part of the day (see p. 70). This can cause problems in pregnancy, because the glucose and insulin (see p. 73) in the mother's bloodsteam will be used up, which may cause brain damage in the growing baby. Pregnant women should not fast for more than 6–8 hours.

Food poisoning

Some types of food poisoning are particularly dangerous to pregnant women. The bacterium *Listeria monocytogenes* (see p. 157) is common in unpasteurized soft cheeses (e.g. Brie, goat's cheese), pre-cooked chicken, pâté, and ready-prepared salads. It may lead to an illness called listeriosis, which can cause stillbirth or miscarriage. Women should avoid these foods altogether during pregnancy.

Salmonella bacteria (see p. 157) can also cause severe food poisoning. It is common in dishes that contain raw or partially cooked eggs, such as mayonnaise, cold soufflés, and mousses. Notices warning women to avoid these foods during pregnancy are often displayed in shops where the foods are sold.

food
safety
in pregnancy

Food poisoning and other infections can occur in pregnancy and on rare occasions can damage your growing baby. By taking a few simple precautions, you can help to protect yourself and your developing baby from infections like listeriosis, salmonellosis and toxoplasmosis.

LISTERIOSIS

Listeriosis is caused by the bacterium *Listeria monocytogenes*. This is a rare illness causing flu-like symptoms in pregnant women which can be mild in the mother but can severely affect her developing baby.

FOODS TO TAKE CARE WITH
MOULD RIPENED SOFT CHEESE

Mould ripened soft cheeses eg Camembert, Brie, Blue Veined Cheese. *Listeria* may occasionally be present in soft mould ripened cheeses. Avoid eating all these types of cheese.

SALMONELLOSIS

Salmonellosis is caused by bacteria called *Salmonella*. It causes sickness and diarrhoea but rarely causes damage to the unborn baby.

FOODS TO TAKE CARE WITH
RAW OR LIGHTLY COOKED EGGS

Raw or lightly cooked eggs and uncooked dishes containing raw egg. It is best to avoid dishes that contain raw eggs, for example; home-made mayonnaise, mousses, cheesecakes as there is a risk that they may contain *Salmonella*. Eat only hard-boiled eggs, cook egg dishes thoroughly or use pasteurised egg products.

RAW POULTRY AND RAW MEAT

These products may occasionally contain *Salmonella* and other food poisoning bacteria which are destroyed by cooking at high temperatures. Poultry and meat should be cooked thoroughly. Keep cooked meat separate from raw meat and always use different preparation utensils.

UNPASTEURISED MILK

May contain a variety of dangerous bacteria and should be avoided. Only consume pasteurised, sterilised or UHT milk.

TOXOPLASMOSIS

Toxoplasmosis is a rare illness which may affect the unborn baby. It is due to the parasite *Toxoplasma gondii* which may be found in raw meat and cat faeces.

Post-natal (after the birth of the baby)

After the birth, the mother's nutrient requirements increase. Her body needs more nutrients to cope with the demands of breast-feeding and the increased activity associated with rearing a baby.

Any weight gained during pregnancy will usually take a few months to go. Weight loss is helped considerably if the mother is breast-feeding, and breast-feeding mothers should increase their intake of liquids.

Infancy (up to one year)

An infant's diet for the first few months of life consists solely of milk.

Breast-feeding (lactation)

Human breast milk is specifically designed to feed human babies. It is the best milk to give babies because:

1 It provides the correct mix and quantity of nutrients for the infant to grow normally.
2 The milk is at the right temperature and consistency.
3 The baby lies close to the mother to feed, and forms a strong bond with her, and she with the baby.
4 The action of sucking produces hormones in the baby's body that help the intestines to develop and to absorb nutrients more efficiently.
5 The baby digests virtually all the milk which gives it a feeling of satiety (fullness) and drowsiness.
6 The baby takes only what it needs, and is therefore less likely to become overweight.
7 Immunity from certain diseases is passed to the baby from the mother.
8 No preparation is needed, so breast-feeding is very convenient especially when going out, and when there are other children to look after.
9 There is little chance of the baby picking up gastric infections (stomach upsets), because the milk is sterile and does not come into contact with the outside air.
10 Breast-fed babies are less likely to be sensitive to foods, or have eczema and asthma.

For the first 5 days, the mother produces a watery substance called **colostrum**. This provides essential nutrients and immunity to the baby. After this, the milk 'matures', and the volume produced increases as the baby demands more of it.

Breast milk provides babies with just the right mix of nutrients for the first months of life.

Mothers are advised to feed 'on demand' rather than keep to a rigid feeding timetable, as babies need different amounts at different times of the day. Gradually, the baby establishes its own feeding timetable, and the mother can predict when to feed.

Breast-feeding takes time to become properly established, and the mother may have problems with sore and cracked nipples, infection of the breast (mastitis), and engorgement (over-full breasts leading to lumpiness and discomfort). Midwives and health visitors can offer help, support, and encouragement to new mothers who may want to give up breast-feeding when problems arise.

Once breast-feeding is established, it can go on for many months, and give great pleasure and good health to both baby and mother.

Bottle-feeding

Not every mother is able to or wants to breast-feed her baby, and she should not be made to feel bad about this.

Instead, she needs careful guidance on bottle-feeding. Her partner and other members of the family can also enjoy the pleasure of feeding the baby.

Powdered milk preparations for bottle-feeding babies are made from modified cow's milk. Ordinary cow's milk must not be given because it is too high in mineral salts and protein, and would put a great strain on the baby's kidneys.

Bottle-fed babies are not at any disadvantage, as long as the milk is prepared exactly as instructed. Using too much powdered milk to make up a feed can lead to obesity, great thirst, and strain on the kidneys. The mother may interpret the baby's distress as being hungry rather than thirsty, and give it more milk, thus causing more problems. Bottle-fed babies should therefore be offered plain cooled, boiled water to drink as well as milk.

Powdered milk, bottles, teats, and sterilizing equipment are all expensive, and bottles and teats must be sterilized after each use. Milk is the perfect medium for bacteria to grow, and poorly cleaned equipment can cause dangerous infections. Some babies cannot tolerate cow's milk, and may become ill or affected by eczema. (see p. 72).

Babies under 4 months should not have sweetened fruit juices or other drinks, as the sugar in them can cause tooth decay, even when the teeth have not yet erupted (come through). They should have plain cooled, boiled water as a supplementary drink if the weather is hot. This will encourage them to drink water when they are older.

Babies should *not* be given dummies that have been dipped in sugar or syrup. The sugar would be in prolonged contact with the gums and would cause tooth decay.

Weaning

Weaning is the gradual introduction of solid foods into the baby's diet, to supplement milk which still forms the main part of the diet. The following advice about weaning babies comes from the Department of Health.

Most babies should not have any solid foods before they are 4 months old. Below that age the kidneys and digestive system may not be developed sufficiently to cope with solid food.

Children should be encouraged to develop healthy eating habits from an early age.

By 6 months, all babies should have a mixed diet (a variety of solid foods and milk).

Foods should be offered from a spoon rather than a bottle. This will encourage the baby to try more solid foods, and the food will be in contact with the gums and teeth for a much shorter time.

Different foods should be introduced a little at a time, and should be sieved or puréed so that the baby can swallow them without choking. Suggested introductory foods include:

1   Low-sugar rusks or unsweetened ground rice in milk. Breast milk can be expressed (squeezed out) by the mother into a sterile bottle and kept in the refrigerator for this.
2   Puréed cooked vegetables, e.g. carrot and potato, parsnip and peas.
3   Puréed cooked meat and fish with unsalted gravy.
4   Puréed fruit, e.g. banana and fresh orange juice, cooked apple, pear, and mango.
5   Sieved, cooked egg yolk (hard boil the egg first).

It is not necessary or advisable to add sugar or salt to these foods. This would encourage a taste for salty and sweet foods, which can be undesirable and unhealthy. Salt also puts extra strain on the kidneys.

As the baby eats more solid foods it will drink less milk, and can drink water with a meal instead. From 6 months babies should be encouraged to drink from a trainer beaker.

As the baby's teeth start to erupt, coarser foods can be introduced, similar to those listed above but less finely puréed. Foods to encourage chewing and to help teething can be given, such as:

dry low-sugar rusks

toasted bread

commercially made bread sticks (grissini)

pieces of fruit, e.g. apple with skin removed

Babies and children should *never* be left alone while eating in case they choke on the food.

Foods for a baby can be prepared from family meals using a liquidizer, processor, sieve, or special baby-food grinder.

The recommendation to reduce fat intake (see p. 38) does not apply to babies and children under 2 years of age, and full-fat milk should be given to this age group. Dietary fat should be reduced gradually between the ages of 2 and 5 years.

Apart from the natural sugar found in milk (lactose), sugar should not make up more than 10% of the total energy intake. Parents need to know the names of the various sugars used in food products and to check food labels carefully (see p. 81).

Sweets and chocolates are often used as treats or to encourage the child to behave well. They can become habit forming as they are very palatable, often brightly coloured, interestingly shaped and packaged, and very appealing. Small children cannot understand the effect of too much sugar on their teeth, so the parent or child minder must restrict the number of sweets they eat. Eating sweets at the end of the meal, just before teeth are cleaned, will do little harm. The same advice applies to sweetened soft drinks (see p. 49).

A variety of protein food should be offered, including plant proteins (e.g. beans, pulses, soya products). Non-vegetarians should also have animal proteins (meat, fish, dairy products, and eggs).

Gradually, more carbohydrate foods (e.g. starchy vegetables, pasta, cereal products, bread, and fruit) and less fatty foods should be offered as the child approaches 2 years of age.

Infants need adequate calcium and iron, along with vitamins D and C to help absorb them. Many commercially prepared baby foods are enriched with vitamins and minerals, and the labels should declare this. However, breast-fed and bottle-fed infants should not need vitamin supplements before 6 months providing the mother has a good diet, and the mixed weaning diet contains plenty of fruit, vegetables, pulses, cereals, milk, and, if eaten, meat and fish.

Toddlers and young children (up to 5 years)

Different foods in various forms should continue to be introduced, so that the child does not become too limited in its food choice. At this age, growth and activity are greatly increased, and meals should provide plenty of the following nutrients to cope with this:

protein – for body growth

calcium – for bones and teeth

fluoride – for teeth

iron – for red blood cells

The diet should be well balanced in all respects.

Children should be discouraged from eating between meals, especially sweets and snacks such as crisps, as this may lead to a poor appetite at mealtimes (and therefore an unbalanced diet), tooth decay, and obesity.

At this age, a child's appetite may vary from day to day, and parents should make allowances for this. Rather than try to force a child to eat, give small portions with the option of a little more if desired.

The child's appetite may be poor for any of these reasons:

1 Teething – gums can be very sore and uncomfortable.

2 Illness – the child may be unable to explain how it feels in words, but show it by refusing food.

3 Assertiveness – children like to assert their independence, and so may refuse to eat even if hungry.

Parents should try to stay calm but firm, and indicate clearly the behaviour they expect at the meal table. The child is then unlikely to refuse food for long.

Children often refuse to eat a food which they have previously enjoyed. This may merely be one of the many phases that children go through, and should not cause great concern.

It is unwise to give children food such as a biscuit or sweet every time they are upset or unhappy about something. This could start a habit that becomes hard to break and can even continue into adulthood, possibly leading to obesity.

A calm, 'matter of fact', and happy attitude towards food by parents is probably the best way to encourage good eating habits in children. Attractively served food in small portions, with new foods introduced gradually, will encourage eating. Suggested meals for this age group are given below:

Breakfast

wholegrain, unsweetened cereal with milk, and perhaps fruit or yogurt or porridge

eggs – boiled, poached, or scrambled
or a small piece of fish, boned
or a small rasher of bacon and a tomato
or a small vegetable burger and a tomato

toast (preferably wholemeal bread)
or a small croissant or toasted bun
butter or margarine
yeast extract or a little jam or marmalade

milk, fruit juice, or water

Midday meal

a small piece of baked or poached fish
or a small portion of meat or bean stew
or a cheese and vegetable omelette
or a salad
or a piece of savoury flan, e.g. quiche Lorraine
or mild vegetable or meat curry
with vegetables, potatoes, rice, or pasta

or pasta in tomato and vegetable sauce
or lentil and vegetable soup with crusty bread
or a baked potato with cheese, tuna, baked
   beans, or cottage cheese
or savoury rice with mixed vegetables

fresh fruit, fruit in jelly, fruit crumble, mousse,
   fool, or yogurt
egg custard, rice, or other milk pudding

drink – e.g. water, fruit juice, milk

Evening meal

egg – boiled, poached, or scrambled
or fish cakes, lentil burger
or small salad with meat, egg, or cheese
or small piece of fish in sauce
or small piece of pizza and salad
or bowl of vegetable soup
or small round of sandwiches
or bowl of mixed 'finger foods', e.g. cheese
   cubes, pieces of cucumber, apple, tomato,
   dried fruit, celery and carrot sticks, cooked
   sausage, beansprouts
or baked beans with toast
wholemeal bread with butter or margarine

fruit juice, water, or milk

small piece of cake or fruit
or yogurt

School-age children

Activity and body growth continue to increase at this period of life. Meals must therefore provide ample energy, and nutrients for body growth and maintenance. New foods will continue to be introduced, and by this stage mealtimes should be well established.

School meals may supply about one third of the child's total daily requirements for nutrients. If a child takes a packed lunch, care should be taken to ensure that it is well balanced (see p. 63).

Children are easily influenced by their peers (children of the same age), and may refuse to eat a food they have previously enjoyed because a friend does not eat it. This is often a passing phase, and as long as the parent ensures that the child eats a mixture of other foods, there is no cause for worry.

Adolescents

Adolescence is a period of rapid growth and body development, and nutrient requirements increase at this stage.

The hormones for adulthood start to be produced during adolescence. They may cause skin disturbances, so adolescents should eat plenty of fresh fruit and vegetables and avoid fatty foods which may aggravate these conditions. The diet must provide sufficient protein and sufficient iron. Iron is particularly important for girls to prevent anaemia developing at the onset of menstruation. About 45% of the adult-sized skeleton forms during adolescence, so plenty of calcium-rich foods and vitamin D (see p. 13) must be eaten.

Alcohol is often available to teenagers, even though it is illegal to sell it to people under 18 years of age. It can cause social problems and health problems, including severe damage to the liver, stomach, and other vital organs. It also has a high energy value and can be a cause of obesity. Adolescents must be warned of the dangers of over drinking, and be set a good example of moderate drinking by adults.

Snacks for school-age children and adolescents

School-age children and adolescents often have large appetites, so they are likely to eat between meals. They should avoid eating too much 'junk food', i.e. food that provides little except fat or sugar. Such food adds to the total energy intake but not to body building or maintenance. Fatty foods, such as potato chips, fall into this category. Their high fat content and satiety value are likely to affect the appetite, so that other more nutritious foods are not eaten at mealtimes.

The following foods are preferable as snacks between meals:

fresh fruit

raw vegetables, e.g. carrots, celery

yogurt or fromage frais

crispbreads/wholemeal bread rolls with a
little butter/margarine

Adolescents should avoid drinking too many carbonated drinks and squashes as their sugar content is often high. Fruit juice, milk, or water are preferable.

The snacks industry advertises its products to young people in many ways. These products are often high in fat, sugar, or salt. It is therefore

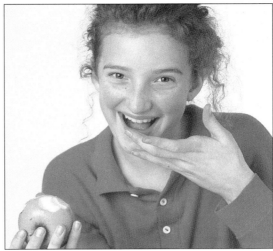
Choose fresh fruit for a healthy snack.

difficult to impose sensible eating habits on this age group. However, if sound eating habits are established when children are very young, they are less likely to be broken at this age. Children must be guided by their parents, carers, and teachers about choosing a healthy and varied selection of food.

Adults

Body growth declines in adulthood. Adults need food to maintain and repair the body and to keep it healthy.

The amount of daily activity affects energy and nutrient requirements, and meals should be planned according to these needs. Energy requirements for different activities were discussed on p. 31. Nutrient requirements are determined to some extent by body size. On the whole, women need less food than men, but they need more iron because of menstruation. Their nutrient requirements change during pregnancy and after the birth of a baby (see p. 57).

Active lifestyle

Meals for active people must provide sufficient energy while keeping to the dietary goals of reduced saturated fats and increased carbohydrate foods. Extra water and salt (sodium chloride) should be taken in very hot weather.

Suitable foods include:

Breakfast
wholegrain cereal and/or fresh fruit salad
or porridge

grilled bacon, egg, sausage, tomato
or omelette with cheese, mushrooms, or meat
or poached fish with eggs

toast, croissants, or warm bread rolls, with butter and marmalade or jam

coffee or tea

Midday meal (packed)
vegetable or meat pasties, pulse-based soup
or sandwiches or rolls with fillings such as eggs, cheese, or meat
or pitta bread filled with salad and cheese, fish, or meat
or lentil, meat, or fish pâté on rolls with salad

fresh fruit
yogurt or fromage frais
a piece of cake or biscuit

soup, coffee, tea, or other drink

Evening meal (or midday cooked meal)
soup, e.g. lentil, onion, potato, vegetable
or vegetable, meat, or fish pâté with crusty pitta, nan, or chappati bread
or bhajias, samosas, or vegetable pancake roll

meat, poultry, or fish in stews, pies, curries, or roasted
or pasta with meat, vegetable, or cheese sauce
or savoury flan
or savoury crumble (e.g. vegetable in cheese sauce with cheese, nut, and wholemeal flour crumble)
or vegetable, meat, or fish burger
or pizza with various toppings
or nut or pulse roast with savoury sauce
or grilled or fried fish

all served with cooked fresh or frozen vegetables, or salad

fresh fruit
or pancake filled with fruit
or fruit crumble
or steamed pudding, fruit pie, mousse, milk pudding, with custard or other sauce

drink

It is important to try and spread the energy intake throughout the day.

Diet and sports training
People who train intensively for sport have to ensure that their diet satisfies their needs before, during, and after training and competing. For most sports, a diet of 60–70% carbohydrate, 12% protein, and the rest fat is suitable.

During sporting activities, muscle glycogen stores are used up, large volumes of sweat are excreted (with loss of body salts), and muscles, joints, and ligaments are subjected to stresses and need to be repaired by the body.

Sports people have to be careful to obtain enough iron, B vitamins, and calcium from food to ensure efficient energy release and good maintenance of the skeleton.

Increased fluid intake is essential to avoid dehydration.

Sedentary lifestyle
People with a sedentary lifestyle need to pay careful attention to their energy input, as it can easily exceed their energy output, leading to weight increase.

Energy-dense snack foods, such as chocolate, pastries, cakes, biscuits, and crisps, should be eaten only in moderation. They are highly palatable and convenient, but can increase energy intake markedly.

Meals should also not be too bulky as they may take longer to digest in an inactive job. Suggested foods include:

Breakfast
fresh fruit or fruit juice
a small amount of cereal or yogurt
or grilled bacon and tomatoes
or poached fish or egg

toast, butter, marmalade

tea or coffee

Midday meal (packed)
a round of sandwiches with various fillings,
    e.g. egg, canned fish, cottage cheese

fresh fruit
yogurt
a small piece of cake

drink

Evening meal (or cooked midday meal)
soup or fruit juice

meat or fish (e.g. as a stew or grilled)
or egg and cheese dish
or pulse- or nut-based dish e.g. lentil curry
fresh vegetables

mousse, yogurt, fresh fruit, or small portion
    of steamed or baked pudding

drink

A healthy packed meal for an office worker

Drinking alcohol increases the energy intake, as alcohol yields 29.3 kJ (7 kcal) per gram. Many people have a drink with a meal and this adds to their energy intake considerably.

Packed meals

Many people take a packed midday meal to work or school, or as a picnic in preference to buying a meal in a canteen or restaurant. Such meals are an important part of the daily food supply, and so should be well planned and prepared. The following list of rules for packed meals should be considered.

1 The meal should be substantial and should supply one third of the daily intake of nutrients and energy.

2 The meal should be well balanced. Foods that supply energy and little else should be kept to a minimum.

3 The food should be easy to eat, using minimum of cutlery and producing the minimum of waste, bearing in mind that it may have to be eaten in an awkward place, such as a building site.

4 The food should be carefully packed, so that it is not crushed or damaged in transit. Delicate items should be packed above more robust foods. A sturdy package, e.g. a plastic box with a lid, is ideal for transporting the food. Items inside the box should be individually wrapped

5 If the meal is to be left in a warm place, such as a car, foods such as cooked meats should not be included to avoid the possibility of bacterial growth. Special lunch boxes with insulation and spaces for ice packs can be used to keep food at a safe temperature for a time.

6 A variety of textures and flavours should be included.

7 The meal should also include a drink. Drinks and soups can be kept hot in vacuum flasks.

Suggested foods for packed meals include:

soups

sandwiches or rolls, preferably wholemeal with low-fat spread or thinly spread butter with e.g. lentil pâté, mixed salad, cottage cheese and chives, sardine and watercress, egg and cress, cheese and tomato, tuna fish and cucumber, meat, peanut butter

small pots of salads, e.g. chopped celery and apple, grated carrot in low-fat salad dressing, coleslaw salad, and sweetcorn, bean, and spring onion salad.

pasties (meat, fish, vegetable)

egg and cheese flan

fresh fruit, e.g. kiwi fruit, plums, apples, small citrus fruits, grapes, banana, nectarines

cake or biscuit

wholegrain cereal or muesli snack bar

small savoury biscuits

yogurt or fromage frais

fruit juice, milk, or hot drink

People living on low incomes

People who have little money to live on may be found in any of these groups:

single-parent families
unemployed men and women
disabled people
house-bound people
homeless people
people unable to work because of illness
students living on a grant
school-leavers setting up home
people in low-paid jobs

Research has shown that people with low incomes are more likely to suffer from heart disease, strokes, and some types of cancer. They are more likely to be overweight, which is also a risk to health (see p. 46).

Eating less fat, sugar, and salt, and more fruit and vegetables, pasta, wholegrain cereals, and bread can be difficult on a low income.

Many people prefer to buy foods high in fat and sugar, which satisfy hunger for longer, rather than fresh fruit and vegetables, even if the fruit and vegetables cost less. Surveys (e.g. The National Food Alliance, 'Food and Low Income') show that many low-income families eat far more fat and sugar per week than fruit and vegetables.

Healthy alternatives, such as low-fat products, high-fibre (NSP) foods (e.g. breakfast cereals), and reduced-sugar foods (e.g. jams) may be more expensive. Some fruits and vegetables and their products, e.g. fruit juices, can also be expensive.

People on low incomes may also face the following problems:

1   Limited local shopping facilities which may be expensive.
2   Limited access (e.g. no car, infrequent and expensive public transport, or a long walk) to out-of-town supermarkets where prices may be cheaper.
3   Poor facilities for food storage, preparation, and cooking.
4   Poor motivation and frustration caused by the difficulties of trying to stretch the money to cover a whole week's meals.
5   Difficulty paying for fuel to cook food.

There is concern about the health and food intake of people on low incomes, and a variety of projects have been started to encourage and help people to eat more healthily. These include:

Food co-operatives

Groups of people organize the purchase of food in large quantities (in bulk), then sell it cheaply to members of the co-op. Food may be delivered to people's homes or sold in a community centre where the co-op also provides an important social role.

Some co-ops buy foods for particular ethnic groups, if they are not sold in local shops. Some produce recipe leaflets using more unusual foods to encourage people to try them.

Community cafés

These are often linked to food co-ops, and provide cheap meals and snacks. They often try to introduce healthy eating e.g. by having one day a week where they do not serve chips, or preparing and cooking foods in new ways to widen people's tastes.

School tuck shops
Food co-ops may organize the selling of fruit or other healthy snacks at local schools.

Food voucher schemes
These aim to help homeless people, by giving them vouchers paid for by donations from the public. The organizers arrange for them to be exchanged in local cafés and food outlets. This can be better than giving out food, which makes some homeless people feel they are begging.

Cook and taste projects
Local health workers sometimes arrange these to encourage lonely people on low incomes to come to a community centre. They can watch or take part in a cookery demonstration, and taste the finished results. Healthier ways of providing foods can be introduced, although the main aim is to provide a social service.

It is important to remember that changing eating habits takes time and gentle persuasion. People will not alter long-held habits overnight, even if their health is being affected by what they are eating.

Suggested foods include:

Breakfast
porridge (with dried fruit)
or breakfast cereal and milk

toast with jam or savoury spread

egg, boiled, poached or scrambled

glass of fruit juice

Midday meal (packed)
sandwiches with corned beef and tomato, sardines, pilchards, tuna or similar fish (mashed with a little vinegar, salad cream, and pepper), hard-boiled egg and mustard and cress, thinly sliced ham (maybe offcuts) with mustard, or tomato
or meat, fish or vegetable pie or pasty
and/or vegetable soup (home-made if possible) containing pasta, beans, or cereal grains

yogurt
piece of fruit
cake or biscuit

drink

Evening meal (or cooked midday meal)
meat, poultry, or fish stew, pie, burger, curry, or pasty with vegetables, pulses, pasta, or cereal grains
or vegetable curry or savoury crumble
or savoury egg and cheese flan containing vegetables, e.g. sweetcorn or peas
or pasta with tomato, vegetable, or cheese sauce
or savoury rice with vegetables, pulses, cheese, or nuts
or thick vegetable soup with pulses and/or cereals and crusty bread
or savoury sausage casserole made with a tomato and baked bean sauce served with rice or pasta

all served with vegetables in season, or cooked frozen vegetables, or salad in season

fruit crumble, fruit in jelly, sponge pudding, milk pudding (e.g. rice), fresh fruit in season, fruit pie or flan

drink of water, milk, tea, coffee

Senior citizens

As people grow older, they become less active, especially after retirement from an active job. Food is required to maintain the health and state of the body, as in younger age groups, but less energy is needed.

Many elderly women and some men suffer from a condition called osteoporosis, which is the result of gradual loss of calcium and other minerals from the skeleton (see p. 22). Bones become brittle, may break easily, and are painful. To help prevent this problem everyone, but especially women, should have plenty of calcium and vitamin D in their diet when younger, and take regular exercise. There is evidence that taking hormone replacement therapy (HRT) at, and for a few years after, the menopause can help prevent osteoporosis in women.

The size of meals should decrease as people become less active, but the quality should not. There is no need for the elderly to eat soft or smooth foods only, unless they have a digestive disorder which makes this necessary; they can still enjoy crisp, crunchy, and hard foods, even if they wear dentures, providing that the dentures fit into the gums properly.

It may be necessary to increase the intake of fibre to avoid constipation, which is a common disorder in this age group, Many elderly people resort to using laxatives to prevent or ease constipation. This is undesirable and usually unnecessary if the diet contains sufficient fibre.

A reduced income may mean that it is not possible to buy much meat or other protein foods, and this poses problems to many senior citizens. Pulses and cereals can be eaten as cheaper alternatives to meat and other animal protein foods, or to supplement them. Mobility problems may also influence where food is purchased and how often, and the elderly may require help from the social services department or from willing neighbours. The loss of a partner may also affect the motivation to cook and eat well, and this often leads to poor health among the elderly.

Senior citizens' luncheon clubs are run by many churches and charities to enable the elderly to meet in a social atmosphere, and enjoy

a meal together. This is good for their quality of life and happiness, and provides the chance to enjoy a cooked meal which they may not have at home. The meals are usually subsidized.

Meals on wheels are provided in many areas, and offer daily social contact for elderly people, as well as a regular hot meal. In some areas, people now receive a weekly delivery of frozen meals which they reheat in a microwave oven. This saves costs, but limits the important social contact.

Illness and convalescence

When someone is ill or recovering from an illness, accident, or operation, it may be necessary to adjust their normal diet to compensate for body weakness, poor appetite, or poor digestion.

If the illness is serious or complicated, the doctor may prescribe a strict diet, which should be followed carefully.

When the patient is convalescing (recovering from an illness or operation) they need food that will compensate for the loss of nutrients and strength that has occurred, e.g. loss of calcium and protein from a bone fracture, or loss of iron as a result of losing blood.

Feeding a patient during illness

In the initial stages of an illness, the body temperature may rise while an infection is being fought. This will increase body water loss through sweating, and must be compensated for by an increase in liquid consumption. Often the appetite at this stage is poor, so liquids taken should provide energy, vitamins, and protein to make up for the reduced food intake. Suggested liquids include:

soups and broths
fruit juice (for vitamin C)
glucose-based drinks (for energy)
milk
water

There should always be a supply of fresh water by the patient's bed, as they may want to drink often.

As the patient gradually recovers, the appetite slowly returns, and solid foods can be given, but remember that:

1 The appetite is likely to be poor, so the food must contain a good balance of nutrients so that it is useful to the body.
2 Small portions should be served with the option of extra if the patient wants it.
3 The food should be easy to eat and digest.
4 Greasy foods should be avoided as they may be indigestible. Strong flavours may be unpalatable.
5 The patient will generally be using less energy while in bed, so the energy value of the food should be lower than normal.
6 The food should tempt the patient's appetite. This can be achieved by attractive serving, variety of colour and texture, and food which is well cooked and well presented.
7 The patient's likes and dislikes for food should be taken into account.
8 Careful attention to hygiene in the preparation and serving of the food is important, and the food must be very fresh.
9 Left-over food should not be served to avoid the possibility of contamination.
10 Food preparation should be carried out away from the patient as the smell of cooking may affect the appetite.

Suitable foods to serve include.

Breakfast

wholegrain cereal with milk or fresh fruit salad

egg, poached, boiled, scrambled (garnish with toast, tomato, parsley)
or fish, poached (white fish is more digestible than oily fish)

toasted wholemeal bread, lightly buttered

a drink, e.g. milk, fruit juice, malted milk

Midday meal

minced meat in a savoury sauce
or fish, steamed and served in a sauce
or casseroled or grilled chicken with salad
or omelette with cheese, mushrooms, or meat
or soup, containing meat or pulses
fresh vegetables or salad in each case

fresh fruit salad or stewed fruit
or mousse or fruit fool
or individual steamed pudding with a sauce
or egg custard or crème caramel
or milk pudding (rice, tapioca, semolina)
or jelly made with milk and fresh fruit

Evening meal or tea

a small piece of cake
plain biscuits, made with wholemeal flour
bread, butter, jam or honey
fresh fruit
yogurt
a drink, e.g. milk, fruit juice, malted milk

The following foods should be eaten rarely, if at all, during most illness:

1 Oily or fatty foods, e.g. oily fish, pork, lamb, and fried foods, as these may be indigestible.
2 Energy-dense, filling foods, e.g. suet puddings, rich cakes.
3 Highly spiced or strongly flavoured foods.
4 Rich pastries and biscuits.

Feeding a patient during convalescence

The guidelines for feeding convalescents are similar to those for feeding patients who are ill, except that the appetite is likely to be better and serving is easier because the patient may be able to eat at a table instead of in bed.

Patients with a broken limb, should eat foods that contain good supplies of calcium (e.g. cheese, milk), so that the bone heals strongly. They will also need extra protein and vitamin D.

If the patient is recovering from an accident or operation, they should eat extra protein for body repair, and iron to replace that lost in blood.

Vegetarians

Vegetarians are people who will not consume animal food, for which an animal has had to be slaughtered or has suffered in any way. There are several reasons why a person may become a vegetarian, including:

1 Religious belief.
2 Objection to the slaughter of animals, because it is considered to be cruel, or economically wasteful (rearing animals is expensive and uses a lot of land, which could produce far more food if it were used for growing cereal crops).
3 Dislike of animal flesh.
4 Dietary reasons.
5 Belief that a vegetarian diet is more healthy than a carnivorous (meat-eating) diet.

In recent years the number of vegetarians has increased. Food manufacturers have responded by producing vegetarian versions of some recipes and main meals. New products such as quorn (see p. 130) have been developed to add variety.

Food manufacturers now produce a wide range of vegetarian products.

There is some evidence that a vegetarian diet is better for long-term health, and that vegetarians may suffer less from diseases such as cancer and heart disease.

There are two main types of vegetarian:
   lacto-ovo vegetarians
   vegans (strict vegetarians)

Lacto-ovo vegetarians

Lacto-ovo vegetarians will not eat meat, or meat products, poultry, fish, lard, suet, fish oils, or gelatine, because producing these involves slaughtering the animal or fish.

However, they will eat food products from animals, such as free-range eggs, milk, cheese, butter, cream, yogurt, fromage frais. The animal is not slaughtered to produce these.

Lacto-vegetarians do not eat eggs but do eat milk and dairy products.

Special vegetarian cheese can be purchased. It is made with vegetable rennet rather than animal rennet (see p. 107), which comes from the stomach of a calf.

There are no real problems associated with a lacto-ovo vegetarian diet, and most nutrients are easy to obtain. There may be a slight problem with iron, however, as it is known to be unavailable to the body from certain plant foods (see p. 23) and may be unavailable from egg yolk (see p. 23).

Vegetarians should limit their consumption of dairy foods, e.g. cheese, butter, and whole milk, to avoid a large intake of saturated fatty acids (see p. 6). Reduced-fat versions of these foods, e.g. cottage cheese and skimmed milk, could be used instead. Soya milk can be used instead of milk. It is available in sweetened and unsweetened forms and enriched with calcium. Soya 'cream' toppings and desserts are also available.

Suggested foods for a lacto-vegetarian include:

savoury flans, e.g. eggs, cheese, onion, and mushroom
vegetable pies with cheese shortcrust pastry
cheese Scotch eggs
salads with pulses, cheese, eggs, nuts, and beans to provide extra protein
savoury vegetable crumbles with nuts and seeds in the topping
cheese Scotch eggs made with a vegetarian burger or sausage mix
vegetable, cheese, and nut loaves
burgers or sausages made with ground nuts, breadcrumbs, tofu (see p. 130), quorn, lentils
vegetable curries

pizzas with toppings such as mushroom, peppers, sweetcorn, pineapple, tomato, onion, herbs

vegetarian lasagne or bolognese using lentils, beans, peas, and nuts in place of meat

savoury pancakes with vegetable and cheese or mushroom sauce fillings

savoury rice with nuts, beans, peppers, pineapple, onion, beetroot, sweetcorn, peas, carrots

stuffed vegetables, e.g. peppers, courgettes or marrow, using breadcrumbs, ground nuts, herbs, spices, onion in the stuffing

cheese and potato pie with vegetables

layered potato, cream, cheese, and onion bake

baked jacket potatoes with toppings such as cheese, cottage cheese and chives, chopped vegetables (e.g. cooked carrot, broad beans, kidney beans, peas, sweetcorn) in mayonnaise

Vegans (strict vegetarians)

Vegans will not eat any food that is made directly or indirectly from an animal, even if the animal has not been slaughtered for that purpose. They also refuse to use products such as soaps, cosmetics, and polishes, which involve the use of animal oils or fats.

With careful planning, vegan meals can be made appetizing and good to eat; and with a knowledge of the value of foods, they can be nutritionally well balanced. There are several important points that must be taken into consideration when planning vegan diets:

1 Protein is found in relatively small amounts in plant foods, so a large bulk may have to be eaten in order to provide enough. The richest sources are:

soya beans   cereals
other beans   nuts
pulses

As many plant proteins are of low biological value (see p. 3), it is necessary to eat a mixture of plant protein foods to make up for the deficiencies of essential amino-acids in each.

The extra bulk from carbohydrates, cellulose, and water in these foods may lead to indigestion and fullness after a meal, so it may be necessary to spread the intake of foods through the day.

2 **Vitamin D** is found in few plant foods in useful amounts, so the action of sunlight on the skin is an important source. Vitamin D is added to margarine, but many margarines contain animal products.

3 **Vitamin A** is present in plants as ß-carotene (see p. 12).

4 **Calcium** can be provided by pulses, cereals, nuts, fruit, and vegetables, but some may be unavailable to the body because of the presence of phytic acid (see p. 21). This may pose problems for young children whose bones are still developing, and who may not be able to eat large enough quantities of such foods to obtain sufficient calcium.

5 **Vitamins B and C** can be provided by fruit and vegetables, and vitamin B is also found in wholegrain cereals, yeast extract, and bread.

6 **Fat** is provided by vegetable oils and is also found naturally in nuts.

Extra vitamins and minerals can be taken in the form of tablets and drops, providing that they are made synthetically (man-made) and do not come from animals originally. Vitamin B_{12} is only found in animal foods. Vegans may be at risk of developing a deficiency anaemia and may need to take it in tablet form to avoid this.

There are many varieties of nuts, pulses, and cereals which can be used to produce satisfying and interesting meals for vegans. The use of spices, herbs, unusual vegetables, and fruits adds variety and flavour, and there is no need for the diet to become monotonous. Many recipe books give ideas for vegan meals, and there are several restaurants and eating houses which produce solely vegetarian food.

Suggested meals for vegans include:

bean and vegetable stews (made with vegetable stock)

salads with nuts and cooked pulses

nut roasts with vegetables

soups with cereal (e.g. barley, rice)

vegetable curry and rice

egg-free pasta with vegetable sauces

soya milk used in place of cow's milk for rice pudding, and added to e.g. soups, vegetable sauces, scones

burgers or rissoles made with nuts, beans, rice, breadcrumbs, herbs, and spices

savoury rice with beans and vegetables

Religious groups

Religious beliefs are important to many people, and some religions have rules about what should and should not be eaten. These include:

The Jewish faith

Jewish food customs and dietary laws are set out in the Old Testament of the Bible (in Leviticus Chapter 11). Foods that fulfil the requirements of the laws are called Kosher foods. Jews who observe these laws may eat only clean birds (these are listed in a collection of writings called the Talmud); only meat from cud-chewing, cloven-footed animals, i.e. beef, venison, and lamb; and only fish with scales and fins.

Forbidden foods, which must not be eaten, include shellfish, crustaceans (crab, lobster), pork, bacon, ham, eels, eggs with bloodspots, and gelatine.

Some Jews will not eat milk and meat together, and may have separate cooking utensils for these.

The Christian faith

Christians remember and celebrate the life and teaching of Jesus Christ in a number of festivals. Jesus is also remembered in the celebration of Holy Communion, when bread (symbolizing his body), and wine (symbolizing his blood) are taken.

The Islamic faith

Muslims follow the religious teachings of Islam, and are not allowed to eat food from pigs. Other meat must be slaughtered by a special ritual, known as Halal. Muslims are not allowed to drink alcohol.

The Hindu faith

Hindus are not allowed to kill cows as they are considered sacred, but they do eat milk and milk products. Strict Hindus are vegetarian and do not eat meat, fish, or eggs.

The Buddhist faith

Buddhists follow five rules for everyday life. The first instructs them to be sympathetic and helpful to all things that have life, and to be careful not to harm or kill any living creatures.

As a result, many Buddhists are vegetarian.

Customs, traditions, and festivals

Many occasions and ceremonies (funerals, marriages, religious festivals, harvests, etc.) are celebrated with feasts or fasts (not eating food for a specific amount of time), or special meals and foods only prepared at that time. Some examples are given below.

The Jewish faith

Purim is celebrated in late February/early March. The special foods served include turkey, cakes and biscuits, filled pastries, and fruit.

Passover is celebrated for a week, and special foods include unleavened bread (not risen with yeast) and haroset (a sweet paste).

Shavuot (sometimes called Pentecost), is celebrated in May or June, and a variety of dairy foods are eaten at this time.

At **Rosh Hashanah**, the Jewish New Year, Jews eat a special meal, including sweet foods such as apples dipped in honey, dates, and dried fruits. Ten days later, at **Yom Kippur**, Jews eat a meal before sunset, and then fast for 24 hours. The meal usually includes chicken and rice, bread, and water.

Hannukkah is the Jewish festival of lights, and lasts for eight nights. Each night a fried food is eaten, to remember oil which was used to light a holy temple in Jerusalem.

The Christian faith

Shrove Tuesday is the day before the beginning of the 40 days of Lent, which lead up to Easter. Traditionally, people were meant to eat and live simply during **Lent**, so they had to use up

Special foods for Shrove Tuesday

certain foods before it began. Pancakes were made to use up milk, eggs, and fat.

On **Mothering Sunday**, the fourth Sunday in Lent, a simnel cake (a fruit cake covered with marzipan) is made.

Hot cross buns are eaten on **Good Friday**, and at **Easter**, eggs – symbolizing new life – are eaten.

The birth of Jesus is celebrated at **Christmas**, which is a time of goodwill and enjoyment. Traditional Christmas foods in the UK include roast turkey, stuffing, vegetables, sauces, Christmas pudding, and mince pies.

The Islamic faith

Ramadan is a very important Muslim festival. It lasts for a month, during which no food or drink is taken from sunrise to sunset. At the end of Ramadan, special feasts are held.

The Hindu faith

Holi is a festival to celebrate the beginning of spring. Feasts and parties are held, and foods such as coconuts are roasted on fires.

Divali – the festival of lights – is held in October or November. Feasts, carnivals, and parties are held and favourite family foods are prepared.

Food intolerance

Most people can eat many different foods without any problems. However, some people cannot tolerate certain foods and react badly if they eat them.

There are different types of food intolerance.

Enzyme deficiency

This is is when the body is missing one or more of the enzymes needed to digest and use nutrients in food.

Lactose intolerance is an example. Normally, the enzyme lactase digests lactose in the small intestine (see p. 35). If the enzyme is missing, the person will experience nausea (feeling sick), bloating (swollen abdomen), pain in the abdomen, and diarrhoea. People with this condition must avoid milk and milk products, as these contain lactose. It is possible to buy lactose-reduced foods.

Phenylketonuria (PKU) is another example. It is caused by a lack of the enzyme phenylalanine hydroxylase, which the body needs in the liver. If it is not treated, the brain gradually becomes damaged.

PKU can be detected by taking a small sample of blood from the heel of a baby, between 6 and 14 days old. (This is often called the heel-prick test, or Guthrie test after the person who invented it.) If the result is positive, action must be taken quickly.

PKU is treated by giving a low-phenylalanine diet, with regular checking of the blood and progress of the patient. Advice on feeding will be given by a hospital dietitian who will work closely with the patient and the parents. Lists of the phenylalanine content of foods are available, but it can appear in unexpected foods such as the sweetener **aspartame** (which is sold under the brand names of Nutrasweet and Canderel). This sweetener is put into many different food products, so labels must be checked carefully.

Malabsorption

This is when nutrients are not absorbed after digestion, but pass through the body. There are many causes, including defects in the intestines, drugs, conditions such as diabetes (see p. 73), surgery, infections, and enzyme deficiencies.

One example is **coeliac disease**. It is caused by sensitivity to the protein **gluten**, which is found in many cereal plants, especially wheat. In sensitive individuals, gluten damages the lining of the intestine (the mucosa). Why this happens in some people and not others is not clear. The damage prevents nutrients from being absorbed.

Children become unhappy, lethargic (no energy), and have no appetite. They produce pale and bulky faeces, and the abdomen swells. The rest of the body becomes thin, and the child fails to grow properly. Adults with coeliac disease often have anaemia, weight loss, and diarrhoea.

Gluten is found in barley, rye, and oats, as well as wheat, so patients must not eat these in any form. Wheat protein is often added to foods, so it is important to check food labels. Some foods are labelled to indicate that they are gluten-free.

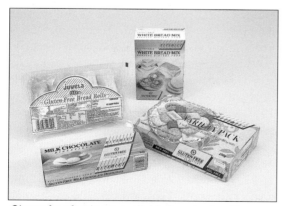

Gluten-free foods are available for people with coeliac disease. They carry a special symbol to show that they contain no gluten.

Food allergies

The body has an immune system to protect it from harmful things such as viruses. Sometimes a person's immune system will react strongly to a particular substance. The person is said to be allergic to the substance, and the substance is called an allergen. In foods, the allergen is often a protein.

Allergies to cow's milk, eggs, soya, and monosodium glutamate (a flavour enhancer) are fairly common. The symptoms can include eczema, asthma, skin irritations, headaches, and sickness.

Some allergic reactions may cause changes in behaviour. There is some evidence that certain food colours and preservatives may cause hyperactivity (uncontrollable activity and violent changes of mood) in some young children.

Some allergic reactions can be very serious. For example, certain people have an anaphylactic reaction to an allergen in peanuts. This means that a tiny quantity of the allergen causes their whole body to react immediately and severely. Their blood vessels leak, the linings of the bronchial tubes in the lungs swell making breathing difficult, lips and face swell, and blood pressure falls. The patient will collapse and die unless treated immediately with an injection of adrenalin.

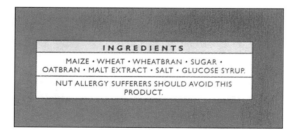

INGREDIENTS
MAIZE • WHEAT • WHEATBRAN • SUGAR • OATBRAN • MALT EXTRACT • SALT • GLUCOSE SYRUP.
NUT ALLERGY SUFFERERS SHOULD AVOID THIS PRODUCT.

Small amounts of peanut cause very serious reactions in some people, so many manufacturers now print a warning on their product labels.

Diabetes mellitus

Glucose is carried in the blood to all body cells to supply them with energy. In order for glucose to enter the cells, a hormone, **insulin**, is required to act as a chemical 'key'.

Insulin is produced by the pancreas. If it does not make enough, the glucose will stay in the bloodstream and will eventually spill over into the urine. The lack of glucose in the cells means they will have to obtain energy from the body fat stores, which will result in a loss of weight and general weakness.

This condition is called **diabetes mellitus** (diabetes for short), and the patient is said to be diabetic. It may be present at birth or may develop at any age.

There are 2 types of diabetes:

1 **Insulin–dependent diabetics** do not make any insulin in their body. They must have daily injections of insulin, and regular, healthy meals to keep the diabetes under control.

2 **Non–insulin–dependent diabetics** do not produce enough insulin to control their blood sugar level properly. They must eat regular, healthy meals, and, if necessary, try to lose some weight. They may also need to take tablets.

The British Diabetic Association (BDA) gives advice to diabetics, and keeps them informed about developments in treating the condition. It currently advises diabetics to eat:

1 Regular, healthy meals including a variety of different foods.

2 More high–fibre, starchy carbohydrate foods, e.g. wholemeal bread, pasta, jacket potatoes, pulses, brown rice, and beans. The BDA recommends that at least 50% of the daily energy needs should be provided by these foods.

3 Less sugar and sweet foods, and to choose reduced–sugar or artificially sweetened alternatives.

4 Less high–fat and fried foods.

5 Less salt, to help reduce the risk of high blood pressure.

6 A maximum of 3 units of alcohol per day for men and 2 units for women. (1 unit of alcohol is 1 measure of spirits, or 1 glass of wine, or 275 ml (half a pint) of beer, cider, or lager, or 1 small glass of sherry.)

Diabetics are encouraged to attend regular clinics to check their blood sugar levels and general health. They also do tests at home to check how much sugar there is in their urine, and many patients do blood tests as well.

Special diabetic foods

A variety of foods, including biscuits, jams, and chocolates, are produced specially for diabetics. They use a sugar alcohol, sorbitol, instead of sucrose and glucose. Sorbitol is absorbed slowly and converted to fructose in the liver, which prevents a rapid rise in blood sugar levels.

The BDA does not recommend these products as they are not especially beneficial, and tend to be expensive. By following the advice on diet given above, and taking insulin or drugs if necessary, most diabetics should be able to control their condition effectively.

Revision questions

1 Why do people vary in their needs for food?

2 What affects a person's appetite?

3 Why have peoples' food habits altered in recent years?

4 Why is the diet of a pregnant woman important, and how can she ensure that she produces a healthy baby?

5 What is the function of the placenta as far as food is concerned?

6 Give six reasons why breast milk is best for a baby.

7 What is weaning, when should it be started, and what foods are suitable?

8 Why is it inadvisable for children to eat between meals?

9 Why is it important that adolescents have a well-balanced diet?

10 What are the dangers and disadvantages of eating too many sweet and fried foods?

11 Why is it important that a very active person has a satisfying and nutritious diet?

12 What are the important points to remember when preparing packed meals?

13 What important points should be remembered when preparing foods for people who are:
a ill in bed
b recovering from a bone fracture?

14 What is the difference between a lacto-ovo vegetarian and a vegan? Suggest suitable meals for each.

15 Briefly describe the food customs of Jews, Muslims, and Hindus.

16 Why do people on low incomes have difficulty in following the dietary guidelines?

17 Why are meals on wheels and luncheon clubs so important for senior citizens?

18 Why are babies given a Guthrie test?

19 Why shouldn't people with coeliac disease eat wheat?

20 What causes an anaphylactic reaction? Why is it dangerous?

21 How should diabetics modify their diets?

Questions and activities

1 The pie chart below shows the results of a survey on the number of food advertisements shown in one week, during children's television viewing hours (4–5.10 pm on weekdays, and 8–1 pm on Saturdays).

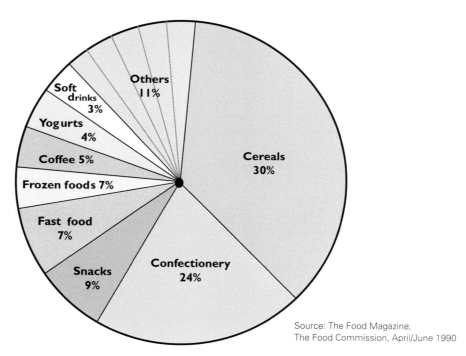

Source: The Food Magazine,
The Food Commission, April/June 1990

a Which group of foods/drinks was most advertised?

b Which group of foods/drinks was least advertised?

c The survey showed that about 78% of the products advertised were high in fat or sugar, or both. Make a list of examples of high-fat and high-sugar products in each group likely to be advertised.

d Why do you think food and drinks companies like to advertise their products to children?

e Make a small survey of your own on food and drinks advertising during children's television viewing time. Find out and comment on the following:

i) the number of advertisements for each group in the pie chart

ii) the types of breakfast cereal advertised (sugar-coated, high-fibre, novelty shaped, etc.)

iii) how many advertisements are associated with:
- sport, energy, health
- winning, or goodies versus baddies
- space, dinosaurs, favourite cartoon characters, adventures, computers, fantasy
- special offers to collect or send away for

Why do you think advertisers use these themes and ideas to help advertise their products?

iv) The Independent Broadcasting Association (IBA) has a Code of Advertising Standards and Practice. Find out about the section of this which deals with advertising to children.

v) British dentists and health education experts are concerned about food and drinks advertising aimed at children. Why do you think this is?

vi) What recommendations would you make to the IBA about advertising to children if you had the chance?

2 Living on a low income makes eating a healthy diet difficult.
The table shows the costs of different foods per 100 kcal of energy (see p. 29). Use the information in the table to answer these questions:

a Which food in each group costs the most and which costs the least?

b Health experts recommend that people of all ages should eat at least 5 portions of fresh fruit and vegetables per day. What problems would someone on a low income have with following that advice?

c Children, like adults, need enough energy from food to ensure that they can be active, but must also have enough to make them grow normally. If a parent has very little money to buy food (perhaps as little as £1 per day for each child), what foods are they likely to buy to meet the energy needs of their children?

Cost of 100 kcal

Group 1

Custard cream biscuits	2p
White sliced bread	3p
Wholemeal rolls	4p

Group 2

Frozen chips	4p
Boiled potatoes	7p
Carrots	20p
Broccoli	74p
Lettuce	76p
Tomatoes	80p
Celery	£1.03p

Group 3

Pork sausages	10p
Meat pie	11p
Lean pork	33p
Fish fingers	13p
Frozen cod fillet	95p

Group 4

Chocolate bar	8p
Corn snacks	12p
Apples	19p
Oranges	30p

Group 5

Full-fat milk	7p
Skimmed milk	13p

Source: 'Food and Low Income' (National Food Alliance)

d The cheaper foods tend to have a high fat and/or sugar content. What long-term health problems might arise for someone living on a low income, whose first priority is to satisfy their hunger and meet their energy requirements?

3 Luke and Sarah have been married for a year, and are planning to start a family. They are both 22 years old. What steps can they both take to ensure that their diet is healthy, so that they have the best chance to produce a healthy family? Where can they find out about health care for themselves and their family?

4 Here is a recipe, issued by Eastbourne Health Authority, Department of Nutrition and Dietetics, from their booklet called Wholefood Recipes.

Lentil soup

Ingredients

1 tbsp oil
1 medium onion
1 small carrot
2 sticks celery
1 tbsp lentils
1 egg-sized potato
575 ml stock
1½ tbsp bran (optional)
herbs
1 clove garlic
salt and pepper

Serves 3
75 kcals per portion

Method

1 Chop vegetables.
2 Gently fry onions, garlic, and herbs in oil for 5 minutes.
3 Add vegetables.
4 Pour over stock.
5 Add lentils and bran.
6 Simmer for 45 minutes.
7 Season to taste.

a What does wholefood mean?
b Suggest what else could be served with the soup to make a healthy and enjoyable 3 course evening meal for a teenager, who takes part in football training, cross-country running, and swimming.
c What does 'optional' mean?
d Who would find the addition of bran useful?
e Is this recipe suitable for a lacto-vegetarian?
f Would the recipe be suitable for a vegan? Give your reasons
g Work out the cost of this recipe per portion. Who would find this information useful?
h Who would find the information on the kcals per portion useful?
i If someone with high blood pressure wants to make this soup, what would they need to do to make it suitable for them?
j Where do you often find a Department of Nutrition and Dietetics?
k Who works there and what do they do?
l Which groups of people might be sent to them, and how can they be helped?

5 Make a list of the priorities the following people might have when choosing their food:
a a mother of two school-age children
b a widowed man, living on a pension
c a student living on a grant
d a pregnant woman
Choose one of the above and write about the other priorities they would have with regard to their weekly income, and the various benefits that are available to help people in certain circumstances.

6 Health food shops are becoming more abundant in shopping centres and towns. If possible, visit a health food shop, and collect some information about the products sold there.
a What kind of image or message do such shops try to promote to the public?
b Why are such shops becoming more popular?
c Compare the prices of some of the products with their equivalents in ordinary supermarkets. Comment on any differences.

③ Foods and food science

Food production, processing, and retail

World food production

Approximately 14% of the world's population (more than 5 billion people) do not get enough food to eat, and suffer from under-nutrition, while many of the rest eat too much. The rich parts of the world (including the UK) produce and consume the most food and have the smallest populations, while the poor parts have the least food and the highest populations.

In poor countries, many people farm their land in order to provide food for themselves, and often have to sell a large proportion of their produce to pay for the rent of the land. The amount of food that they produce is often very small for a variety of reasons, including:

1 **Poverty:** being unable to buy fertilizers, farm machinery, better seeds, etc.
2 **Crop failures:** due to infestation by pests (e.g. locusts), disease, infertile ground, lack of water, etc.
3 **Natural disasters or bad climate:** earthquakes, hurricanes, severe drought, flooding.
4 **Limited agricultural technology:** lack of knowledge and finance to improve their farming methods.
5 **War:** damage to land and belongings.
6 **World economic recession:** leading to rapidly increasing prices for food, seeds, tools, etc., a reduction in trade, and an increase in national borrowing and debt.
7 **Unstable social conditions:** may prevent crop planting and maintainance, and equal food distribution to all parts of the population.

In richer countries, farming and food production are highly mechanized, and technological advances have enabled people to produce high yields of food from crops, and to eliminate many crop diseases.

A large proportion of the plant foods consumed in rich countries are used for feeding animals that are reared to produce meat and dairy foods. In poorer countries plant foods are the main (staple) food of the people, as meat is too expensive.

Poor countries often use large areas of their valuable growing land to grow 'cash crops', e.g. sugar or bananas, for export to rich countries, rather than for growing much-needed food for their own people.

Often the farmer is paid a low price for the crop, and the exporter, transporter, importer, and retailer each make a profit as they pass the crop on to the next person. The consumer pays far more than the farmer receives.

Organizations such as Traidcraft buy food and other items direct from the farmer or community producing the goods, so they receive a fair price. Cocoa, banana chips, coffee, tea, nuts, and sugar are purchased in this way from countries such as Turkey, Mozambique, Peru, Bangladesh, and Vietnam.

As the population of the world increases (especially in poorer countries) much research is being carried out to find ways of producing larger crops and alternative sources of protein (see pp. 129-30). The problem is by no means solved, however, and the distribution of world food supplies remains unfair.

Food production in the UK

Agricultural land in the UK is intensively farmed. Intensive farming produces food – in particular meat and dairy products – at low cost on a large scale.

After the Second World War, farmers received subsidies to encourage production of food as cheaply as possible. This led to:

1   More machinery and fewer farm workers.
2   Large-scale use of fertilizers, pesticides, antibiotics, and growth promoters.
3   Removal of thousands of miles of hedgerow and acres of woodland to make large fields.
4   Large numbers of animals and birds reared in specially built sheds, barns, and houses and fed on concentrated, high nutrient value foods.
5   The loss of hundreds of small farms to be replaced by fewer, large farm businesses.

Intensive arable farming in the UK

Since 1972 Britain has belonged to the European Union (EU). The EU directly influences food supply and production in Europe through the Common Agricultural Policy (CAP).

Common Agricultural Policy

The aims of the CAP are:

1   To increase the productivity and efficiency of farming.
2   To increase and maintain farmers' incomes.
3   To secure supplies of food, and to increase self sufficiency in food and prevent price fluctuations.
4   To provide food at reasonable prices.

Foods from the rest of the world are still imported, as not all foods can be grown within the EU. Some foods are exported. Farmers who are considered to have a good production potential are given subsidies to improve their farming facilities. Intensive farming methods have resulted in large surpluses of some products (e.g. milk, wine, beef, and butter) in the EU. Some farmers are now paid to leave part of their land unused (called 'set-aside' land) so that these surpluses do not increase further.

The EU enforces its own regulations for various aspects of food production and retail, such as hygiene, weights and measures, labelling, and food additives.

Organic farming

Many people object to the use of intensive farming methods for growing crops and rearing animals. **Organic farming**, which is regulated by the Soil Association, is being promoted as an alternative. Organic farming uses traditional, non-intensive methods, without artificial fertilizers, pesticides, or growth hormones. Many supermarkets and other outlets sell organic foods. Although they tend to be more expensive, many people believe they are more healthy and better for the environment in the long term.

Food manufacture and technology

Food manufacture and technology have developed rapidly over the last hundred years. Previously, food was manufactured and sold locally to a small area, and processing and technology were very limited.

Today, a relatively small number of large companies in the UK each produce several kinds of food products. These companies often own large areas of farm land and farmers grow food specifically for the company to process, e.g. vegetables for freezing or canning. They also import foods from around the world.

Food technology influences people's food habits in several ways:

1   78% of the population of the UK live in urban districts, away from the areas where food is produced. These people now have a wide choice of food in good condition, all year round.

2   New foods and food inventions, such as imitation cream, TVP (see p. 130), and instant foods, have been developed and the range of processed and ready-prepared foods has greatly increased. This has widened people's food choice.

3   Food technology also affects the nutritional value of people's diets. In many processing methods, nutrients are lost (e.g. milling of wheat to make white bread), and may not be replaced.

Some food additives may affect people's health in the long term (see pp. 142-4).

Many manufacturing processes are controlled by computer. This is called computer-aided manufacture (CAM). Computers are particularly useful in quality control, i.e. in ensuring that a product is consistent in flavour, colour, appearance, and safety, and that it meets the requirements of the consumer.

Food processing

Food processing is the alteration of food by a series of actions (mechanical or chemical) in a factory or kitchen.

Primary processing involves altering a basic food to preserve it or to prepare it for sale or cooking, e.g.:

milling wheat into flour
descaling and gutting fish
cleaning and jointing a meat carcass
heat treating milk
skimming cream from milk
sorting and washing vegetables
peeling, stoning, slicing, and canning fruit
extracting oil from seeds and nuts

Secondary processing involves turning basic processed foods into food products such as:

making margarine from oil
making bread, cakes, and biscuits from flour, fat, sugar, etc.
making cooking sauces from vegetables, meat, fish, etc.
making jam and preserves from fruit and sugar
making snack foods from starch products and oil

Marketing of food

Every year, many new products are developed, promoted, and put on sale. Not all new products are successful and some are later withdrawn. Products are developed in the following stages.

Market research

Market researchers establish the need for a product by analysing **trends** (e.g. eating habits, working hours, and leisure time), and the **potential market** (i.e. which groups of people would be most likely to buy the product). They study people's behaviour, attitudes, values, and emotions in a variety of ways, including interviews and surveys, and use this information to develop the product.

To be useful and valid, surveys need to be planned and carefully worded. Questions need to be:

brief and clear
answerable in a few words or by ticking a box
in a logical order, e.g. asking the consumer to try the product before asking them if they would buy it

The results of the survey should be easy to present (e.g. as a graph or pie chart) so that they can be interpreted easily.

Product development

Once the need for a product is established, **food technologists** design and develop it. **Machinery designers** develop the most efficient way of making the product on a factory production line, and **packaging designers** present the product to the consumer in a cost-effective, safe, protective, informative, and attractive way. **Home economists** prepare and

Sensory analysis is an important part of food product development.

present the product in a variety of ways to demonstrate its versatility, attractiveness, etc.

A very important part of food product development is **sensory analysis**. This is used to produce, measure, examine, and explain people's reactions to a food through the senses of smell, sight, taste, hearing, and touch (the 'organoleptic' qualities of food). Both trained and untrained assessors examine and eat various food samples. The samples may differ from each other, by having more or less salt, darker or lighter colour, or more or less fat. The assessors record their observations using:

1 **Hedonic descriptions**, which describe likes and dislikes, e.g. horrible, appetizing, delicious, bad, unpleasant, tasty.
2 **Sensory descriptions**, which describe texture, mouthfeel, taste, appearance, and smell, e.g. crisp, crunchy, smooth, greasy, fruity, salty, sweet, watery, shiny, sour.

Market researchers may also ask assessors and potential consumers to give **attitudinal descriptions** which describe beliefs about the product and attitudes to it, e.g. healthy, satisfying, traditional.

Advertising

Advertising agencies promote the product through the media. Their role is to convince consumers to buy the product. Consumers usually choose from a range of products (different breakfast cereals, different chocolate bars) so each agency has to convince consumers that its product is 'better' than the others.

Advertisements are carefully designed to make the product appear attractive, and to make people remember its name so that they buy it.

All advertising is carefully regulated, and advertisers are not allowed to make false claims about their products (see p. 81).

Evaluation

The results of all tests, surveys, market research, feed-back from advertising, and sales of the product (which may be sold only in one area as a pilot study), are carefully analysed, and then decisions are made about its future. The product may be improved, or more varieties developed, or it may be withdrawn from sale.

Genetic engineering

This relatively new technique in biotechnology is being used in the agricultural and food-processing industries.

All the information about a plant or animal, including its colour, size, shape, and growth, is carried in its genes. This information is passed on to the next generation of plant or animal when it reproduces. Using genetic engineering, scientists can alter genes and change certain features of a plant or animal.

Some examples of genetically engineered food products include:

1 Tomatoes that do not go soft during transport and can be left on the plant longer to develop flavour.
2 Potatoes that have resistance to potato leaf roll virus.
3 Yeast that raises bread more quickly.

Some people are concerned about the use of this new technique, so genetically engineered foods are carefully controlled and regulated. The concerns include:

1 Genetically engineered plants and animals could affect the natural ecology of wildlife.
2 The genes from animals that some religions forbid people to eat may be used in foods.
3 The welfare of animals could be at risk.
4 Legislation is needed to require such foods to be clearly labelled.

Food advertising

About 15% of all advertising in the UK is for food. The food industry spends over £600 million every year: chocolate manufacturers spend the most, followed by breakfast cereal and coffee manufacturers.

Recent surveys on advertising during children's TV viewing time, have shown that about 78% of food and drink advertisements showed products high in sugar and/or fat, such as sugar-coated breakfast cereals, chocolate, crisps, and soft drinks. Many are shown in a sporting or 'healthy' context, although manufacturers are not allowed to advertise their product as beneficial to health.

Exposing children to too much advertising like this may have a bad influence on their choice of food and future health.

Advertising is carefully regulated to ensure that all advertisements are legal, decent, honest, and truthful. There are some specific rules about food advertising, including:

1   Excessive consumption of food should not be encouraged or condoned.
2   Good, healthy eating habits should not be criticized.
3   Frequent consumption of foods (e.g. sugary or fatty snack foods) throughout the day should not be encouraged.
4   Claims about nutrition or health must be supported by sound scientific evidence.
5   Children should not be encouraged to eat or drink near bedtime, to eat frequently throughout the day, or replace their meals with snacks and confectionery.
6   Advertisements aimed specifically at children should take into account their immaturity, innocence, and unsuspecting nature.

Advertising is regulated by:

the Independent Television Commission (ITC), which covers all television advertising

the Advertising Standards Authority (ASA), which covers all advertising in magazines, newspapers, posters, cinemas, leaflets

the Radio Authority

Each produces a 'code of practice', and investigates complaints from the public and other advertisers if an advertisement breaks the code.

Food labelling

Food manufacturers invest much money and time in designing packaging to attract customers to their food products. Food labelling laws are set by MAFF and the EU, and their aim is:

1   To inform consumers about all the words, pictures, descriptions, trade marks, symbols, or brand names that appear on a food label.
2   To make sure that labels do not mislead consumers about:
what the food is (its nature and identity)
where it comes from (its country of origin)
who made it (its manufacturer)
what is in it (its composition)
how it was made (its method of manufacture)
how much there is (its quantity)
how long it will safely keep (its shelf-life and durability)
what it will look, taste, smell, and feel like (its properties)
3   To make sure that the label does not make a false claim about the food, e.g. 'aids weight loss', without evidence to support the claim.

Labels must show:

1   The name of the product, including any treatment the food has had, e.g. UHT milk, smoked haddock, freeze-dried coffee.
2   A list of ingredients, including additives, in descending order of weight.
3   The net quantity (for pre-packed foods) – the weight of the food without the packaging. A large letter '**e**' after the weight means that, although the average quantity must be right, the weight in individual packs may vary slightly.
4   Instructions about storage, cooking, or use.
5   How long the food will be at its best. There are two ways of showing this:
'**best before**' or '**best before end**' tells how long the product will be in its best condition if kept according to instructions on the label. It is shown as day/month/year unless the product has a **shelf-life** of less than 3 months, in which case the year is not shown. If eaten after the best before date, the food may not cause food poisoning, but will not be in best condition.

'use by' tells how long the food will be safe to eat if stored correctly. This is used for perishable foods, such as cream and fish, which would become a health hazard if kept too long. Freezing can prolong the safe storage of some perishable foods.

6   The name and address of the manufacturer, packager, or retailer.

7   The place of origin – where the food was originally grown or produced.

Nutritional labelling of food products is discussed on pp. 40–41.

The law requires food labels to carry certain information about the product.

Food retailing

Before the advent of the supermarket in the late 1940s, different types of food were sold in specialist shops (greengrocers, butchers, fishmongers, etc.).

Today, most foods are sold through supermarkets, and most supermarkets belong to a few large 'chain' companies which own many outlets.

Chain companies generally buy their food direct from manufacturers rather than a wholesaler. They often sell their own brand-name products at a lower price than the manufacturing companies' equivalents. They may also own farms and have fruit, vegetables, and other items produced only for them.

Hypermarkets or 'superstores' are large outlets usually situated out-of-town. They often sell houseware, garden goods, petrol, and clothing as well as food. Many have in-store bakeries, fresh fish and meat counters, newsagents, alcoholic drinks sections, and pharmacies. The range of foods available has greatly increased in the last 20 years, and some hypermarkets sell over 13,500 food lines.

A recent development in retailing is the discount food store. These stock fewer types of product than most supermarkets, but at low prices. Many are arranged as warehouses in out-of-town areas.

The use of bar codes and electronic scanning of goods at the checkout has made retailing more efficient.

Many shops now have bar code scanners at the checkout.

It is more efficient because:

1   Most goods are no longer priced before being put on the shelves.
2   Customers can select fresh produce, e.g. fruit, and have it weighed and priced at the checkout.
3   Customers receive an itemized till receipt, giving details of items purchased and money-saving offers.
4   Retailers can check their stock and sales easily and quickly.
5   Scanning generally takes less time at the checkout, so customers are dealt with speedily.

Some shops have introduced a scheme where customers are given a machine to scan their own goods as they place them in the trolley. They then pay at the checkout. The aim is to reduce queueing time.

The chart on p. 84 lists the main types of food retail outlet and the advantages and disadvantages of each type.

Points to look for in food shops

1   A high standard of hygiene.
2   Rotation of goods, so that old stocks are sold first.
3   Efficient, helpful, knowledgeable service.
4   A wide selection of goods, in both range and sizes of products available.
5   Competitive prices.

Budgeting for food

Food is an expensive item in a family budget, so it is important to shop economically and carefully. It helps to follow these guidelines:

1   Plan the weekly shopping before going out, and stick to the plan as far as possible.
2   Look for competitive prices, special offers, and multi-buy savings.
3   Look for good quality food that is good value for money. Some retailers have an economy range of essential food items sold in simple packaging. These are cheap but the quality of the ingredients may not be so high.
4   Buy only the amounts that are required for particular meals, unless the extra food is to be used up on another occasion.
5   Compare prices per unit weight, volume, portion, or pack to get the best value.

A supermarket

An independent grocery shop

A specialist shop

A market stall

Type of outlet	Advantages	Disadvantages
Supermarket or hypermarket	1 A wide range of goods is available. 2 Prices are generally cheaper. 3 Food is usually good quality and fresh. 4 Food is selected by the customer – even fruit and vegetables. 5 Car parking is usually easy and convenient. 6 The standard of hygiene is usually high. 7 Unusual foods may be stocked. 8 Multi-buy (e.g. three for the price of two) and special offers can save money. 9 Many have mother and baby rooms, toilet facilities, packing and carry-to-car service, savings schemes, coffee shops or restaurants, children's play areas, information leaflets and advice, help for disabled customers, and discount card schemes.	1 Do not usually deliver food to the home. 3 It may be hard to get advice. 4 Self service may result in the customer spending more money than intended, and goods are often attractively presented to encourage this 'impulse buying'. 5 There may be long queues at the checkouts, which can increase shopping time considerably. 6 Out-of-town shopping is leading to fewer shops in town centres. High transport costs and difficulty in carrying large amounts of shopping may discourage people on low incomes, the elderly, and the disabled from using superstores. This means they cannot take advantage of the lower prices, special offers, and variety of foods available. 7 It may be difficult to buy small quantities and packs (for single people).
Small independent grocer	1 The personalized service is helpful to the customer. 2 The shop may deliver the goods. 3 Often near to residential areas, and so convenient. 4 Small packs may be available.	1 May be expensive. 2 There may be a limited selection. 3 Food may not be very fresh as turnover may be slow.
Specialist shop	1 Advice on the food being sold is usually good. 2 Food is usually of good quality. 3 The selection of food within the range is normally good.	1 May be expensive. 2 Food may not be very fresh if turnover is slow.
Open market	1 May be considerably cheaper. 2 There is normally a rapid turnover of food, so it is fresh. 3 Local produce is often available. 4 Often a lively, friendly service.	1 Food sold may be of inferior quality to that on display. 2 The food may be open to flies and the standards of hygiene may not be high. If the market is near a road, the food may be exposed to dust and car fumes. 3 It may not be possible to tell how fresh certain foods are, e.g. cheese, cold meats.

Bulk buying

Many people buy food in bulk once a month or less. This saves time and petrol, and may save money.

In order to be able to bulk buy, the following must be available:

1 Sufficient storage space in the home for the food.
2 The initial outlay of money.
3 Transport to and from the shop.

Many large supermarkets and hypermarkets cater for people who wish to buy food in bulk, and often sell large packs of goods at a lower price per unit than smaller packs. Also, many farms and small-holdings allow customers to pick produce such as fruit and vegetables in bulk. Some farms also sell bulk quantities of meat for storage in the freezer, as do many butchers' shops.

Bulk buying can be very useful, but consumers must take care not to buy unnecessary items or to eat more food just because it happens to be in the house.

Revision questions

1 What are the main causes of famine in poor countries?
2 Why are countries such as the UK and USA able to have more than enough to eat?
3 Give three examples of primary and secondary food processing.
4 Why is fast food popular?
5 What are the stages in the marketing of food?
6 How is food advertising regulated?
7 What information must a food label show?
8 What does 'shelf-life' mean?
9 How does electronic scanning of goods in a shop help the customer and the retailer?
10 What points would you look for when choosing which shop to buy food in?
11 Compare the advantages and disadvantages of shopping for food in a superstore, small independent store, and open market.

Cereals

Cereals are the most important single food in nearly every country. Even in wealthy countries, they are eaten in large amounts. In most countries, cereals are the staple foods for most people, because they are quite easy to grow and are cheaper than meat.

Types of cereal

Name	Areas grown
Wheat	USA, Canada, Argentina, Europe, Russia, Egypt, Northern India.
Maize	Southern USA, Italy, India, Egypt.
Rice	Damp tropical areas, e.g. India, China.
Oats	Cold temperate climates, e.g. Scotland.
Barley	Temperate climates, e.g. UK.
Rye	Cold climates, e.g. Scandinavia, Russia, Poland.

The word 'corn' is generally used to describe the most familiar local cereal grown in an area.

Wheat

Wheat is a main cereal food in many countries.

Wheat grains are divided into different layers. Each has a different function in the plant and contains different amounts and types of nutrients.

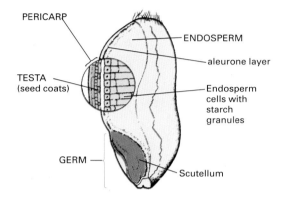

Distribution of nutrients in wheat

Part of grain	Nutrients
Pericarp, testa, and aleurone layer	B vitamins (especially niacin); mineral elements (50% of total grain): iron*, phosphorus, calcium*; LBV protein (concentrated source). Also contains cellulose, in the form of bran.
Scutellum	B vitamins (especially thiamin); protein.
Germ	B vitamins; vitamin E; protein; fat; iron.
Endosperm	B vitamins; protein; starch.

*Calcium and iron are bound to phytic acid in these layers of the wheat. This makes them insoluble and limits their absorption in the body.

Types of wheat

Several varieties of wheat are grown, to produce different types of flour. The most common are:

Winter wheat, which is grown in the UK and Europe, and is sown in autumn and harvested the following summer. It produces soft, weak flour with less than 10% protein.

Spring wheat, which is grown in Canada, and is sown in early spring and harvested the same year. It produces hard, strong flour with more than 10% protein.

Milling and flour production

Wheat is usually ground into flour before it is used as a food. This is achieved by **milling**. Modern milling is carried out using a series of steel rollers. The object of milling is to separate the endosperm from the rest of the grain, and to reduce the grain to fine flour particles. The process is carried out in the following stages:

1 Blending of different varieties of wheat grain.

2 Washing to remove dirt and stones.

3 Breaking the grains between rollers rotating at different speeds.

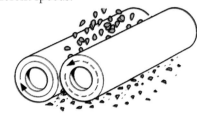

4 Sieving the crushed grain into

a a small amount of flour

b particles of endosperm (semolina)

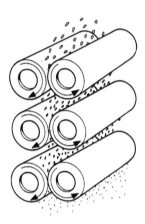

c particles of bran with endosperm attached

5 Removing the bran by further rolling. The bran is used for animal feeds.

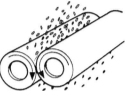

6 Making flour by passing the endosperm through the next series of rollers, each set closer together than the last, in order to produce a fine flour with the minimum damage to the starch granules. (Damaged starch granules produce poor quality flour).

7 Sieving to remove the germ as a powder.

The milling process can be adjusted according to the amount and type of flour required from the original grain. The percentage of the whole grain used in the flour is called the **extraction rate** of the flour.

Type of flour	Extraction rate
Wholemeal (Contains all the components of the original grain, and is brown because of the bran.)	100%
Wheatmeal (Contains 85% of the original grain, with 15% discarded as bran, but is still brown because of the remaining bran.)	85%
White (Contains 70% of the original grain, with most of the bran, germ, fat, and minerals removed.)	70%

Advantages of wholemeal flour
1   The nutrient content of the grain is retained.
2   The bran provides a valuable source of NSP (see pp. 26-8).
3   The flour gives a pleasant 'nutty' flavour to baked items.

Disadvantages of wholemeal flour
1   It does not keep as long as white flour as it contains fat which can become rancid.
2   It contains phytic acid (see p. 21) which may affect the absorption of calcium and iron.
3   It does not have such good baking qualities as white flour for items such as pastry and cakes.

Advantages of white flour
1   It has good baking qualities, producing a fine texture in cakes, bread, and pastry.
2   It contains less phytic acid.
3   It contains less fat, so it is less likely to become rancid.

Disadvantages of white flour
1   It contains less NSP.
2   It contains less calcium and iron, although by law these are added to flour used for making bread.
3   It contains less protein and vitamins.

Loaves made from wholemeal and white flour

The gluten in flour helps dough to stretch.

Protein content and baking quality of flour

Wheat flours which have a protein content of more than 10% (hard, strong flours made from spring wheat) are normally used for bread making; flours with a protein content of less than 10% (soft, weak flours made from winter wheat) are normally used for cake, pastry, and biscuit making. The reason for the difference is the amount of **gluten** formed from the protein in the flour when it is mixed with water. However, not all flours of high protein content produce sufficient or strong enough gluten; **durum wheat**, which is used to make pasta, has a high protein content, but is unsuitable for baking as its gluten is tough and does not stretch.

The gluten of flours used for bread making can stretch and hold pockets of gas produced by yeast during rising and baking. When baked in the oven, the gluten stretches and eventually coagulates, forming a framework in the baked item. The dough should be kneaded thoroughly to develop the gluten and increase its elasticity. The addition of salt helps to strengthen the gluten, whereas sugar softens it. In commercially produced bread, **dough improvers** such as vitamin C are added to help develop the gluten.

The gluten of flours used for cake, pastry, and biscuit making is weaker and less elastic than that in strong, hard wheat flour, and is damaged by over-handling. It can be used to make bread, providing that it is handled less and more yeast is used to raise the dough. However, the volume of bread produced is usually less. When used in cake, pastry, or biscuit making, the gluten stretches and holds pockets of gas produced from raising agents. It sets to form a framework in the baked item, with a finer texture than bread.

Plain cake flour has no raising agent added to it, whereas self-raising flour has baking powder added commercially. Flour with an extraction rate of 80% can also be used for cakes, and may have baking powder added.

Rice

The structure of rice is similar to that of wheat.

Types

Patna: has long, thin grains, and is traditionally served in savoury dishes.
Carolina: has round grains and is traditionally used in puddings with milk.
Flaked: the grains are flaked by machine, and usually made into puddings.
Ground: the grains are crushed into a powder, and used in cakes, puddings, soups, and biscuits.

Importance in the diet

Rice is the staple cereal food in many countries, particularly China, Japan, and India.

Whole-grain rice is a good source of thiamin, 79% of which is found in the pericarp, aleurone layer, and scutellum. The endosperm contains only 9% of the thiamin. Most rice is milled (polished) to remove the outer layers of the grain and make the rice easier and quicker to cook. This results in a large loss of thiamin from the grain, and is the cause of many cases of beri-beri (see p. 16) in poor countries where rice is the main food.

Rice also contains other B vitamins, which are often lost when the rice is washed before and after cooking, and during boiling.

Preparation

Rice should be cooked in the minimum amount of water, for the shortest time possible, until the grains are just tender. If overcooked, the starch gelatinizes and the grains stick together instead of remaining separate.

Rice growing in a paddy-field in Indonesia

Maize

Maize is generally more resistant to drought and gives a higher yield than wheat or rice. It is grown in many countries and there are many varieties.

Sweetcorn (corn on the cob) The freshly picked cobs are usually boiled and served as a vegetable. The grains can also be removed from the cob before being boiled.

A maize plantation in Tanzania

Whole maize meal The grains are crushed into meal and used as a type of flour in some countries, such as Mexico. Some of the germ and pericarp can be removed by sieving if required.

Importance in the diet

The nutrient content of maize is similar to that of other cereals, except that the yellow varieties contain a good supply of β-carotene, which is converted in the body to vitamin A.

The niacin in maize is in a bound form and cannot be efficiently absorbed by the body. This can be overcome, as in the preparation of tortillas in Mexico (see p. 17).

Oats

Oats grow well in the cold climate of Scotland and were at one time the staple cereal food. They were used to make porridge but their consumption has fallen as porridge has largely been replaced by other breakfast cereals.

Oats are usually rolled rather than crushed, and are partially cooked during the process. Coarse, medium, and fine grades are sold. They can be treated to make them quick to cook, and are used mainly in the preparation of breakfast cereals such as muesli and porridge, and in baking cakes and biscuits. Oats have a relatively high fat, protein, and NSP content compared with other cereals. Research suggests that they may help to lower blood cholesterol levels.

Barley

Barley is widely grown, and is a hardy cereal plant. At one time it was eaten in large amounts, but now it is mainly used as cattle food and in the brewing and whisky industries. It is sold for food use as pearl barley, which is the grain with the husk removed, and is used to thicken soups and stews.

Rye

Rye is grown mainly in the north and east of Europe, because it is resistant to the cold. It is made into rye bread, which is dark brown in colour, and also into crispbreads, which are traditionally produced in Scandinavian countries.

Rye crops are prone to attack by a mould called ergot, which is toxic if eaten. It causes 'ergotism', one of the symptoms of which is a burning sensation in the feet.

Cereal products

Breakfast cereals are an easy-to-prepare food, and have become very popular. They are made from various cereals, including wheat, rice, maize, and bran from wheat, by roasting and baking. They may be shredded, rolled, 'puffed' or flaked, and mixed with a number of ingredients such as dried fruit, honey, sugar, or coconut. They are often fortified with vitamins and minerals to increase their food value.

Many popular breakfast cereals have sugar added during processing, or are coated with sugar. This can give them a higher energy value.

Cornflour is made from maize, and is almost 100% starch. It is used as a thickening agent and is the basis of custard powder. It is useful for people with coeliac disease, as it contains no gluten.

Pasta is made from **durum wheat** flour, water, and sometimes egg, which are mixed to a paste, then shaped and partly baked, resulting in a dried product with good keeping qualities.

It is also possible to buy fresh pasta, with or without fillings and sauces. This must be stored in a refrigerator and eaten soon after purchase. Pasta can be made with wholegrain flour, spinach (pasta verdi), and tomatoes, in traditional and novelty shapes. The shapes have names and are served with different types of sauces.

Many different types of fresh and dried pasta are available.

Chappatis are made from wheat flour, mixed with water and sometimes oil. They are cooked on a flat, heated surface.

Popping corn is heated in a little oil, to make the starch burst out of the hard seeds. It is tossed in icing sugar or salt and served as a snack.

Gluten-free products are available for people who have gluten intolerance (see p. 72).

Storage of cereals

Cereals should be stored in cool, dry conditions, to prevent them from becoming mouldy. Wholegrain cereals do not keep as well as refined cereals because of the fat content of the germ. Cereals are prone to attack by insects and should be regularly inspected if stored for long periods.

Cereal-like foods

The following foods are often called cereals but strictly they are not:

Tapioca is made from a tuber vegetable called cassava. It is used in puddings and to thicken soups and stews. It is almost 100% starch.

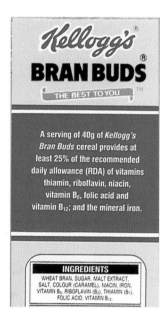

This bran breakfast cereal is fortified with vitamins and minerals. It also contains added sugar.

Arrowroot is made from the maranta plant, which has underground stems from which the arrowroot is obtained. It is a white powder and is used as a thickener. It is also used as a glaze, because it becomes clear when boiled with water.

Sago is made from the sago plant, and is used in milk puddings.

Revision questions

1 Name the six main cereal plants and say where each is grown.
2 Which nutrients are found in the following parts of the wheat grain?
   a scutellum
   b aleurone layer
   c endosperm
   d germ
3 How is winter wheat used in baking and why? What is spring wheat used for and why?
4 How is wheat milled?
5 What is the 'extraction rate' of flour?
6 Why are wholemeal cereals nutritionally preferable to refined ones?
7 How does the protein content of flour affect its baking qualities?
8 How can gluten be developed in a bread dough?
9 Name the two main types of rice and give their uses.
10 Why is beri-beri a common disorder in poor countries where white rice is the staple food?
11 How should rice be cooked, and why?
12 What are the main uses of barley, oats, and rye?
13 How should cereals be stored?

Further work with cereals

1 To examine the gluten content of flour:
   Mix 50g of:
   a strong plain flour
   b ordinary plain flour
   c self-raising flour
   separately with enough water to form a dough.
   Place each in a piece of muslin and rinse out the starch under a gentle stream of water. Squeeze the bag to help. Continue until no more starch is washed out and a small ball of gluten is left.
   Weigh the gluten samples and work out the percentage of gluten in the different flours. Explain why there are differences.
2 Observe wheat grains under a magnifying glass and sketch one. Carefully cut a wheat grain lengthways and observe again, looking for the outer layers, germ, and endosperm.
3 Compare the wheat grain with rice, barley, and maize grains under the magnifying glass.
4 Boil 50g of white patna rice and 50g of whole-grain patna rice, and measure how long it takes for each to become tender. How do you account for the difference?
5 Measure the length and width of rice grains before cooking, and compare these with cooked rice. How do you account for the difference?
6 Observe starch granules (in water) from rice, flour, maize (cornflour), and potato under the microscope. Sketch your observations.

Fats and oils

Fats and oils have many uses in food preparation and are important sources of energy in the diet. The functions, composition, and chemistry of fats and oils are discussed in Chapter 1, pp. 5–8.

Uses
Fats and oils have many uses, including:
   spreading on bread, etc. (butter, margarine, low–fat spreads)
   creaming for cakes (see p. 209) (butter, margarine)
   shortening for pastry (lard, vegetable fat)
   frying deep and shallow (see pp. 187–90) (lard, vegetable oil for deep frying; also butter, margarine for shallow frying)
   oiling baking tins (any melted fat or oil)
   salad dressings (see p. 220) (vegetable oils)
   ice cream (vegetable oils)

Properties

Fats are solid at room temperature and oils are liquid. This is because they have different **melting points** due to the type of fatty acids they contain. In general, the more **saturated** fatty acids a fat contains, the more **solid** it will be, and the more **unsaturated** fatty acids it contains, the more **liquid** it will be at room temperature.

Effect of heat

When a fat is heated, it melts to an oil, then heats up until eventually it ignites. Some fats can be heated to higher temperatures than others, and so are more suitable for frying.

Vegetable oils can generally be heated to higher temperatures because of their fatty acid content and their purity. Fats such as butter and margarine cannot be used for frying at high temperatures as they contain other substances such as water and emulsifiers which make them burn easily.

When a fat is heated, at a certain temperature a thin, bluish haze of smoke is given off which will give food an unpleasant flavour. This is the **smoke point**, and at this temperature the fat molecules start to split up, reducing the keeping qualities of the fat. Soon after this, the fat will ignite and burn fiercely. The temperature at which this occurs is called the **flash point**.

Fat	Smoke point (when fresh)
vegetable oil	227–232°C
lard	183–205°C
vegetable fat	180–188°C

Rancidity

Fats and oils, and foods containing them, can develop 'off' flavours and odours due to the fat becoming **rancid**.

Rancidity is caused by the action of the enzyme **lipase**, or by **oxidation**. Lipase breaks down the fat molecules, and the 'off' flavours and odours develop because of the free fatty acids in the food. Heat can destroy both lipase and the micro-organisms in the food that produce lipase.

In oxidation, oxygen is absorbed by the fat and reacts with the fat molecules to produce substances that give the fat an unpleasant flavour and odour. Oxidation is accelerated by light, impurities in fat, enzymes, and the presence of many polyunsaturated fatty acids. **Antioxidants** are added to foods containing fats, and the foods may be packed in foil-lined containers to prevent light from reaching them.

Rancidity can develop in fat-containing foods that are kept in cold storage or frozen.

Types of fats and oils

Edible fats and oils are obtained from both animals and plants.

The main animal sources are:

milk fat - butter, ghee (clarified butter), cream

meat - dripping, lard, suet, fat under the skin and in muscles

marine - liver oils, oily flesh, whale oil

Animal fats

Butter

Butter is made from cream (see pp. 105-6) which has to be separated from milk. By law, butter must contain at least 82% fat. Cream contains 35-40% fat.

After being separated from the milk, the cream is pasteurized. Undesirable flavours and air are removed, then it is held at 4.5°C to harden the fat globules. It is then held at 15-18°C for three to four hours to develop acidity (for flavour) and to prepare it for churning. It is then cooled to 7°C and churned.

Traditional butter churns are being replaced by butter-making machines which carry out the complete butter-making process. Churning breaks up the seal of milk solids around the fat globules so that they **coalesce** (stick together). The non-fat milk solids then mix with the liquid in the cream to form **buttermilk**, which is drained off and used for cattle feeds or sold as a drink. The fat is then chilled, washed, and hardened, and salt is added. This helps to preserve the butter. Usually 1.5% salt is added, but some butter is sold unsalted. After this, the butter is worked until smooth, and then packed.

Animal fats include butter, suet, dripping, lard, and fish oils. Some people take fish liver oils as a diet supplement, in liquid or capsule form.

Composition

Butter contains:

    82% fat – the fatty acid, butyric acid, gives
      butter its characteristic flavour

    15% water

    0.4% protein

    2.3% minerals

    vitamins A and D: amounts vary with the
      time of year

The colour of butter varies according to the breed of cow, the quality of grass, and the carotenes present. Additional colouring may be added.

Salt and extra flavouring may be added as well as preservative and antioxidant.

Uses in food preparation

Butter is popular because of its flavour. It is used for spreading on bread and biscuits and it is sometimes served with vegetables.

In cookery, butter can be used for cakes, although it takes longer to cream than margarine. It can be used for pastry, together with lard or vegetable shortening, and for shallow frying at relatively low temperatures. Unsalted butter can be used for butter icing, home-made cream, brandy butter, and sauces.

Suet

Suet is obtained from the fat around vital organs, e.g. kidneys, usually from the ox. The fat content varies from 70% to 99%, and it is solid and hard,

composed of mainly saturated fatty acids.

Suet is sold either in cartons, or shredded and mixed with flour to prevent it from sticking together. It is used in making pastry, puddings, dumplings, and sweet mincemeat.

Vegetable suet, made from hydrogenated vegetable oils, is suitable for vegetarians.

Dripping

Dripping is the fat released during the roasting of a joint of meat (usually beef). On cooling, it separates into a layer of fat and a layer of meat extractives in a jelly. The fat can be used for roasting other joints or vegetables, or for shallow frying. Some people eat dripping spread on bread or toast.

Lard

Lard is produced from pigs that are specially bred for this purpose. The fat is obtained from the fatty tissues under the skin. They are cut into small pieces and heated to remove the lard. This is called **rendering**.

The quality of lard depends on where it is on the body. Antioxidants are added to prevent rancidity, and it may be modified to improve its baking qualities.

The taste of lard is bland. It is used as a shortener for pastry, but it is mixed with margarine for added flavour. It is not used in cake making as it has poor creaming properties.

Lard is also used for deep and shallow frying. It must be pure for this purpose so that it can be heated to high temperatures.

Marine oils

Fish-liver oils (e.g. cod, halibut) are rich sources of vitamins A and D, and used to be given to children regularly to supplement their diet. It is now realized that a well-balanced diet can provide all the required fat-soluble vitamins. If too many are given, they are stored in the body and may cause poisoning.

Whale and fish oils contain many polyunsaturated fatty acids and must be refined, as they deteriorate rapidly after being extracted. Whale oil used to be used for margarine manufacture, but in recent years mainly plant and fish oils have been used.

Plant oils

Plant oils are mostly obtained from the seeds of plants such as:

soya bean	cottonseed
sunflower	groundnut
coconut	palm
linseed	olive
sesame	maize
rapeseed	

Apart from their uses in the food industry, plant oils are also used in the manufacture of paints, varnishes, and plastics.

Refining

The plants that produce oil seeds are grown in many parts of the world. All oils that are used for food have to be **refined** first.

Oil is contained in the cells of the seeds. It is **extracted** from them either by squeezing or by dissolving the oil in a solvent, e.g. trichloroethene.

The cell walls of the seeds are hard to penetrate, so expensive machinery has to be used for extracting the oil.

The process involves the following stages:

1 Cleaning the seeds.

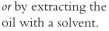

2 Breaking by rollers.

3 Cooking the seeds in steam.

4 Expelling the oil by squeezing (olive oil is cold-pressed, i.e. not cooked first)

or by extracting the oil with a solvent.

5 Removal of natural acids.

6 Bleaching to lighten the colour.

7 Deodorizing and improving the taste and smell.

The oils are sold separately or blended. Some oils, e.g. olive oil, are more expensive than others.

Oils that are exported to colder countries such as the UK have to be treated to stop them forming fat crystals in cold weather. This is called **winterization**.

Oils are used for:

margarine manufacture
frying
salad dressings

They are also used in the baking industry.

Margarine manufacture

It is possible to produce solid fats from liquid oils by a process called **hydrogenation**. This process is used in the manufacture of margarine.

Unsaturated fatty acids have the capacity to take up more hydrogen atoms (see p. 6), which makes them more solid. During hydrogenation, hydrogen is bubbled through oils under carefully controlled conditions. The process can be stopped when the required hardness has been reached.

Margarines made mainly from vegetable oils, such as sunflower or soya oil, have a higher polyunsaturated fatty acid content (see p. 7) than margarines made mainly from animal fats and oils. This information is normally displayed on the labels of margarine cartons, to enable the consumer to choose a product high in polyunsaturated fat, as recommended for following the dietary guidelines (see p. 38).

Hydrogenation causes some polyunsaturated fatty acids (PUFAs) to change to trans fatty acids (TFAs). There is concern that TFAs may affect levels of cholesterol in the blood (see p. 45), and research is continuing into their effects on health. Some manufacturers are attempting to reduce the levels of TFAs in their products.

The manufacture of margarine from plant and marine oils is carried out as follows:

1 The oils are refined.

2 The oils are hydrogenated, then deodorized.

3 Flavours, preservatives, salt, colour, and (by law) vitamins A and D are added.

4 Cultured, pasteurized milk is blended in.

5 The mixture is emulsified and stabilized.

6 The margarine is chilled and textured (e.g. whipped for cake making, or blended with other oils).

7 It is finally packed, either in paper or in plastic tubs.

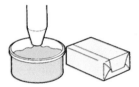

Block margarine is of a similar hardness to butter, and is sold in paper wrapping. It is suitable for pastry making and, if softened, can be used for creaming.

Soft margarine is less hydrogenated than block margarine and is therefore softer and suitable for creaming. It can be spread and used straight from the refrigerator, but is not suitable for pastry making as it is too soft for rubbing in.

Some margarines are sold as butter substitutes, and may have up to 10% butter added. Others are rich in polyunsaturated fatty acids (see p. 6).

Cooking fats

White cooking fats, suitable for making pastry and other dishes, are produced in a similar way to margarine, except that they are nearly 100% fat. They can be used for creaming in cake making, and may be made softer by being whipped. They can also be used for frying.

EU categories of fats and spreads

Name			Fat content
Fats			
Butter	Margarine	Blend	80–90%
³/₄ fat butter	³/₄ fat margarine	³/₄ fat blend	60–62%
Reduced-fat butter	Reduced-fat margarine	Reduced-fat blend	41–62%
Half-fat butter	Half-fat margarine	Half-fat blend	39–41%
Spreads			
Low-fat/light butter	Low-fat/light margarine	Low-fat/light blend	<41%
Dairy spread x%	Fat spread x%	Blended spread x%	x%

Low-energy spreads

Margarine has (by law) at least 80% fat, so food technologists have developed lower-energy alternatives called **spreads**. EU rules govern the composition of these products (see chart above), which must be clearly labelled to show how much fat they contain.

Butter must contain only milk fat.

Margarines and **spreads** may contain vegetable and/or animal fat with no more than 3% milk fat.

Blends may contain vegetable and/or animal fat with 10–80% milk fat.

Many margarines and spreads try to imitate the taste of butter. Some are low in saturated fats; some are low in energy.

Storage of fats and oils

Fats should be stored in a cool place, covered, and away from strong odours which they could absorb.

Oils that have been used for frying should be strained to remove any impurities and food particles which may cause them to become rancid. They should not be used over and over again, as the molecules split up when heated and this may cause rancidity.

Revision questions

1 What are the uses of the following fats and oils in cookery?
   a margarine (soft and hard)
   b butter
   c lard
   d suet
   e vegetable oil
2 What are the main sources of fats?
3 How is butter produced?
4 Where is suet found, and what is its function in the animal's body?
5 How is lard produced?
6 What are the main sources of plant oils?
7 What is the difference between soft margarine, block margarine, and low-energy spread?
8 How are plant oils obtained?
9 How is margarine produced?
10 How do the fatty acids affect the characteristics of the fat?
11 What is hydrogenation?
12 Why do fats become rancid? How can this be prevented?
13 Why is it important not to overheat oil used for frying repeatedly?

Sugar and sweeteners

Sweet foods are highly palatable and very popular. Many processed foods have sweeteners added and much of their success depends on having the right degree of sweetness to attract the consumer.

Foods have been sweetened for thousands of years. The early sweeteners were natural ones such as honey. Sugar (sucrose) has been used as a preservative and flavouring for many centuries in some parts of the world (such as India), but was not used in Europe until about the 13th century. At that time, it was very expensive and it did not become a major item of the diet in Europe until the late 19th century.

Since then, consumption has increased considerably, and many foods are sweetened with natural carbohydrate products such as cane sugar, beet sugar, sucrose, glucose, glucose syrup, hydrolysed starch, dextrose, fructose, maltose, lactose, and invert sugar.

Research into artificial sweeteners has been going on for many years. Initially, the aim was to find a suitable, cheaper alternative to sucrose. Later, it was to find a low-energy substitute for use in energy-reduced diets. Consumers in the UK consume more low-energy sweeteners than any other European country (approximately 10 tonnes per year). Artificial sweeteners used in foods and soft drinks include:

Artificial sweeteners provide a low-calorie alternative to sugar.

Some countries have banned certain sweeteners as research suggests that they may have an adverse effect on health. Some health experts are concerned about the amount of sweeteners consumed by children and young people, particularly in soft drinks.

Sugar (sucrose)

Types

Sugar is made from either sugar cane, which is grown in tropical countries, or sugar beet, which is grown in temperate climates such as the UK.

Name of sweetener	Sweetness index (sucrose=1)
Saccharin	500 (i.e. 500 times sweeter than sucrose)
Sodium saccharin	500
Calcium saccharin	500
Aspartame	150
Acesulphame potassium	150
Xylitol	10
Mannitol	10
Sorbitol	0.6

Sugar beet   Sugar cane

Production

Sugar cane The sugar is found in the soft fibres in the centre of the cane. To extract the sugar, the canes are first crushed, then sprayed with water. This makes a solution containing 13% sugar (sucrose), 3% impurities, and 84% water. The impurities are removed by boiling, adding calcium oxide (lime), and filtering.

A clear, brown solution (molasses) is left. This contains a mixture of sugar crystals and liquid. The liquid is spun off, and raw brown sugar is left.

Sugar beet The sugar is stored in the root of the sugar beet. The beets are shredded and the sugar extracted by soaking them in hot water. The solution obtained contains about 14% sugar (sucrose), 4% impurities, and 82% water. The impurities are removed and the water is evaporated off to leave raw brown sugar, as for cane sugar.

Sugar refining

Raw sugar, from cane or beet, contains about 96% sucrose, as sugar crystals and molasses. The raw sugar is mixed with sugar syrup, and the syrup is then forced out in a centrifuge, leaving crystals which are washed in water. Next, the crystals are dissolved in water and the impurities are removed as before. The liquid is then allowed to filter through a deep layer of bone charcoal to remove all the coloured impurities. A clear liquid is left.

The liquid is then evaporated to produce sugar crystals of the desired shape and size. The crystals are washed again, and centrifuged. The syrup that is spun off is used for the manufacture of golden syrup or soft brown sugar.

Granulated sugar is made as described above.

Caster sugar is made in the same way as granulated sugar, but the process is modified so that very small crystals are obtained.

Golden granulated and caster sugar are made as described above but not all the coloured impurities are removed in the refining process.

Icing sugar is obtained by pulverizing granulated sugar to a very fine powder in a special mill.

Brown sugar is made by crystallizing the syrup obtained at the end of the refining process. It is moister than white sugar. There are several types of brown sugar, including:

> **soft brown sugar** (dark or light)
>
> **demerara sugar**, which has larger crystals and is traditionally served with coffee and used in cake making.

Coffee crystals are large sugar crystals, sometimes made in different colours. They take longer to dissolve than other sugars.

Lump sugar is made by pressing together moistened sugar crystals, and then cutting into lumps.

Preserving sugar with added pectin is available for making jam and other preserves.

Honey

Honey is produced by bees from the nectar obtained from flowers. Bees collect the nectar, which is a solution of sucrose, glucose, and fructose in water. As the nectar passes through the bee's body, enzymes convert these sugars into mainly glucose and fructose. The resulting honey is deposited in honeycombs, and consists of about 75% sugars (glucose, fructose, and some sucrose), 20% water, and 5% extracted flavours peculiar to the flower from which the nectar was obtained.

Honey is sold in both liquid and granulated forms. Honeys are supersaturated solutions, and they tend to granulate because the sugars gradually crystallize out of solution. Honey to be sold liquid is processed by flash heating to 60–71°C.

Importance in the diet

Sugars are an important source of energy to the body, and are relatively quickly digested and absorbed. Artificial sweeteners such as saccharin provide the body with very little energy.

An excess of sugar in the diet is undesirable because it can lead to obesity and tooth decay. It is therefore sensible to limit the amount of sweet foods eaten, particularly between meals.

Revision questions

1 Why is sugar added to so many foods?
2 Why is saccharin used to sweeten foods?
3 How is sucrose obtained from sugar cane and sugar beet?
4 How and why is sugar refined?
5 Describe the different sugar products and what they are used for in food preparation.
6 What is honey and how is it produced?
7 What is the importance of sugar in the diet? Why is it inadvisable to consume too much?

Further work with sugar

N.B. Sugar solutions boil at very high temperatures, so take care when doing these experiments.

1 Mix 1 tablespoon water with 1 tablespoon granulated sugar in an evaporating dish. Heat gently until the sugar has dissolved and boil without stirring. Observe the changes in colour, consistency, and smell of the sugar solution, as the water evaporates. The change in colour is due to the sugar being caramelized (a change in molecular structure due to the removal of water). Continue heating and observe the changes in colour, smell, and appearance and how rapidly these occur. What is left in the dish when all the water has gone?
   Which recipes involve caramelization of sugar? Why is it important not to overcook the solution?

2 Repeat experiment 1 but stir the solution while it is boiling, and observe the changes in texture and appearance. Why does this happen?

3 Repeat experiment 1 but add a pinch of potassium hydrogen tartrate (cream of tartar). Observe the difference in time taken for the sugar to caramelize.

4 Repeat experiment 1 but use 100g sugar and 50ml water. Using a sugar thermometer, drop small samples of the solution into a jug of cold water at 10°C intervals from 110°C to 180°C. Squeeze the cooled samples and observe their textures and flavour. Why is temperature important in sweet making?

Milk

Milk and its products are known as dairy foods. The main milk products are:
   butter
   cream
   cheese
   yogurt
Butter is discussed in the section on fats and oils as its main component is fat (see pp. 92-3). Cream, cheese, and yogurt are discussed later in this chapter.

History of milk production

Today, it is taken for granted that milk supplies are always available and that they are clean and safe to drink. However, before the 1850s, there was no legislation to prevent the sale of unhygienic or untreated milk. Milk supplies were produced on a very small scale and were often contaminated with bacteria from diseased cows and dirty utensils.

In the 1860s, the demand for milk increased as the population of the UK grew. Dairy farmers increased their production accordingly; but frequent outbreaks of diseases such as cattle plague and foot and mouth disease caused serious problems. In 1866, the government took steps to control the situation, by introducing the Cattle Diseases Prevention Act. Also at this time, the transportation of milk by railway became increasingly common, so towns were able to receive more regular supplies.

In 1870, the first dairy foods manufacturing factory was opened in Derby, and by 1900, a whole system of factories was in operation throughout the country.

It was not until 1884 that the first milk was sold in bottles. In 1894, the heat treatment of milk by sterilization was tried, but the results were not popular. Louis Pasteur's experiments on heating milk to destroy harmful bacteria (see pp. 155-7) in the late 19th century paved the way for the hygienic production and distribution of milk and dairy products.

Production

In the UK, most of the milk we buy comes from cows. Milk from goats and sheep is also available.

Milk is made from water plus the nutrients in the grass and other foodstuffs which make up the cow's diet. Some of the nutrients are used for the growth and maintenance of the cow's body and the rest are used for milk production. A cow can eat up to 70kg of grass a day, and extra nutrients in the form of supplements can also be given.

The nutrient content of the grass may vary according to:

1   The time of year – more vitamin A (as β-carotene) is found in summer grass.
2   Soil fertility.
3   The variety of grass.

The amount and quality of milk produced by a cow depends on:

1   The quality and amount of food eaten.
2   The breed of cow; Friesians as a breed are high producers of milk.
3   The health of the cow.

Cows are usually milked twice a day, in the early morning and late afternoon. Most milk is produced after calving, and the production gradually decreases until it stops about 10 months after calving. Over 20 litres a day can be obtained from one cow at the height of milking.

Treatment and processing

Milk produced by a healthy cow contains few harmful bacteria, but cows can catch a variety of diseases which could be passed on to humans, e.g. tuberculosis, brucellosis. All dairy herds have to be inspected by a vet to ensure that they are healthy before they are used for milk sales, and at regular intervals thereafter.

Rules of hygiene must be strictly followed at all stages from production to retail to the consumer.

Hygiene rules

These are laid down by the government and the EU. There are rules for each stage of processing.

Milking premises Rooms for cooling, storage, and milking should be airy and light, with good drainage and easily cleaned surfaces. They must be supplied with adequate water, and must be cleaned every day.

Cows must be clean and free from disease. Their teats and udder must be washed before milking.

Equipment and containers The milk must be covered and all equipment and containers must be thoroughly cleaned after use.

Farm workers must have proper washing facilities. They must cover cuts on their skin, and they must not spit or smoke.

Milk collection

Milking machines for the hygienic and efficient collection of milk are in use on nearly all dairy farms. A record is kept of the milk yield from each cow, and samples are taken to check the fat and protein content of the milk. This helps the farmer to assess the food intake of the cow.

Once collected, the milk is cooled to 4.5°C and put into a large vat. A road tanker collects the milk from several farms and transports it

Fresian cows are the most popular breed for milk production. Milk is collected . . .

. . . and transported quickly and hygienically.

rapidly to a depot or manufacturing creamery. Each batch is checked for quality, quantity, and hygiene. If it fails the tests, the batch is rejected. The tanker is cleaned after use.

Processing

Milk can be made safer to drink and will keep longer if it is heat treated. 96% of milk sold in the UK is subjected to heat treatment. The farmer must obtain a special licence to sell untreated ('raw') milk.

Pasteurized milk

Louis Pasteur believed that milk soured because of the presence of bacteria. He showed by experiment that heating the milk delayed the souring process and made the milk safer to drink by destroying harmful bacteria.

It took several years for legislation to be brought in and for the process to be perfected before pasteurization of milk became standard practice.

The aim of pasteurization is to destroy harmful (pathogenic) bacteria without adversely affecting the quality of the milk.

Pasteurization is usually carried out by heating the milk in a heat exchanger. There are two main methods:

1 The milk is heated to over 72°C for at least 15 seconds, then cooled rapidly to below 10°C. This is the **flash process**.
2 The milk is heated to 63°C for half an hour, then cooled rapidly as above. This is the **Holder method**, and is less common.

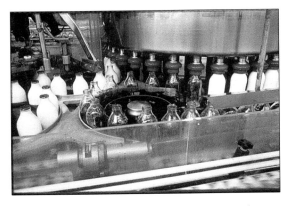

Milk bottles are automatically filled and capped.

The milk must be cooled rapidly, otherwise the nutritional value is affected, and bacterial growth is encouraged.

After cooling, the milk is put into insulated stainless steel tanks and bottled as soon as possible.

Homogenized milk

To **homogenize** is to produce a substance which is of a uniform consistency. In homogenized milk the cream does not rise to the surface as it does in pasteurized milk, but remains evenly distributed throughout the milk in tiny droplets.

The milk is first pasteurized, and then forced through a tiny mesh under pressure. This breaks up the fat globules in the milk into very small droplets. It is then cooled and bottled.

Channel Island and South Devon milk

Jersey, Guernsey, and South Devon breeds of cow produce very creamy milk, with a minimum fat content of 4% (other breeds have a fat content of about 3%). It is heat-treated, cooled, and bottled in the same way as milk from other breeds.

Sterilized milk

Sterilization kills harmful and souring bacteria more completely than pasteurization, and the milk will therefore keep for several weeks if unopened.

The milk is first homogenized, put into glass bottles with long necks, and sealed with a metal cap. It is then sterilized inside the bottles in one of the following ways:

1 In a **batch process**, where the milk is heated in bottles in an autoclave (a large industrial pressure cooker) at up to 113°C for 15-40 minutes.
2 In a **continuous process**, where the bottles pass on a conveyor belt through hot water tanks, into a steam chamber (under pressure) at 113°C for 15-40 minutes, then into cooling tanks.

Ultra heat treated milk

Ultra heat treated (UHT) milk can be kept in sealed packs for several months. The milk is heated in a heat exchanger at 132°C for not more than one second. It is then rapidly cooled and packed into foil-lined containers which are sealed. The rapid treatment does not adversely affect the colour or nutritional value of the milk. It can be stored at room temperature until it is opened.

Dried milk

Milk can be preserved by removing water so that the resulting powder contains 5% or less moisture. Before drying, the milk is homogenized and heat treated. It may be skimmed (i.e. most of the fat may be removed) or left as whole milk.

Spray drying

The milk is sprayed through a very fine jet into a chamber in which hot air is circulating. The water is quickly evaporated and the drops of milk fall to the bottom as a powder. The milk reconstitutes easily with water.

Milk is dried in a spray-drying chamber like this one.

The dried milk is packed into foil-lined cardboard drums or tins, which are made airtight to prevent any fat present from becoming rancid (see p. 92).

Dried milk which contains less than 26% fat should not be given to babies, and manufacturers are required to state this on the label.

Condensed milk

Milk can be preserved by the addition of sugar and the removal of water. Condensed milk is made with whole, partly skimmed, or skimmed milk. The milk is homogenized and heated to 80°C for 15 minutes. Sugar is then added and it is heated under a vacuum to evaporate some of the water until the milk is approximately 22 times more concentrated than fresh milk. It is then cooled and put into sealed cans.

Evaporated milk

Evaporated milk is prepared in a similar way to condensed milk, but no sugar is added. It is approximately twice as concentrated as fresh milk. It is put into sealed cans and sterilized for 20 minutes at 115.5°C.

Skimmed milk

The fat content of milk can be skimmed off to reduce the energy value of the milk. Skimmed milk is available in cartons or bottles, or in a dried form, and is useful in low-fat or energy-reduced diets.

Semi-skimmed milk

This has a fat content of slightly less than half that of whole milk, and is sold as pasteurized and UHT.

Frozen milk

Pasteurized homogenized milk can be frozen in polythene bags for up to a year. Ordinary, whole pasteurized milk is not suitable as it tends to separate on thawing.

Dried milk substitutes

It is possible to buy dried milk substitutes where skimmed milk and non-milk fats (e.g. from plants) are combined, and used in the same way as dried milk.

Dried artificial cream for coffee ('whiteners')

Artificial creams have been developed using vegetable fat, glucose syrup, and sodium caseinate. These are dried into granules or powder and are used in coffee drinks instead of milk or cream.

Storage of milk in the home

Fresh milk should be stored in a cool, dark place, preferably a refrigerator, and covered to prevent exposure to dust, bacteria in the air, and contamination by strong flavours from other foods. It should be used within two to three days, if pasteurized or homogenized. Sterilized, canned, and UHT milks should be treated as fresh once opened.

Dried milk should be stored in a cool, dry place with the lid firmly in place to prevent absorption of moisture. Once opened, it should be used up within the time stated by the manufacturer, and when reconstituted with water, should be treated as fresh milk.

The importance of milk in the diet

Milk is the single most complete food known to exist naturally. It is designed by nature to feed the offspring of mammals, (cows, goats, sheep, humans, etc.), so contains sufficient nutrients in the right proportions for the animal it was designed to feed. Milk is, however, deficient in ascorbic acid (vitamin C) and iron, containing only traces of these. Human babies are born with a supply of these in the body to last them for the first few months of life, until they can be provided by food.

The nutrients in milk are in a readily digestible form, and little is wasted during digestion. Milk is a valuable food not only for babies, but for people of all ages.

Nutrients in milk
Protein
Milk proteins are of a high biological value (see p. 3), and the chief ones are:

> caseinogen
> lactalbumin
> lactoglobulin

Caseinogen accounts for about 80% of the protein in milk, and in fresh milk it is combined with calcium and phosphorus as **calcium caseinate**. If an acid is added to the milk, or if it is soured naturally by lactic acid bacteria, the casein coagulates and separates from the calcium and phosphorus. This happens in cheese making. During digestion, it is coagulated by rennin to form a clot (see p. 35).

Lactalbumin accounts for about 8% of the protein in milk, and **lactoglobulin** for about 3.5%. When milk is heated, they both coagulate and form a 'skin' on the surface of the milk. They are not coagulated by rennin in the stomach during digestion, or by acid.

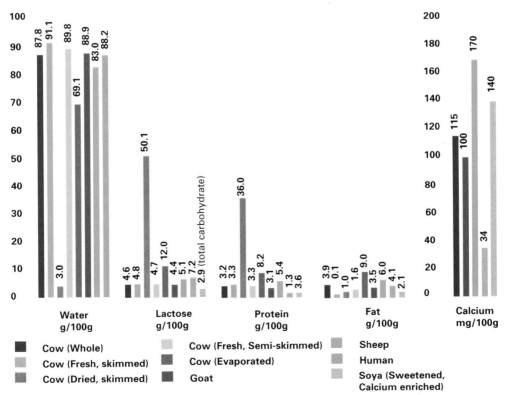

Nutrient content of various types of milk

Cow (Whole)
Cow (Fresh, skimmed)
Cow (Dried, skimmed)
Cow (Fresh, Semi-skimmed)
Cow (Evaporated)
Goat
Sheep
Human
Soya (Sweetened, Calcium enriched)

Fat

The fat content of milk is often used as a guide to the quality of the milk, and may affect its price. By law, whole milk must contain a minimum of 3% fat and that produced by Channel Island and South Devon cows must contain a minimum of 4% fat.

The fat is present in the form of tiny globules or droplets, which are lighter than water, and rise to the surface to form a cream layer (unless the milk has been homogenized).

Milk fat contains both saturated and unsaturated fatty acids, in varying proportions, according to the feed given to the cow.

Milk fat is used in the production of butter (see p. 92) and cream (see p. 105).

Dietary guidelines encourage us to reduce our saturated fat intake, so there is an increasing demand for low-fat dairy products. Sales of skimmed and semi-skimmed milk (see p. 102), and low-fat yogurts, cheeses, creams, and spreads have increased, with many new products becoming available each year.

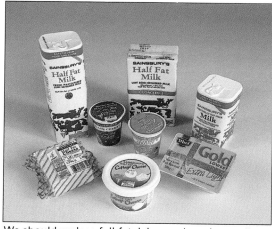

We should replace full-fat dairy products in our diet with low-fat ones like these.

Carbohydrate

The only carbohydrate in milk is the disaccharide, lactose (see p. 9). Cow's milk contains about 5% lactose, whereas human milk contains just over 7%. Lactose is less sweet than sucrose, and is therefore not easy to detect. Lactic acid bacteria readily ferment lactose to lactic acid, thus causing the milk to go sour, and curdle.

Vitamins

Fat soluble Milk contains a relatively good supply of retinol (vitamin A). The amount varies according to the time of year. In the summer, when cows can graze on fresh grass, milk contains more vitamin A and carotene than in the winter. Skimmed milk contains less vitamin A as it is removed with the milk fat.

Milk contains more vitamin D in the summer, when the cows are exposed to sunlight for longer periods. It is not a rich source of this vitamin.

Water soluble Milk is an important source of riboflavin, but this is destroyed if the milk is left exposed to sunlight. Milk is a relatively good source of thiamin.

It is a poor source of ascorbic acid (vitamin C), and this is usually destroyed when the milk is heat treated.

Minerals

Milk is an excellent source of calcium, and milk and milk products are important suppliers of this mineral in the diet. Milk also contains a good supply of **phosphorus**, plus smaller amounts of **sodium**, **chlorine**, and **potassium**. Milk is a poor source of **iron**.

Two-thirds of the minerals in milk are combined with milk solids (e.g. calcium and phosphorus with caseinogen), and the rest are dissolved in water.

The effect of heat on the nutritional value of milk

Pasteurization causes a slight loss (up to 10%) of the thiamin, and a 25% loss of the vitamin C.

UHT and dried milk The nutrient losses are similar to those of pasteurized milk.

Sterilization leads to a loss of 20% of the thiamin and 60% of the vitamin C. The sugar lactose is partially caramelized and this accounts for some of the flavour and colour change.

Condensed milk The nutrient losses are similar to those of pasteurized milk.

Evaporated milk About 40% of the thiamin and 60% of the vitamin C are lost.

Uses of milk in food preparation

Milk is a cheap and versatile ingredient for a variety of recipes, including:

sauces
beverages
soups
milk puddings
custards (egg or cornflour)
batters
cold sweets, e.g. fruit fool, blancmange
scones

Revision questions

1 What affects the amount and quality of milk produced by the cow?
2 Why is milk such a valuable food?
3 How should fresh milk be stored in the home?
4 Why is it inadvisable to leave milk standing on the doorstep for too long?
5 List the minerals found in milk.
6 Why is milk so useful in food preparation?
7 Why was milk often unsafe to drink before the 1860s?
8 How was this situation changed?
9 Why is milk heat treated?
10 List the heat treatments given to milk.
11 What hygiene rules do milk producers have to abide by?
12 Describe the principles behind, and the processes involved in, the various heat treatments given to milk.
13 How else can milk be preserved? Describe each method and give the advantages and disadvantages of each.
14 Why does the nutrient content of milk vary slightly throughout the year?
15 What does the amount and quality of milk produced depend on?
16 Describe the proteins found in milk and their reactions to heat and acids.
17 How is the fat in milk distributed? How is this different in homogenized milk?
18 What is lactose?
19 Why does the retinol content of milk vary throughout the year?
20 How does heat affect the nutritional content of milk?

Cream

Cream contains all the main components of milk, but the fat content is higher, and the quantity of non-fat solids and water is lower. Channel Island and South Devon cows produce the most cream.

Types of cream

The fat contents of different creams are defined by law. The minimum percentages of fat which the different types of cream must contain are:

clotted cream	55%
double cream	48%
whipping cream	35%
single cream	18%
half cream	12%
sterilized cream	23%

Production

Milk is left to stand for 24 hours. During this time, the cream forms a layer on the surface, and can be skimmed off by mechanical separators, at a temperature of 35–54°C. The cream is then cooled to 4.5°C and stored until processed.

The cream is then pasteurized in a similar way to milk, to improve its storage qualities and make it safe to eat.

Single and **half** cream need to be homogenized to prevent separation, because of their relatively low fat content.

Sterilized cream is heated either in bottles or cans, at 116°C for 20 minutes. It has a different flavour to fresh cream.

Ultra heat treated cream is treated in a similar way to UHT milk, and can be kept unopened in foil-lined cartons for several months. Once opened it should be treated as fresh cream.

Long-life cream is sold in jars, in which it is pasteurized at 65.5°C for 30 minutes, then cooled to 4.5°C for storage. This will keep longer than fresh cream but for less time than sterilized cream.

Cultured (soured) cream is prepared in a similar way to yogurt, and has a nutrient content similar to that of normal cream except that the lactose has been converted by bacteria to lactic acid. It is used in both sweet and savoury dishes.

Long-life double and **whipping** cream is available in pressurized cans. They are used in restaurants and in the home to produce a swirl of 'whipped' cream, expanded by an inert gas. The cream remains in shape for only a short time as the gas escapes from it.

Cream substitutes

Other products can be used in some recipes in place of cream. They are often lower in fat and may be cheaper. They include:

crème fraiche
fromage frais
quark
Greek yogurt
soya cream

Uses of cream in food preparation

Cream that has a fat content of 35-42% can be whipped until stiff and used for decorating cakes and flans, serving with scones and fruit, and incorporating into dishes such as mousses, soufflés, and cheesecakes. The cream should be kept in a cold place (4–5°C) for several hours before use. It should be gently whipped, and care taken not to overwhip it, as it will separate into large fat globules and liquid whey. This separation is irreversible.

Single cream will not whip, but can be used for pouring over fruit or in coffee, and for adding to casseroles and soups.

Storage of cream in the home

Fresh cream should be stored in a cool, dark place, away from strong odours, and covered up. It should be used within the time recommended by the manufacturer.

Single cream should not be frozen, as it separates when thawed. Whipping and double cream should only be frozen if they are lightly whipped first. Rosettes of whipped cream can be frozen on greaseproof paper, for use on trifles, cakes, and cold sweets.

Revision questions

1 Why is the nutrient content of cream different from that of milk?
2 List the different types of cream and their fat contents.
3 How is cream produced commercially?
4 Why is cream used in food preparation?
5 How should cream be stored in the home?

Cheese

Cheese making is a method of preserving the nutrients of milk when it is in plentiful supply. Cheese has been made for centuries throughout the world.

At least 400 varieties of cheese are known, and most are now made on a large scale in creameries. In the past, they were made in farmhouses, but increased demand for cheese has led to large-scale production, and import and export all over the world.

Types of cheese

Cheeses are classified according to how they are manufactured and the ingredients used:

1 Hard-pressed cheeses, e.g. Cheddar, Derby, Cheshire, Double Gloucester, Leicester.
2 Lightly pressed cheeses, e.g. Caerphilly, Lancashire, Wensleydale.
3 Blue-veined cheeses, e.g. Blue Stilton, Blue Wensleydale.
4 Acid curd cheeses, e.g. curd cheese, cottage cheese.
5 Processed cheeses.
6 Cream cheeses.

Many traditional foreign cheeses are sold in the UK. Examples include Mozzarella, Feta, Camembert, Mascarpone, Edam, Parmesan, Brie, and Gruyére.

Production

The production of Cheddar cheese is described here, but the process is basically the same for most cheeses, with slight variations in the temperatures, ingredients, and processes used.

1 Pasteurized fresh milk is pumped into large vats.

2 A special bacteria culture is added to the milk, to convert the lactose to lactic acid. The lactic acid helps to preserve the cheese.

Adding the starter culture to the milk

3 The milk is heated to 30°C and the enzyme rennin, in the form of rennet, is added, to make the milk clot (set). The caseinogen coagulates with the acid and rennet. Vegetarian cheeses use a non-animal enzyme called chymosin instead of rennet to set the milk.

4 The rennet is left to react for 30-45 minutes, during which time a solid **curd** and liquid **whey** form.
   The curd consists of the coagulated caseinogen, plus about 80% of the calcium in the milk, plus fat and fat-soluble vitamins and some thiamin.
   The whey consists of most of the water, water-soluble vitamins, lactose, some minerals, and the proteins lactalbumin and lactoglobulin.

Draining the whey from the curd

5 The curd is cut with special knives to release the whey, which is drained off.

6 The curd is then scalded to 37–40°C for 40-45 minutes, while being stirred, to help to expel the whey and gain the correct consistency. Lightly pressed cheeses do not have such a solid curd, and less whey is drained off.

7 Drainage of the curd continues as the curd settles, and it is cut into blocks. The blocks are piled on top of each other and re-piled at regular intervals to complete the draining - this is known as **cheddaring**. The acidity of the cheese at this stage has increased.

8 The curd may then be cut in a mill into small chips, and 2% of **salt** is added for flavour and to preserve the cheese.

9 The salted curd is then packed into metal moulds, lined with cheesecloth. Traditional moulds are cylindrical but, for large-scale production, square and rectangular moulds are used.

10 The curd is pressed hard for 24 hours, and the moulds are sprayed with hot water to form a rind on the cheese for protection.

11 The cheese is then removed, date stamped, and left to **ripen** at 10°C for about four months, during which time the characteristic flavour, smell, and texture of the cheese develop as a result of enzyme and bacterial activity. Mature Cheddar is left to ripen for about 12 months.

12 At the end of the ripening period, the cheese is graded according to its flavour, texture, appearance, and colour.

Testing and grading cheese

Cottage cheese

Cottage cheese is made from pasteurized skimmed milk, to which a special starter is added to develop the texture and flavour brought about by the natural souring of the milk by lactic acid bacteria. The curd is cut into small pieces and slowly heated. The whey is drained off, and the curd is washed and cooled.

Cream may be added and blended in. Additional ingredients such as pineapple, chives, or peppers can also be added.

Cottage cheese has a short shelf-life, and must be kept in a cold place. It is useful in energy-reduced and low-fat diets, and is a good source of protein, riboflavin, calcium, and phosphorus.

Processed cheese

Processed cheese is made by thoroughly mixing Cheddar and other cheeses. Sometimes colouring and flavouring are added. It is packed in foil.

Cream cheeses

Cream cheeses are not true cheeses, but are made from cream with a fat content of 30–60%. They have a similar composition to cream, but contain less water and more fat.

Blue-veined cheeses

Blue-veined cheeses, e.g. Stilton, are produced by inoculating the curd with a harmless mould which grows in the air spaces in the curd. The mould produces the characteristic flavour of the cheese.

Storage of cheese in the home

Hard cheeses should be wrapped in foil or plastic to prevent them drying out, and then stored in a cool place.

Lightly pressed cheeses have a shorter storage life than hard cheese. They should be stored in a similar way.

Acid curd cheeses and cream cheeses should be eaten within a few days of purchase and stored in a cool place.

Hard cheeses can be frozen if wrapped in foil. They become rather crumbly on thawing.

Importance of cheese in the diet

Cheese is a relatively concentrated source of protein, and an important source of calcium, retinol (vitamin A), and riboflavin. Over 90% of the cheese is digested, so there is little wastage. Cheese can be included in most meals for all age groups, and is a useful food for snacks and packed meals.

In response to advice to reduce the amount of fat in the diet, it is now possible to buy reduced-fat cheeses.

Nutritive value

	Cheddar cheese	Cottage cheese
	%	%
Protein	26.0	13.6
Fat	33.5	4.0
Carbohydrate	trace	1.4
Minerals	3.4	1.4
Water	37.0	78.8

Effect of heat on cheese

When hard cheeses are heated, the fat first melts, and the protein (caseinogen) continues to coagulate. Overheating causes the protein to toughen and become stringy, reducing its digestibility. Eventually the cheese will burn.

Uses of cheese in food preparation

Apart from its use in salads and snacks, cheese is used in the following ways:

as a garnish for soups, meat sauces, cauliflower cheese, etc.

grated on salads, meat dishes, etc.

in sauces

in savoury flans, e.g. quiche Lorraine

in cheesecakes

in shortcrust pastry and scones

Revision questions

1 List the main types of English cheese and gives examples of each.
2 Why is cheese an important food in the diet?
3 How should cheese be stored in the home?
4 How is cheese used in food preparation?
5 What happens when cheese is heated?
6 How is Cheddar cheese produced?
7 What is whey?
8 What are curds?
9 Why is salt added to cheese?
10 What happens during the ripening stage of cheese making?
11 Why is cottage cheese different from Cheddar cheese?
12 What is processed cheese?
13 What is vegetarian cheese and how is it different?

Yogurt

Yogurt is a cultured milk product. In the UK it is usually made from cow's milk, but goat's or ewe's milk can also be used. Yogurt is eaten all over the world, and originates from West Asia and Eastern Europe.

Fruit and fruit-flavoured yogurts are particularly popular in the UK. The most popular varieties (in order of popularity) are:

strawberry

black cherry

raspberry

peach melba

Types of yogurt

Yogurt is divided into two categories according to its consistency and method of manufacture:

set yogurt

stirred yogurt (either thick or pouring consistency)

In the UK the stirred variety is the most popular.

Composition

Yogurt can be made from milk in any of the following forms:

whole milk – minimum fat content 3.5%*

partially skimmed milk – minimum fat content 1–2%

skimmed milk (concentrated or normal) – minimum fat content 0.3%*

evaporated milk

dried milk

or any combination of these.

*as recommended by the Food Standards Committee in 1975.

Concentrated skimmed milk is most often used in commercial yogurt manufacture.

The Food Standards Committee also recommends that yogurt should contain not less than 8.5% **non-fat solids**, which consist of casein and whey proteins. The more solids there are, the firmer the yogurt will be and the less likely it is to separate.

The milk used must conform to the same high standards of hygiene and composition as liquid milk, and it must also be free from the antibiotics that are given to cows to treat udder infections. These antibiotics affect the bacteria used in yogurt production.

Bacteria culture

The taste and texture of yogurt are brought about by the carefully controlled addition of a special harmless bacteria culture. The bacteria used belong to the lactic acid bacteria group which ferment the disaccharide sugar lactose in milk. Under the right conditions of temperature, moisture, and food they produce lactic acid.

The two bacteria used are:

Lactobacillus bulgaricus

Streptococcus thermophillus

During fermentation, the milk proteins coagulate and the yogurt sets. A colourless, volatile (evaporates easily) liquid called acetaldehyde is also produced. It is acetaldehyde which is mainly responsible for the characteristic flavour of yogurt.

Commercial manufacture

The process outlined below is a general one, and it may vary according to the manufacturer.

1 The milk is homogenized (see p. 101) to give the finished yogurt a smooth, creamy texture. This also helps to prevent the final product from separating.

2 The milk is then pasteurized at 85-95°C for 15-30 minutes. This helps to stabilize the proteins and results in a nearly sterile product.

3 The milk is then cooled to 40-43°C, which is suitable for the fermentation process to take place.

4 The two bacteria (the 'starter' culture) are added to the milk in equal proportions, usually as 0.5-2% of the total finished product.

5 The culture is then incubated at 37-44°C for 4-6 hours, during which time fermentation takes place, the product becomes acidic, the flavours develop, and the proteins coagulate.

6 Once the level of acid reaches 0.8-1.8%, the bacteria growth stops, although the bacteria remain alive.

7 The yogurt is then cooled to 4.5°C, and held at this temperature during storage and distribution to shops.

8 Additives may be included in the yogurt:
vitamins A and D
stabilizers, e.g. gelatine, agar, pectin, to prevent the yogurt from separating into curds and whey
sucrose
colour
preservatives
flavourings, e.g. lemon, chocolate
All additives are strictly controlled by legislation.

The manufacture of set and stirred yogurt is slightly different.

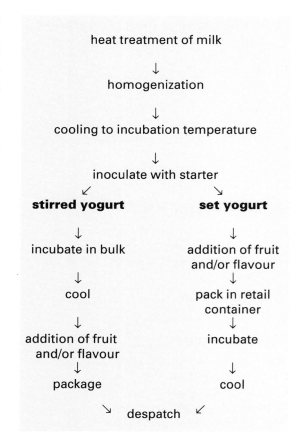

Storage of yogurt

Yogurt should be stored at 4.5°C. At this temperature the bacteria remain alive, but grow and multiply very slowly. After about 10 days, they raise the acid content to a point at which the yogurt becomes unpalatable, and separates.

Sometimes the lid of a yogurt may 'blow' and the yogurt will be gassy. This happens when yeast cells from the added fruit ferment the sucrose and produce CO_2 gas and alcohol.

Preparation of yogurt at home

Yogurt can be made in the home with either a yogurt-making machine or a vacuum flask. If using a yogurt machine, the manufacturer's instructions should be carefully followed to achieve satisfactory results.

The following method can be used for making yogurt in a vacuum flask. All equipment used must be sterilized with boiling water.

575 ml sterilized or UHT milk
50 g dried skimmed milk
1 tbsp natural yogurt

1   Heat the milk to 43°C, and blend in the skimmed milk and yogurt.
2   Warm a flask with hot water, empty, and pour in the milk mixture and seal. Leave for 7 hours to incubate.
3   Cool rapidly, refrigerate for 4 hours.
4   Flavour and sweeten as required.
5   Use within 5 days, storing in the refrigerator.

Yogurt products

It is possible to buy a range of yogurt-based products including:

bio-yogurts
yogurt drinks
yogurt ice creams
soya yogurts

The importance of yogurt in the diet

Yogurt contains all the nutrients found in the milk from which it is made, plus any that are added in the form of fruit, sucrose, vitamins A and D, etc.

Low-fat yogurt contains the following nutrients (with approximate percentages):

| | Type of yogurt | | |
Nutrient	Fruit	Flavoured	Plain
Water	75%	80%	86%
Protein	4.8%	5%	5%
Fat	1.0%	0.9%	1.0%
Minerals	0.8%	0.8%	0.8%
Lactose	3.3%	4.8%	4.6%
Other sugars	14.6%	9.2%	1.6%
	(mostly sucrose)		(galactose)

Very low fat or diet yogurts are available, usually containing artificial sweeteners to reduce their energy value still further. Some manufacturers use gelatine to improve the texture and make the yogurt thick and creamy. This can be a problem for vegetarians and those who do not eat cows or pigs, as it may not be declared on the label. Yogurt is useful in the diet for:

1   Energy-reduced diets.
2   Weaning babies on to solid foods.
3   Convalescents.
4   Alternatives to puddings.

Uses of yogurt in cooking

1   As a substitute for double cream in cheesecakes, cold soufflés, mousses, etc.
2   Salad dressings, as a substitute for mayonnaise.
3   For certain meat dishes, e.g. goulash.
4   For cold drinks with fruit.

Revision questions

1   What is yogurt?
2   What is the difference between a set yogurt and a stirred yogurt?
3   How should yogurt be stored?
4   What is the value of yogurt in the diet, and why is it so popular?
5   How can yogurt be used in food preparation?
6   Describe the manufacture of yogurt.
7   How are the taste and texture of yogurt brought about?
8   What additives are put into yogurt?

Further work with dairy foods

1   Test some fresh pasteurized milk with universal indicator paper to measure the pH. Leave some in the refrigerator and some in a warm room. Test the pH daily and observe the changes in the appearance and smell of the milk. Comment on the time taken for each sample to sour and the reason for the changes in pH. Discard the milk afterwards.
2   Add two teaspoons of lemon juice to four tablespoons of fresh milk and observe the reaction. Comment on this, and compare it with the effects of adding tomato juice, water, and bicarbonate of soda.
3   Place a small amount of grated Cheddar and processed cheeses in separate test tubes. Heat gently and observe the changes that take place. Allow the cheese to bubble, then cool it and observe the texture. Account for the change in texture after heating.
4   Collect samples of different cheeses and compare them for flavour, appearance, cost, smell, and colour. Set up a tasting panel to establish the most popular types.

Eggs

Eggs have been used as a food for centuries. As long ago as 1400BC, natives in South-East Asia kept poultry, and throughout history eggs have not only been eaten, but have been involved in rituals and used as currency all over the world.

Production

Traditionally, eggs were produced by **free-range** farming. This meant that hens were allowed to roam loose in the farmyard, eating grain and other food from the ground. The eggs were laid in a hen house. The sale of free-range eggs has increased again in recent years as concerns about animal welfare have grown.

Free-range farming

As the demand for eggs grew, large-scale production in the form of **battery farms** was developed. Thousands of hens are kept in cages in large hen houses which are artificially lit and heated. The hens remain in the cages at all times and the eggs they lay are collected, usually on a conveyor belt, graded, and checked for quality.

Battery farming

Deep-litter farming

Another form of large-scale egg production involves keeping large numbers of hens together in huge heated sheds, but not in cages. The hens lay their eggs in nest boxes. This is called **deep-litter**, **barn**, or **perchery** farming.

Four-grain eggs are produced by hens that receive a totally vegetarian cereal diet. They are usually barn produced.

Types

Most eggs eaten in this country are hens' eggs, but duck, goose, and quails' eggs can be eaten, providing they are very fresh.

Eggs are graded according to size:

Size of egg	Weight/g	Old sizing
large	70	0–1
medium	60–70	2–3
small	50–60	4–5

Eggs are also graded according to quality:
Extra eggs have been packed in the previous 7 days and are of high quality.
Class A are good quality and are the grade usually sold to the consumer.
Class B are of lower quality and may have dirty shells.
Class C are usually sold to cake manufacturers as they have weak or damaged shells.

All egg cartons should state the week in which they were packed during the year, and the supplier. Some producers now stamp a use-by date on each egg.

Structure and composition

Eggs are composed of three main parts:

shell

egg white

egg yolk

88.5% of an egg is edible.

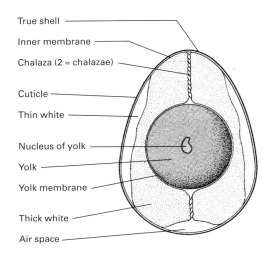

True shell

Inner membrane

Chalaza (2 = chalazae)

Cuticle

Thin white

Nucleus of yolk

Yolk

Yolk membrane

Thick white

Air space

The structure of a hen's egg

Shell

The shell consists of an outer **cuticle** (a transparent, protective coating), a **true shell**, and **inner membranes**. The true shell forms 11.5% of the whole egg. It consists of:

97% calcium carbonate ($CaCO_3$)

3% protein

The shell is **porous** (pores are tiny holes), and therefore allows the developing chick to obtain oxygen. The pores also allow bacteria and odours to enter, and water and carbon dioxide to escape. The membranes that line the shell inside act as filters to bacteria to protect the inside.

At one end of the egg, the membranes separate into an **air space**, to supply the chick with oxygen.

The colour of the shell varies according to the breed of bird and does not influence the nutritional value of the egg in any way. The shell is relatively strong, but older birds tend to produce weaker shells.

White

Egg white has two visible layers:

the **thick white** (nearest to the yolk)

the **thin white** (nearest to the shell)

The white forms 58.5% of the whole egg, and consists of:

88.5% water

10.5% protein

riboflavin and other B vitamins

a trace of fat

The main proteins in egg white are **ovalbumin** and **mucin**.

Yolk

The yolk is covered by a membrane to separate it from the white, and support it. The yolk forms about 30% of the whole egg. It consists of:

16.5% protein

33% fat

50% water

fat-soluble vitamins A, D, E, and K

mineral elements, including iron (see p. 23)

lecithin (an emulsifier)

The colour of the egg yolk is related to the diet of the hen and is due to the presence of carotenes (see p. 12) and any colourings added to the hen's feed. The nutritional value of the egg is not affected by the colour of the yolk.

The yolk is supported by the **chalazae** which are attached to the egg white, and help to keep the yolk away from the shell where it could pick up bacteria. The yolk is more vulnerable to bacterial attack when it is older, as the yolk membranes weaken.

Testing an egg for freshness

Before eggs are packed they are checked for defects by being passed over a strong light. This process is known as **candling** because wax candles were originally used as a light source.

As an egg gets older, several changes take place:

1   Water moves from the white into the yolk.
2   The yolk membranes weaken.
3   The thick white becomes thinner.
4   The size of the air space increases.
5   Moisture is lost through the shell.
6   Bacteria enter through the shell.
7   The bad smell of hydrogen sulphide is

produced by the reaction of sulphur from the egg white and phosphoric acid in the yolk.

8 The egg eventually decomposes as bacteria contaminate the contents.

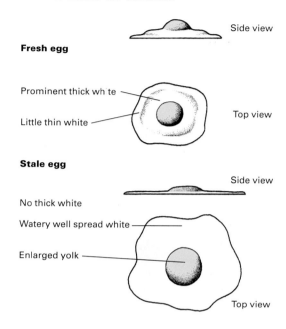

Fresh egg

Side view

Prominent thick white

Little thin white

Top view

Stale egg

Side view

No thick white

Watery well spread white

Enlarged yolk

Top view

Eggs can be checked for freshness in the home by placing them in a jug of brine (2 tbsp salt dissolved in 575 ml water). If the egg sinks, it is fresh. If it floats on the surface, it is stale, because the air space has enlarged and water has evaporated from the egg, making it lighter.

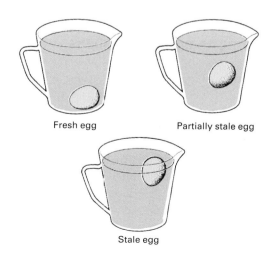

Fresh egg

Partially stale egg

Stale egg

Importance of eggs in the diet

Eggs are a good source of high biological value protein, and are easily digested by most people, especially when lightly cooked. As they are used in so many different ways in food preparation, they make a valuable contribution to the diet.

However, there is no carbohydrate in eggs, and the iron in the yolk may be unavailable to the body (see p. 23). They are also a poor source of calcium because it is concentrated in the egg shell which is not eaten.

The effect of heat on eggs

Ovalbumin in the egg white starts to coagulate at 60°C, until the whole white is solid and opaque. The proteins of the egg yolk start to coagulate at 70°C and continue until the yolk is dry and hard. If overcooked, the protein becomes tough and difficult to digest.

If an egg is boiled for some time, a green/black ring of **iron sulphide** forms around the yolk. This is due to the reaction of sulphur in the egg white with iron in the egg yolk, particularly in eggs that are not very fresh. This reaction can be partly prevented by cooling the egg rapidly as soon as it has been cooked.

If eggs are heated too quickly, the proteins will coagulate and shrink rapidly, causing any liquid that the egg contains to be squeezed out, and the protein to become tough. This is called **syneresis**.

Uses of eggs in food preparation

Eggs are used for a variety of processes in food preparation, and are very versatile. Their uses include:

1 **Trapping air** Both the egg white and the whole egg can trap air, because of the ability of ovalbumin to stretch (see p. 205).
This ability is utilized in:
Cake making Eggs are used as a raising agent.
Lightening mousses, soufflés, etc., as meringue or whole egg.

2 **Thickening** Eggs are used to thicken custards, sauces, soups, etc., because of the coagulation of the egg proteins.

3 **Emulsifying** Egg yolk contains lecithin which is an emulsifier and enables oil and

water to be mixed to an emulsion without separating. This is made use of in:

Mayonnaise (see p. 218).

Cake making, when eggs are added to the fat and sugar in a creamed mixture (see p. 209).

4 **Binding** Ingredients for rissoles, croquettes, and meat or fish cakes can be bound together with egg, which when heated will coagulate and hold the ingredients together.

5 **Coating** Eggs are used as a coating for fried food, either on their own, or combined with flour or breadcrumbs. They form a protective layer on the outside of the food which sets and holds it together and prevents it from overcooking.

6 **Glazing** Egg yolk, egg white, or whole egg can be brushed over pastries, bread, etc., to produce a golden brown shiny glaze during baking.

7 **Enriching** Eggs can be added to sauces, milk puddings, soups, etc., as a way of including extra protein.

8 **Garnishing** Hard-boiled egg white and yolk can be used to garnish salads, etc.

Eggs are also used as a main ingredient in a variety of dishes, and provide an important supply of protein in the diet. They can be cooked by the following methods:

baking – in small dishes or with vegetables in custards and flans

frying – normally shallow fried

boiling

poaching

scrambling – over a gentle heat with a small amount of fat and milk

As they are easily digested, they are a valuable food for convalescents if lightly scrambled or boiled.

In 1989, some eggs were found to be infected with *Salmonella* bacteria, which can cause food poisoning. The government advised consumers not to eat foods containing raw or partially cooked eggs. Pasteurized, dried egg white or whole egg can be used in recipes where raw egg is traditionally used, e.g. royal icing, meringue.

Storing eggs

Eggs should be stored in a refrigerator, away from strong-smelling foods. They should be removed an hour or so before use if they are to be whisked, because cold eggs do not whisk well.

Eggs should not be washed as this destroys the protective cuticle. They will normally stay in good condition if stored correctly for two to three weeks.

Eggs cannot be frozen whole, but the whites and yolks can be frozen separately.

Eggs are commercially stored in rooms of high humidity and low temperature (just above $-2°C$) to prevent moisture loss and deterioration. They can be kept for up to 6 months.

Eggs can be preserved by pickling.

Revision questions

1 What sizes of egg are sold?
2 Why are eggs used in food preparation?
3 How should eggs be stored in the home?
4 How are eggs checked for defects?
5 How can an egg be tested for freshness?
6 What is the importance of eggs in the diet?
7 What are the differences between free-range, deep-litter, and battery egg production?
8 What function do the following parts of an egg have?
   a chalazae
   b cuticle
   c yolk membrane
   d air space
   e yolk
9 Why does the shell have pores in? How do the pores affect the keeping qualities of the egg?
10 What is the food value of the egg white?
11 What is the food value of the yolk?
12 What changes take place in an egg when it gets older?
13 How does heat affect eggs?

Further work with eggs

1 Place three clear glass lids over squared paper and break an egg on to each. Use:
   a a six-week-old egg
   b a two-week-old egg
   c a very fresh egg
   Measure the area covered by each and observe the height of each egg. Comment on these observations.

2 To test the stability of egg whites: Whisk 100g of egg white until stiff. Divide into four equal quantities and to the four samples add:
   a ⅛ tsp cream of tartar
   b ⅛ tsp salt
   c 1tsp sugar
   d nothing
   Set up four funnels with filter papers into 100 ml graduated cylinders. Put each sample of egg white into a funnel and measure the amount of liquid lost from each at 10 minute intervals for one hour. Which addition gives the most stable foam? Why is this?
   Try the test with egg whites from stale eggs and record the amount of liquid lost at regular intervals.

3 Boil three fresh eggs in water in the following ways:
   a Boil for 10 minutes then plunge directly into cold water; leave until cold.
   b Boil for 10 minutes, then leave to cool in the hot water.
   c Boil for 10 minutes, remove from the water and leave to cool.
   Repeat using eggs that are at least four weeks old.
   Repeat using fresh eggs, but boiling for half an hour each time.
   Observe the formation of the green/black ferrous sulphide ring between the white and yolk in each case. Account for the differences.

4 Prepare five egg custard mixtures as follows:
   200 ml fresh milk
   1 egg
   25g sugar
   Warm the milk to 60°C. Do not boil. Beat the egg and sugar and add the warm milk. Pour into a small ovenproof dish and bake as follows:
   a Stand the dish in a tray of hot water and bake at gas 3, 160°C for approximately 40 minutes or until set.
   b Repeat **a**, but do not use a tray of water.
   c Repeat **a**, but bake at gas 9, 240°C (475°F).
   d Repeat **c**, but do not use a tray of water.
   e Repeat **a**, but boil the milk before adding it to the egg.
   Compare the cooked custards for texture, appearance, and flavour. Account for the differences. What difference does the tray of water make to the finished result?

Meat

Meat has been a principal food for centuries, and is still in great demand, despite its expense.

The main reason for the high price of meat is the amount of time, effort, and feed it takes to rear animals for meat. Large amounts of food, e.g. pulses, cereal grains, nuts, vegetables, fish meal, and grass have to be provided, and the conversion of these into meat is inefficient. Some people feel that this is a waste of food that could be used to feed humans, particularly in poor countries.

When they reach the right age, animals for meat are slaughtered in abattoirs. The cleaned and gutted carcases are hung in cold store, inspected, and graded, ready for sale to a butcher.

The butcher cuts the meat into joints or cuts, according to the amount and position of bones, lean meat, and fat in the various parts of the body. Lean, tender joints are more popular and difficult to produce and therefore cost more, so the butcher must separate these accurately.

Meat is sold in specialist butchers' shops, supermarkets, or direct from farm shops. It can be bought in bulk for freezing (e.g. as a half or whole animal) and many butchers joint it for the customer. Pre-frozen meat joints can also be bought in bulk from freezer centres. Good butchers should have a sound knowledge of what they sell and should be able to advise customers about the suitability of different joints for cooking.

Types of meat

The main meats eaten in the UK are:

beef	mutton
veal (calf)	pork
lamb	bacon

Rabbit and hare are also eaten, but less often.

Structure and composition

Lean meat is composed of the **muscles** that move the body in an animal. Muscles are composed of **cells** in the form of long, slender **fibres**. These muscle fibres are made of two main proteins, myosin and actin.

The size of muscle fibres affects the **tenderness** of cooked meat:

slender, small fibres are associated with tender meat;

large, long fibres are associated with tougher meat.

Muscle fibres increase in size as the animal gets older, so the older the animal, the tougher the meat from it.

The parts of the animal's body that do the most physical work, e.g. neck, shin, forearm, have the largest muscle fibres, and so make tougher meat.

Individual muscle fibres are formed into **bundles**, surrounded by a substance called **connective tissue**. The bundles are then formed into groups which are also surrounded by connective tissue. Whole muscles are attached to bones by **tendons**.

Connective tissue is made of two proteins, collagen and elastin.

Collagen is the main component of tendons, and the connective tissue surrounding muscles, particularly those that do the most work. Collagen is less flexible than elastin, and when heated in the presence of moisture, it is converted into soluble **gelatine**, which greatly increases the tenderness of connective tissue and therefore of the meat. Traditionally, tough cuts of meat were cooked by slow, moist methods such as stewing, to allow this conversion to gelatine to take place. However, if tough cuts of meat are roasted slowly at Gas 3, 160°C (325°F), there is sufficient moisture within the meat to convert the collagen and make the meat tender.

Elastin is a main component of ligaments (in between bones), and has the ability to stretch and return to its original shape. It is an insoluble and tough protein, but there is less elastin than collagen in muscles, so it does not have a major influence on the toughness of meat.

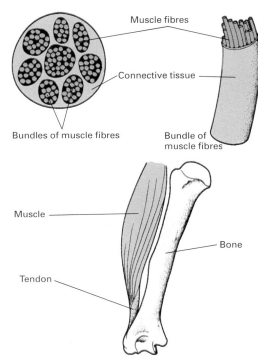

The structure of muscle

Fat

In meat, fat is found in the following places:

under the skin in **adipose tissue**

around vital organs, e.g. kidneys (suet)

between bundles of muscle fibres (invisible fat)

The fat under the skin may be yellowish in colour, because of the presence of **carotenes** from plants, depending on what the animal was fed on. The fat between the bundles of muscle fibres gives the meat a **'marbled'** effect. Marbling in lean meat is an important requirement when the meat is graded, and large amounts of feed are required to produce it. This is one of the reasons why lean meat is so expensive.

The fat content of meat helps to give flavour, moisture, and texture to the cooked meat.

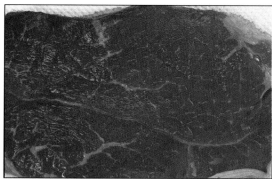
Fat between the bundles of muscle fibre gives the meat a marbled appearance.

Colour of meat

The colour of meat is mainly due to the presence of **myoglobin**, which is a purple/red tissue protein, and **haemoglobin** from the blood, some of which is left in the meat after slaughter.

In a living animal, haemoglobin takes oxygen to the muscles, and myoglobin holds it there, so that the muscle can work. There is therefore more myoglobin in well-used muscles such as the heart and shin, and in older animals, and the colour of the meat is darker in both cases.

When oxygen is taken to the tissues, the myoglobin is converted to **oxymyoglobin** which is bright red. After slaughter, the meat remains dark red until it is cut and exposed to the oxygen in the air, when it becomes bright red.

When fresh meat is stored for a few days, its colour changes to a brown/red, due to the formation of **metmyoglobin**. This does not seriously affect its palatability when cooked. If storage is continued, the meat may become green/brown through the effects of enzymes and bacteria. This will spoil the palatability.

Choosing meat

As meat is an expensive food, it is wise to choose it carefully, considering the following factors:

Value for money
1   There should not be too much bone in a joint as this reduces its value for money. However, some is needed to produce flavour when cooking.
2   Cheaper cuts of meat, which are generally tougher, are just as nutritious as more expensive, leaner cuts. If cooked well, they can be made into appetizing and nutritious meals.
3   There should not be too much visible fat on the joint.

Appearance
Meat should have the following physical characteristics:

1   Colour

Meat	Colour of lean	Colour of fat
Lamb	pink/brown	cream/white
Mutton	dark pink/brown	white
Beef	red/brown	cream/pale yellow
Pork	pink	white
Veal	pink	white

2   It should be moist but not dripping.
3   It should smell fresh.
4   Lean meat should have a marbled appearance.
5   It should be slightly springy to the touch.

Intended use
1   Allow for possible shrinkage during cooking when choosing a joint.
2   It is uneconomic to use expensive, lean joints of meat for stewing or casseroling.
3   As a general guide, allow about 100g of meat per person, unless it is for a dish such as risotto where vegetables, cereal grains, or pulses form a major part.

The effect of heat and changes during cooking

Texture and tenderness
The proteins of meat denature at temperatures of 40°C to 65°C. As the proteins denature, the structure of the meat tightens and the meat becomes firmer.

The protein of muscle fibres (actin and myosin) may toughen during some cooking methods.

The connective tissue is tenderized during cooking. It becomes shorter and thicker so that the meat shrinks in size. The collagen is converted to gelatine in the presence of moisture which greatly increases the tenderness. The elastin is only softened slightly.

Meat can be partially tenderized before cooking by:

1 Mechanically pounding, scoring, and cutting across the muscle fibres to reduce their length.
2 The use of enzymes, such as **papain** (from the pawpaw plant) which partially digest the protein.
3 Marinading in vinegar or alcohol.

Fat

The adipose tissue becomes more tender when cooked. The fat melts, and penetrates the lean meat during cooking, which increases the energy value of the lean meat. The fat content may also make the meat appear more juicy. On the skin of roasted meat, the fat becomes crisp and brown.

Colour

During cooking, the colour of meat changes from red to brown, due to the oxymyoglobin being converted to **haemochrome**.

Flavour

Cooking meat improves its palatability. In dry cooking methods, **extractives** containing flavour are squeezed out of the meat on to the surface as the protein denatures and shrinks. These extractives give meat its characteristic taste. The fat melts and gives a crisp surface to the meat.

In moist methods of cooking, the extractives are leached into the cooking liquid, which should be served with the meat to give it flavour.

Nutritive value

Protein The nutritive value of proteins in meat is little affected in normal methods of cooking. But, if overcooked, they become less digestible.

Vitamins The fat-soluble vitamins remain stable, but the water-soluble B vitamins may be leached into the cooking liquid in moist methods of cooking. Thiamin is particularly heat sensitive and may be destroyed in dry methods of cooking.

Minerals There may be some leaching of minerals into the cooking liquid in moist methods of cooking. The liquid should be served with the meat.

The importance of meat in the diet

Meat is an important food as it is a good source of protein, B vitamins, iron, and zinc. It is a main source of high biological value protein for many people. The nutritional value of lean meat of most types is on average:

protein	20%
fat	5%
minerals	1%
water	74%

Modern techniques of breeding and feeding have been adopted by British livestock farmers. These produce meat with a lower fat content than traditional methods. Pressure from health

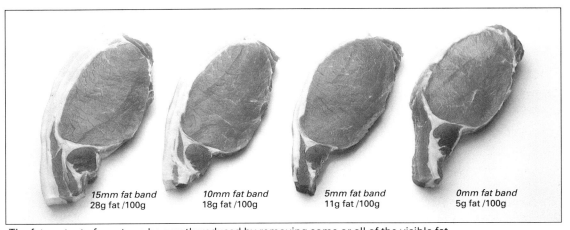

15mm fat band
28g fat /100g

10mm fat band
18g fat /100g

5mm fat band
11g fat /100g

0mm fat band
5g fat /100g

The fat content of meat can be greatly reduced by removing some or all of the visible fat.

experts and consumers has increased demand for meat with a lower fat content, so all farms now produce animals with less fat, and butchers prepare lean cuts of meat by removing some or all of the fat.

The minerals found in meat include iron and zinc. Meat also contains B vitamins in useful quantities, and pork is a particularly good source of thiamin.

Both the protein and fat in meat are readily digested and absorbed in the body.

Uses of meat in food preparation

Meat is used in a vast range of recipes all over the world. The various cuts of meat are used for different purposes, according to their suitability for each cooking method (see notes on tenderness, p. 117). As a rule, lean, tender cuts are suitable for dry methods of cooking, e.g. grilling, roasting, and frying, whereas tough cuts of meat require long, slow, moist methods of cooking to tenderize them (see pp. 181–2).

BSE

BSE (bovine spongiform encephalopathy) or 'mad cow disease' is a fatal disease which attacks the brain and spinal cord of cattle. It was first identified in the UK in 1986.

Some health experts are concerned that a form of BSE could be transferred to humans if they eat the meat of affected animals, although this is by no means certain. Since 1988, very strict measures have been in place in the UK to control the disease and make sure that meat from affected animals does not enter the food chain.

The cause of BSE in cattle is unclear, but it is thought that using brain and offal from sheep in cattle feeds may have been the prime factor. This practice has now been stopped, and the government also ordered that all affected cattle must be destroyed when the disease was made notifiable in 1988. Much is still unknown about BSE, and research is continuing into its causes and effects.

Lamb and mutton

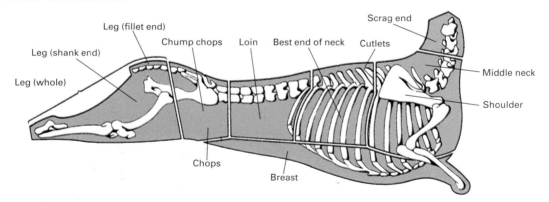

Joint	Method of cooking	Joint	Method of cooking
Scrag end	Stew, braise	Chump chops	Grill, fry, roast, barbecue
Middle neck	Stew, braise	Leg (fillet end)	Braise, pot-roast
Shoulder	Roast, braise, barbecue	Leg (shank end)	Roast, boil
Cutlets	Grill, fry, barbecue	Leg (whole)	Roast, braise
Best end of neck	Roast, braise	Chops	Grill, fry, roast, barbecue
Loin	Fry, grill, roast	Breast	Stew, roast, braise

Pork

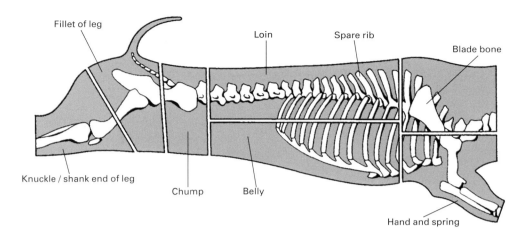

Joint	Method of cooking	Joint	Method of cooking
Blade bone	Pot-roast, braise	Chump	Fry, grill, barbecue
Spare rib	As chops – fry, grill, roast, barbecue	Knuckle/ shank end of leg	Roast Salt and boil
Loin	As chops – fry, grill, roast, barbecue	Belly	Pot-roast, boil, braise As slices – fry, grill
Fillet of leg	Roast – slice and salt skin Salt and boil	Hand and spring	Roast, braise Salt and boil

Bacon and ham

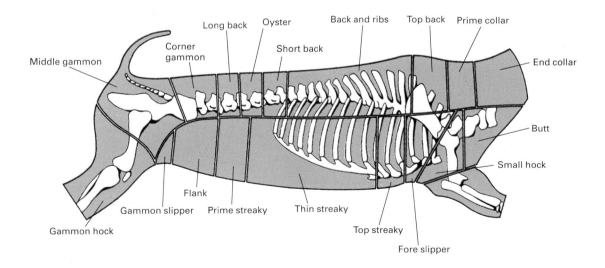

Bacon rashers are normally fried or grilled, and whole joints are roasted or boiled.

Beef

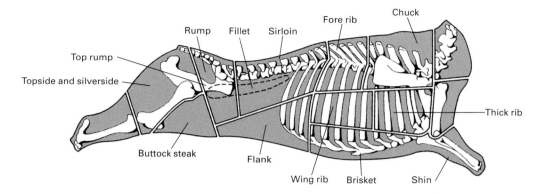

Joint	Method of cooking	Joint	Method of cooking
Chuck	Braise, stew	Buttock steak	Braise, pot-roast, stew
Fore rib	Roast	Top rump	Pot-roast, braise
Sirloin	Roast As steak – grill, fry, barbecue	Flank	Salt and boil, stew
		Wing rib	Roast
Fillet	Grill, fry, barbecue	Brisket	Braise, pot-roast Salt and boil
Rump	Grill, fry, barbecue		
Topside	Roast, pot-roast, braise	Thick rib	Roast
Silverside	Roast, pot-roast, braise Boil, salt and boil	Shin	Stew, braise

Veal

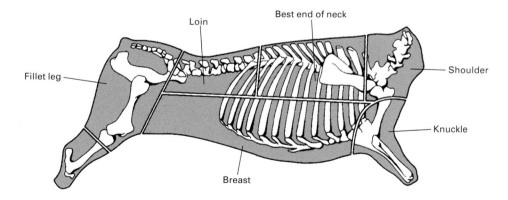

Joint	Method of cooking	Joint	Method of cooking
Shoulder	Roast, braise	Fillet leg	Roast, barbecue
Best end of neck	Roast, stew As cutlets – grill, fry	Veal escalopes	Fry
		Breast	Roast, stew
Loin	Roast As chops – grill, fry, barbecue	Knuckle	Stew, braise

Poultry

Poultry is the name given to birds eaten for food and includes:

chicken   goose   duck
turkey   pigeon

At one time, chicken and turkey were a rare treat, but intensive rearing has made them more readily available. Chicken is now generally less expensive than other meat.

Structure and composition

Poultry meat has the same basic structure as other meat, except that there is less connective tissue, so the meat is more tender. The legs and wing muscles which do the most work are generally tougher and darker in colour, because of the presence of myoglobin.

With the exception of goose and duck, there is less fat in the meat of poultry, so it is drier when cooked.

The flavour of poultry is generally not strong, and develops during cooking in a similar way to that of other meat.

Choosing poultry

Poultry should be chosen according to the following factors:

Appearance

1   Poultry meat (except for pigeon which is darker) should be pink/white, with darker meat on the wings and legs.
2   It should be plump and springy to the touch.
3   It should have a fresh smell.

Inside a chicken processing factory

Intended use

Poussins are very young birds that are cooked and served whole or in half.

Turkeys are available in a range of sizes, particularly at Christmas and other festive occasions. Medium-sized birds tend to be more tender than larger ones.

Nutritive value

The protein of poultry is easily digested and of high biological value. With the exception of goose and duck, poultry contains less fat than red meat. There is also less iron, thiamin, riboflavin, and nicotinic acid than in red meat.

Uses of poultry in food preparation

Chicken

Whole or joints – roast, braise, boil, casserole.

Joints – coat in egg and breadcrumbs and fry; grill, casserole.

Cooked chicken can be eaten cold, in salads, snacks, and picnic meals.

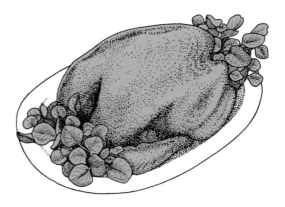

Turkey

Turkey can be cooked in a similar way to chicken. Boneless turkey rolls can be roasted to provide three to four servings.

Duck and goose

Duck and goose are usually roasted. To reduce the fattiness of the meat, they can be placed on a rack during cooking and pricked with a knife at regular intervals to release the fat. They are often served with a sharp, acidic sauce, e.g. orange, to counteract the greasiness.

Bones can be boiled to produce stock for use in soups, stews, and sauces.

Poultry products

A variety of poultry products is available, including:

chicken nuggets and nibbles
chicken wing nuggets
poultry burgers
poultry sausages
chicken Kiev
rissoles

They are often made from poultry pieces pressed together or from mechanically recovered meat (MRM). This is a slurry made by sucking tiny scraps of flesh under high pressure from the carcases, and the technique is used in processing poultry and other meat.

Storage of poultry

Freshly killed birds should be hung in a cool, dry place, with all the internal organs in place. This is to ensure that the meat becomes tender before it is cooked. Chickens are normally hung for one day, turkeys for up to five days, and geese and ducks for up to two days.

Fresh poultry should be kept in a cold place after the giblets (internal organs – neck, gizzard, and liver) and other organs have been removed. It should be eaten soon after purchase (two to three days if kept in the refrigerator).

Frozen poultry should be allowed to thaw completely before being cooked, and then thoroughly cooked to avoid salmonella food poisoning (see pp. 155-8).

Offal

The following internal organs of an animal count as offal: liver, kidney, heart, brain, tongue, sweetbreads (pancreas and thymus glands), tripe (the stomach of an ox or sheep), chitterlings (pig's intestines, often used as sausage casings).

The following parts of the body are also offal: tail (e.g. oxtail), feet (e.g. pig's trotters), ears, head, eyes.

As a result of concern over BSE (see p. 120), certain offal from cows (the brain and spinal cord) has been banned from use in animal feeds and in meat products.

The term is derived from the two words 'off fall', because the parts are removed from the carcase. In America, offal is now called 'variety meats' to make it sound more appetizing.

Choosing offal

All offal, particularly the kidneys, liver, and heart, should be bought very fresh. It should be eaten within 24 hours of purchase, and carefully washed and prepared before eating. Thorough cooking is necessary to prevent food poisoning and to tenderize the offal.

Some types, e.g. tripe and tongue, are prepared by the butcher before purchase. Tripe is cleaned and boiled for 12 hours and tongue is soaked and salted (except lamb and calf tongue).

Importance of offal in the diet

Protein The protein of offal is of high biological value, and if well cooked is readily digested.

Fat There is less fat in offal than in muscle meat in general.

Carbohydrate Liver may contain a little glycogen, but is not an important source.

Vitamins Retinol (vitamin A) is stored in the liver, so liver is a very rich source. Pregnant women are advised to avoid eating liver, as high intakes of vitamin A in early pregnancy can cause birth defects. Kidney and heart also contain some retinol.

Heart and liver contain useful amounts of thiamin. There is some vitamin C in liver, but it is not a valuable source.

Minerals Tripe contains a useful amount of calcium. Liver and, to a lesser extent kidney, are important sources of iron.

Storage

Offal should be kept in a cold place and used as soon as possible after purchase. It can be frozen for long-term storage.

Uses in food preparation

Offal	Cooking method	Uses
Liver	*Lamb's:* grill or fry. *Pig's:* fry, braise, or stew. *Ox:* stew or braise gently.	Pates, casseroles, pastes.
Kidney	Remove central core. *Lamb:* fry or grill. *Pig* or *ox:* stew or braise.	Steak and kidney pie, casseroles, breakfast.
Heart	Stew or braise with a stuffing.	
Brain	Grill or fry gently, or braise.	
Sweet-breads	Stew, grill, fry, or steam.	
Tongue	Boil gently until tender, then press until cold.	Salads, sandwiches.
Tripe	Stew or braise.	Serve with onions.
Tail	Stew or braise.	Soups, stews.

Meat products

A variety of meat products are available and are very popular. These include:

pâtés
sausages
faggots
meat extractives
cold cooked meats
burgers
pies
pasties
pastes and spreads

Sausages

Sausages have been made for many years, originally as a method of preserving and packaging meat.

There are many different types, but the basic ingredients are a mixture of meat and cereal, such as bread. Flavourings, herbs, and spices are also added, and the mixture is encased in specially prepared intestines or edible synthetic casings.

Meat extractives

These are sold as thick pastes, cubes, or powders, for use as drinks or in gravies, soups, and stews. They contain flavouring from meat, plus salt and spices. They have little nutritional value and are mainly used for their flavour.

Cold cooked meats

A large variety of cold meats can be bought. They are useful for packed lunches, picnics, and salads. Corned beef is a popular cold meat which contains a useful supply of iron. Cold meats are usually prepared from meat, cereal, flavourings, and spices.

Cooked cold meats should be sold and stored separately from uncooked meat to prevent cross-contamination by bacteria. They should be stored in a cold place and eaten within a few days of purchase.

Sausages and cooked meats normally have preservatives added, and some cold meats are sold in cans for long-term storage.

Labelling of meat products

Complicated UK regulations cover the definitions of meat products. For example:

Sausages

Pork sausages must be not less than 65% meat, half of which can be fat. All other sausages must not be less than 50% meat, half of which can be fat.

A similar product, not called a sausage, can have as little meat in it as the manufacturer wishes.

Lean meat

Includes flesh, fat, skin, rind, gristle, and sinew, in amounts naturally associated with the meat used (i.e. the manufacturer may not add any). It can also include heart, kidney, tongue, tail, some head meat (but not brain), spinal cord, spleen, thymus, tonsils, and intestines.

Meat products may also contain mechanically recovered meat. It does not have to be labelled on the product, and is used in cooked pressed cold meats, ravioli, and chicken and turkey burgers.

People who do not eat beef or pork need to check the labels of meat products carefully as they are sometimes present.

Revision questions

1 What are the main types of meat eaten in this country?
2 How should meat and poultry be stored?
3 Give three examples of poultry birds.
4 What points should influence your choice of meat when shopping?
5 What points should influence your choice of poultry?
6 What is offal? Give five examples.
7 Why is it important that offal is very fresh when purchased?
8 Describe some meat products and give their uses in food preparation.
9 What is lean meat?
10 Where is the fat in meat found?
11 Describe the changes that take place when meat is cooked.
12 How is the colour of meat produced and how is it affected by heat?
13 How is the flavour of meat developed during cooking?
14 What is the nutritive value of meat, and how is this affected by heat?
15 What are myosin and actin, and where are they found?
16 How do muscle fibres affect the tenderness of meat?
17 How does the age of the animal affect the tenderness of meat?
18 What is connective tissue, and what is its connection with the tenderness of meat?
19 What is collagen?
20 What is the effect of moist heat on collagen?
21 What is elastin?
22 How can meat be tenderized?
23 Which methods of cooking are suitable for
   a lean
   b tough
   cuts of meat?
24 Why is poultry meat more tender than red meat?
25 What is the food value of offal?
26 What is BSE and why is it controversial?

Further work with meat

1 Compare the cost per kilogram of different cuts of meat from one animal and comment on the difference.
2 Observe some different meat cuts with a magnifying glass and find the muscle fibre bundles, fat marbling, and connective tissue. Comment on the differences between each cut.
3 Using a small amount of shin of beef, cut it into cubes and boil one piece, grill another, bake another in the oven, and pressure cook the last. Compare each for flavour, colour, texture, and tenderness.
4 Observe the changes that occur in fresh meat stored in the refrigerator for a few days in a glass dish (covered), on a plate (uncovered), and closely wrapped in polythene. What are the reasons for the changes?

Fish

There are a great many varieties of fish, and at one time they were profusely available. However, since the Second World War, there has been a great increase in fishing (partly to feed humans directly and partly to feed animals reared for food), and this has given rise to much concern about the dwindling of supplies of some varieties. Some countries have imposed fishing limits around their shores to regulate the number of fish being caught (particularly young fish), but the problem still exists.

At sea, fish is gutted, cleaned, and frozen on board special boats, before it reaches the shore, as it deteriorates very rapidly once caught.

Types

Fish are classified in two ways:
1 According to their origin:
   Freshwater fish, e.g. salmon, trout;
   Seawater fish, which are further divided into:
      pelagic fish (which swim near the surface), e.g. herring, pilchard, mackerel;
      demersal fish (which swim near the bottom), e.g. plaice, cod, hake.

Structure and composition

Fish has a muscle composition similar to that of meat, but there is far less connective tissue, so it is much easier to tenderize and quicker to cook. It is important not to overcook fish as the protein easily becomes tough and the flesh dry. The muscle is formed into flakes which separate on cooking.

There is a lot of wastage with fish, i.e. the bones, head, fins, and often the skin. The only internal organ to be eaten is the roe of some species, which contains the eggs. Cod and herring roe are often eaten, and the roe of the sturgeon fish (caviare) is a prized and very expensive delicacy.

Choosing fish

As fresh fish deteriorates rapidly, it is important to choose it carefully. Fresh fish should have:
1 Bright eyes, not sunken.
2 Plump, firm flesh.
3 Plenty of bright scales, firmly attached to the skin.
4 Moist skin.
5 A fresh, sea smell.
6 Bright red gills, not sunken.

Shellfish is normally sold cooked. As several species are scavenger feeders (i.e. they feed from sediment on rocks and pipes, often near sewage outlets), they may harbour food-poisoning bacteria and must be eaten as soon as possible after purchase.

A catch of fish on a deep-sea boat

2 According to their fat content and type:
Oily fish have more than 5% fat in their flesh, which is therefore quite dark. Examples: mackerel, herring, pilchard, sprat, sardine, salmon.

White fish have less than 5% fat in their flesh, which is therefore white. They have oil in their liver. Examples: halibut, cod, whiting, coley, plaice, haddock, sole, hoki.

Shellfish, which are divided into:
molluscs (small, soft-bodied sea animals which live inside a hard shell), e.g. cockles, mussels, winkles;
crustaceans (soft-bodied, jointed sea animals which are covered by a hard protective 'crust' or external skeleton), e.g. lobster, crab, shrimp.

Clockwise from top right: turbot, tuna steaks, bass, Dublin Bay prawns, trout, plaice, sole, mackerel

Fish are sold in various ways:

Large fish, e.g. cod, coley, haddock, are cut into fillets, steaks, or cutlets.

Small and medium fish, e.g. herrings, mackerel, rainbow trout, are usually sold whole, and can be filleted by removing the backbone, tail, head, and fins.

Very small fish, e.g. sprats and whitebait, can be fried and eaten whole.

Importance of fish in the diet

For many people, e.g. Eskimos, Japanese, fish is a major source of protein. Like meat, the protein is of high biological value, and is readily digested and absorbed with little waste. White fish in particular is more easily digested than meat and is a useful food for people with digestive disorders.

Unlike meat, the fat in fish consists mostly of oils containing unsaturated fatty acids. The essential fatty acids in oily fish are of benefit to health (see p. 7).

Nutritive value

The approximate nutritive value of fish is:

	Oily fish	White fish	Shellfish (edible part)
Protein	19.0%	17.5%	15%
Fat	15.0%	0.9%	4%
Water	67.5%	80.0%	8.5%
Carbohydrate	none	none	trace
Minerals	2.5%	1.2%	1.4%

Vitamins

Fat soluble Oily fish contain useful amounts of vitamins A and D in their flesh. Canned oily fish contains the most vitamin D.

White fish contain vitamins A and D in their liver oils, not in their flesh.

Shellfish are not good sources of these vitamins, as they have a low fat content.

Water soluble Fish does not contain any vitamin C. Most fish contain small amounts of the B-group vitamins.

Mineral elements

Calcium Most calcium in fish is found in the bones. If the bones of canned fish, which have been softened, are eaten, they provide a useful source of calcium.

Iodine and **fluoride** Seawater fish are good sources.

Iron Fish are poor sources of iron.

Sodium, **chlorine**, **potassium**, and **phosphorus** are found in all fish.

Methods of preparation and cooking

Fish can be used in many dishes, but is most popular in the UK fried in batter and served with potato chips. Overcooking tends to lead to dryness and breaking up of the flesh.

Fish	Uses
White	Steamed, poached, grilled, fried, baked. Serve in a roux sauce, or in pastry (e.g. Russian fish pie), curry, with sweet and sour sauce, etc.
Oily	Bake, fry, grill, poach. Serve with a sharp sauce, e.g. tartare; fry in oatmeal; stuff with breadcrumbs, herbs, orange, etc., and bake.
Shell	Serve as a starter, e.g. prawn cocktail, or in soups, salads, fried in batter, with rice, etc.

Storage

Fish should be eaten as soon as possible after purchase,. and should be stored in the coldest part of the refrigerator (but not the ice box), well wrapped, to prevent the strong odours from contaminating other foods.

It is not advisable to freeze fresh fish bought from a shop as it must be frozen while very fresh.

Preserving fish

Apart from being frozen, fish can be preserved by:

Curing

Smoking is carried out over wood smoke in carefully controlled conditions. The smoke develops flavours in the fish and has a preservative action. Some fish are cooked and smoked (e.g. smoked mackerel), others are left raw.

Examples of smoked fish:

Haddock is sold as golden cutlets, Finnan haddock, or fillets. It sold either undyed, or coloured yellow (e.g. with annatto).

Salmon Smoked salmon is ready to eat, and is expensive.

Herrings are prepared in different ways:

> **kippers** – produced by splitting herrings open, soaking in brine, then smoking.

> **bucklings** – the heads are removed, and the fish is salted, then smoked and cooked at the same time.

> **bloaters** – the fish are salted whole, then smoked.

> **roll mops** – the filleted fish are marinaded in vinegar and brine for ten days, then rolled with pickling spice, and pickled.

Salting Some varieties of fish are salted and dried, e.g. cod.

Canning

Several varieties of oily fish are canned (e.g. tuna, sardine, pilchard, herring), and may be served with oil or tomato sauce. The bones are softened and can be eaten, providing a good source of calcium.

Fish products

A variety of fish products are available including:
> fish fingers
> ready-prepared fish pieces for oven baking
> fish nuggets and rissoles
> ready-prepared meals, e.g. seafood pie

Revision questions

1 How are fish classified? Give examples under each classification.
2 What points should influence your choice of fresh fish?
3 Why is fish an important food in the diet?
4 How can fish be prepared and cooked?
5 Why does fish take less time to cook than meat, and how does its structure differ?
6 How should fresh fish be stored in the home?
7 How is fish preserved?

Further work with fish

1 Weigh out four equal portions of the same fish and cook as follows:
   a grill
   b steam
   c fry
   d wrap in foil and bake.
   Note the changes in appearance, size, and texture in each case. How do you account for the differences?
2 Grill a piece of meat and a piece of fish of equal weight together. How long does each take to cook? Why is this? Continue cooking the fish. What happens to it?

Alternative protein foods

There have been many attempts to manufacture foods that are rich in protein as alternatives to meat, for the following reasons:

1 Meat is expensive to produce, and has risen in price over recent years due to:
   a shortage of good pasture land on which to rear animals;
   increases in the price of feeds for animals.
2 In countries where there is a shortage of food (particularly protein-rich food), there is an urgent need for new protein foods to be manufactured, especially for babies and young children who suffer most under conditions of famine.
3 Cheaper feeds for animals are required, as meat is in high demand in many countries.
   Several different raw materials have been used for the preparation of new protein foods, including:
   micro-organisms – bacteria, yeast, algae, plankton
   plants – seeds, legumes, cereals, seaweed

Micro-organisms

Micro-organisms can be made to grow on industrial or agricultural waste materials (e.g. paper, wood, cotton, sugar-refining waste) and the production of protein is fast and efficient. Bacteria can double their weight in 30 minutes, and 80% of this is protein (yeast, algae, and plankton are slightly less efficient).

Protein products from micro-organisms, e.g. the mycoprotein quorn, are useful for vegetarians. Quorn is sold as chunks or mince and can be stir-fried, or used in casseroles, bolognaise, etc. It is also available in ready meals, sausages, burgers, and oven-bake fillets. It is more expensive than some meats.

Plants

Seeds and legumes (pulses) can be used to produce protein-rich food. The main types used are soya bean, sunflower seed, groundnut, and sesame seed.

Soya is one of the most important sources of HBV plant protein. The soya plant comes from the Far East, but different varieties have been grown successfully in different climates. Soya beans must be well cooked to destroy the toxin soyin.

Soya beans were originally grown for the oil industry, but it was discovered that, once the oil was extracted, the residues contained up to 50% protein and could be made into flours or flakes for various uses. The flakes can be further refined and concentrated so that they contain up to 70% protein.

The extracted protein can be textured and flavoured to resemble meat. This is known as **textured vegetable protein** (TVP). The TVP can be shaped into 'meat' cubes or minced granules and used as a meat substitute in a variety of dishes. Usually other nutrients are added, e.g. iron, thiamin, and riboflavin, to bring the nutritive value close to that of meat.

TVP products are used in commercially prepared meat pies, stews, etc., and in canteen meals and vegetarian meals. They are a cheap alternative to meat but are unlikely to replace it because of the popularity of meat and the reluctance of people to change their eating habits.

Several other soya bean products are also important. Soya beans and flour are often added to vegetarian burger and sausage mixes, and soya flour can be used in baking in place of eggs.

Soya bean products are often used in stir-fry meals and other Chinese cooking. Soya bean

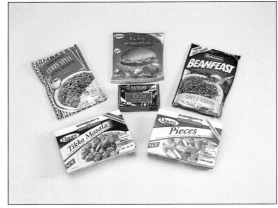

Quorn and soya products are good sources of protein and are popular alternatives to meat.

curd (tofu), which can be bought plain or smoked, is a good source of protein. Tempeh, specially fermented and cultured soya beans, has been produced in China for 2000 years. It is easy to digest and is rich in protein and vitamin B_{12}, but low in fat. Soy sauce (tamari) and soy bean paste (miso) are made from fermented soya beans, and are both high in salt.

Soya milk is a substitute for cow's milk but needs to be fortified with vitamins and minerals. Soya desserts, cream substitutes, and yogurts are also available.

Pulses are a rich source of protein and other nutrients (see p. 136–7) and are therefore a valuable food in their own right.

Research into alternative protein foods is ongoing, particularly for use in poor countries. With a growing world population and less land on which to rear animals, they are likely to become more important as foods in the future.

Revision questions

1 Why have there been attempts in the recent past to find alternative sources of protein to meat, fish, and dairy foods?
2 What raw materials have been used for the preparation of new protein foods?
3 Why is soya a useful food for this purpose?
4 What is TVP? How is it used in meal preparation?
5 What is quorn? How is it used in meal preparation?

Further work with alternative protein foods

1 Prepare a variety of main course dishes, e.g. spaghetti bolognese, goulash, meat stew, meat pie, using **a** meat and **b** TVP meat substitutes. Compare the results according to these criteria:

> texture before and after cooking
> flavour
> colour
> cost
> consistency of dish

2 Using the dishes made above, set up a tasting panel, asking participants to assess each dish according to the criteria set out in number 1. Draw up a chart to show the results, concluding which dishes were most popular and why.

Gelatine

Gelatine is a protein which is extracted from the collagen present in the skin, tendons, bones, and connective tissue of cattle that have been slaughtered for meat.

Gelatine is available in leaf and powder forms.

Properties

Gelatine is a tasteless, transparent, odourless, brittle solid which is faint yellow in colour. When mixed with water, the gelatine absorbs it and swells, because the protein molecules in it

form a three-dimensional network which entangles the water and immobilizes it:

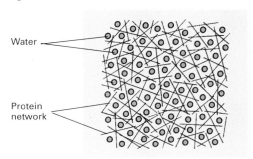

When the water is trapped in this way, it forms a **gel**. If the gel is then heated above 35°C it becomes a liquid and is called a **sol**. When cooled, the sol becomes solid, and this process is called **gelation**.

The ability of gelatine to cause liquids to set in this way is used in food preparation for several purposes.

Domestic uses

1 Jellies: clear or plain, sweet or savoury.
2 Whips: made by beating plain jelly into a froth until it thickens.
3 Sponges: made by adding whipped egg whites to a plain jelly, to form a spongy-textured sweet.
4 Bavarian: made by folding in whipped cream to a plain jelly.
5 Creams: made with gelatine, milk, or cream and eggs.
6 Soufflés: cold.
7 Sweets: e.g. marshmallows, Turkish delight.
8 Aspic: for setting meat, fish, and vegetables in a savoury jelly.

Industrial uses

1 Ice cream: as a stabilizer, to ensure a smooth texture.
2 Meats: for canned hams and pressed meat, meat loaves, pates, pies, sausages, and brawn.
3 Thickening agent: for soup, cream.
4 Crystallized fruits: e.g. cherries.
5 Medicines: as a coating for pills and capsules.
6 Yogurt: as a stabilizer to stop separation.

Using gelatine in food preparation

Proportions to use

12.5 g or 3 rounded tsp gelatine

575 ml water or other liquid

To dissolve gelatine

1   Sprinkle the gelatine into the liquid in a jug.
2   Stand the jug in a pan of hot water, stir, and leave to dissolve.
3   The gelatine is ready for use when it is clear and transparent.
4   Do not boil the gelatine liquid.

Adding gelatine to a mixture

The dissolved gelatine should be poured slowly into the mixture, stirring all the time, to incorporate the gelatine completely. The mixture should not be icy cold as the hot gelatine liquid will not mix well and will form 'ropey' globules. This will prevent it from setting properly.

Fresh pineapple should be cooked first if used in a dish that is to be set with gelatine. This is because pineapple contains an enzyme called **bromelain** which prevents gelatine from setting. Heating inactivates the enzyme.

Gelatine should not be added to very hot milk as it will cause it to curdle.

Gelatine can be used to help jam to set, but it will not keep so long if this is done.

Storing gelatine

Gelatine absorbs moisture readily and so should be stored in a cool, dry place. It will also absorb odours from other foods, and so should be kept in an air-tight container.

The importance of gelatine in the diet

Gelatine is a protein, but although it is an animal protein, it has a low biological value (see p. 3). It is not, therefore, as useful in the diet as was once thought.

Gelatine can be used to set jam for people suffering from diabetes, where sugar intake has to be limited.

Revision questions

1   What is gelatine?
2   What is gelatine used for in food preparation?
3   How should gelatine be added to a mixture?
4   How should gelatine be stored?
5   What is the food value of gelatine?
6   What are the properties of gelatine?
7   How does gelatine set liquids?
8   What is a gel?
9   What is a sol?
10 What is gelatine used for in food manufacture?
11 What effect does fresh pineapple have on the setting of gelatine?

Further work with gelatine

1   Dissolve 12.5 g gelatine in 575 ml water. Divide equally into five beakers, with the following additions:
    a no addition (control)
    b 25 g fresh crushed pineapple
    c 25 g fresh crushed pineapple that has been boiled for 10 minutes
    d 25 g canned crushed pineapple
    e 25 ml (1 tablespoon) canned pineapple juice
2   Leave in a cold place for at least 1 hour, then observe the differences in the way they have set.
3   Account for the difference between samples **b** and **c**, and between **b**, **d**, and **e**.

Vegetables

A wide variety of fresh vegetables can now be purchased. Many of them are imported and have only been available in the UK for a relatively short time. Vegetables are also available in a preserved state, frozen, canned, or dried. Many can be grown in domestic gardens.

Vegetables are usually served as accompaniments to main meals, but with imagination and good cooking, they can be used as the main part of a meal in a variety of interesting ways.

Types

Vegetables can be classified according to the part of the plant from which they come, as described below. Some people distinguish vegetables from fruit by their inclusion in savoury parts of a meal, while fruits are eaten with sweet parts of a meal. However, some foods which are called vegetables, e.g. tomatoes, are really fruits.

If vegetables are grown out of doors in the UK, they are only available or are at their best and cheapest at certain times of the year. They are then said to be 'in season'. Many vegetables are grown in hothouses or are imported from all around the world, so it is possible to obtain a wide variety at all times of the year.

Chemicals

Over 400 different chemicals are approved for use on plant crops in the UK. They include pesticides, insecticides, herbicides (weed killers), fungicides, and growth regulators. There is evidence that some may cause cancer, birth defects, asthma, and other disorders if eaten, so all vegetables and fruits should be washed before eating.

Some chemicals are systemic (they work by going right into the plant) and cannot be washed off.

Pressure groups are trying to encourage farmers to produce plant crops using fewer chemicals, and the Soil Association promotes organic farming where no chemicals are used.

Types of vegetable

Leaves

cabbage – green, red, white

spring greens

kale

Brussels sprouts

spinach

cress and watercress

chicory

endive

lettuce – cos, Webbs, iceberg, little gem

kohl rabi

Chinese leaves

Seeds and pods

peas

runner beans

broad beans

French beans

mangetout

Stems

celery

Fruit

tomatoes

cucumber

marrows

corn on the cob (strictly a cereal but eaten as a vegetable)

capsicum (sweet red, green, yellow, or white pepper)

aubergine

courgettes (sometimes called zucchinis)

okra (ladies fingers)

ackee

squash

spaghetti squash

Flowers

cauliflower

purple or green broccoli

calabrese

Roots

carrot, beetroot

swede, parsnip

turnip

radish

celeriac

mooli (white radish)

salsify

Bulbs

onions

pickling onions

spring onions

shallots

leeks

Tubers

potatoes

Jerusalem artichokes

cassava

sweet potato

yam

eddoes

Colour of vegetables and fruit

Leafy vegetables are green because of the presence of **chlorophyll**. The yellow/orange colour of fruits and vegetables is due to **carotenoids**. The red/blue colour of others is due to **anthocyanins**.

Many fruits and vegetables are brightly coloured.

Preparation and choice

Vegetables should be chosen carefully:
1   Damaged, wilted, and bruised vegetables should be avoided, as there is likely to be waste and loss of nutrients.
2   Leaf vegetables should be crisp, firm, and of a good colour, and root vegetables should be firm and free of spade marks.
3   Insect- or mould-infected vegetables should be avoided.

To preserve the vitamin and mineral content, vegetables should be prepared as follows:
1   If the vegetable requires peeling, peel it very thinly, as there are vitamins and minerals under the skin which could easily be removed. Young potatoes, carrots, and other vegetables often do not require peeling and can be served with their skins on. They should be scrubbed thoroughly beforehand, to remove chemicals.
2   Prepare vegetables just before cooking to prevent the destruction of vitamins by enzymes. They can be placed in a plastic bag in a cool place to prevent the oxidation of vitamins.
3   Wash the vegetables but do not soak them in water, as this will cause water-soluble vitamins and minerals to be lost.
4   Cook the vegetables in the minimum amount of boiling water. Placing them in boiling water destroys enzymes, and so helps to preserve the vitamins. They should be cooked for the minimum time, with a lid on the pan.
5   When vegetables are just tender, they should be drained and served immediately. If kept hot, there will be further losses of vitamin C.

Conservative method of cooking vegetables

Vegetables, except for leaf types, can be chopped and sautéed in fat, then placed in a covered casserole with a little liquid in the oven, and cooked until tender. The juices should be used for gravy. This conserves most of the flavour, colour, and shape of the vegetables. Microwave cooking of vegetables in a minimum of water also conserves nutrients.

Effect of heat

Vegetables are cooked to reduce their bulk and make them more digestible by cooking the starch they contain. Some vegetables, e.g. potatoes, increase in bulk when cooked as they absorb water. Vitamins and minerals, particularly vitamin C, are destroyed by heat, so vegetables should be cooked carefully to keep such losses to a minimum.

Importance in the diet

Vegetables are eaten in a variety of ways as part of main meals and as snacks. The nutrient content of different types varies considerably. With the exception of pulses, vegetables provide little protein and fat.

Vitamins

Water soluble

Vitamin B group Most vegetables contain some riboflavin and nicotinic acid, and pulses provide a good supply of thiamin.

Vitamin C The richest sources are Brussels sprouts, kale, cabbage, green peppers, watercress, spinach, cauliflower, tomato, and asparagus (in that order). Potatoes contain a reasonable amount, and as they are eaten in large amounts, are a useful source.

Fat soluble

Vitamin A (as β-carotene) Carrots and dark green vegetables contain the most. Potatoes, onions, and cauliflower contain none.

Vitamin D Vegetables do not contain vitamin D.

Vitamins E and K Green vegetables and peas contain a little.

Carbohydrate

Plants produce starch during photosynthesis (see p. 9). The starch is stored in various parts of the plant, notably the roots and tubers. Some of the starch is converted into sugar in vegetables such as beetroot, onion, peas, leeks, tomatoes, and parsnips.

Minerals

Calcium and iron are found in various vegetables including watercress, cabbage, lentils, and spinach, but the presence of cellulose and **oxalic acid** reduces their availability to the body.

Storage of vegetables

Potatoes should be stored in a dark, cool, dry place to prevent them from becoming mouldy and green (due to a reaction to light), and to stop them sprouting in warmth. Root vegetables should be stored in a similar way.

Leaf vegetables lose vitamin C and water rapidly during storage and should be stored for the minimum time in a cool place, in a plastic bag.

All vegetables should be used as soon as possible.

Revision questions

1 Why are vegetables an important food in the diet?
2 How can vegetables be used in a meal to add interest and variety?
3 How are vegetables classified? Give three examples for each main group.
4 Why is it best to buy vegetables in season?
5 How should vegetables be chosen?
6 How should vegetables be prepared in order to preserve their nutrient content?
7 What is the conservative method of cooking vegetables?
8 What effect does heat have on vegetables?
9 How should vegetables be stored?

Further work with vegetables

1 Weigh out five 50 g samples of a leafy green vegetable. Place each into a small pan of boiling water (about 150 ml), with the following variations:
   a no addition (control)
   b 3 tsp salt
   c 1 tsp vinegar
   d pinch of bicarbonate of soda
   e no addition
   Simmer samples **a** to **d** for 10 minutes. Plunge sample **e** into the water for a few seconds only, then remove. Drain the water from each into a beaker and observe the colour of the water and the vegetable. Account for the changes in colour. Why is it bad practice to add bicarbonate of soda to green vegetables?

2 Repeat the above experiment with sample **a** only, and boil rapidly for half an hour, observing the changes in colour, smell, and texture of the cooked vegetable at 5 minute intervals.

3 Repeat experiments 1 and 2 with carrots (simmer for 15 minutes) and observe the colour and texture changes.

4 Peel four old potatoes of similar size. Leave one whole, chop one into two, chop the third into four, and the fourth into small dice.
   Cook each in boiling water for 5 minutes and then test with a skewer or fork. Which sample is the softest? Why?
   Continue cooking the potatoes for a further 20 minutes. Observe the textures of each and account for the differences.
   From the results of experiments 2, 3, and 4 write a short account of the importance of correct timing and cooking conditions for vegetables.

5 Repeat experiment 1 using red cabbage and observe the changes in colour and texture. Then add a pinch of bicarbonate of soda to the water from sample **c**, and observe the colour change. Add more bicarbonate of soda until a constant colour is maintained. Add a few drops of vinegar to the water from sample **d** and observe the colour change. Add more vinegar until a constant colour is maintained. Account for the changes in colour.

Pulses and nuts

Pulses

Pulses are the dried seeds of the legume plant family, which includes:

beans

peas

lentils

Many varieties are grown all over the world, in different climates.

Types

There are many types of pulse grown, but the most familiar ones in the UK are:

Beans

Seeds: lentils (orange and brown)

Peas: whole, or split without skins (yellow or green)

Peanuts and **groundnuts** (strictly pulses)

Pulses (clockwise from top): red lentils, green lentils, haricot beans, kidney beans, butter beans, peanuts, green split peas

Preparation

All pulses, except for lentils, should be soaked in water for approximately eight hours before cooking, to allow water to be taken up by osmosis. This causes the pulse to swell and soften. The addition of bicarbonate of soda to the water hastens this process without significantly affecting the nutritional value.

It is inadvisable to use pulses that are more than one year old, as the skins tend to harden during storage and are difficult to soften.

Once softened, pulses should be boiled gently in the minimum amount of water until tender. Red kidney beans *must* be boiled for at least 15 minutes, to destroy a natural toxin (poison) they contain. If eaten raw or partially cooked this toxin can cause food poisoning. Some people are allergic to peanuts and even the smallest amount can cause a severe reaction (see p. 72).

Uses

Pulses are included in meals in a variety of ways:

Soups and stews – to thicken and add extra protein.

Vegetable accompaniment – served in a sauce with meat and other vegetables.

Salads Cooked pulses can be served cold in a dressing or with other salad vegetables.

Soya Soya beans are ground into flour or made into other products (see pp. 129–30).

Vegetarian meals Pulses are a main source of protein in vegetarian meals.

Importance in the diet

Pulses make an important contribution to the diet in many Eastern countries, where they may be the main source of protein and can be produced relatively easily. In Western countries such as the UK, where a greater variety of foods are available, pulses are less important in the diet. However, in the UK approximately 300,000 tons of baked beans (haricot beans) in tomato sauce are consumed each year, which is more than in most other Western countries.

Nutritional value

Protein Most pulses contain approximately 20 g LBV protein per 100 g (dry weight). Soya beans contain up to 40 g per 100 g (dry weight) of

HBV protein, so are an exceptionally good source compared with other pulses.

Fat Soya beans and groundnuts contain up to 20% and 40% fat respectively, so are a good source of fat compared with other pulses.

Carbohydrate Most pulses contain up to 20% carbohydrate.

Vitamins In general, pulses are a good source of B vitamins, except for riboflavin. They have no vitamin C in their dry state, but on germination, they provide a rich source. Bean sprouts provide a valuable source of vitamin C. Aduki and mung beans form sprouts within a few days if put onto damp kitchen paper and kept moist.

Because pulses are relatively easy to grow and have a high nutritional value, it has often been suggested that more should be eaten, particularly in poor countries. However, it may be difficult to change people's food habits, and in poor countries people may not have the facilities to prepare pulses for consumption.

Nuts

Most people only eat nuts in small amounts because they are expensive, so their contribution to the diet is small.

Types

coconut palm	brazil	pistachio
walnut	hazelnut	pecan
almond	cashew	
chestnut	macadamia	

Uses

Nuts are used in baking and confectionery, chiefly for their flavour and texture. They can also be used in poultry stuffings, served in salads, nut roasts, casseroles, and croquettes, and used as a garnish for vegetables.

Importance in the diet

Most people eat nuts in such small amounts that they do not feature significantly in the nutrient content of the diet. However, they are a useful source of LBV protein and fat to vegetarians, and add variety to their diet. They also supply some carbohydrate, calcium, iron, plus a little thiamin.

Revision questions

1 What are pulses?
2 Give some examples of beans, seeds, and peas.
3 How should pulses be prepared?
4 How can bicarbonate of soda help in the preparation of pulses?
5 How are pulses used in meal preparation?
6 Why are pulses an important food in poor countries?
7 What is the food value of pulses?
8 Give some examples of nuts, and their uses in food preparation.
9 What is the importance of nuts in the diet?

Fruits

Fruits are a unique group of foods because there is such a wide variety of types, flavours, colours, and textures.

Apples and pears were grown as far back as Roman times, and in the 16th century, many types of fruit, including apricots, grapes, figs, plums, and peaches were introduced into the UK.

Relatively recent preservation techniques and modern transport facilities have increased the variety of fruit available.

Botanically, fruits are the part of the plant that carries the seeds for future generations of plants. They are often attractively 'packaged' by nature to encourage animals and birds to eat them and scatter the seeds.

Types of fruit

Hard fruits

apples (eating), e.g.
Cox's Orange Pippin,
Starking, Golden
Delicious, Granny
Smith, Worcester,
Russet, Laxton Superb

apples (cooking), e.g.
Bramley

pears, e.g. Conference,
William

Stone fruits

plums, e.g. Victoria,
Golden

damsons

apricots

greengages

peaches

cherries

grapes – black, green,
red

nectarines

avocado pear

mango

Citrus fruits

oranges

lemons

limes

grapefruits

tangerines

clementines

satsumas

Berry fruits

strawberries

raspberries

blackberries

gooseberries

Currants

black and red currants

Dried fruit

sultanas

currants

raisins

dates

prunes

Miscellaneous

melon – water melon,
honeydew, galia,
canteloupe

star fruit (carambola)

lychees

figs

kiwi fruit (Chinese
gooseberry)

paw paw (papaya)

grenadillo

passion fruit

cape gooseberry
(physalis)

pomegranate

sharon fruit
(persimmon)

fresh figs

nashi pear

kumquat

bananas

rhubarb (strictly a stem,
but eaten as a fruit)

pineapples

Preparation

Most fruits can be eaten raw when ripe, but they are cooked for various dishes, often by stewing them in a little water. Fruit should be cooked over a gentle heat for the minimum time. Very little water should be used as most fruits produce a fair amount of juice when cooked. This should be served with the fruit to conserve the nutrients.

Fruit should be chosen carefully:

1 Choose fruit that is just ripe, and has no bruising or blemishes.
2 Wash the fruit carefully, as it may have been sprayed with chemicals before or after harvesting, and may be dusty.
3 Store the fruit carefully, taking care not to crush it as this will cause bruising.

Importance in the diet

Fruits are eaten mainly for their flavour, texture, and the variety they give to the diet. Their high water content makes them refreshing, particularly when eaten raw.

The nutrient content varies considerably between different varieties. In general, fruits are very low in protein and fat, their main contribution to the diet being vitamins, carbohydrate, and minerals.

Vitamins

Fruits are an important source of vitamin C (ascorbic acid). However, not all fruits are good sources. The richest sources are rose hips and blackcurrants. Citrus fruits (especially oranges, lemons, and grapefruits), gooseberries, strawberries, and raspberries provide a good source. Apples, damsons, peaches, apricots, and cherries provide some. This only applies to fresh or frozen fruit, not canned or stewed fruit as heat destroys much of the vitamin C content.

A reasonable amount of vitamin A is present as β-carotene in apricots, but there is very little in other fruits.

Fruits do not contain any vitamin D and very little of the vitamin B group.

Carbohydrate

Plants produce starch during photosynthesis, and, in unripe fruits, most of the carbohydrate is present as starch. As the fruit ripens, the starch is converted to fructose, and the fruit becomes sweeter in taste. Fruits are generally eaten before this conversion is complete, so they provide a mixture of carbohydrate.

Fruits are a useful source of dietary fibre (NSP), which is found in the skins, seeds, pith, and fibrous parts of the fruit. Pectin also helps to remove waste products from the body.

Minerals

Fruits supply a small amount of iron and calcium, plus some of the trace elements.

Storage of fruit

Fresh fruit should be stored in a cool, ventilated place, and used as soon as possible. Soft fruits are best kept in the refrigerator, as they deteriorate rapidly in warm weather.

Revision questions

1 How are fruits classified? Give three examples of fruits in each category.
2 Why are fruits a valuable food in the diet?
3 Describe the food value of fruits.
4 How should fruits be prepared and chosen?
5 How should fruits be stored in the home?
6 Which fruits are the best sources of vitamin C? How should they be prepared to conserve the vitamin C?
7 What happens to the carbohydrate in fruit as the fruit ripens? How does this affect the taste of the fruit?

Further work with fruits

1 Place samples of fresh fruits in the freezer for a few days, then remove and thaw. Observe the change in colour, texture, and overall appearance. Account for these changes.
Suggested fruits:
apple   raspberry
banana   tomato
orange   cucumber
strawberry   plum
melon
2 Peel and chop five samples each of apple, banana, and orange.
a Leave one sample of each exposed to the air.
b Wrap one sample of each tightly in plastic cling wrap.
c Sprinkle one sample of each with lemon juice.
d Sprinkle one sample of each with bicarbonate of soda.
e Plunge one sample of each into boiling water for a few seconds and then remove.
Account for the differences in appearance. What causes the browning in the apple and banana, and why is the orange not affected? What is the best substance to use to prevent browning in a fresh fruit salad, and why?

Herbs

Herbs have long been used to flavour food, and are believed by many people to have medicinal properties. Normally the leaves are used in food preparation, as they contain aromatic oils which are released when the leaves are crushed or chopped. Occasionally flowers, roots, or seeds are used.

Herbs usually grow in temperate climates, and can easily be grown in gardens or indoors in pots. They can be dried or frozen for use all year round and can be used raw or cooked.

A bouquet garni is made from a variety of fresh or dried herbs (tarragon, mint, rosemary, sage, parsley, thyme) tied in muslin. It is added to soups, stews, etc., for flavouring, then removed before the dish is served.

Some commonly used herbs include:

Herb	Uses
Angelica	The stems are candied (preserved in sugar) and used to decorate cakes, etc. The root can be used to flavour drinks.
Basil	The leaves are used for salads; tomato, egg, or mushroom dishes; pasta dishes; and in sauces.
Bay	The leaves are used in meat and fish stews, soups, and marinades.
Chives 	The leaves are used for salads, vegetable soup, omelettes, cream cheese, and meat broths.
Dill 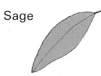	The leaves are used with fish, salads, and sandwich fillings. The seeds can be used in stews and bean soups.

Herb	Uses
Garlic	The bulb is used and is divided into cloves. It has a strong flavour and is used sparingly in stews, soups, salads, butter, mayonnaise, etc.
Mint	The leaves are served chopped in vinegar with roast lamb, and used in water ices, drinks, and fruit salads.
Oregano	The leaves are used for meat loaves, marrows, stuffed green peppers, pizzas, and pasta dishes.
Parsley	The leaves are used for stuffings, sauces, soups, and salads. It is a good source of vitamin C if used in large quantities.
Rosemary	The leaves are served with roast lamb or chicken, fish, eggs, and cheese.
Sage	The leaves are used for stuffings, sage and onion sauce, and sage Derby cheese.
Tarragon	The leaves are used to flavour vinegar, sauces, and mustards, or are cooked with chicken dishes.
Thyme	The leaves are used in stuffings, soups, stews, herb sauces, and with vegetables.

Spices

Spices have been used throughout history all over the world, and have for many centuries been an important trading commodity.

Spices are mostly grown in tropical countries, and tend to be derived from dried roots, seeds, or barks. They are used in food preparation either whole, crushed, or powdered. They generally have a strong aromatic flavour. They are used in small quantities so they do not contribute significantly to the diet, although curry powder contains a useful amount of iron, probably partly obtained from the iron pots in which it is prepared.

There are many spices in use, and these are some of the most common:

Spice	Uses
Allspice	Savoury sauces, marinades, Middle-Eastern meat dishes, pickling.
Caraway seeds	Used in bread, cakes, and cheeses, particularly in German and Jewish cooking.
Cayenne pepper	Made from ground chillies. A hot, fiery pepper, used sparingly in cheese dishes and with shellfish.
Chillies	Used in hot pickles, curries, spicy dishes, chilli and tabasco sauces, and chilli con carne.
Chinese five spice	A mixture of star anise, anise pepper, fennel, cloves, and cinnamon. Used in Chinese cookery.
Cinnamon	Comes from the bark of a tree. Used in mulled wines, cakes, apple pies, biscuits.

Spice	Uses
Cloves	These are flower buds from the myrtle tree. Used for bread sauce, baked gammon, etc.
Coriander	The seeds and leaves are used in curries and other spicy dishes.
Curry powder	A mixture of several hot spices. Used in mulligatawny soup and savoury dishes.
Ginger	The root is used powdered, crystallized, or whole, in cakes, with melon, etc.
Mustard	The seeds are used for mustard powder and in pickles. Mustard is served with meat, cheese, etc, and used in salad dressing.
Nutmeg	The seed is sold whole or powdered. Used in egg custards, cheese sauce, milk puddings, moussaka.
Paprika	Ground sweet red peppers; not usually very hot. Used in Hungarian cookery, e.g. goulash, and with egg and shellfish as a garnish.
Peppercorns	Can be white, black, green, or red. Served with most meals, powdered or freshly ground.
Turmeric	This is made from the root of a plant and is used in curries, or for colouring rice yellow.
Vanilla	Vanilla plants are a type of orchid and the dried seed pods are used either whole or as an essence for cakes, puddings, etc.

Food additives

Manufactured foods often contain certain food additives for the following reasons:

1   To preserve them from decay and spoilage (see pp. 154-62).
2   To improve their keeping qualities.
3   To improve or enhance the flavour, colour, and texture of a food.
4   To produce a uniform food during large-scale manufacture.
5   To provide easy-to-prepare convenience foods in a society that is busy and spends less time in the kitchen than in the past.
6   To produce new food products, e.g. snacks and confectionery in novelty shapes and colours.

Additives such as salt, alcohol, spices, and sugar have been in use for a long time, and there are now many synthetic additives used in a variety of ways. The use of both natural and synthetic additives is strictly controlled by law.

INGREDIENTS, WHEN RECONSTITUTED: VEGETABLES (LEEK ,ONION), WHEAT FLOUR, MODIFIED STARCH, HYDROGENATED VEGETABLE OIL, SALT, FLAVOURINGS, CHICKEN FAT, FLAVOUR ENHANCERS (MONOSODIUM GLUTAMATE, SODIUM GUANYLATE), STABILISER (SODIUM TRIPOLYPHOSPHATE), CASEINATES, SOY SAUCE, YEAST EXTRACT, SUGAR, HERBS, ACIDITY REGULATOR (SODIUM HYDROGEN ORTHOPHOSPHATE), SPICES, CITRIC ACID, ANTIOXIDANT (BHA).		
NUTRITION INFORMATION - TYPICAL VALUES		
	PER 100g	PER SERVING
ENERGY kJ.	1751	350
kcal.	418	84
PROTEIN	6.9g.	1.4g.
CARBOHYDRATE	54.1g.	10.8g.
FAT	19.3g.	3.9g.

How many additives does this soup mix contain?

Important requirements of food additives

For an additive to be acceptable for use in a food, it must conform to certain principles:

1   It must be safe to use.
2   It must be effective in its intended use.
3   It must only be used in the minimum quantity required for it to work.
4   It must not mislead the consumer about the quality or a nature of a food.

5   It should, where possible, be of nutritional value to the body.

Natural versus synthetic additives

Much concern has been voiced about the use of synthetic additives in food. They are considered by some to be less safe than natural additives (i.e. those produced by plants and animals). However, many of the most dangerous poisons occur naturally in plants and animal foods, and it is not possible to establish accurately what other chemicals they contain.

Synthetic additives, on the other hand, are generally pure and can be tested for their effects on the body by animal experiments. Also, the amount added to food can be strictly controlled.

There are approximately 6,000 food additives in use in the UK, many of which are flavourings. There has been little research into their long-term effects but the increase in cases of asthma, eczema, headaches, hyperactivity, digestive complaints, and skin rashes has been linked to additives in food.

Types of additives and their uses

Preservatives and **antioxidants**, see pp. 169-70.

Emulsifiers and **stabilizers** are used to ensure that food products remain in a good stable condition for a certain period of time after they are manufactured (this may be several months). Emulsifiers work in the following way:

An oil in water emulsion

separates after a time.

Emulsifier molecules have a water-loving (hydrophilic) head and a water-hating (hydrophobic) tail.

The water-loving head is attracted to the water and the water-hating tail to the oil droplets.`

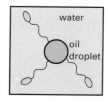

So the emulsifier molecules surround the oil droplets and prevent them from separating out from the water.

An example of an emulsifier is:

glyceryl monostearate

(water-loving part of molecule)   (water-hating part of molecule)

Emulsifiers are used in products such as salad dressings, low-fat spreads, and ice cream. Emulsifying salts are used to change the proteins in processed cheese into a smooth mixture with the fat and water.

Acids are used to develop an acid flavour in sweets, for setting jam, and in baking powder. Types of acid used:

citric acid (from lemon juice)
tartaric acid (from grapes)
malic acid (from apples and grapes)
acetic acid (in vinegar)
lactic acid (from dairy foods)

Acidity regulators are used to control how acid or alkaline a food is.

Non-stick agents are used to prevent powdery foods from sticking together, e.g. magnesium carbonate is used in salt.

Colourings Natural food colours are chemicals produced by plants and animals.

When food is coloured during food manufacture, natural or synthetic colourings can be used. The colour of food has a great influence on people's desire to eat, so firms spend a lot of time and money on research to get the right colour in their food. Some foods have to be coloured after processing as they lose their natural colour, e.g. canned peas go grey, as does blackcurrant cordial. There is a list of permitted food colours that may be used, and food manufacturers must abide by this.

A group of colours called azo dyes, cause allergic reactions in some people. Consumer pressure has persuaded some food manufacturers to use alternative colours. Azo dyes include:

E102 tartrazine
E110 sunset yellow FCF
E128 red 2G
E124 ponceau 4R

Flavours and sweeteners The flavour of a food product is an important factor in its success. The most widely used sources of food flavours are:

herbs	roots
fruits	seeds
berries	barks

Many flavours are extracted from oils, e.g. peppermint, clove, citrus oils. The addition of a flavour enables the manufacturer to produce a consistent product.

At least 3500 flavourings are used in the food industry, and at present they do not have to be listed on a label. Many are produced in the laboratory, and have not been obtained from the food they are described as tasting like. On food labels, flavours must be correctly described, for example:

raspberry-flavour yogurt has no raspberry in it at all

raspberry flavoured yogurt must have some real raspberry in it

raspberry yogurt must be made with real raspberries

Flavour enhancers, e.g. monosodium glutamate, are used to bring out the flavour of an ingredient of the food, e.g. meat, cheese.

Sweeteners such as saccharin are often added to foods instead of sucrose, as they are more concentrated and produce the desired sweetness at a lower cost.

Nutrients During the processing of some foods (e.g. cereals), nutrients are lost, and may be replaced by the manufacturer. This is called restoration. Nutrients may also be added to foods to enrich or fortify them. For example, vitamins A and D are added to margarine, and calcium is added to white bread by law. Fruit juices often have extra vitamin C added, and salt may have iodine added. The Food Standards Committee also recommends that TVP foods intended to replace meat should be fortified with nutrients to make them similar to meat in food value.

Foaming agents are used to ensure that bubbles are evenly distributed, e.g. in ice cream.

Glazing agents give a shiny outer layer, e.g. to sweets.

Humectants stop foods drying out, e.g. in soft centres of chocolates.

Sequesterants stop reactions such as off-flavours in fruits, and discoloration of foods.

Modified starch is added to dry foods such as soups and baby foods to add bulk and enable liquid to be incorporated easily.

Gelling agents enhance texture, e.g. in soya milk.

Propellants are gases that are used to make aerosols work, e.g. for decorating cream.

Thickeners improve the texture and mouthfeel e.g. in yogurts.

All manufactured food products in the UK have to bear a label stating exactly what is in the food, including any additives, which may be described by their chemical name or listed as, e.g. 'permitted antioxidants', or by their 'E' number from a list prepared under EU (see p. 78) regulations.

Strict controls and checks are made on food additives, but some products (including alcoholic drinks, medicines, take-away and fast foods, and unwrapped bread and cakes) do not have to declare the additives used in their manufacture. Various consumer groups have put pressure on the food industry and government to reduce the use of additives in food.

Revision questions

1 Why are additives put into foods?
2 Why are colourings added to food?
3 What are the most common flavours used in foods?
4 Why are nutrients added to foods?
5 What important principles must food additives conform to?
6 What is the difference between natural and synthetic additives? Give some examples of each.
7 What are emulsifiers and stabilizers, and how do they work?

Convenience foods

Convenience foods are usually described as foods that are processed and partly or totally prepared by a food manufacturer, so that they are either ready to eat, or require minimal preparation by the consumer.

These foods have gained in popularity in recent years, for a number of reasons, including:

1 Less leisure time being spent in food preparation.
2 More women going out to work and so having less time to prepare food.
3 Advances in food technology.
4 Increased freezer ownership (so people can store ready-prepared foods at home).
5 The influence of advertising on people's food habits.

Many different foods are now available as convenience foods, which require little or no preparation by the consumer.

Years ago, most foods, including butter, cheese, and bread, were prepared in the home, and many hours were spent in food preparation. Food technology was limited, as were the means of preserving food and distributing it over a wide area. Today, a wide range of convenience foods is available. They can be loosely classified as in the following table.

Type of food	Examples
Dehydrated	
'Instant foods' (quickly and easily prepared by reconstituting with water or other liquid)	mashed potato; custard; cold desserts; soups; coffee; baby foods; porridge; snacks (pasta or rice based)
Foods requiring reconstituting and a short cooking time	soups; main meals, e.g. curries, stews; sauces; custard; pie fillings, e.g. lemon meringue; TVP foods (see p. 130)
Ingredients for main dishes requiring the addition of extra ingredients and liquid	mixes for cake, batter, scone, bread, crumble, cheesecake, icing
Ready-to-eat	
Sweet	cakes; biscuits; fruit pies and tarts; puddings; sweets
Savoury	meat pies; pasties; cold meats; pâtés; salads, e.g. coleslaw; pastes (fish and meat); cheese spreads; preserves
Canned	
Foods requiring heating	pasta or pulses in sauce, e.g. beans; baby foods; stews; puddings; sausages; soups; milk puddings
Foods requiring no cooking	fish; cold meats; custard; fruit
Foods requiring some cooking	vegetables; pies; meat; puddings
Foods used as part of a main dish	meat and fruit pie fillings; special sauces, e.g. bolognese
Frozen	
Foods ready-to-eat on thawing	cold sweets, e.g. mousses, trifle; ice cream; fruit juice
Foods ready to cook	pastry; yeast doughs; sausage rolls; mince pies; burgers; meat pies; fish fingers
Foods cooked and ready to heat	fish in sauce; casseroles; pies
Cook-chill foods	
Food cooked to destroy food poisoning micro-organisms, then quickly chilled, and kept cold during transport and storage. Must be thoroughly heated by consumer.	fresh pasta; main courses, e.g. bolognese, chilli con carne, curry, lasagne, seafood pie; sauces; soups
Ready-prepared meals	
Food cooked to destroy micro-organisms, then packed in modified atmosphere (see p. 166), and stored at room temperature. Heated by microwave oven, or by standing in boiling water.	main courses, e.g. lasagne, curry, bolognese, rice dishes

Advantages of convenience foods

1 Convenience foods are quick and easy to prepare and save time and fuel.
2 They are easy to store and useful for taking on holiday.
3 They can be kept for emergencies.
4 A wide variety is available.
5 There is usually little waste.
6 They often have extra nutrients added.

Disadvantages of convenience foods

1 They may be more expensive than fresh foods, but the time and fuel required to cook fresh foods and the wastage from them must be taken into account.
2 Too many processed and refined foods in the diet may limit the intake of NSP.
3 Servings in convenience meals may not be adequate, making it necessary to buy extra, which defeats the object.
4 Nutrients may be lost during processing and not replaced.
5 They may have high levels of fat and sugar.

Using convenience foods

In theory, it is possible to live entirely on convenience foods, without suffering from any nutritional deficiencies. However, in practice, most people would not be able to tolerate such a diet and it would become monotonous. In terms of flavour, texture, and appeal, there is no substitute for fresh foods.

In a broad sense, most foods in the shops are convenience foods, as they have been made and prepared by a manufacturer to save the consumer time.

Some people object to processed and refined convenience foods on the grounds that they are not as nutritious as fresh foods and contain many additives which are not naturally found in foods. A sensible approach is to use both fresh and convenience foods in proportions that suit the individual in terms of money, time, likes, and dislikes.

There is no doubt that convenience foods have a place in modern eating habits and are likely to be developed further in the future.

Revision questions

1 What are convenience foods?
2 Why are they so popular?
3 Describe some different types of convenience food and give examples of each.
4 What are the advantages of convenience foods?
5 What are their disadvantages?
6 Why do some people object to convenience foods?

Further work with convenience foods

1 To assess the value of convenience foods to the consumer, prepare and cook a variety of convenience foods plus their home-made equivalents, e.g.:
bread mix
cake mix
scones
batters
soups
meat dishes, e.g. spaghetti bolognese
canned sauces
dried sauces
cold puddings
2 Compare the convenience foods and the home-made equivalents according to the following criteria:
total cost of ingredients
length of preparation and cooking time
processes required during preparation, e.g. whisking, creaming, beating
consistency and appearance before baking or cooking
appearance after cooking, e.g. size, volume, texture
flavour after cooking
additives used, e.g. preservatives
total amounts of ingredients used
keeping qualities before and after preparation
number of servings
versatility of mixture
3 Make constructive criticisms of the results and decide which foods are best value for money, most appetizing, and most useful to the consumer.

Fast food

'Fast food' has become increasingly popular in many countries, including the UK, and fast food outlets have grown rapidly in number and type. In 1989 UK consumers spent about £4 billion on fast food. The most popular types include:

sandwiches
burgers
fish and chips
pizzas
Chinese food
chicken and chips
Indian food

There is concern about the nutritional value of fast foods, particularly as many of the products have a high saturated fat and sugar content. Fast food companies are not required by law to declare the ingredients used in their products, so consumers cannot always be sure of what they are eating. For example, beef fat is commonly used for frying, but may not be declared. The fast food industry is also criticized over:

1   Loss of rain forest to grazing land for beef cattle for the burger companies.
2   The use of polystyrene containers which pollute the environment.
3   Litter pollution at take-away outlets.
4   The effect of fast food on the long-term health of young people.

Food packaging

Food is packaged for the following reasons:

1   For hygienic storage and transport.
2   To protect it from damage during storage and transport.
3   To give information to customers.
4   To attract customers.
5   For customers' convenience.

Strict rules of manufacture and hygiene must be followed for all packaging products. The manufacturer must choose a suitable packaging for each food, as some of the chemicals in packaging may migrate into food, e.g. plasticizers from cling film migrate into fatty foods.

New developments in packaging include:

1   Tamper-proof seals (e.g. for squash bottles, jam jars) to prevent the deliberate contamination of food.
2   Ring-pull cans (e.g. for pet foods, canned fish).
3   Easy-pour spouts (e.g. for cartons of fruit juice, milk).
4   Modified-atmosphere packaging (e.g. for ready meals, meat, fish, crisps). Food is sealed in an atmosphere of an inert gas such as carbon dioxide or nitrogen, which slows food spoilage reactions (including the growth of micro-organisms) because there is no oxygen present.
5   Vacuum packaging (e.g. for bacon rashers, ground coffee). The air is removed, so food spoilage reactions are slowed.

Recent developments in packaging include easy-pour spouts, ring-pull cans, tamper-proof seals, and vacuum packing.

Recycling

An enormous amount of household waste is produced each year (about 18 million tonnes in the UK) and much of it is packaging. Disposing of this waste is a major problem. In response to consumer and political pressure, many foods are packaged in recycled or recyclable materials, and many local authorities and some supermarkets have set up recycling centres.

Recycling centres take many different types of household waste for recycling.

Glass, cans, paper, fabric and some plastics can be recycled, and many carry a logo to indicate this.

Questions and activities

1 Study the graph below and answer the questions.

  a Which foods have shown an increase in consumption since 1971?

  b Which foods have shown a decrease in consumption since 1971?

  c What factors may have influenced the change in the consumption of each group of foods on the graph?

  d Find out about the National Food Survey and why its findings are useful to:

  health experts and nutritionists

  food manufacturers and retailers

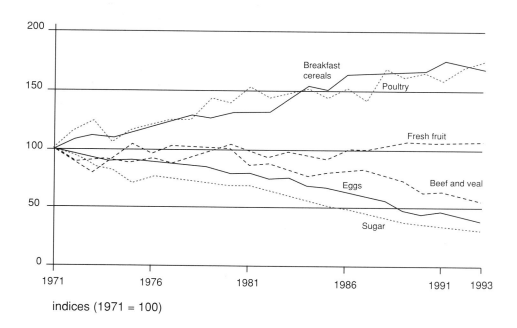

Changing patterns in the consumption of foods at home (Great Britain)

indices (1971 = 100)

2 Make a survey of fresh and processed foods in a supermarket, and list the ways in which the supermarket and the food manufacturer are encouraging the consumer to eat a more healthy diet. List the ways in which they help the following groups to select suitable foods:
    vegetarians
    religious and ethnic minorities
    people with food intolerance, e.g.
        coeliac disease

3 **a** What do the following mean:
    battery egg production
    free-range products (e.g. eggs, pork)
    organic produce
    intensive farming
  b Discuss each topic in class and list your opinions and comments about each.

4 Study the graph below:
  a Which types of convenience foods come into the group called 'other'?
  b Why has there been an increase in the consumption of frozen convenience foods?
  c Why has there been a decrease in the consumption of canned foods?
  d Which groups of people are likely to buy the most convenience foods? Why?

Consumption of convenience foods at home (Great Britain)
Ounces per person per week

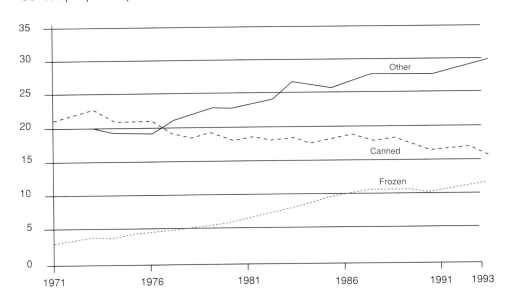

4 Practical food preparation

Principles behind the cooking of food

Heat

Heat is a form of energy, and is continually used in the home to:

cook food

heat water

heat rooms

In the body, some of the energy released from food during digestion is converted into heat to maintain body temperature.

Heat is produced when the molecules in a substance vibrate and move rapidly. The faster the movement, the more heat energy is produced.

Measurement of heat

The amount of heat energy produced is measured on a **temperature scale**, using a **thermometer**, which indicates the degree of heat.

Temperatures are normally measured on the **Celsius** scale. The **Fahrenheit** scale is also sometimes used.

Heat transfer

Heat energy can be transferred from one point to another. This is the underlying principle in the cooking of food: heat must pass from the cooker to the food at a suitable rate.

Heat flows from a **high** temperature to a **lower** one, until a **constant** temperature is reached (this process is reversible). Heat can be transferred by conduction, convection, and radiation.

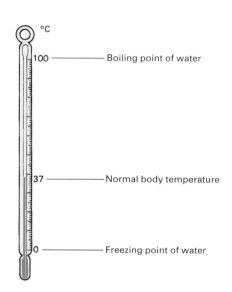

°C

100 ——— Boiling point of water

37 ——— Normal body temperature

0 ——— Freezing point of water

Conduction

If a metal spoon is placed in boiling water, its handle quickly becomes hot. This is because the molecules in the bowl of the spoon start vibrating rapidly as the heat energy from the surrounding water is transferred to them. As they vibrate, neighbouring molecules start to vibrate too, so the heat energy is transferred along the whole length of the spoon.

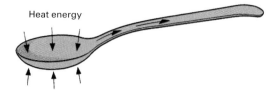

Heat energy

Heat is conducted at different rates through different substances.

Good conductors of heat conduct heat rapidly and efficiently, e.g. metals.

Poor conductors of heat (heat **insulators**) conduct heat slowly and inefficiently, e.g. glass, plastic, wood, cotton cloth, wool, still air.

Examples of conduction and insulation in food preparation

Ovens Insulated with glass fibre or a similar poor heat conductor to prevent heat loss.

Oven gloves Made of a thick insulating material to prevent heat conduction.

Pans Made of metals which are good conductors of heat. Copper can be welded to the base of a stainless steel pan to conduct heat rapidly (see p. 259).

Pan handles Made of an insulating material, e.g. plastic or wood, to prevent heat conduction.

Wooden spoon Poor conductor, so useful in the preparation of hot liquids.

Double-based cake tins Layer of air prevents rapid heat conduction and reduces risk of burning.

Oven-proof glass cooking utensils These are poor conductors of heat. This may affect cooking time and the finished result.

Cool boxes Insulation prevents heat entry into box, so useful for transporting frozen foods.

Food Some foods, e.g. meat, are poor conductors of heat and require a long time to cook. Metal skewers placed in a joint, or bones, help to conduct heat to the centre.

Frying, stewing, boiling Heat is mainly transferred by conduction in these methods.

Convection

Liquids and gases are poor conductors of heat but heat can be transferred rapidly through them by convection. As a liquid is heated, it expands and rises. Cooler liquid moves to take its place. The cooler liquid is heated in turn, and it then

rises. In this way, convection currents are set up, until a constant temperature is reached.

Exactly the same thing happens in gases. Heat energy is actually transferred by the movement of the gas or liquid molecules.

Examples of convection in food preparation

Cooking methods: Several cooking methods rely partly on convection for the transfer of heat.

1   Baking and roasting – movement of air molecules in the oven sets up convection currents.
2   Boiling, steaming – movement of liquid molecules sets up convection currents.

Foods Semi-liquid/solid mixtures, e.g. sauces, have slow convection currents because they are less fluid. If not stirred while heating, they burn at the base of the pan as the heat is not carried away fast enough.

Ovens In most gas and electric ovens, convection currents are set up from the heat source. This produces different zones of heat:

1   Middle shelf – corresponds to the thermostat setting.
2   Top shelf – hotter than the middle shelf.
3   Bottom shelf – cooler than the middle shelf.

Advantage can be taken of this to cook items requiring slightly different cooking temperatures at the same time.

Fan-assisted ovens have a heating element and a fan. The fan distributes hot air evenly throughout the oven, so the food cooks more quickly. It is not always necessary to pre-heat the oven, and most items are cooked at a lower temperature (see p. 277).

Radiation

In conduction and convection, heat energy is transferred from one place to another through a **medium**, which may be a gas, liquid, or solid. In radiation, heat energy can pass from one point to another without the aid of a medium. It passes through space or a vacuum.

This is possible because of the existence of **electromagnetic waves**. There are several types, including:

X-rays   light waves
heat rays   microwaves

Heat rays are called **infra-red rays**, and when they come into contact with an object, some of them are **absorbed** and are felt as heat, while others are **reflected**. The space between the object and the source of the heat rays is not heated.

Dull, black surfaces absorb and emit heat rays well, whereas white, shiny surfaces reflect and do not emit them well.

Examples of radiation in food preparation

Grilling Grilling relies partly on radiation to heat the food. Gas grills have radiants made of fire clay. Electric grills have heater elements with radiants or metal reflectors.

Roasting Roasting food on a spit relies partly on radiation.

Infra-red grills Infra-red grills have electrically heated wire elements, enclosed in a silica tube for protection. This method grills food efficiently and rapidly.

Microwave ovens Food can be cooked by microwaves, which are a form of radiation (see pp. 190–4).

Prevention of radiation

Vacuum flask No heat is conducted across the vacuum and heat rays are reflected off the silvered interior into the liquid.

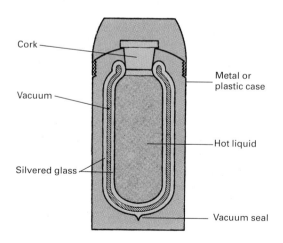

Cork

Metal or plastic case

Vacuum

Hot liquid

Silvered glass

Vacuum seal

Summary of heat transfer in the cooking of food

The different methods of cooking food each rely mainly on one method of heat transfer, although in some cases two or more transfers are involved:

Boiling an egg

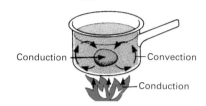

Conduction — Convection

Conduction

Grilling a chop (bone in)

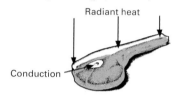

Radiant heat

Conduction

Roasting a rib of beef

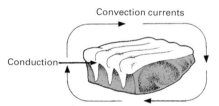

Convection currents

Conduction

Baking a cake

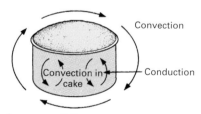

Convection

Convection in cake

Conduction

Steaming a pudding

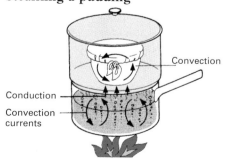

Convection

Conduction

Convection currents

Deep-frying fish

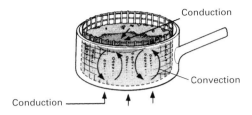

Heat transfer in a cooker

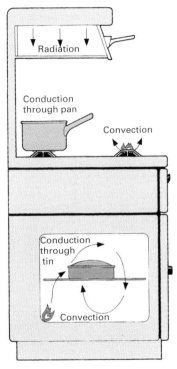

least 15 minutes to destroy the natural toxin they contain.

4   To aid digestion, e.g. the coagulation of egg protein enables it to be broken down efficiently by gastric enzymes.

5   To make it easier to eat, e.g. cooking meat tenderizes it, making it easier to chew and swallow.

6   To make the food more appetizing and attractive, e.g. cooked fish or offal is more appetizing than raw.

7   To enhance the flavour of food, e.g. roasting meat develops extractives which add to the flavour.

8   To give variety in the diet, e.g. potatoes can be fried, boiled, creamed, roasted; chicken can be casseroled, fried, roasted, boiled.

9   To reduce bulk, e.g. green leafy vegetables reduce considerably when cooked so that more can be eaten.

10   To provide hot food in cold climates.

11   Necessary for some processes, e.g. thickening of sauces, dissolving gelatine, preparation of cakes and biscuits.

Revision questions

1   What is heat and how is it produced?
2   Give five reasons why food should be cooked.
3   How can heat be transferred from one place to another?
4   Name three good and three poor conductors of heat.
5   Name the ways in which conduction is used in the kitchen.
6   How are convection currents set up in liquids?
7   Why is the top of the oven hotter than the bottom, and how can this be used to advantage when baking?
8   Why are fan-assisted ovens different from conventional ovens?
9   How do heat waves heat up objects?
10   How is heat transferred in the following?
   a   boiling an egg
   b   baking a cake
   c   deep-frying fish

Reasons for cooking food

Many foods can be eaten raw, but cooking is a highly developed art and science, with basic principles underlying the different methods. The main reasons for cooking food are:

1   To destroy or inactivate pathogenic (harmful) micro-organisms present in the food (see pp. 154-6).

2   To preserve the food from natural and microbiological decay (see pp. 154-9).

3   To destroy natural toxins (poisons) in foods; e.g. red kidney beans must be boiled for at

Food spoilage

Once food has been harvested, gathered, or slaughtered, it starts to deteriorate until eventually it becomes unfit for consumption. This deterioration is known as decay and leads to food spoilage.

Food spoilage is caused by two main factors:
1   Natural decay within the food itself.
2   Contamination by microscopic forms of life (micro-organisms).

Foods that spoil rapidly are known as **perishable foods** and usually contain relatively large amounts of water and nutrients. Examples are milk, fruit, and meat. Processed and cooked foods (e.g. frozen, canned, dried) are also easily susceptible once thawed, opened, or reconstituted. Foods that contain relatively low amounts of water or high concentrations of salt, acid, or sugar are less readily affected.

Natural decay

Natural decay in food is the result of:
    moisture loss
    the action of enzymes.

Moisture loss

Moisture loss is most easily demonstrated in vegetables and fruit, which contain large amounts of water. After harvesting, they continue to **respire**, i.e. their metabolic functions continue, and this results in loss of moisture through leaves and skins. Before harvesting, such water loss would be replaced from the soil through the roots, to retain the structure of the cells of the plant. After harvest, however, lost water is not replaced, and the vegetable or fruit shrinks and becomes limp, and its skin becomes wrinkled and 'leathery'.

As the carrot dries out, it becomes limp and wrinkled.

Moisture loss also occurs in other foods, (e.g. meat, fish, cheese), because of **evaporation** from the surface.

Action of enzymes (see pp. 33–4)

Many enzymes are present in foods, and some are inactive until a food is harvested or slaughtered. Once activated, such enzymes speed up the process of decay by breaking down the tissues and components of the food in different ways, including:

1   **Oxidation** Oxidase enzymes cause the destruction of certain nutrients, e.g. vitamin C, thiamin, and carotene. (Oxidation also occurs without enzymes, see p. 92).

2   **Browning** If some foods, e.g. apples, are cut or bruised, the damaged surface will discolour and turn brown due to the activity of enzymes.

3   **Ripening** Enzymes are involved in the process that causes ripening in foods such as fruits and vegetables, e.g. unripe bananas contain starch which is gradually converted to sugars, until the banana becomes very sweet, and its skin colour changes from green to yellow and eventually to dark brown.

Contamination by micro-organisms

Micro-organisms are microscopic plants or animals, many of which are single-celled. Microbiology is the study of such organisms.

The main micro-organisms responsible for the contamination of food are:
    bacteria
    moulds
    yeasts

Each group has many members (species) which are responsible for different forms of contamination. All three groups require a medium in which to grow and reproduce, and food is an ideal medium as it provides nutrients and moisture. Micro-organisms contaminate food by producing waste products or toxins (poisons), or simply make the food inedible by their presence. In some cases, eating contaminated food causes illness (food poisoning). Micro-organisms which cause food poisoning are called pathogenic (harmful) micro-organisms.

Not all micro-organisms are harmful, however. Some are used in the food industry to produce foods such as cheese, yogurt, and soy sauce.

Food poisoning and its prevention are discussed on pp. 157-8.

Bacteria

Bacteria are microscopic forms of life – as many as one million can fit on to a pin head. They are single-celled organisms and are found in many places including:

air	plants
water	animals (including humans)
soil	dust
sewage	food

There are many thousands of different species of bacteria, some of which are harmful to humans. They can be classified according to their shape:

Spherical bacteria are called **cocci**. They include:

streptococci (cause diseases such as scarlet fever and tonsillitis)

diplococci (cause pneumonia)

staphylococci (cause boils, septic wounds, and food poisoning)

Rod-shaped bacteria include:

bacilli (cause diseases such as diphtheria, tuberculosis, and food poisoning)

clostridia (cause food poisoning)

Spiral-shaped bacteria can cause diseases such as cholera, syphilis, and infectious jaundice.

Reproduction of bacteria

Under suitable conditions of temperature, moisture, and food supply, bacteria can reproduce (multiply) very rapidly. They reproduce by dividing into two, and in the space of 12 hours, under the right conditions, a single cell can give rise to 16 million others simply by dividing in this way.

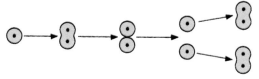

When a large number of bacteria are present in one place, they form a **colony**, which is usually visible to the naked eye.

If conditions for division are unfavourable, e.g. if moisture is lacking, then bacteria are able to form **spores** which remain dormant until the right conditions return, when the spores will germinate. Spores are often very resistant to heat.

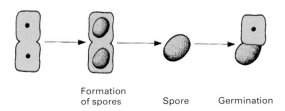

Formation of spores   Spore   Germination

Many bacteria do not require a source of oxygen to grow and multiply. They are called **anaerobic bacteria**, and they can grow in food and intestines, where oxygen supplies are limited. Some bacteria do require oxygen and are called **aerobic bacteria**.

The effect of heat on bacteria

Some bacteria can withstand extremes of temperature, but most are destroyed at around 60°C. Bacteria multiply most rapidly at around 37°C, and this has important implications for the preservation of food by heat (pp. 163-5). At very cold temperatures, most bacteria stop multiplying and become dormant until the temperature conditions become favourable again. This has important implications for the freezing and cold storage of foods and their use (pp. 166-9).

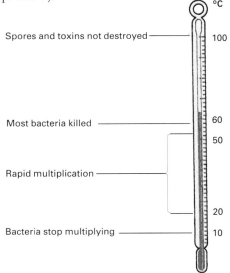

Other effects on the growth of bacteria

Many bacteria are affected by high concentrations of salt, acid, or sugar. These interfere with the normal life processes of the bacteria cells, and either destroy them or prevent reproduction. Such substances are used for food preservation (pp. 169–70). However, some bacteria thrive in such conditions and may therefore require different treatment to prevent their growth.

Contamination of food by bacteria

As bacteria are so small, it is often difficult to see when they are present in food. Also, the flavour, physical appearance, and smell of the food may remain unchanged, so it is easy to consume contaminated food without realizing it.

However, many species of bacteria cause food poisoning, often with serious outcomes, so it is important to know what causes food poisoning and how to prevent it:

1   **Physical presence of bacteria** If bacteria have been able to multiply in large numbers in a food, then their physical presence in the intestine may cause irritation and food poisoning symptoms.
2   **Production of waste products (toxins)** Bacteria, like all living things, have to dispose of waste products which are the result of metabolic processes. These can cause irritation to the intestine and food poisoning symptoms even when only a small number of bacteria are present. The toxins are not destroyed by normal cooking temperatures.
3   **Germination of spores** The germination of bacterial spores is usually accompanied by the production of highly poisonous substances (exotoxins). They can cause severe illness or death even in very small quantities. In some cases, just one spore can produce sufficient toxin to cause food poisoning.

Food poisoning

Bacteria can be transferred to food by several means, including:

1   Using the same utensils to serve contaminated food and other foods.
2   Careless attention to personal hygiene while handling food, e.g. not washing hands after visiting the toilet, touching nose while preparing food.
3   Leaving skin infections and cuts uncovered while preparing food.
4   Coughing, sneezing, or spitting while preparing food.
5   Incomplete cleansing of food utensils and serving dishes.
6   Pests, e.g. houseflies, cockroaches, beetles, certain moths.
7   Rodents, e.g. rats, mice.
8   Household pets, e.g. dogs, cats, hamsters.
9   Infected or diseased cattle and dairy cows.
10 Contaminated water supply.
11 Soil and dust.

Once bacteria have been transferred to a food, they will grow and multiply under the following conditions:

1   Incomplete thawing and cooking of certain foods, e.g. poultry, pork (see p.202).
2   Holding cooked foods, e.g. chicken, shellfish, at room temperature before serving.
3   Incomplete or repeated cooking of leftover food (see p. 204).
4   Careless storage of food.

In the UK, food poisoning is a notifiable disease, i.e. all cases should be reported by a general practitioner to the Local Health Authority, so that they can inspect food-serving premises and shops to identify the cause of the illness and prevent its recurrence.

Quite often, however, the symptoms of food poisoning are relatively mild and may not require medical attention. Such cases are not reported, so it is difficult to know how many cases there are each year. From the number of cases which are reported, however, it is clear that food poisoning is a widespread problem.

Government guidelines, which should be displayed in food shops, state:

Babies, elderly people, people recovering from illness, and pregnant women should never eat raw egg in any form. Eggs should be well cooked so that both white and yolk are solid. Pregnant women and people with a

Main causes of bacterial food poisoning

Bacteria type	Name	Illness Incubation	Duration	Symptoms	Sources	Notes
Cocci	*Staphylococcus aureus*	1–6 hrs	1–6 days	Severe vomiting, diarrhoea, exhaustion.	Nose, skin, cuts, sores, cooked meat, pies, custards, ice cream.	Poisoning due to toxins. Heat does not destroy toxin.
Bacilli	*Salmonella typhimurium*	12–48 hrs	7 days	Headache, fever, vomiting, abdominal pain.	Faeces, sliced or cooked meat, poultry, pies, sausages, eggs.	Main cause of poisioning in UK. Can be fatal.
Clostridia	*Clostridum botulinum* (botulism)	12–36 hrs	Fatal within 7 days	Double vision; difficulty with breathing, talking, and swallowing.	Improperly canned food, especially meat, vegetables.	Rare, but fatal in most cases. Exotoxin produced.
Clostridia	*Clostridium welchii*	8–24 hrs	1–2 days	Diarrhoea, abdominal pain, headache.	Meat pies, gravy, canned meat, soil.	Poisioning due to toxin from bacteria in gut.
Bacilli	*Salmonella typhi*	1–3 weeks	1–2 months	Headache, tiredness, fever, rash, haemorrhage.	Sewage, water, flies, cream cake, watercress, canned meat.	Can be fatal. Slow recovery.
Bacilli	*Bacillus cereus*	2–18 hrs	1–3 days	Vomiting, diarrhoea, abdominal pain.	Faeces, cold meats, gravy, cream, sausages.	Poisioning caused by bacteria in body.
Bacilli	*Campylobacter jejuni*	2–5 days	2–5 days	Profuse diarrhoea (blood stained), abdominal pain, nausea, exhaustion.	Unpasteurised milk, under-cooked poultry, raw meat.	A major cause of food poisioning in UK.
Bacilli	*Listeria monocytogenes*	5 days– 5 weeks	Varies	Like flu, still-birth, miscarriage, blood poisioning, pneumonia, meningitis.	Widespread in water, manure, soil, milk, milk products, soft cheeses, pâté, meat, poultry, prepared salads, cook/chill products.	Pregnant women, new-born babies, elderly and sick people, and diabetics at high risk. Often fatal. Poisioning due to toxin.
Bacilli	VTEC 0157	12–60 hours	Varies	Abdominal cramps, vomiting, diarrhoea.	Farm animals; under-cooked minced beef, beefburgers, untreated cow's milk and cheese; infected people; untreated water.	Can be fatal. Children and elderly at risk. Poisioning due to toxin.

low resistance to infection should avoid eating soft, ripened cheeses (e.g. Brie, blue-veined, Camembert), pâté, or under-heated cook-chill ready-made meals (see p. 56).

Reasons for the increase in the number of cases of food poisoning

1 More ready-prepared foods are eaten, e.g. meat pies, pasties, partly cooked breads.
2 More people eat out at restaurants, take-away shops, and hotels. Large-scale catering may result in outbreaks of food poisoning.
3 Increased importing of food, from countries where food hygiene laws may not be strictly enforced.
4 Increased importing of animal feeds, which may be contaminated and will infect the animals that eat them.
5 Insufficient training of staff who handle food.
6 Failure by consumers to store food correctly and use it by the recommended date.
7 Temperature too high in domestic freezer or refrigerator, leading to the growth of bacteria.

Moulds

Moulds are tiny plants, which are just visible to the naked eye. They grow on many types of food, especially cheese, bread, and fruit. They grow best in warm, moist conditions, but will grow at a slower rate in cool places.

Moulds reproduce by means of sporulation.

Moulds can grow easily on cheese, fruit, and bread.

Spores are released into the atmosphere and carried in the air. If they land on a suitable food, the spores germinate, and a new mould appears.

There are many types of mould, but among the more common are:

Pin mould (mucor)

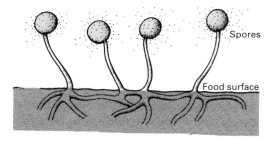

Spores

Food surface

Pencillium

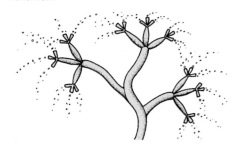

Food that is contaminated with mould often looks safe to eat as only the outer part is affected by mould growth. However, substances produced by the mould may migrate into the food and be harmful to many organs of the body. These substances are called mycotoxins. It is therefore advisable to discard mouldy food completely, rather than just to remove the mouldy part.

Mould growth is prevented by:
    cool, dry storage
    heating to destroy moulds and spores
    acidic conditions

Mould in cheese

Not all moulds are harmful. Specially produced moulds are added to certain cheeses, e.g. Stilton, Danish Blue, to develop characteristic flavours.

Yeasts

Yeasts are microscopic single-celled fungi, which are found in the air and soil, and on the surface of fruits. Some can tolerate fairly high acid, salt, and sugar concentrations, and can grow without the presence of oxygen.

Yeast cells reproduce by budding:

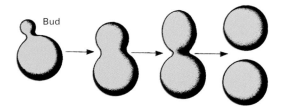

Yeast cell

In order to do this, they need a supply of water, warmth, and food (see p. 206). The cells remain dormant in very cold conditions, and are killed at temperatures approaching 100°C. Growth is inhibited by high salt concentrations.

Yeasts can spoil foods such as jam and fruits by fermenting the sugars, to produce alcohol and carbon dioxide gas. The time that this takes will depend on the concentration of sugar in the food and the length of time it is stored. Fruit-flavoured yogurts may also be affected in this way.

Food contamination from other sources

Food can become contaminated by other agents besides micro-organisms, e.g.

chemicals
radiation
pollution

Chemicals

Chemicals are used in modern food production for a variety of reasons. The aim is to obtain good supplies of high quality food.

1 **Insecticides, pesticides, fungicides, and weed killers** are used to protect crops from attack by various organisms and plants. Many of these chemicals are toxic, so their use is carefully controlled.
    To reduce the risk of harm to the consumer, chemicals are usually applied to the plants well before harvesting. However, traces are left on food and in the soil, and even found in the air and water supply. People are concerned about this, as it is not known what becomes of these

chemicals once they are in the body. Fruit and vegetables should be washed thoroughly before use. Use a dilute detergent as some of the sprays leave a greasy residue. Root vegetables such as carrots should be peeled.

2 **Antibiotics** are given to cattle, pigs, and sheep to prevent them from contracting diseases which would affect their health or their ability to produce. Antibiotics are carefully controlled, because bacteria can become immune to them if they are used too much. Traces of antibiotics in food can cause allergic reactions in some people.

Radiation

Nuclear power stations are carefully controlled, because if radioactive material was allowed to leak out, food and water supplies would become polluted. Radioactive materials are released into the atmosphere when nuclear weapons are tested, so efforts are being made to encourage all countries to stop testing.

Pollution

If industrial waste is poured into rivers and the sea, the chemicals and metals it contains are taken in by fish and other animals which drink the water. Food supplies can become polluted in this way. Attempts have been made to control industrial waste disposal, but it is still a problem in many countries.

Bovine spongiform encephalopathy (BSE)

This disease affects cattle, and there are fears that it could pass to humans through meat and meat products (see p. 120).

The Food Safety Act 1990

This act must be followed in all sectors of the food industry in the UK, including:

1 **Production** - farming, market gardening, fishing.
2 **Processing** –factories, bakeries, butchers, restaurants, cafés, canteens, roadside snack bars, self-employed small home businesses, burger bars, public houses, passenger ships, aircraft.
3 **Storage** - refrigeration units, warehouses, shipping companies.

4 **Distribution** – transport businesses, warehouses, shipping companies.

5 **Retail (sale)** – shops, markets, hypermarkets, mail order companies, farm shops, non-profit making organizations (charities), restaurants, cafés, self-employed caterers.

The Act covers:

food

sources of food (i.e. crops, animals)

drinks

slimming aids

food supplements (e.g. vitamin tablets)

water used in the food industry (but not the water supply, which has separate laws)

what comes into contact with food (e.g. packaging, cling film, machinery, cooking utensils)

sale of food at money raising events

Under the Food Safety Act, it is an offence:

1 To sell food which does not meet food safety requirements, i.e. food which could make people ill, because it is infected with bacteria or other micro-organisms (the Act does not cover allergic reactions to an ingredient), or food that is unfit to eat, e.g. because it contained a dead animal, a piece of glass, antibiotic residues.

2 To deliberately make food harmful by adding to it or removing something from it.

3 To sell food which is 'not of the nature, substance, or quality demanded by the purchaser' (i.e. the food must be exactly as described, and of good quality).

4 To mislead consumers deliberately by giving a false or exaggerated description of the food, e.g. picturing a gateau decorated with lots of strawberries and cream, when the actual item has 1 strawberry and 2 whirls of cream.

The Food Safety Act is enforced by:

Central government

1 Devises the laws, in conjunction with the EU.

2 Oversees the work of the local authorities.

3 Can make emergency control orders to remove a food or close down a part of the food industry if there is a risk to public health.

Local government (local authorities)

1 Responsible for enforcing the law in their own areas.

2 Trading standards officers deal with food labelling, composition, chemical contamination.

3 Environmental health officers deal with food hygiene, poisoning, contamination by micro-organisms, food that is unfit for human consumption.

Under the law, these officers can:

1 Enter premises (e.g. factory, shop, farm, market stall, kitchen, private home, lorry, take-away bar, or shop).

2 Inspect food and take samples for analysis.

3 Seize (remove) food they suspect is a problem.

4 Ask for the food to be condemned (judged as unfit to eat) by a judge, magistrate, or sheriff.

5 Require a business to improve its operation within a certain time. This may mean that part or all of the business must close (by court order) while improvements are made.

6 Require a business to close immediately (by court order) if there is an immediate danger to public health.

People who break the laws of the Food Safety Act may be fined or imprisoned, and may have to pay compensation to members of the public who have been affected by the offence.

People handling food in shops and restaurants must be trained in food hygiene and follow the hygiene rules.

Other requirements of the Food Safety Act are:
1 Premises used by food businesses on 5 or more days in 5 consecutive weeks, must be registered with the local authority, so that they can be inspected.
2 People handling food should be trained in food hygiene at the appropriate level for their job. Training courses are run by local authorities, colleges, and other institutions.

People who handle food must follow the hygiene rules:
1 Always wash your hands before handling food and after using the toilet.
2 Tell your boss at once of any skin, nose, throat, or bowel trouble.
3 Ensure cuts and sores are covered with waterproof dressings.
4 Keep yourself clean and wear clean clothing.
5 Do not smoke in a food room. It is illegal and dangerous. Never cough or sneeze over food.
6 Clean as you go. Keep all equipment and surfaces clean.
7 Prepare raw and cooked food in separate areas. Keep food covered and either refrigerated or piping hot.
8 Keep your hands off food as far as possible.
9 Ensure waste food is disposed of properly. Keep the lid on the dustbin and wash your hands after putting waste in it.
10 Tell your supervisor if you cannot follow the rules. Do not break the law.

Hygienic practices in the handling and preparation of food

The hygienic handling and preparation of food are of great importance in the prevention of food contamination and food poisoning. Catering establishments and retailing premises must obey the regulations of the Food Safety Act (see pp. 159–61).

In the home, it is the duty of the person handling the food to ensure that food is prepared as hygienically as possible. This can be achieved by following a few basic rules.

Personal hygiene
1 Before preparing food, tie hair back, wash hands, and scrub nails clean.
2 Always wash the hands after visiting the toilet.
3 Never cough, sneeze, spit, or smoke over the food.
4 Cover up skin infections, cuts, and grazes.
5 Wear a clean apron.
6 Do not lick fingers or spoons and then touch the food with them.

Food purchase
1 Buy food from clean, reputable shops, where the assistants handle the food hygienically, and the food is stored properly.
2 Check that there are no animals in food shops.
3 Check the date stamps on fresh foods.
4 Choose fresh foods wisely (see individual foods for factors affecting choice).
5 Be wary of fresh foods sold on market stalls – they should be covered to protect them from dust and flies.

Food storage at home
1 Store fresh foods in a cool place. Use them up fairly rapidly, and certainly within the time recommended on the label or pack.
2 Use up old stocks of dried and canned foods before new ones.
3 Cool left-over foods rapidly and eat within 24 hours (see p. 204).
4 Keep food protected from flies, pests, and rodents, by the use of muslin cloth, plastic film, or a food net.

Kitchen hygiene
1 Regularly wash and clean work surfaces, the cooker, and the floor.
2 Keep utensils clean and well stored when not in use.
3 Wipe up spills as they occur.
4 Do not allow pets to sit on work surfaces or to eat from utensils and dishes that will be used for humans; some animals carry viruses and bacteria which can be passed on to humans, especially young children whose resistance is not well developed.
5 Rinse out the dishcloth after use and leave to air so that it does not become stagnant. Immerse in diluted bleach or disinfectant regularly.

6 Do not use the dishcloth to wash the floor.

7 Use very hot water and a good detergent for washing dishes, so that all food traces are removed. Nylon brushes are useful for washing intricate pieces of equipment, e.g. cheese graters, bottle necks.

8 Sterilize infant feeding bottles carefully.

9 Make sure that frozen poultry, pork, cream, and fish are completely thawed before cooking, and then thoroughly cooked to destroy salmonella bacteria which may be present. Incomplete thawing and cooking will provide a suitable temperature for the growth and multiplication of such bacteria, and lead to food poisoning.

Waste disposal

1 Keep dustbins well away from the kitchen, in a cool, shaded position. Protect from flies, cats, and vermin by ensuring that food wastes are wrapped and the lid fits tightly.

2 Disinfect the dustbin regularly, especially in summer. Use a bin liner if possible.

3 Empty kitchen pedal bins every day, and wash out.

4 Keep nappy pails out of the kitchen; leave them in the bathroom. Wrap disposable nappies hygienically in plastic bags before disposal.

5 Do not allow the sink waste pipe to become clogged. Disinfect the sink regularly, to kill germs and prevent stagnation.

Experiments on food spoilage

Wear disposable plastic gloves while carrying out experiments, and wash hands with disinfectant afterwards. Only carry out experiments in a laboratory, not in a room where food is prepared.

1 Prepare several sterile agar plates with agar-agar broth (as directed by the manufacturer), and leave to set. Wipe swabs of sterile cotton wool over various surfaces and quickly smear over the agar jelly, without opening the lid of the plate for too long.
Alternatively, contaminate the plates with some of the following:

cough or sneeze	hands
dirty dishcloth	rubbish bin
sink plug	floor or bottom
dust	of a shoe
the air	soil
a house fly	top of a milk bottle

Cover the plates and label. Leave in a warm place for two days. Observe the results, and compare with an unused agar plate. *Destroy plates after use.*

2 Leave a piece of bread in the following conditions:
a a warm, moist, bread bin
b a refrigerator
c a dry warm place.
Observe and compare the growth of moulds on the bread.

3 Leave some carrots or other root vegetables in a sealed plastic bag at room temperature for four days, and observe the evaporation of water from the vegetable on to the plastic. Note the changes in the vegetable texture and appearance.

Revision questions

1 Where are bacteria found?
2 How do bacteria multiply, and what conditions do they require for this to take place?
3 How do bacteria cause food poisoning?
4 How are bacteria transferred to food?
5 How can bacteria be prevented from multiplying in food?
6 How do moulds reproduce, and what conditions do they require for growth?
7 How does food spoilage occur?
8 What are enzymes, and how do they cause food spoilage?
9 How can enzymes be made inactive?
10 What are pathogenic micro-organisms?
11 What are mycotoxins?
12 In what other ways can food become contaminated?
13 How does the Food Safety Act protect the consumer?
14 How can the consumer ensure that the kitchen and the food that is served are hygienic?

Preservation of food

Food is preserved to prevent natural and microbial decay, by modifying the conditions that favour enzyme activity and the growth of micro-organisms.

In the past, food was preserved to provide a store of food during winter, when there was no other source of food. Today, food is preserved for the following reasons:

1   To add variety to the diet, by making foods available out of season.
2   To make use of food when it is cheap and plentiful and to store it for later use.
3   To vary the diet by preserving food in ways that make a new product out of the food (e.g. pickling, jam making).

The aims of preservation

While preventing decay, preservation also aims to retain as many of the qualities of the fresh food as possible, e.g.:

flavour
texture
colour
appearance
nutritional value

Preservation also aims to prevent micro-organisms from contaminating the food once it is preserved, by sealing it from the outside air.

Methods of preservation

Food decay can be slowed by:

1   **Heating** to destroy micro-organisms and enzyme activity.
2   **Removal of moisture** to inhibit microbial growth.
3   **Removal of air** to prevent further entry of micro-organisms.
4   **Reduction of temperature** to inhibit microbial and enzymatic activity.
5   **Addition of a chemical preservative** to destroy or inhibit microbial and enzymatic activity.
6   **Irradiation**

Heat preservation

Most bacteria, yeasts, moulds, and enzymes are destroyed by heating at 100°C. However, some bacteria and bacterial spores are resistant to such temperatures and higher temperatures are required to destroy them.

Some bacterial toxins are resistant to heat, so that a food which is already contaminated with them may not be made safe to eat by heat treatment.

The main methods of heat treatment are:
sterilization
pasteurization
canning and bottling

Sterilization

At the beginning of the 19th century, a Frenchman, Nicolas Appert, discovered that if food was heated in a sealed container at a high temperature, it would remain edible and free from decay for some time, unless the seal was broken. This is because prolonged heating will destroy harmful micro-organisms, which are naturally present in the food, and the food will only start to decay when new organisms contaminate it.

Today, sterilization is a commonly used form of heat preservation. Since Appert's early attempts, the process has been much improved, and the flavour and colour of sterilized foods are not so greatly impaired as they used to be. In particular, the ultra heat treatment of milk (see pp. 101–2), which is now common, gives a much better product than the original sterilization process.

Uses of heat sterilization
Milk (see p.101).
Canned or bottled foods.

Effects on nutritive value
The heat-sensitive vitamins thiamin and vitamin C (ascorbic acid) are destroyed to a large extent.

Pasteurization

Another French scientist, Louis Pasteur, later discovered that less severe heat treatment than that used in sterilization could be effective in destroying pathogenic and souring microbes, without adversely affecting the appearance or flavour of a product.

This process, known as pasteurization, has been successfully developed, and many items are now treated in this way. However, as pasteurization only destroys the harmful microbes, the food will not keep for very long, as other naturally occurring microbes in the food will begin to cause decay.

Uses of pasteurization

Milk (see p. 101).
Milk products
Fruit juices
Liquid egg for bakery products
Vegetable juices
Beer
Vinegar
Wine

Canning and bottling

Today, canning is one of the most widely used methods of preservation. A huge variety of foods are canned and bottled, providing a safe and convenient method of preserving food.

Both methods rely on heat sterilization to destroy microbes and enzymes and sealing to prevent contamination during storage.

Cans

Modern cans are made of **steel** which is coated in a very thin layer of **tin**, and often lacquered to prevent corrosion.

The cans are first filled with food, then air is removed, and the cans are sealed. They are sterilized under pressure for a carefully calculated

Cans on a production line

length of time, and then removed and cooled. Most cans are cooled by water. They are then labelled and packed.

Many sizes and shapes of can are produced and some cans have aluminium ends for easy opening. Aluminium cans are expensive to produce, but they are used for some canned drinks. They have a ring-pull so are opened without a can opener.

All cans now carry a date stamp to show when they should be used by.

Uses of canning

Cans are used for the following products:

fruit	pâtés
milk	desserts
vegetables	soups
fish	pet foods
meat	coffee
nuts	sausages

complete meals (stews, curries, etc.)
meat pies and puddings
sponge puddings
pasta and pulses in sauce
alcoholic and non-alcoholic beverages

Using canned foods

Store in a cool, dry place, and rotate the stock so that old cans are used first. Do not buy rusty or 'blown' cans. Rust can weaken the metal and may create a small hole where bacteria can enter and contaminate the food. Blown cans indicate that bacteria are present, as they produce gas which distends the can. Dented tins should also be avoided as they may have tiny punctures in the metal, or damaged seams.

Once opened, canned food should be treated as fresh food and it will deteriorate. Left-overs should be removed from the can and put in a covered container in a cool place.

Bottling

The principles and methods of preservation for bottling food are similar to those used in canning. The glass used must be free from minute cracks which could allow bacteria to enter, and should be heat proof and strong enough to cope with transport and retail handling.

Glass is heavy and prone to breakage, so bottling is not used as much as canning.

Removal of moisture (dehydration)

Dehydration is a very old method of food preservation and there is evidence that it was used as long ago as 2000 BC.

Micro-organisms depend on water for growth and reproduction. Removing water from their cells relies on the process of osmosis. Osmosis is the movement of water from a dilute solution to a concentrated one, through a semi-permeable membrane. When water is removed from food by evaporation, the concentration of sugars and salts in the food increases. If there are any micro-organisms in the food, water will pass from their cells (a dilute solution) into the more concentrated solution surrounding them, and this dehydration will destroy them. Experiments with osmosis are given on p. 166).

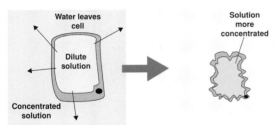

Cell placed in concentrated solution

Cell becomes dehydrated

Evaporation of water used to be achieved by leaving food to dry in the heat from the sun, but today it is carried out by passing carefully controlled warm air over food.

Dehydrating solid foods

Food is usually placed on large perforated trays, through which hot air is blown. This is called a **hot air bed**, and is carefully controlled. The product at the end will keep for up to a year quite satisfactorily.

Dehydrating liquid foods

Liquids are usually dried by **spray drying**, which is used for products such as milk and eggs. A fine spray of liquid is passed into a hot air chamber or tunnel, and the droplets dry almost instantly and drop to the bottom of the chamber. The moisture is removed before it settles. The temperature of the hot air is carefully controlled to prevent coagulation of the protein and alteration of flavour.

Another method of dehydration is **accelerated freeze drying**. The food is quick-frozen and tiny ice crystals are formed, which are rapidly removed by turning to vapour when the food is heated in a vacuum. There is less damage to the food structure and the water content is extremely low in foods dried by this method. Reconstitution is usually very good. This method is used for coffee, mashed potato, instant meals, etc.

Uses of dehydration

Milk
Coffee, tea
Fish, meat
Vegetables
Pulses (peas, beans, lentils)
Eggs
Soups, instant snacks and meals
Herbs

Using dried foods

Dried foods should be stored in a cool, dry place. Moisture in the atmosphere may be readily absorbed by some dried foods, e.g. coffee, milk, potato, and this will affect the keeping qualities.

Some dried foods must be packed in foil-lined containers to prevent rancidity (see p. 92) and oxidation from occurring.

Dried foods are very convenient as they are lightweight, take up little storage space, and can be stored for long periods as emergency foods.

Many different kinds of food can be dried.

Effect on nutritive value and flavour

The heat-sensitive vitamins, thiamin and vitamin C are the most affected, and they may be further destroyed when the food is reconstituted and cooked. Freeze-dried foods usually retain slightly more vitamin C than conventionally dried foods.

Flavour and texture changes may be noticeable in many dried foods, and the use of additional flavourings may help to improve this.

Experiments to demonstrate the action of osmosis

1   Place a piece of dried fruit (e.g. a prune, apricot, or raisin) in a bowl of water, and another in a bowl of sugar and water, and leave overnight.
    You will see that the fruit in the plain water has swollen, and that the other is still shrunken. This is because water has been absorbed into the first fruit by osmosis, whereas in the second fruit there has been little movement of water as the concentration inside the fruit is similar to the sugar and water solution.
2   Cut radishes into thin slices almost all the way through and place in water (see
    p. 226). Cut celery into thin strips and repeat.
    The cut parts will curl as the cells absorb water by osmosis.
3   Cut some potatoes into chips and soak them in salt and water before frying them. Some water will leave the potato cells by osmosis, and this will help the chips to remain crisp when they are fried.
4   Sprinkle some fresh strawberries with sugar two to three hours before serving and compare them with some others prepared in the same way just before serving.
    The first strawberries will become soft. This is because water leaves the strawberries by osmosis, forming a syrup with the sugar and leaving the fruit without a firm structure.

Removal of air

The removal of air from canned foods has already been discussed. Some foods can be temporarily preserved by **vacuum packaging** and **modified atmosphere packaging** (see p. 147). Cold meats, cheese, sausages, fish, etc. can be wrapped in an impermeable plastic film, and the air can be removed under a vacuum. This prevents the entry of micro-organisms until the seal is broken. Such foods are normally stored in a cool place and may have chemical preservatives added to them so that they keep for longer.

Vacuum packaging and modified atmosphere packaging both involve removing air from food. This helps to keep it fresh.

Reduction of temperature

When the temperature is reduced, the activities of most micro-organisms are slowed down, until they become dormant (inactive), and growth and multiplication cease. Some types are destroyed at low temperatures.

Once the temperature is raised, growth and multiplication of the micro-organisms that are not destroyed by low temperatures starts again.

Some micro-organisms are resistant to low temperatures, and can continue to multiply and remain active, although probably at a slower rate.

Refrigeration

As long ago as the mid-19th century, attempts were made to chill meat and other foods by packing them with ice, but this did not prove very successful. Domestic refrigerators were not available on a large scale in this country until the 1920s, but today most homes have one. More details on refrigerators and how they work are given in Chapter 5, pp. 253-4.

It is only possible to store foods for short periods in domestic refrigerators, which are normally set at 5°C. This is because at this temperature, microbial activity still takes place, although it is slowed down. Thus, food decay will still occur.

However, refrigerators are useful as they enable a few days' supply of fresh foods to be stored, reducing the need to shop every day.

The temperatures used in refrigerators are:

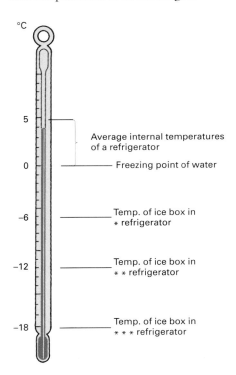

°C

Average internal temperatures of a refrigerator

Freezing point of water

Temp. of ice box in ∗ refrigerator

Temp. of ice box in ∗ ∗ refrigerator

Temp. of ice box in ∗ ∗ ∗ refrigerator

Foods to be kept in a refrigerator should be suitably wrapped before storage (see p. 254), and used up fairly quickly.

Foods that are purchased ready frozen can be stored in the freezer compartment of the refrigerator.

Follow the manufacturer's instructions on the maximum storage time. The star ratings on a refrigerator indicate the temperature of the freezer compartment and the length of time for which frozen foods can be stored.

Star rating	Temperature	Storage time
∗	–6°C	up to 1 week
∗∗	–12°C	up to 1 month
∗∗∗	–18°C	up to 3 months

Commercially frozen foods normally give this rating on the packet as a guide.

It is not possible or safe to attempt to deep-freeze food in a domestic refrigerator, as the temperatures are not low enough.

Many foods that are sold in the shops are held in refrigerated storage during transit or at a warehouse. This is done to preserve the quality of the food before it reaches the consumer. Some foods are stored at low temperatures in an atmosphere of carbon dioxide. This slows the growth of micro-organisms because they need oxygen to grow. Foods stored in this way include the following.

Eggs
If eggs are stored in normal air, carbon dioxide and water vapour are lost through the pores in the shell. This results in the white becoming thinner and deteriorating. In an atmosphere of carbon dioxide gas, this does not happen, and eggs can be stored in a cold atmosphere containing 60% carbon dioxide for up to nine months.

Meat
Beef can be kept in a cold place in an atmosphere of 10-15% carbon dioxide for up to ten weeks.

Some fruits and vegetables
Some fruits and vegetables continue to ripen (see p. 154), after they are harvested. This can be delayed if they are stored in carbon dioxide gas at a temperature of between 0°C and 3°C. This applies to, for example, apples and pears, and root vegetables such as carrots and turnips.

Freezing
The basic principles of refrigeration also apply to freezing, but as the temperatures are much lower

in freezing, food can be stored for much longer periods.

Deep-freezing is the reduction of temperature in a food to a point where not only does microbial activity cease, but the natural decay and deterioration of the food is halted for a considerable time.

The temperatures used in freezing are:

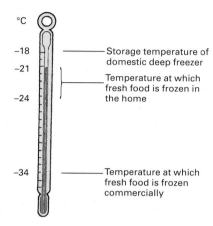

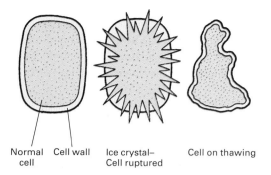

Normal cell   Cell wall   Ice crystal–Cell ruptured   Cell on thawing

Large ice crystals are formed in food if it is frozen too slowly. If food is **quick-frozen**, however, the ice crystals are formed rapidly, and are much smaller in size. They remain within the cells without rupturing them.

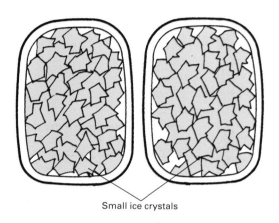

Small ice crystals

Many foods can be frozen successfully (see pp. 200–203 for more details), and freezer ownership has increased considerably in the last few years in most affluent countries. The advantages of this method of preservation, the types of appliance available, and the methods and rules for freezing foods are discussed on p. 200.

Principles involved in freezing

Most foods contain relatively large amounts of water. When a food is frozen, **ice crystals** are formed in it.

Foods such as fruit and vegetables, which are made up of many cells, can be damaged by the ice crystals, if they are too large. This is because the cells **rupture** if the ice crystal exceeds the size of the cell.

Once the food is thawed, its structure will collapse, releasing most of the liquid in it, because the cells no longer form the framework of the food.

Quick-freezing is defined as a drop in temperature from 0°C to -4°C in 30 minutes in the centre of a pack of food.

Using a home freezer

Most home freezers have a special section where food to be frozen should be placed, to ensure a rapid reduction in temperature, and less risk of structural damage by ice crystals. A switch for fast-freezing is used to lower the temperature. This should be operated two to three hours before the food is put in. During this time the temperature will fall to -24°C. The recommended amount of food to be frozen at one time will vary according to the freezer, and the manufacturer's instructions should be followed. The food should be put separately into the fast-freeze section, and the switch should be left on for 24 hours. The close contact of the food with the refrigerated plates will ensure rapid temperature reduction.

Commercial freezing

Food can be quick-frozen in several ways.

1 **A blast of very cold air**, which cools the food rapidly.

2 **Close contact with refrigerated plates**. The food is passed into a cabinet called a multi-plate freezer, and is rapidly frozen to -18°C.

3 **Immersion in a very cold liquid**, such as brine (salt and water solution) or liquid nitrogen. When liquid nitrogen is used, the process is known as **cryogenic freezing**. It is used for foods such as strawberries, which do not freeze well using conventional quick-freezing methods. Liquid nitrogen is extremely cold (it boils at -196°C) and food placed in or sprayed with it freezes instantaneously, with tiny ice crystals being formed.

Peas are frozen commercially in a freezing tunnel.

The effect of freezing on food

Low temperatures do not significantly affect the nutritional value of food, but thiamin and vitamin C may be destroyed when vegetables are blanched (briefly immersed in boiling water) before freezing.

If meat is frozen too slowly, some of its cells may rupture, and release nutrients into the liquid that drips from the meat when it thaws. In this way there may be losses of protein, thiamin, riboflavin,

and nicotinic acid, but these losses are unlikely to affect the nutritional value of the meat greatly.

Some flavours become weaker and some become stronger when food is frozen. This has implications for the preparation of cooked foods for the freezer (see pp. 201–2).

Addition of a chemical preservative

Substances called **preservatives** can be added to food to inhibit the action of enzymes, and either destroy or inactivate micro-organisms which may contaminate the food.

Preservatives such as vinegar, salt, sugar, and wood smoke have been used for many years for this purpose. Most chemical preservatives work by surrounding the microbial cells with a concentrated solution which draws water out of the cell by osmosis (see p. 165). This renders the cell inactive. Enzyme activity is also affected by the presence of high concentrations of salt, acid, sugar, etc.

The use of chemical preservatives in manufactured foods is strictly controlled. A permitted list of such chemicals is issued, and no other chemical may be used. Stringent safety tests are carried out on preservatives, to determine the maximum permitted amounts for use in food.

There are many different chemical preservatives in use. The more common ones are given below.

Antioxidants

These are put into foods for various purposes.

1 To prevent fat rancidity (see p. 92).

2 To prevent destruction of vitamins A and C.

3 To prevent the browning of food by enzymes (see p. 154).

Some foods contain natural antioxidants, (e.g. vitamin E is an antioxidant), but these are not usually present in sufficient amounts to be effective.

Antioxidants are added to the following types of foods:

oils and fats

baked goods containing fat, e.g. cakes and biscuits

apples and pears

dried foods such as milk and meat

Sodium chloride (common salt)

Salt is an effective preservative. It not only prevents food decay, but also adds flavour and nutritional value to the food. Many foods have salt added or are preserved in salt, including:

cheese
sausages
dried fish
canned vegetables (in brine)
bacon

Acids

Some acids are used as preservatives, including:

ethanoic acid (vinegar)
citric acid
lactic acid
tartaric acid

The acidity of a substance is measured by its pH value on a scale of 1 to 14. Substances that have a pH value of 1 to 6 are acidic, 1 being the strongest acid and 6 the weakest; those that have a pH value of 7 (such as water) are neutral; and those that have a pH value of 8 to 14 are alkaline, 8 being the weakest and 14 the strongest alkali.

Acids that are used for preserving, such as vinegar for pickling, are usually fairly strong (about pH 2-3), and are therefore suitable for preserving less acid foods. Some foods are naturally acidic, and can be preserved by other methods. These include:

lemon juice	pH 2.4
apples	pH 3.0
rhubarb	pH 3.1
pineapple	pH 3.7
tomatoes	pH 4.2

Most bacteria only grow well at pH 7. Yeasts grow well at pH 4-4.5, and some moulds can grow at pH 2, so the strength of an acid used to preserve a food has to be adjusted according to the type of micro-organisms that normally contaminate it.

Nitrates and nitrites

These are added to ham, pickled meats, and bacon, to preserve them and to improve the colour of cured meat.

Sulphur dioxide

Sulphur dioxide is a commonly used preservative for many foods, including:

beer
fruit for jam making
flour for biscuits
fruit juices
pickles
sauces
sausages
soft drinks
tomato puree
dehydrated vegetables

When dissolved in water, sulphur dioxide forms sulphurous acid, which accounts for its preservative action. It also prevents both the oxidation of vitamin C and enzymatic browning.

Sugar

Sugar is an effective preservative and adds flavour and energy value to food. It is used to preserve many foods, including:

fruit in jam making (see pp. 171-4)
canned and bottled fruit
dried fruit (naturally present)

Irradiation

Ionizing radiation can kill micro-organisms, so it can be used to preserve food. When food is irradiated, energy passes through it and kills harmful bacteria. The energy is similar to ultraviolet light. It does not make the food radioactive.

Two levels of radiation are used:

Low dose will stop vegetables (e.g. potatoes) sprouting; prevent insect damage to cereals, pulses, spices, etc.; destroy parasites (e.g. tapeworm in pork); delay the ripening of fruits (e.g. bananas, mangoes); and allow longer storage of foods such as shellfish and strawberries.

Medium dose will kill most spoilage and harmful bacteria, moulds, and yeast, and will enhance the storage of some foods.

There is concern that some nutrients may be lost when food is irradiated. Also, although the food may look fresh, chemical and enzyme changes may continue, so the consumer may be buying an inferior product.

This internationally recognized symbol can be used to label irradiated foods. Regulations to control the processing, sale, and labelling of irradiated foods are being established in the UK and other countries.

This symbol shows that food has been irradiated.

Revision questions

1 Why is food preserved?
2 How does heating preserve food?
3 How should canned, dehydrated, and sterilized food be stored?
4 Describe the following and give examples of foods treated by these processes:
   a sterilization
   b pasteurization
   c canning
5 How does dehydration affect micro-organisms?
6 What are the effects on the nutritive value of food when it is preserved by:
   a dehydrating
   b heating
7 What chemical preservatives can be added to food?
8 What is osmosis? Why is it important in the chemical preservation of food?
9 What are the principles behind the freezing of food?
10 Why is it necessary to quick-freeze foods?
11 Why are refrigerators used only for the temporary storage of food?
12 What is food irradiation?

Home preservation of fruit

Jam making

Jam is prepared by boiling fruit with a sugar solution until it forms a 'gel' which sets on cooling.

In order for a gel to form, the jam should contain:
   pectin
   acid
   sugar
and it is important that these are present in the right concentrations.

Pectin

Pectin is a polysaccharide (see p. 10). During jam making, its molecules form a three-dimensional network (which is the framework of the gel) with the water, sugar, and solid matter from the fruit.

Pectin will not form a satisfactory gel until the pH (see p. 170) of the mixture is about 3.5 (acidic). It is found in the cell walls of fruits and vegetables. The amount present depends on the type of fruit and its age. Unripe fruit contains more acid and pectin (which is released during the stewing of the fruit). Over-ripe fruit contains pectin which has been converted into a form which is unable to form a gel.

Acid

Acid is needed to extract the pectin from the fruit during stewing, and fruits that have a high pectin content are normally acidic. Acid also improves the colour and flavour of the jam, and prevents the sugar from forming crystals during storage.

Sugar

Sugar is added as a preservative (see pp. 169–70), and to form the gel. It must be accurately measured, as too much will cause crystallization of the sugar, and too little will prevent proper setting and will encourage fermentation to take place. The sugar should be about 60% of the total finished weight of the jam.

Preserving sugar is specially made for this purpose. It is composed of large crystals which are purer than ordinary granulated sugar, and so cause less scum to form during boiling. Some brands have added pectin. Granulated sugar is an acceptable alternative, however, and is cheaper.

Choice of fruit

The fruit used for jam making should be:
slightly under-ripe
free from blemishes and mould growth
clean

Fruits rich in pectin
cooking apples
damsons
gooseberries
bitter oranges
lemons
blackcurrants
redcurrants

Fruits with a good pectin content
blackberries
plums
apricots
raspberries

Fruits with a poor pectin content
strawberries
cherries
pears

In order to make a successful jam from fruits with a poor pectin content, other fruits that are rich in pectin can be added, or a commercially prepared pectin concentrate can be used.

Proportions of ingredients required

Fruits with a rich pectin content

575 g sugar	Expected yield of jam:
450 g fruit	950 g
150 ml water	

Fruits with a good pectin content

450 g sugar	Expected yield of jam:
450 g fruit	750 g
150 ml water	

Fruits with a poor pectin content

350 g sugar	Expected yield of jam:
450 g fruit	575 g
20 ml lemon juice	
No water	

Equipment required for jam making

Pan A large, thick-based pan should be used, to allow space for the boiling mixture to rise, and to prevent the jam from burning on the base. Special preserving pans are most suitable, and they normally have a large handle and lip for easy pouring.

Wooden spoon, with a long handle, for easy stirring.

Measuring jug A heat-proof jug should be used for transferring the jam to the jars.

Jars Empty, used jars are suitable, providing that they have no cracks or chips in them. They must be well cleaned, and warmed in the oven before use, so that they do not crack when the hot jam is put into them.

Jam jar covers can be bought in different sizes, and consist of:
1   Small waxed circles of paper, which are placed, waxed side down, on to the hot jam. The wax melts, and forms an airtight seal over the jam, to prevent mould growth.
2   Larger cellophane circles which fit over the neck of the jar, and are kept in place with a rubber band. They are placed over the jar while the jam is hot, and on cooling, they shrink to form a second seal over the jam.

Equipment to test for setting A sugar thermometer, a cold plate or saucer, or both.

Equipment to test for pectin Two glasses, methylated spirits.

Labels Self-adhesive labels are best, and should indicate the contents of the jar and the date of preparation.

Method
1   Wash the fruit, and remove bruised or over-ripe pieces. Dry it.
2   Prepare the fruit:
remove stalks and leaves,
remove stones or cores,
chop the fruit as required.
The stones of plums, apricots, etc., can be included while the fruit is being stewed as they usually have some pectin in and around them. They should be removed at the end of the stewing process.

3 Grease the preserving pan with margarine or butter, to prevent the fruit from sticking and to reduce the amount of scum produced when the jam is boiled.

4 Add the water (if included) to the fruit and simmer until the fruit is very tender. This stage is important, as the pectin is extracted from the fruit with the help of the acid which is either added or is already present in the fruit.
Fruits that are rich in pectin have water added to soften them properly, and to prevent the jam from setting too hard because of the high pectin content.
Fruits that have a good pectin content have water added to soften them, and it should all evaporate at this stage.
Fruits which have a poor pectin content have lemon juice added to assist the extraction of the pectin that is present.
The amount of time required for stewing at this stage varies:
Soft fruits (raspberries, strawberries, etc.) need up to 20 minutes.
Apricots, plums, and similar fruit need up to 30 minutes.
Hard fruits with tough skins (blackcurrants, oranges, etc.) need between 40 minutes and 3 hours.

5 After stewing the fruit, test it for pectin. Cool some of the fruit and juice for a few minutes, in a glass. Add three parts methylated spirit to one part of the fruit liquid, and leave for one minute. Gently pour this into another glass, and observe its consistency.
A high pectin content is indicated by the liquid forming one large clot with the methylated spirit.
A medium pectin content is indicated by the liquid forming several smaller, firm clots with the methylated spirit.
A poor pectin content is indicated by the liquid forming small, thin clots with the methylated spirit.

6 If the pectin content is poor, the fruit may be stewed for longer, and retested, or fruit with a high pectin content can be added, but this must have been stewed separately first.

7 Whilst the fruit is stewing, wash the jars well and warm them in the oven so that they are completely dry and ready to take the hot jam.

8 Add the sugar all at once. It can be prewarmed in the oven to make it dissolve more quickly. Stir it over a gentle heat until dissolved.
If the sugar is added before the fruit has been sufficiently stewed and softened, it will cause the skin to become tough.

9 Bring the mixture to the boil quickly, and stir it occasionally. Boil rapidly to reach setting point quickly, and thus prevent the spoilage of flavour and colour by overcooking.
Remove any scum that appears on the surface with a draining spoon.
When testing for setting point, remove the pan from the heat to prevent overcooking, which will result in a hard jam.

To test for setting point:
Temperature When jam is at setting point, it should reach 105°C. This can be checked with a sugar thermometer, which should be kept in a pan of boiling water, so that it is ready to take a reading.
Wrinkle test Have a cold plate or saucer ready. Place a little of the jam on it and leave to cool. Push the jam with the finger; if it wrinkles, the jam has reached setting point.
Flake test Dip a clean, dry, wooden spoon into the jam. Allow it to cool slightly, then let the jam run gently over the side of the spoon. If it comes off in wide flakes it is ready; if it pours off in a thin trickle, it needs more boiling.

10 When setting point is reached, pour into the hot jars, fill to the top, seal, and cover while still hot, and leave the jam to cool and set at room temperature. Label when cool, wiping the jars if necessary.

Qualities of a good jam

Well-made jam should have the following qualities:

a good flavour

a bright colour

a clear appearance

evenly distributed fruit

a firm, but easy-to-spread texture.

Storing jam

Jam should be stored in a cool, dry, dark place. Screw-on lids can be used as an extra seal. If the jam is stored in warm, moist conditions, the growth of moulds will be encouraged.

Faults in jam making

Jam has crystallized

Causes

1   Insufficient boiling of jam.
2   Overcooking of jam.
3   Too much sugar used.
4   Insufficient acid in the mixture.

Jam has mould growing on top

Causes

1   Incorrect storage.
2   Poor quality or over-ripe fruit was used.
3   Insufficient sugar used.
4   Incorrect filling of jar and sealing, resulting in a layer of air at the surface of the jam.

Jam has fermented

Causes

1   Insufficient boiling of jam, so that it does not set properly.
2   Insufficient sugar used.
3   Poor quality fruit used.

Jam has not set

Cause

Insufficient pectin or acid. The jam may need reboiling, or the addition of more acid or commercial pectin. Reboiling should be carried out with care to avoid spoiling the flavour of the jam.

Fruit is tough

Causes

1   Insufficient stewing.
2   Sugar added too soon.

Marmalade making

Marmalade making is similar to jam making in most respects, except that in the first stage of extracting the pectin from the fruit, a longer stewing time and more water are required. The fruit can be pressure cooked in the first stage, to save time.

> 450 g fruit
> 1150 ml water
> 900 g sugar

Suitable fruits

lemons

limes

oranges – Seville oranges are best for flavour

grapefruit

tangerines

Oranges, grapefruits, and tangerines usually require additional acid from lemons or limes (citric acid), so that they form a proper gel.

Preparation of the fruit

The skins of the citrus fruit should be shredded coarsely or finely, depending on the required texture of the finished result, and the pith and pips should be separated and placed in a muslin bag which can be removed after stewing the fruit.

The skins must be stewed until very tender, otherwise they will spoil the finished result.

A large, heavy-based pan is suitable for making preserves.

Choosing, preparing, and cooking food

Choosing, preparing, and cooking food is a worldwide activity, and a highly prized skill in many communities. Many people find it creative, enjoyable, satisfying, and an important part of their lives.

Changes in the pattern of working, leisure, and meal times and the development and popularity of ready-made convenience and fast foods have contributed to a decline in home cooking. Appetizing, economical, nutritious, and satisfying meals can be prepared at home by most people, with a little imagination, experimentation, and the confidence that comes from practising.

Using recipes

Most recipes are developed around basic or foundation recipes, which use a set of main ingredients in particular proportions, and prepared in a certain way. They can be used for more than one dish by varying or adding other ingredients or flavours. For any recipe, it is important to:

1 Weigh and measure ingredients (dry and liquid) accurately.

2 Vary ingredients that are added for flavour, e.g. herbs, spices, seasoning, garlic, stock.

3 Avoid combining too many flavours which might be confusing and spoil the effect.

4 Follow the method of preparation carefully.

Measurements

From October 1995, UK Government regulations have required food manufacturers and retailers to use the metric system of measurements for weight, size, and volume. Certain goods, e.g. fruit and vegetables sold loose, can be sold in imperial measures until the year 2,000.

A chart of measurements is on p. 277. It includes cup and spoon measurements which are often used in recipes.

Adapting and changing recipes

Many recipes can be adapted by reducing or omitting an ingredient, or substituting one or more ingredients for another. This may be necessary because:

1 A particular ingredient is not available.

2 The cost needs to be reduced.

3 It needs to be adapted to suit someone on a special diet, e.g. low fat, high fibre, low salt.

4 It needs to be adapted to suit a vegetarian, Hindu, Muslim, Jew, etc.

5 It needs to be prepared and cooked in less time.

Adaptations may produce a slightly different result, e.g. using wholemeal flour in a cake may reduce its finished volume.

Although a particular recipe may contain a large proportion of fat or sugar, its effect on the daily intake of fat, sugar, and other nutrients depends on how much is eaten, and how often.

Adapting recipes makes meals more interesting and develops the cook's confidence. Recipes can be served or used in different ways from the one described in a book, for example:

Spaghetti bolognese sauce Use for shepherd's pie, lasagne, pasties; add curry spices; add beans.

Macaroni cheese Use the sauce for a vegetable crumble, vegetable flan, poured over cooked chicken joints, with cooked leeks or mushrooms.

Tomato/onion pizza topping Mix with cooked spaghetti and sprinkle cheese on top (add mushrooms, ham, pineapple, salami, pepper, etc. as optional extras); spread on sliced bap rolls, top with cheese, and grill; add cooked sausages, herbs, cooked peas, and baked beans, and serve with pasta shells or jacket potatoes for a main meal.

Lemon meringue pie Carefully mix together whipped meringue and cooked lemon filling and chill in small dishes; make small tartlets instead of a large pie.

Vegetable curry Serve in pasties; cold in a chilled rice ring; in vol au vents (hot or cold); as a filling for jacket potatoes.

Methods of cooking

The preparation of many foods involves the application of heat (cooking) in a certain way, for the reasons given on p. 153.

The choice of cooking method to be used will be influenced by:

1   The food to be cooked.
2   The amount of preparation required.
3   The facilities available: fuel, storage, equipment, etc.
4   The time available.
5   The needs of the individual being catered for, e.g. state of health, age.
6   Individual preference.

Methods of cooking can be classified according to how heat is applied:

Moist methods: heat applied through the medium of a liquid.

Dry methods: heat applied directly to food.

Frying: heat applied through the medium of fats or oils.

Microwave: heat generated by electromagnetic waves.

Moist methods of cooking

Relatively low temperatures are used, which may prolong the cooking time of some foods. The liquid medium may be water, steam, stock, milk, fruit juice, wine, or beer.

Effects on the nutrient content of food

Starch is softened and made more digestible. The **water-soluble vitamins** (B complex and C) are the most significantly affected by:

1   **Leaching** or diffusion into cooking water, especially in boiling. Some mineral elements may also be affected. As the amount of liquid used increases, more water-soluble nutrients will diffuse out of the food and into the liquid.
2   **Oxidation** Vitamin C is destroyed by heat in the presence of oxygen.
3   **Oxidation by enzymes (oxidases)** The presence of oxygen in water encourages the destruction of vitamin C by oxidases. This effect can be reduced by putting food into boiling water, which inactivates the oxidases.
4   **Prolonged cooking and keeping food hot** encourages heat destruction of vitamin C and thiamin.
5   **Preparation for cooking** Slicing, shredding, or chopping vegetables increases their surface area. This leads to a greater loss of water-soluble vitamins by leaching and releases more oxidase enzymes. Vegetables should therefore be chopped quickly with a sharp knife or torn into pieces just before cooking to avoid too much damage to the tissues and the release of enzymes. (See preparation of vegetables, p. 134.)

Boiling

Boiling is a common method of cooking. The liquid (usually water) is heated to boiling point and the heat is then lowered until the liquid is bubbling evenly and rapidly. This is used for rice, pasta, etc.

Simmering Foods that are cooked in hot water but require gentler treatment than boiling to prevent toughening (e.g. fish, meat), or to prevent the food breaking up (e.g. potatoes) should be simmered.

When a liquid is simmering, few bubbles rise to the surface, and the temperature is just below boiling point.

Advantages

1 The transfer of heat by convection is fairly rapid and efficient.
2 Water is readily available.
3 Food is unlikely to burn, though it may disintegrate if overcooked.

Disadvantages

1 Nutrient loss may be high.
2 Soluble matter may be lost into the liquid.
3 Some flavour is lost from meat.

The disadvantages can be partly overcome by serving the cooking water as gravy, sauce, or stock with the meal.

Suitable foods

Most vegetables
Muscular cuts of meat:
    lamb – middle neck
    beef – brisket (salted), silverside
        (salted), oxtail
    pork – knuckle, ham
Eggs
Pasta, rice, cereals
Fish

Poaching

Poaching is the cooking of food in water at just below the temperature used for simmering. It is therefore a very gentle method of cooking.

The water should only come half way up the food, and the heat should be applied slowly until the right temperature is reached.

Suitable foods

Foods containing protein which would become tough or curdled at higher temperatures, e.g. eggs, fish.

Par-boiling

Par-boiling is the part-cooking of certain foods which are then cooked by another method, e.g. potatoes and parsnips can be par-boiled before being baked (roasted) in fat in the oven.

Par-boiling quickly softens the outside of the food and reduces the amount of time needed for baking.

The food should be placed in boiling water and simmered for five to ten minutes or until the outside is soft. It should then be drained and cooked as desired.

Steaming

Food that is steamed does not come into direct contact with the water, but is cooked in the steam rising from boiling water. Steaming can be carried out in a variety of ways:

1   **Plate method**, e.g. for fish.

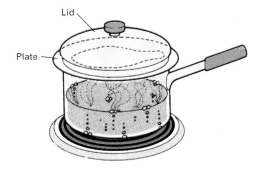

2   **Saucepan method**, e.g. for puddings.

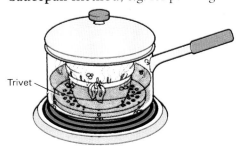

3 Tiered steamer, e.g. for cooking a whole meal.

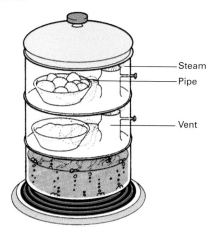

Steam
Pipe
Vent

4 Stepped steamer, e.g. for puddings.

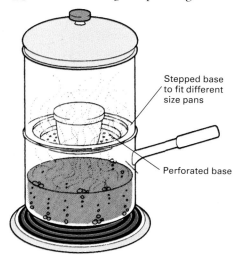

Stepped base to fit different size pans

Perforated base

5 Electric steamers and rice cookers are also available.

Fuel economy

Steaming food is economical on fuel if a small item or whole meal is being prepared in this way. However, food that requires several hours' steaming, e.g. Christmas puddings, is not very economical.

Points to remember when steaming

1 Cover the food with a waterproof lid or wrapping, to prevent condensed water vapour from spoiling the finished result. Steamed puddings rise, so a pleat should be made in the covering to allow for this.

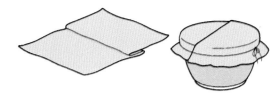

Some pudding basins (plastic) are specially designed to withstand boiling water and have domed lids to allow for the rising of flour mixtures.

2 Keep a kettle of boiling water nearby to replenish the steamer when the water evaporates.
3 Allow water to come to the boil before placing food in the steamer, and ensure that a steady flow of steam is produced.
4 Stand well back when removing the lid of the steamer, to prevent scalding.

Advantages

1 Loss of nutrients by leaching is reduced as the food does not come into direct contact with the water.
2 Food cooked in this way is easy to digest and has a light texture. This is therefore a suitable method to use for convalescent cookery (see pp. 66–7).
3 Little attention is required while the food is cooking, except to replenish the water supply.
4 Food is unlikely to be overcooked.

Disadvantages

1 Food takes a long time to cook, so the heat destruction of vitamin C is more likely to occur.
2 Even with a well-fitting lid, the kitchen is likely to be filled with moisture and so should be well ventilated.

Suitable foods

Puddings – suet, sponge, meat
Fish
Potatoes and other vegetables

Pressure cookery

At normal atmospheric pressure, water boils at 100°C. But if the pressure is increased, the water will boil at a higher temperature. This forces steam through food so that it cooks more rapidly and saves energy.

Types of pressure cooker

Most pressure cookers are made of aluminium, which is thicker than an ordinary pan. It is possible to buy stainless steel pressure cookers, but these tend to be more expensive. All pressure cookers have the following features:

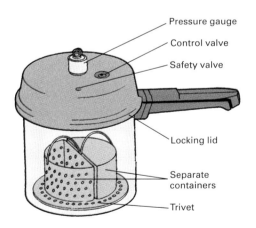

Pressure gauge
Control valve
Safety valve
Locking lid
Separate containers
Trivet

Safety valve

If the pressure becomes too great inside the cooker (e.g. if the control valve becomes blocked), then it will be released through the safety valve which will either be pushed out or melt. This should not happen if the cooker is used properly and the control valve is kept clear.

Pressure gauge

This is fitted over the control valve and either has separate weights which allow different pressures to be built up (see below) or has a central pin which rises as pressure builds up and indicates this by means of marks.

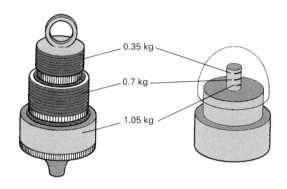

0.35 kg
0.7 kg
1.05 kg

Pressure	Boiling point of water
Normal atmospheric plus:	100°C
Low 0.35 kg/sq cm	107°C
Medium 0.7 kg/sq cm	112°C
High 1.05 kg/sq cm	120°C

Locking lid and rubber seal (gasket)

These prevent steam escaping from the rim of the cooker so that pressure will build up inside. The locking lid is also for safety purposes, as it cannot be opened when under pressure.

Control valve

This allows a small amount of steam to escape to prevent too much pressure building up inside the pan.

Trivet

This allows food, e.g. chicken, to stand in the steam but not in direct contact with the base of the pan.

Separate containers

These can be used to cook different types of food at the same time, e.g. vegetables.

Pan type

This has a slightly domed lid and can be used to cook most foods, except large puddings and poultry.

High-domed type

This has a larger capacity, and can be used for pot-roasting a joint with vegetables or for other large foods.

Automatic type

These have a timer which is set according to how long the food is to be cooked, and releases the steam automatically once cooking is completed. There is also an alarm to indicate that the heat should be turned off.

A pressure cooker

Points to remember when using a pressure cooker

1 A minimum of 250 ml water should be used to ensure that sufficient steam builds up inside the cooker.
2 The cooker should be no more than two-thirds full with solid foods (meat, puddings, etc.) and no more than half full with liquids. Exceeding these amounts may result in the control valve being blocked.
3 Lock the lid in position and heat the cooker *without* the pressure gauge in position, until the water has boiled and steam is escaping. This ensures that all the air in the cooker is expelled. Any air left inside will affect the cooking temperature and may cause discoloration of some vegetables (e.g. potatoes), due to oxidation.

4 Once a steady jet of steam is coming from the control valve, place the pressure gauge in position and allow pressure to build up to the desired level. A steady hissing sound indicates that pressure has built up.
5 Lower the heat to maintain the desired pressure and cook for the correct time. Timing should start when the pressure has been reached.
6 When cooking time is completed, turn off the heat and allow the pressure to fall, either by leaving the cooker at room temperature or by pouring a gentle stream of cold water over it.

Never attempt to open the lid or remove the pressure gauge before the pressure has fallen to normal.

Examples of cooking time and pressure

Manufacturers usually supply a recipe leaflet with the cooker and their instructions should be followed carefully. The examples below are a guide:

Food	Pressure	Cooking time
Beef casserole	high	20 minutes
Brisket of beef (1 kg weight)	high	60 minutes
Steak & kidney pudding	medium	60 minutes
Potatoes	high	5 minutes
Carrots	high	5 minutes
Crème caramel (individual)	high	3 minutes

Sponge puddings should be given ten to fifteen minutes cooking time at normal pressure to allow them to rise properly and should then be cooked at medium or low pressure for the stated length of time.

Advantages

1 Economical on fuel.
2 Meals can be prepared quickly.
3 Nutrient loss by leaching is reduced, though heat destruction still occurs.

4 Whole meals can be cooked in one pan.

5 Tough cuts of meat can be cooked quickly and tenderized in the pressure cooker.

Disadvantages

Careful timing is important to prevent foods such as vegetables from being overcooked.

Suitable foods and uses

Jam making, fruit bottling
Stews and casseroles
Vegetables
Meat joints
Puddings
Milk puddings
Soups and stocks

Slow cookers

Slow cookers are operated by electricity and can be used for cooking stews, braises, and other dishes that require long, slow, moist cooking. They can also be used to cook pâtés, soups, fish, and desserts.

A slow cooker is useful for dishes that require long, slow cooking.

There are several types available, but they all have the same basic design. They have a metal or plastic case into which an earthenware or stoneware pot is fitted. The heating element is located under the base or around the sides of the pot. There is no thermostat to control the temperature as very little power is used to operate them (about 55 watts). Food can be left to cook for up to 14 hours on some models. Some models also have two heat settings. If the cooker has to be left on for longer than originally

planned there is usually no adverse effect on the food, unless it is a rice or pasta dish which may become sticky if overcooked.

As the build-up of heat is slow, some models have to be pre-heated for about 20 minutes before food is placed in them. This avoids the risk of food-poisoning bacteria multiplying as the food warms up.

Advantages

1 Once the cooking starts the pot can be left unattended, except for rice dishes which should be stirred occasionally.

2 Little fuel is used.

3 Tough cuts of meat can be tenderized by the moist, slow cooking.

4 Pots that can be lifted out allow a topping (e.g. potato, cheese) to be put on top of the dish, so that it can be grilled.

Disadvantages

1 Pulses and beans may not cook completely at the temperature of the slow cooker. Red kidney beans should be boiled for 10 minutes beforehand to destroy the toxin they contain (see p. 136).

2 Meat and poultry may have to be browned in a pan beforehand, although some models have a flameproof pot which can be put on the hob for this purpose.

Stewing

This is a slow method of cooking, which is similar to boiling, but the food is cooked below boiling point. It can be carried out on the hob in a pan with a lid, or in the oven in a covered dish (casserole), on a low heat (Gas 2-3, 150-160°C, 300-325°F). The liquid in which the food is cooked is normally served with the food.

Advantages

1 Tenderizes tough cuts of meat (see pp. 118-20).

2 Relatively economical in use of fuel.

3 Nutrient losses are kept to a minimum as the liquid is served with the meal.

4 The flavour is retained as the liquid is served with the meal.

5 Improves certain fruits, e.g. plums, rhubarb, as the cellulose is softened. The fruit acids help to keep vitamin C and thiamin losses to a minimum.

6 A whole meal can be prepared in one container, which saves time and clearing up.

7 A large variety of stews and casseroles can be prepared.

Disadvantages

1 Stewing is a long, slow method of cooking. The use of an automatic oven is helpful, as a stew can be prepared in advance and left to cook as required.

2 There is little variation in texture and consistency, so crisp foods should be served with a stew.

Suitable foods

Beef – flank, chuck steak, oxtail, leg, shin
Lamb – middle neck, breast, liver, kidney
Mutton and veal – breast, neck, kidney, liver
Poultry – chicken
Fruit – plums, rhubarb, apricots, apples

Braising

Braising is a combination of stewing and roasting. Cuts of meat or poultry are placed on a bed of fried vegetables, bacon, and herbs (a **mirepoix**) with sufficient liquid to cover the mirepoix and keep the food moist. A well-fitting lid is placed on the pan to prevent loss of liquid, while the food is cooking in the steam rising from the stock. When the food is tender, it is browned in a hot oven with the lid off.

During cooking, the liquid should simmer, not boil, to avoid toughening the meat.

Advantages

1 A whole meal can be cooked in one pan, which saves time and fuel.

2 Tough cuts of meat can be used.

Disadvantages

Meat may not develop a good colour and may need to be grilled at the end of the cooking time.

Suitable foods

Beef – brisket, flank, topside
Lamb, mutton, or veal – loin, neck, breast
Rabbit
Offal – hearts, liver
Poultry – chicken joints or whole small bird

Revision questions

1 Describe the effect of moist methods of cooking on the nutrients in food.

2 Why is boiling a common method of cooking?

3 What are the disadvantages of boiling?

4 Name five foods suitable for boiling.

5 What is the difference between boiling and simmering?

6 Why is poaching a suitable method of cooking for delicate foods such as fish and eggs?

7 Why are potatoes par-boiled before being roasted in the oven?

8 Why is steaming a suitable method of cooking for people who are suffering from digestive upsets?

9 Why is steaming a useful method of cooking for retaining water-soluble nutrients?

10 What points should be remembered for successfully steaming food?

11 What safety measures are needed when steaming food?

12 What are the advantages and disadvantages of steaming food?

13 What is the principle behind pressure cooking?

14 What are the safety features on a pressure cooker?

15 What are the advantages of pressure cooking?

16 Why should all the air be excluded from the pressure cooker before building up the pressure?

17 How do slow cookers work, and what are the advantages of owning one?

18 What are the advantages of stewing, and why is it suitable for cooking tough cuts of meat?

19 What is braising? Name five foods suitable for this method.

Dry methods of cooking

Higher temperatures are used in dry cooking, and this has different effects on the nutritive value and physical appearance of the food.

Effects on the nutrient content of food

All nutrients, except for most of the mineral elements, are affected to some extent, particularly the heat-sensitive vitamins, thiamin and vitamin C.

1 **Fats** At high temperatures, fat molecules decompose into their component glycerol and fatty acid parts, which affects the nutritive value and keeping qualities of the fat (see p. 92).

2 **Proteins** are very sensitive to heat, but their nutritive value is not seriously affected by dry heat, except if they are heated to very high temperatures (e.g. in roasting) for a prolonged time. In this case some amino-acids may be destroyed, and toughening of the protein may reduce digestibility (see p. 4).

3 **Carbohydrates** The effect of heat on starch and sugar has already been described (see p. 11). There is little effect on nutritive value, except for the increased digestibility of starch in the presence of a liquid.

4 **Non-enzymatic browning (Maillard reaction)** If a food containing protein and carbohydrate is dry heated, a reaction occurs between the two. This results in the production of substances that cannot be digested and which therefore cause the loss of a small amount of protein and carbohydrate. Such losses are insignificant, and the substances contribute to the appearance of the cooked product as they are brown in colour. Foods that demonstrate this reaction include bread, roasted nuts, breakfast cereals, and biscuits.

Baking and roasting

Baking is the cooking of foods such as flour mixtures (cakes, pastries, bread, biscuits), and fruits and vegetables (baked apples, potatoes) by convection in the oven, without the addition of fat, except to prevent mixtures sticking to cooking vessels, e.g. baking tins, flan cases.

Roasting was traditionally carried out over an open fire, with the meat being rotated on a spit. Nowadays, roasting is generally described as the cooking of meat or vegetables in the oven, basting them with hot fat to prevent drying and to develop colour and flavour.

In either case, account must be taken of the heat variation in an oven resulting from convection currents (see p. 151). In most types of oven the upper part is the hottest and the lower part the coolest. Items such as cakes, pastries, and bread should not be placed on the floor of the oven as there is insufficient heat to bake them properly. However, egg custards, fish, fruit, and other foods that require slow cooking can be baked there. Fan ovens provide more uniform heating regardless of shelf position, and food on different shelves will brown evenly.

The source of heat in an oven will affect the way in which baking tins should be placed and the evenness of baking.

In a **gas oven**, the source of heat is usually at the back, so that the heat circulates from back to front:

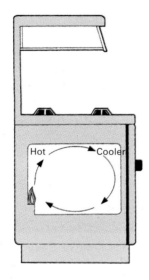

So the correct way to position food to be cooked in a gas oven is as shown below:

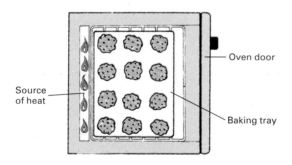

The oven temperature is controlled by the thermostat (see p. 250) and the temperature required depends on what is being baked (see p. 277). If the temperature of the oven appears to be hotter or cooler than the oven setting (because a dish cooks more quickly or more slowly than expected), then it is wise to have the thermostat checked. Using aluminium foil to line the ceiling of the oven to reduce food spattering may affect the evenness of baking, as heat may be reflected on to the food more intensely.

In an **electric oven** (not fan assisted), the source of heat is usually at the sides, so that the heat circulates from side to side.

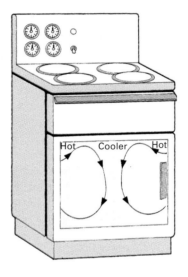

So the correct way to position food to be cooked in an electric oven is as shown below:

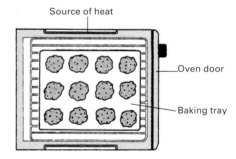

Points to remember when baking

1   Several items can be baked at once to save fuel, if they require slightly different temperatures. Careful timing will ensure that all the items cook evenly and successfully.

2   Pre-heat the oven for at least 10 minutes before placing items in it to bake. This is important for cakes, pastries, and bread, where raising agents need heat to work efficiently.

3   When the baking time is nearly complete, you can open the door to check items, without adversely affecting the finished result. Do not open the door too soon or too often, or the temperature will fall.

Methods of roasting meat

There are four main methods of roasting meat in the oven.

Method A: searing method

The meat is put into a very hot oven (Gas 8-9, 230-240°C, 450-470°F) for the first 20 minutes to sear the outside and develop the flavour and extractives. The heat is then lowered to complete the cooking. This method is only suitable for tender joints of meat, e.g. topside of beef, leg of lamb or pork, and care should be taken not to overharden the meat.

Method B: meat thermometer

The meat should be cooked at Gas 6-7, 200-225°C (400-425°F). A meat thermometer, which is stuck into the thickest part of the joint, is used and the internal temperature of the joint is registered on the dial. This indicates when the meat is cooked inside. Any cuts of meat can be cooked by this method. Different meats become cooked at different temperatures:

Beef, well cooked	70°C (160°F)
Lamb and mutton	80°C (175°F)
Pork	85°C (180°F)

Method C: slow roasting

The joint is baked at a cool temperature (Gas 3, 170°C, 325°F) for double the usual time, resulting in a tender joint which does not, however, develop such a full flavour. This method is suitable for cuts such as breast of lamb, belly of pork, or brisket of beef.

Method D: cold oven method

The meat is put into a cold oven, set at Gas 7, 220°C (425°F), and the gradual rise in temperature tenderizes the meat and develops the flavour as heating continues. Any cuts of meat can be cooked by this method, but it is particularly suitable for the less tender cuts, e.g. shoulder of lamb, brisket of beef.

Timing the roasting of a joint

It is important to follow the recommended cooking time for a joint of meat to ensure that it is well cooked. This is especially important with poultry and pork joints, which must first have been well thawed, to prevent the risk of food poisoning.

The chart below indicates how long joints should be cooked, according to their weight and the method used to roast them.

Suitable joints for roasting

Beef – Fore ribs, sirloin, topside, silverside, top rump.

Pork – All main cuts can be roasted.

Veal – All main cuts can be roasted.

Lamb – Best end of neck (crown roast), loin (whole), saddle, leg, breast, shoulder.

Type of meat		Method A	Method D	Method C
Beef:	large joints	20 mins per 450 g + 20 mins		30 mins per 450 g
	small joints	15 mins per 450 g + 15 mins		25 mins per 450 g
Pork:	all joints	35 mins per 450 g + 30 mins	Same as for method A in all cases, but allow an extra 20 minutes overall for heating the oven.	55 mins per 450 g
Veal:	large joints	35 mins per 450 g + 30 mins		45 mins per 450 g
	small joints	25 mins per 450 g + 25 mins		40 mins per 450 g
Lamb:	large joints	25 mins per 450 g + 20 mins		35 mins per 450 g
	small joints	15 mins per 450 g + 15 mins		25 mins per 450 g
Stuffed meat		extra 10 mins per 450 g		
Covered joint		extra 20 mins for any weight		Allow 20 minutes extra for oven to heat up.
Poultry		20 mins per 450 g + 20 mins		

Suitable vegetables for roasting

Potatoes	Turnips
Parsnips	Onions

These should all be par-boiled first.

Advantages of roasting

1 Tenderizes suitable joints of meat (see pp. 118–19), and develops their flavour.
2 Little attention is required while the meat is roasting, except to baste the joint.
3 Fuel can be saved if other items are baked in the oven at the same time.

Disadvantages of roasting

1 A lot of moisture is lost by evaporation and the joint may dry out.
2 Fat from the meat will spatter at high temperatures, making the oven dirty. Self-cleaning ovens (see p. 252) help to reduce this problem, and the meat can be covered by foil, or placed in a roasting bag, or a roasting dish with a lid.
3 Meat may shrink markedly as a result of moisture loss and protein denaturation.
4 High temperatures may result in toughening of protein and reduced digestibility.

Roasting bricks

Special clay crocks or roasting bricks can be used for roasting most types of meat and poultry and for baking fish. The meat is placed in one half of the brick with little or no additional fat, the lid is placed on top, and the brick is put into a cold oven, set at Gas 7-8, 220-230°C (425-450°F). No basting is required, as the joint self-bastes inside the brick and develops extractives and colour on the surface. A substantial volume of juices is also collected, which can be used for gravy. Oven cleaning is reduced, as the meat is covered. Roasting bricks should be cleaned with hot water and vinegar, as detergent will soak in and taint the food.

Microwave roasting

Meat can also be roasted in a microwave oven (see pp. 190-4).

Pot-roasting

If no oven is available, meat can be pot-roasted, i.e. cooked in a pan with a lid on, over a gentle heat and with a little fat. The meat should be turned occasionally so that it browns on all sides and cooks evenly. Slow cookers and pressure cookers can also be used for pot-roasting.

Grilling

Grilling is the cooking of food by radiation under a gas or electric grill (see p. 249). The surface of the food is quickly sealed, and the flavour is well developed. The food must be moistened with fat to prevent it from drying out and turned frequently to ensure even cooking. The food to be grilled should not be more than 2.5-3.5 cm thick, to allow heat penetration. The use of skewers or bones in meat joints helps heat penetration by conduction.

Grilling can also be used to brown foods such as cheese, potatoes, sauces, and crumpets, and to toast bread.

Advantages

1 Grilling is a quick method of cooking and is therefore suitable for snacks, and for time-saving meals.
2 It is a healthy method of cooking because the fat from meat, bacon, etc., drains away.

Disadvantages

1 Grilling requires careful timing to prevent overcooking.
2 Meat to be grilled must be tender and will therefore be more expensive.

Suitable foods

Tender meat cuts (see pp. 120–2), e.g. chops (chump, loin), steaks (rump, sirloin), rashers
Cutlets, poultry breasts
Sausages, beefburgers

Offal, e.g. kidney, lamb's liver
Fish fillets
Tomatoes, mushrooms

Barbecueing

Barbecues are now a popular way of cooking food. Food is laid on a wire rack over hot, glowing charcoal, and cooks by radiant heat from underneath. The charcoal imparts a flavour to the food which adds to the enjoyment of eating it.

The charcoal must not be too hot or the food will burn on the outside but be undercooked inside, which could lead to food poisoning. The charcoal should glow red, and not have high flames reaching the food above. During cooking, food should be turned at regular intervals and basted in a moist marinade to prevent drying out and to add flavour.

Suitable foods

Sausages
Small meat and poultry joints
Oily fish
Corn on the cob (wrapped in foil)
Burgers (meat or vegetarian)
Kebabs

Revision questions

1 Give four examples of foods that are suitable for grilling.
2 What are the advantages of grilling?
3 What is the difference between baking and roasting?
4 Why should the oven be pre-heated for baking foods such as cakes and bread?
5 What are the effects of roasting meat on the texture and protein content?
6 How is pot-roasting different from oven roasting?
7 Why must food that is to be grilled be moistened with fat and turned frequently?
8 Describe the methods of roasting meat.
9 Name two cuts of beef, lamb, and pork that are suitable for roasting.
10 What precautions should be taken when barbecuing food?
11 How are the following affected by dry methods of cooking?
   a fats
   b carbohydrates
   c proteins
   d vitamin C
12 What is the Maillard reaction, and how does it occur?

Frying

Frying is a quick, convenient, and popular method of cooking, which involves high temperatures. Solid fats or oils are used (see pp. 91–4).
There are four types of frying:
   deep frying   dry frying
   shallow frying   stir-frying

Effect on nutritive value

1 When food is fried, some fat is absorbed (see p. 33) and this increases the fat content of the food and consequently its energy value. Dietary guidelines recommend a reduction in the amount of food cooked by frying.
2 The temperatures are higher than those used in boiling, etc., and this leads to the destruction of heat–sensitive nutrients.

Choice of fat or oil

The fat or oil used in deep frying must be suitable for heating up to 200°C without burning. Some fats and oils are especially produced for this purpose (see pp. 91–4). Vegetable oils and lard are suitable. For shallow frying, the temperatures are lower and butter or margarine can also be used.

Reduced fat spreads have a high water content and are not suitable for frying. The water causes the fat to spit when heated and so is dangerous.

Deep frying

Deep frying involves the immersion of a food in a pan of hot fat, so that the food is covered by the fat while frying.

Use a strong, deep pan, with a frying basket. Electric fryers, with built-in thermostats can be purchased for domestic use; they are safer as there is less risk of causing a fire.

A domestic electric deep fat fryer

Preparing food for deep frying

Foods that are to be deep fried, e.g. fish, meat, fruit, should first be coated to prevent over-cooking and the loss of juices from the food, and to prevent the food breaking up and absorbing too much fat. Suitable protective coatings include:

   beaten egg
   beaten egg and breadcrumbs
   beaten egg and seasoned flour
   beaten egg and oatmeal
   egg, flour, and milk batter

When the food is placed in the hot fat, the egg in the coating coagulates rapidly and thus forms a protective layer around the food, which becomes crisp and golden brown. The food inside continues to cook by conduction and retains its flavour and texture.

Preparing fat for deep frying

Clear, fresh fat or oil should be used. It must be free from water and impurities as far as possible. The presence of moisture in the fat will affect the keeping qualities and will cause the fat to spatter when it becomes hot. Impurities, such as crumbs or flour from previous fryings, will decompose at high temperatures and cause 'off' flavours and odours. They will also affect the keeping qualities of the fat (see p. 92).

Fat should not be heated beyond the required temperature, as fat molecules decompose at high temperatures. This leads to the release of **free fatty acids** which affect the keeping qualities and flavour of the fat. Free fatty acids also reduce the temperature at which the fat will ignite (see p. 92).

The fat should be heated gently to the required temperature, which is indicated by the use of a food or sugar thermometer. The appropriate temperatures for deep frying are shown below:

Food	Temperature of fat	Time
Meat or poultry portions	180–185°C	Meat: up to 8 minutes Poultry: up to 12 minutes
Doughnuts	180–185°C	4–5 minutes
Fish fillets	180–185°C	Up to 6 minutes, if coated with batter. Up to 8 minutes, if coated with egg and breadcrumbs.
Fritters	180–185°C	3 minutes
Potato chips	150°C then increase to 185°C	5 minutes, until soft. Remove chips. Cook at higher temperature for about 2 minutes until crisp and golden.

Important rules for deep frying

1   Do not fill the pan more than half-way with oil or fat, as the oil or fat will rise rapidly when food is placed in it, and could boil over.
2   Lower the food gently into the hot fat. Do not drop it in as it will splash and cause burns.
3   Do not overfill the pan with food, as this will considerably lower the temperature of the fat and affect the finished result.

4 Heat the fat to the required temperature before putting the food in, so that it starts to cook immediately. If the temperature is too low, fat will be absorbed and this will affect the texture and finished result of the food.

5 Do not overheat the fat, as the outside of the food will cook too quickly and the inside will not cook sufficiently. The keeping qualities of the fat will also be reduced (see p. 92).

6 Turn the food over carefully as it is frying to ensure even cooking.

7 Have ready a plate with a piece of absorbent kitchen paper on which to drain the food when it is cooked, and a perforated spoon with which to lift the food out. Cooking tongs can also be used. A frying basket is useful for helping to drain the fat when the food is lifted out.

8 When the food is cooked, turn off the heat and allow the fat to cool before straining it through a piece of muslin to remove impurities.

9 Store the fat in a cool, dry, dark place, to prevent it from becoming rancid due to oxidation (see p. 92). Use a suitable container, e.g. a bottle or can.

Safety rules for deep frying

1 *Never* leave a deep-fat frying pan unattended when cooking.

2 Do not heat the fat beyond the required temperature (see p. 92).

3 Keep the pan handle turned towards the side of the cooker to prevent it being knocked over.

4 If the fat starts to smoke, turn the heat off immediately as this means it is near to its flash point (see p. 92).

If the fat catches fire:

Do not attempt to carry the pan outside. Turn the heat off and smother the flames with either a lid, a thick damp towel, a flat baking tin, or a fire blanket.

Do not attempt to extinguish the flames with water, as this will cause the flames to flare up and the burning oil may float on top and spill over.

Do not touch the pan until the fat has cooled down.

Never add water to burning fat: the results can be disastrous.

Suitable foods for deep frying

Scotch eggs, rissoles, fish cakes
Fruit and meat fritters
Doughnuts, choux pastry aigrettes
Small poultry joints
Fish portions
Potato chips and crisps
Onion rings

Shallow frying

Shallow frying involves the cooking of food in a layer of hot fat that comes about half-way up the food. A strong, large, flat frying pan is used.

Heat is conducted from the base of the pan to one surface of the food at a time. This means that the food has to be turned at regular intervals to ensure even cooking and heat penetration.

Food that is to be shallow fried does not necessarily have to be coated beforehand as the frying can be fairly gentle. Foods with a high moisture content may cause the fat to spatter and a lid or spatter guard can be used to prevent this.

In general, the rules given for deep frying (see pp. 188-9) also apply to shallow frying.

Suitable foods for shallow frying

Tender meat joints, e.g. chops, cutlets
Offal, e.g. liver, kidney
Fish cakes, rissoles, beefburgers
Sausages, bacon rashers
Vegetables, e.g. mushrooms, onions
Eggs
Fish, e.g. herrings in oatmeal

Dry frying

Some foods, e.g. bacon and sausages, can be fried without the addition of fat, as they contain sufficient fat to prevent them from sticking to the pan.

It is possible to buy oil sprays, which spray a very thin layer of oil on to the pan for frying. This reduces the energy value of the fried food. Non–stick pans are most suitable for this form of frying, as there is less risk of the food sticking to the pan.

Stir-frying

Stir-frying originated in the Far East, and is traditionally done in a wok. All ingredients should be finely chopped and prepared before cooking commences. A little oil (about 1 tbsp) is heated in the wok, and the food is put in and stirred continuously to ensure even and thorough cooking. Few nutrients are lost, and the food remains crisp and well flavoured. It is a quick, healthy, and energy–saving method of cooking.

Suitable foods

Vegetables	Lamb
Chicken	Nuts
Beef	Beans
Pork	Seafood

Revision questions

1 Why must the frying pan be only half-filled with oil or fat, and why is it important not to overfill it with food when hot?
2 What safety precautions should be followed when frying?
3 Why is it important to regulate the temperature of the fat carefully when frying?
4 Give five examples of foods that are suitable for deep-fat frying and five suitable for shallow frying.
5 Why must some foods that are to be deep fried be coated first? Give three examples of suitable coatings.
6 What causes fat that is used for frying to deteriorate?
7 Why is stir-frying a healthy method of cooking?

Microwave cookery

Microwave ovens are now commonly used in many homes, catering kitchens, shops, offices, and canteens.

A typical domestic microwave oven

Electromagnetic waves

Energy can be transmitted in the form of electromagnetic waves. This process is known as **radiation**. It is the process by which light and heat from the sun reach the earth.

If produced in sufficient intensity, certain waves can cause a rise in temperature in an object with which they make contact. These include:

heat radiation

infra-red waves

microwaves

Microwaves move at the speed of light and have a very **high frequency**, i.e. they vibrate millions of times a second. If absorbed into an object, the vibrations of the microwaves agitate the molecules within the object, causing friction. If you rub your hands together, the friction makes them become warm. Similarly, the vibration of microwaves within an object will cause a rise in temperature as their energy is converted into heat energy.

Microwaves are **reflected**, **transmitted**, or **absorbed** by different materials.

Reflection

Microwaves are reflected from metal, which does not heat up. Inside an oven, microwaves bounce off the metal walls, hit the food, and are absorbed by it.

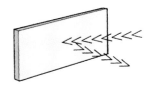

Transmission

Some materials, e.g. paper, china, and some plastics, allow microwaves to pass through them, but do not heat up.

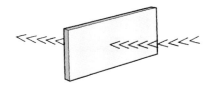

Absorption

Some materials, e.g. food, absorb microwaves and become hot.

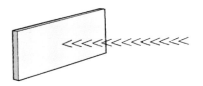

How food is cooked by microwaves

Microwaves can penetrate up to 4 centimetres into food. They agitate molecules throughout the food, so the food heats up rapidly. Traditional methods of cooking rely on conduction to get energy from the surface of the food to the inside, and this is much slower.

Conventional microwave ovens, unlike ordinary gas or electric ovens, do not heat up. The only heat produced is that generated within the food.

In a conventional microwave oven, moisture from the food evaporates and condenses on the outside, as the oven itself is cool. This means that the outside of food is cooler than the inside.

Microwave ovens

Several types of microwave oven are now available. They all have the same basic design and parts:

Cavity The food is placed in here, on a plate or dish.

Magnetron This is the valve that generates the microwave.

Guide This determines the length of the waves and guides them into the cavity.

Mode stirrer This distributes the microwave energy evenly in the cavity.

Door The door has a safety seal to prevent leakage of microwaves to the exterior.

Power supply This converts the mains supply to the required voltage for the correct operation of the magnetron valve.

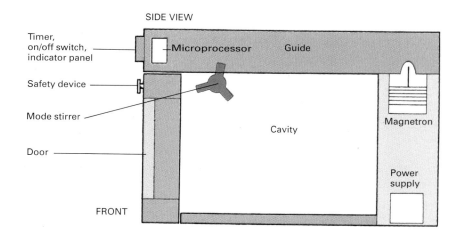

SIDE VIEW

Timer, on/off switch, indicator panel

Microprocessor   Guide

Safety device

Mode stirrer

Door

Cavity

Magnetron

Power supply

FRONT

Safety device This ensures that the microwaves cease to be emitted once the door is opened.

Timer This controls the time during which microwaves are emitted, and switches the cooker off at the end of the set time.

On/off switch This may be in addition to a mains output control switch.

Indicator panel This may include a time chart for different foods as well as operating instructions.

Microwave ovens may also have the following features:

Quartz grill Rapidly browns and crisps foods when used with the microwave, or can be used on its own like an ordinary grill.

Radiant grill Similar to those found in traditional cookers.

Convection oven Can be used on its own like a traditional oven, or with the microwave to cook foods quickly.

Weight sensor Sends information to a microprocessor, which selects the correct cooking time, power, and oven temperature for the food being cooked.

Auto-sensor cooking A microprocessor detects the amount of steam produced by food during cooking, and adjusts the remaining cooking time.

See-through oven door and internal light Make it easy to view the progress of cooking.

Combination ovens Combine two or more of the above features. This makes them very useful in situations where a traditional gas or electric cooker might not be available or appropriate, e.g. in a small kitchen, bedsitting room, caravan, boat, small take-away food outlet.

The instruction leaflet for individual ovens should be studied, but the following rules apply to most models.

Microwave
with various power settings, including defrost.

Grill
browns and cooks food such as toast, bacon.

Convection oven
allows quick preheating and even cooking.

Combination: Convection and Microwave
for cooking cakes, meat, etc. quickly

Combination: Grill and Microwave
For cooking chops, chicken portions, etc.

Combination: Convection and Grill
for reheating items needing a crisp coating, e.g. battered fish.

Combination ovens combine a number of features.

Containers for food

Suitable containers:

oven-proof glass   china
ceramics   paper

Some plastic films and containers are also suitable, but not all, as the heat from the food may cause some plastics to distort or melt, particularly when fat or syrup is heated to a temperature above 150°C.

Polythene products, such as those used to hold frozen foods, can be used as long as they are pierced beforehand. Otherwise they may burst during cooking.

The following containers are *not* suitable:

Metal foil dishes and dishes with a metal trim reflect the microwaves back to the magnetron and cause 'arcing'. This may cause permanent damage to the cooker.

Melamine plastic ware may scorch and char.

Polystyrene containers deform and give off a strong odour if heated for too long.

Timing and cooking the food

1. Different foods need different cooking times, and this should be taken into account.
2. The greater the volume of food, the longer the time required to cook it as penetration by the microwaves will take longer.
3. If the food is very cold to begin with, it will take longer to cook than if it is at room temperature.
4. Thick portions of food (more than 3–5 cm thick) take longer to cook as the microwaves lose their power to heat the deeper they penetrate into the food. This may produce uneven cooking in items such as bread and pastries.
5. Light, porous foods absorb microwaves more readily than more compact, moist foods such as meat.
6. The greater the moisture content of the food, the longer the cooking time.
7. Food should be separated, not stacked up in the oven, as this will affect the penetration of the waves.
8. Foods that are traditionally eaten browned or crusty, e.g. meat, cakes, and bread, may need to be finished off in an ordinary oven or grill,

as they will not develop these characteristic in a conventional microwave oven.

Special 'browning' plates can be purchased for the microwave oven. These are heated in the cavity, before food such as meat is placed on them. When the food comes into contact with the hot plate, it will brown, as in frying or roasting. Combination ovens may have this facility built in.

A voluntary labelling system is used on microwave ovens and food packs to advise consumers on how to cook food properly. By matching the information on the two, consumers can easily work out the heating time required.

The oven label shows the following information:

Power output is the amount of energy available to heat or cook food. The power ratings are:

500 W
600 W
700 W
800 W
1000 W

The higher the power output, the shorter the heating time.

All microwave oven manufacturers measure the maximum power output of their products by a standard method called IEC 705 (International Electrotechnical Commission specification number 705). This appears on the label.

The **heating category** indicates how efficiently the oven will heat a small amount of food (500 g). The categories are:

A   B   C   D   E

A needs the longest heating time, and E the shortest.

The consumer needs to match the information on the oven with the label on a food pack.

MICROWAVE COOKING

Preparation guidelines: All appliances vary. The following are guidelines only. Adjust times for your particular oven. Remove outer packaging and pierce film lid before cooking.

To Microwave	Cook on Full Power	Shake and Stand	Cook on Full Power
650W or Category B	2½ minutes	1 minute	2½ minutes
750W or Category D	2 minutes	1 minute	2 minutes

Cooking from frozen: Thoroughly defrost before cooking, then follow microwave guidelines from chilled.

Instructions for microwave heating are given on many food labels. This label is from a sausage and bean hotpot.

Check the food temperature after heating. It should be at least 70°C ('piping hot'). Some foods, e.g. soups and stews, must be stirred during and after cooking to ensure even heating and cooking. Others, e.g. chicken pieces, must be repositioned at intervals to ensure even cooking. Large portions of food, e.g. meat joints must be turned over at intervals.

Advantages of microwave cooking

1 Food is cooked very quickly. This cuts down on fuel costs, preparation time, and wastage (food is only heated as required).
2 In a conventional microwave oven, the food heats up but the oven does not. This prevents the kitchen from becoming uncomfortable to work in, and is safer for elderly or disabled people to use.
3 It is useful for preparing foods and meals that are required quickly, and for entertaining.
4 There is less heat destruction of nutrients as cooking time is short.
5 Some foods, e.g. vegetables, are improved in colour and flavour as cooking time is shorter.
6 There is less danger of food poisoning as food does not have to be kept warm, providing it is thoroughly cooked or reheated.
7 Food spills do not burn on the oven as it does not become hot (unless it is a combination model with a convection oven).

8 The oven is usually portable (although it is heavy) and can be placed on an ordinary worktop and operated from a normal mains supply.
9 Frozen foods can be defrosted.
10 The food can be cooked and served in the same dish, which saves washing up.
11 The serving dish or cooking utensil is not heated by the microwaves, and can therefore be handled. It may become hot by the conduction of heat from the cooked food, in a conventional microwave oven.

Disadvantages

1 It is easy to overcook the food, so careful attention must be paid to timing.
2 In a conventional microwave oven, food will not become crisp, and may not develop characteristic flavours, colours, or textures.
3 Irregular-shaped foods may affect the cooking time and finished result of foods cooked on the same plate. This may necessitate separate cooking, in order to reduce the risk of food poisoning due to incompletely cooked food.

Suitable foods

Most foods can be cooked in a microwave oven. The main exceptions are pastries and some cake mixtures, which need to be baked in an ordinary oven or combination microwave oven.

Whole eggs cannot be cooked in a microwave oven as they explode.

Safety regulations

Safety regulations on the manufacture and design of microwave ovens operate in several countries. Much research has been carried out to ensure that there is no possibility of accidental leakage of microwaves while the oven is in use.

Revision questions

1 What are microwaves and how do they heat food?
2 Why do conventional microwave ovens stay cool when in use?

3 In a microwave oven, what do the following parts do?
   a magnetron
   b guide
   c mode stirrer
   d safety device
4 Give three examples of suitable containers to use in a microwave oven, and give reasons for your answers.
5 What are the advantages and disadvantages of microwave cookery?
6 How do the thickness and temperature of food affect their cooking time in a microwave oven?
7 Which foods cannot be successfully cooked by conventional microwave ovens? Give reasons for this.

Freezer cookery

The principles underlying the freezing of foods as a method of preservation are discussed on pp. 166-9.

Freezer ownership is both convenient and time saving, but freezer management should be studied carefully in order to achieve the best results as economically as possible.

Advantages of owning a freezer

1 Freezing is a simple and effective way of preserving food, and, providing the basic rules are followed, it is safe. There is very little effect on the flavour, colour, appearance, and nutritive value of most foods.
2 Whole meals, snacks, and parts of meals can be stored in a freezer to use at any time.
3 It is usually cheaper to buy foods such as meat in bulk, and store them in the freezer for long-term use.
4 Home-grown or 'pick-your-own' produce can be frozen at home, which saves money.
5 Foods can be eaten out of season.
6 Parties and other special occasions can be catered for in advance and the foods stored until they are needed.
7 'Emergency' foods can be stored for unexpected guests or for when the larder is depleted.

8 Freezers are inexpensive to run, if used wisely; on average they use one unit of electricity per 15 litres per week.
9 Various sizes and types of freezer are available to cater for varying needs and family size.
10 Time can be saved on shopping if food is bought in bulk for the freezer.
11 Left-over foods and items such as stock or fruit juice can be frozen for later use, to avoid wastage.

Disadvantages of owning a freezer

1 The initial cost of a freezer is high, but by sensible use, this cost can gradually be retrieved.
2 In order to work and run efficiently, a freezer should be well stocked, which means that plans should be made to buy or freeze more food as stocks run down.
3 To prepare a bulk buy or harvest of foods may entail a good deal of work in a short space of time.
4 There may be a tendency to fill the freezer with uneconomic commercially frozen food.
5 A family may find that it is eating more foods such as meat, shellfish, etc., just because they are in the freezer, and this may be unnecessary and expensive.
6 If storage space is limited, the freezer may have to be housed outside the kitchen and this may be inconvenient.

Types of freezer

There are several types and makes of freezer available, and a study of consumer association reports on these is often a valuable guide to buying one. It is important to evaluate your needs before buying a freezer, based on:
1 How much you can afford to pay.
2 What types of food you are likely to freeze (home-grown or commercially frozen).
3 The number of people in the family, allowing approximately 55 litres per person.
4 How much entertaining you do.
5 How much floor space is available.
6 Your preference for style.

There are three main types of freezer:
>   chest freezer (left)
>   upright freezer (centre)
>   refrigerator/freezer (right)

Chest freezers

Chest freezers have a top-opening lid, and their sizes range from 150 to 500 litres. Removable baskets and open trays make the packing and removal of food much easier. All models stand on the floor, and some, which are table-top height, can be used as work surfaces.

Most models have a separate compartment for fast-freezing food.

Advantages

1   Chest freezers are slightly more economical to run, and need defrosting less often.
2   Large, bulky foods, e.g. meat joints, can be stored more easily.

Disadvantages

1   It may be difficult to reach the bottom of the freezer or to see the contents at a glance.
2   Chest freezers take up more floor space than other types.

Upright freezers

Upright freezers have a front-opening door, and the food is placed on shelves, which are usually adjustable to cope with different foods. Their sizes range from 60 to 120 litres for small, free-standing models, and from 120 to 600 litres for floor-standing models. The larger types often have two doors, and the lower half can be used for long-term storage.

As upright freezers take up less floor space than chest freezers, the weight they hold is more concentrated on one small area. It is important to check that the floor is strong enough to withstand such constant weight.

Some models have one or two fast-freeze shelves for quick freezing of foods.

Advantages

1   It is easy to pack and unpack the goods from the freezer and to check the contents.
2   Some models have spaces and racks on the inside of the door to hold small items.
3   Little floor space is taken up.

Disadvantages

1   When the door is open, heavy, cold air falls out quickly, so the motor must work more to maintain the temperature.
2   They need defrosting more often, and the shelves may become iced up easily, which makes the removal of food difficult.
3   They are slightly more expensive to run.
4   Bulky foods may be more difficult to store in upright models.

Refrigerator/freezers

Refrigerator/freezers usually consist of two separate cabinets, joined together, with separate doors. Normally, the freezer compartment is below the refrigerator. It may operate independently or in conjunction with the refrigerator.

These models are particularly useful to single people or small families, and there is a range of sizes available.

The advantages and disadvantages are similar to those for the upright models, although the refrigerator/freezer may be slightly more economical to run.

It is often possible to buy second-hand **conservators** from shops or ice cream manufacturers. These are not designed to freeze food, only to store foods which are already frozen at -18°C. They should not be considered if food is to be frozen at home. Appliances that are suitable for freezing food will carry the following symbol:

Storage capacities of freezers

The maximum storage capacity of a freezer may be more than the actual storage space available, because space is wasted when uneven-shaped packages are used. The approximate holding capacity of 30 litres of freezer space is:

16–20 identical, tub-shaped, 500 ml cartons
or 8 kg poultry or meat
or 35–40 identical, square or rectangular 500 ml cartons

Siting the freezer

For the freezer to operate efficiently it must be placed in a suitable position. The following points should be considered when choosing a site:

1   Dampness may damage the motor and the exterior of the freezer, so the site must be dry.

2   If air cannot circulate, heat will not be removed from the condenser, so the freezer will not work properly. There must be at least 25 mm of space around the freezer.

3   It must be kept in a cool place. A site that is always hot will cause the motor to work overtime to maintain the temperature inside the freezer.

Suitable sites include:
a cool dry kitchen
utility room
a dry garage, conservatory, or outhouse
spare living-room or bedroom

Running costs of freezers

Several factors help to determine the running costs of the freezer, including:

1   The size and type of freezer.

2   How often the door or lid is opened.

3   How much food is stored in the freezer; leaving large gaps increases running costs as the motor has to operate more often to maintain the temperature.

4   How often the freezer is defrosted; if too much ice is allowed to build up the work of the motor will be increased.

5   Where the freezer is kept, and the climate; more electricity will be used in warm weather to maintain the temperature.

6   How often fresh food is frozen; food to be frozen raises the temperature of the freezer and causes the motor to work more often.

Insurance

A full freezer may contain food worth a great deal of money. It is wise to insure the contents against power failures, breakdown of the motor, or theft of the contents.

Many insurance companies will insure against such losses, often as part of the house contents insurance, but many do not cover the loss incurred if the freezer is accidentally switched off. It is useful to cover the mains switch with tape or a label to prevent this happening. These insurance policies are usually fairly inexpensive. It may also be possible to insure the freezer itself for repair costs.

Power failure or moving house

In the event of a power failure, the freezer should be left closed. The food will remain in perfect condition for at least six hours, or longer if the freezer is well packed and full. It is also possible to buy alarms which will sound if the temperature rises in the freezer cabinet, before any damage is done to the food. If the freezer has to go for repair, it may be possible to hire another from the firm carrying out the work.

If moving house, it is advisable to run down the stocks of food in the freezer for a few weeks in advance so that there is not so much to move on the day. The freezer should be the last item to be put into the van and the first to be removed, so that it can be connected immediately. If the food has to be unpacked, it is possible to buy dry ice to surround the food in a packing box, with newspaper to provide extra insulation. The food should remain frozen for several hours in this way.

Equipment

Apart from packaging materials, little special equipment is required for running a freezer, and many of the items may already be in the home. The following are needed:

- a large saucepan for blanching (see p. 201)
- a fine wire-mesh blanching basket
- a large bowl for cooling blanched foods
- a liquid measuring jug
- a funnel for filling bags with food
- a sharp knife, fork, and draining spoon

Packaging materials and labels

Food that is to be frozen must be well packaged to prevent:

1 **Dehydration and oxidation** Cold air is very drying and if dehydration occurs, oxidation reactions will take place in the food. This will cause foods such as poultry and meat to develop 'freezer burn' (visible greyish, fibrous patches on the surface of the meat), and fats to become rancid (see p. 92).
2 **Contamination** by dirt, insects, and moulds.
3 **Transfer** of flavours from one food to another.

A suitable packaging material should be:

- moisture/vapour-proof
- greaseproof
- waterproof (for liquids and odours)
- odourless and odour-proof
- strong and durable
- economical of storage space
- easy to use
- able to withstand very low temperatures

Some of the packaging materials used for home freezing

There are three main groups of packaging materials:

- sheet wrapping materials
- bags
- rigid containers

Sheet wrapping materials

Aluminium foil

This is sold in rolls of varying widths and lengths. It is fairly expensive, and is often not reusable. It is suitable for most foods except those that contain acid (e.g. fruits), and is flexible enough to be moulded around foods of different shapes.

Aluminium foil makes a good outer wrapping for foods, but it is easily punctured. Extra-thick foil can be bought, but is more expensive.

Polythene sheeting

This is also sold in rolls of varying lengths and widths. It needs to be sealed with special freezer tape that does not lose its adhesiveness at low temperatures.

The thin, self-clinging films that are available are not suitable as outer coverings, but can be used to wrap individual foods that are part of a pack.

Freezer papers

These are strong, moisture-proof papers which are coated on the inside and can be written on on the outside. They have to be sealed with freezer tape.

Bags
Polythene bags

Polythene is made in different thicknesses or gauges. Ordinary household bags are not usually suitable. For freezing, 120-150 gauge polythene bags should be used, which are specially produced for freezing and are available in a range of sizes.

Polythene bags should be sealed with paper-covered wire ties. They can be re-used providing there are no punctures in the polythene and the bag is completely clean.

Most foods can be stored in these bags, and liquids can be frozen into easy-to-store blocks, by placing the bag in an empty carton, filling it, and freezing it in the carton. Once solid, the bag can be removed and easily stored.

Rigid containers
Plastic or polythene boxes or tubs

These are fairly expensive but can be reused many times. They usually have tightly fitting lids, which make the boxes air-tight.

Square or rectangular shapes take up the least space and are easy to pack into the freezer; round ones are less useful. Empty ice cream and margarine containers can also be used, but these should be made air-tight with freezer tape if necessary.

The food should be cooled before it is placed in these containers, as the hot plastic may release toxic substances, or may 'deform' into a permanent shape.

Waxed cartons or tubs

These are only suitable for cold foods, as the wax coating will melt easily. They are useful for storing small amounts of food.

Aluminium containers

These are available in many shapes and sizes, and can be used for heating the food once it has thawed. Acidic foods should not be frozen in these containers as they will cause corrosion. These containers are reusable, but they must be thoroughly cleaned after use, as food residues can become trapped in the folds of metal at the corners of the dishes.

Ceramic containers

Ceramic casseroles can withstand cold temperatures, but they are a waste of space in the freezer and once put in, will be out of use for some time. It is therefore wise to line the casserole with foil, cook the food, and freeze it until solid. The frozen block can then be removed and the casserole released for further use. The casserole can be thawed in the casserole dish when required.

Labels

It is important to label food packs in the freezer, as they often become unrecognizable once frozen. The date on which the food was frozen should always be marked on the label, to indicate when the food should be used. The label should also indicate how many servings it contains.

Tie-on or adhesive labels can be bought in different colours, to make identification easier in the freezer.

Care of the freezer

It is important to take care of a freezer so that it works efficiently and gives value for money.

The outside of the freezer should be kept clean and free from rust, and the hinges of the lid or door may require oiling from time to time.

Defrosting

It is important to defrost the freezer when the frost reaches a thickness of about 1cm inside the cabinet. The manufacturer's instructions should be followed carefully, but the following points generally apply:

1   Chest freezers normally require defrosting only once or twice a year; upright freezers require defrosting two or three times a year.
2   Try to defrost the freezer when the food stocks are low.
3   Remove the food, wrap it in newspaper and blankets, and put it in a cold place.
4   Switch off the electricity, leave the freezer open, and place bowls of hot water inside, so that the steam speeds up the melting of the ice.
5   Gently scrape off the ice with a plastic or wooden spatula; do not use sharp or pointed tools which could damage the interior walls.

6   Use a towel to catch water at the bottom of the freezer. Some models have a drain plug which can be opened to release the water.

7   When all the ice has been removed, wash the inside with a clean cloth and a solution of bicarbonate of soda and water (1 tablespoon to 4 litres water). *Do not* use detergent as this may leave a smell in the freezer which could taint the food.

8   Allow the freezer to dry, then replace the food neatly. It is a good idea at this point to make an inventory of the contents. Do not open the freezer once it has been switched back on until it has reached the required temperature.

Using the freezer

There are several basic rules to follow for the successful use of a freezer. Specific rules for freezing individual foods are usually supplied in recipe books.

Basic rules

1   Freeze only fresh foods.
2   Freeze food when it is at the peak of quality; i.e. when just ripe or ready for eating.
3   Once prepared or harvested, freeze the food quickly to avoid deterioration.
4   Handle and freeze the food hygienically.
5   Use suitable packaging materials and wrap the food properly.
6   Pack food in single or multiple portions according to family size and needs.
7   Remove as much air as possible from the package before freezing, e.g. by sucking out the air through a straw, to prevent oxidation of the food during storage.
8   Label the packs clearly. Keep a record of what has been frozen and when.
9   Chill the food in a refrigerator before freezing so as not to raise the temperature inside the freezer too much.
10 Use the fast freeze switch to reduce the temperature quickly when freezing fresh food.
11 Only freeze food in the quantities recommended by the manufacturer for the capacity of the freezer.

12 Store the food only for the recommended storage time (see p. 203).
13 Aim to use up stocks of food before they come into season again.
14 Do not allow the temperature of the freezer cabinet to rise above –18°C. A thermometer which can be placed inside the freezer is useful for checking this.
15 Never refreeze foods that have been thawed, unless they have undergone a process of cooking, e.g. thawed meat made into a casserole can be frozen.

Choice of food for freezing

Most foods can be frozen, but some are more suitable than others. The length of time that food can be stored varies, and no food can be frozen indefinitely. Once a food has passed its storage life, i.e. the length of time it can be kept frozen in perfect condition, chemical changes start to affect the flavour, quality, and edibility of the food.

Some foods which are available for most of the year and have a long storage time in a fresh state are not worth freezing, e.g. potatoes.

Some foods react poorly to freezing and are therefore unsuitable. These include:

Vegetables

Lettuce, **cucumber**, and **radish** become mushy and discoloured on thawing, as their high water content results in large numbers of ice crystals being formed. These rupture the cells, even if quick-frozen (see p. 168).

Boiled potatoes become 'leathery' when thawed, if frozen whole.

Celery has a high water content and loses its structure on thawing, but it can be used as a cooked vegetable in casseroles, soups, etc.

Fruit

Strawberries tend to become mushy on thawing, due to ice crystals rupturing their cells, but they can be used in fruit salads, flans, soufflés, mousses, etc., as their flavour is not impaired.

Bananas and **avocado pears** turn black if frozen, because of enzyme activity.

Pears tend to lose their texture if frozen, because of the effect of ice crystals on the cells.

Dairy products

Whole pasteurized milk (non-homogenized) separates out when frozen.

Cream with less than 40% fat separates (e.g. single cream). Whipping or double cream should be whipped lightly before freezing.

Eggs: whole fresh eggs crack and become gluey. However, egg white and yolks can be frozen separately.

Mayonnaise separates.

Cornflour-based soups and stews tend to separate.

Icings (except buttercream) crumble and become soggy.

Preparation of food for freezing

Vegetables

Vegetables should be prepared for freezing as soon as possible after harvest, so it is best not to try and handle too many at one time. Most vegetables have to be **blanched**. After washing, peeling, and cutting, the vegetables are plunged into boiling water for a specific length of time (1), then cooled rapidly in iced water (2). Blanching retards the activity of enzymes in the vegetables which would discolour them and spoil their flavour.

Blanching should be carried out in a large saucepan, and no more than 450 g of prepared vegetables should be blanched at one time, as it is important to bring the water back to boiling point within one minute. Blanching should be timed from the moment the water comes back to the boil. Blanching times for various vegetables are given below:

runner beans	1 minute
broccoli	3 minutes
Brussels sprouts	3 minutes
cauliflower	3 minutes
sweetcorn	5 minutes
peas	1 minute
root vegetables	3 minutes

A blanching basket or large sieve makes the transfer of vegetables from the pan to the iced water easy. The blanching water can be used for about six batches of vegetables. After blanching, the vegetables should be well drained and packed for freezing (3).

Fruit

Fruit for freezing should be just ripe and free from bruises. Some fruits (e.g. peaches, apricots) discolour when frozen raw, so they should be frozen in a sugar syrup. Some fruits, e.g. apples, must be blanched to prevent discoloration by oxidase enzymes. Fruit can be prepared in three ways:

1 **In syrup** Use 225–450 g sugar to 575 ml water, and allow the syrup to go cold. Use 275 ml syrup for every 450 g fruit. Leave headspace in the container, as the liquid will expand when frozen.

2 **Loose** Spread fruits such as strawberries and raspberries out on shallow trays and freeze open (without a cover) until solid, then pack into a container. In this way they do not stick together.

3 **In dry sugar** Use 100 g caster sugar to 450 g fruit. Sprinkle the sugar over the fruit until it is well coated, then pack into containers and freeze.

Dairy produce

It is a waste of space to freeze butter or cheese as they can be stored satisfactorily in a refrigerator, unless you buy them in bulk. Double or whipping cream should be lightly whipped before freezing to prevent separation. It is possible to pipe cream into rosettes on paper and freeze them separately for use on cakes, cold sweets, meringues, etc.

Baked foods

Cakes should be frozen open until solid, then packed in containers. This applies particularly to cakes that have been decorated with cream or butter icing.

Pastries can be frozen raw, then cooked when thawed. It is possible to prepare pies in this way. Batches of raw pastry, or portions of rubbed-in mixtures without liquid, are useful to have in the freezer. Frozen cooked pastry may become soggy when it is thawed.

Bread should be well wrapped to prevent it from dehydrating. Sliced bread can be toasted while still frozen, but whole loaves should be thawed at room temperature.

Fish

Fish should be frozen as soon as possible after being caught. With the exception of fish sold locally from the port, fresh fish should not be frozen at home as it deteriorates rapidly and will not be completely fresh.

White fish freeze better than oily fish (see p. 127). Small fish can be frozen whole (after gutting and cleaning), and larger fish can be filleted or cut into steaks.

Meat and poultry

It is often possible to buy whole sides of meat, cut into joints for the freezer. Meat and poultry should be frozen quickly, and it may be better to buy large joints already frozen as the domestic freezer may not freeze them quickly enough.

All joints and poultry should be closely wrapped with all the air removed to prevent freezer burn. Small joints, such as chops and cutlets, can be wrapped individually or separated with small sheets of greaseproof paper.

Boned joints save room in the freezer.

Offal

All offal should be very fresh for freezing, and is best packed into tubs or cartons as it tends to be messy when thawing.

Cooked foods

Pre-cooked meals and dishes can be frozen successfully, but it is better not to include potatoes, pasta, or rice as these tend to lose their texture and flavour, unless they are covered with a sauce. It is also a waste of space to freeze these foods as they can be stored well in cupboards and are relatively quick to cook.

Fresh ingredients should be used, and food should be prepared quickly and hygienically, to prevent contamination by micro-organisms. The food should be cooked quickly and for the minimum time necessary, and should then be cooled rapidly before freezing.

Seasoning and the use of spices should be minimal, as their flavours tend to intensify during storage. They can be added afterwards.

Packed lunches

It is possible to freeze ready-made sandwiches and rolls or pies for packed lunches, which saves time during the week. Sandwich fillings must be suitable for freezing. Foods such as tomato, egg, or cucumber should not be included.

Thawing frozen food

Some frozen foods, e.g. vegetables, beefburgers, fish, can be cooked from frozen. Foods such as cakes must be thawed so that they can be cut.

Some foods *must* be thawed completely before cooking, for safety reasons. This includes meat (especially pork) and poultry, shellfish, and cream. Such foods may harbour bacteria (especially salmonella - see pp. 154–8), and if insufficiently thawed, the food will not get properly hot when it is cooked. This will encourage bacterial growth and reproduction, which may cause food poisoning if the cooked food is kept warm. This is more likely in large volumes of food, such as poultry. Large turkeys should be thawed for at least 24 hours in a cool place, and chickens for at least eight hours. There should be no signs of ice when the poultry has been thawed.

Most foods should be thawed at room temperature. This takes several hours for large packs, and must be allowed for when using foods from the freezer.

Once thawed, raw food *should not be refrozen*, unless it is cooked first, as this may lead to microbial growth and food poisoning.

Storage times for frozen foods

Different foods will keep for different lengths of time in the freezer, and it is important not to exceed storage times. The following list gives storage times for foods stored at –18°C:

Food	Storage time
Vegetables	12 months
Fruit	12 months
Raw meat	
beef and lamb	12 months
mince and offal	2 months
pork	9 months
unsmoked bacon	6 weeks
sausages	6 weeks
smoked bacon	4 weeks
vacuum-packed rashers	3 months
bacon joints	3 months
Poultry	
chicken	12 months
duck	6 months
Fish	
white, filleted	8 months
oily	4 months
Shellfish	2 months
Whipped cream	2 months
Hard cheese	3 months
Cakes	
fatless	6 months
with fat	4 months
Pastry	
cooked	6 months
uncooked	3 months
Bread	3 months
Soups, sauces	4 months
Stews	2 months
Meat loaves, pâtés	1 month
Ice cream	3 months

Revision questions

1. What are the advantages of freezing?
2. Describe the types of freezer that are available, and list the advantages and disadvantages of each.
3. What are conservators, and why are they unsuitable for freezing food?
4. Where and how should a freezer be sited?
5. What factors affect the running costs of a freezer?
6. In the event of a power failure or moving house, how should the food be handled to keep it in good condition?
7. What are the features of a good packaging material for frozen foods?
8. Name five containers or materials suitable for storing frozen foods?
9. How should a freezer be defrosted?
10. What are the basic rules for freezing foods successfully?
11. Name five foods that are unsuitable for freezing.
12. Why must some foods be blanched before freezing?
13. How should the following be prepared for freezing?
    a cakes   d bread
    b pastries   e fish
    c meat joints
14. How long can the following foods be stored in the freezer?
    a cheese   e sausages
    b bread   f whipped cream
    c meat   g stews
    d vegetables
15. Why is it important that poultry, shellfish, and pork are completely thawed before use?
16. How should foods be thawed?

Use of left-over foods

As food is an expensive item in a household budget, it makes sense to use left-over items of food from one meal to prepare another. It is possible to produce tasty and nutritious meals by adding other ingredients to left-over foods, and by careful preparation.

However, it is necessary to follow some important basic rules to ensure that the left-over food is safe to eat as well as appetizing and nutritious. Left-over foods such as meat and fish can harbour bacteria if stored incorrectly or not cooked thoroughly, and can be a major cause of food poisoning (see pp. 156–8). The reheating of left-over foods is called **réchauffé** cookery.

Rules for preparing left-over foods

1 Use the left-over food preferably within 24 hours and certainly within 48 hours.
2 Cool the left-over food within 1½ hours, and store in a covered container in the refrigerator.
3 Reheat the food quickly: it should be cut up finely or minced to facilitate heat penetration.
4 Do not recook the food, as this will toughen the protein and make it indigestible. Just reheat it, to a safe temperature of at least 63°C.
5 Cook additional ingredients, e.g. vegetables, before adding them to the food.
6 Never reheat food more than once.
7 During the first cooking, moisture will be lost and should therefore be replaced when reheating, by the addition of a sauce, stock, or gravy.
8 Include additional flavouring in the form of herbs, spices, or seasoning, as much of the original flavour may be lost in the first cooking.
9 Serve the reheated food immediately it is ready. Do not keep it warm as this will encourage bacterial growth.
10 Heat-sensitive nutrients, e.g. vitamin C, will have been destroyed in the first cooking and should be replaced, e.g. by adding fruit or vegetables to the meal.

Methods of cooking used for réchauffé dishes

Some left-over foods, e.g. fish, some meat and poultry, should be protected from being recooked by one of the following means:
  coating in batter
  covering with a layer of sauce or potato
  coating with egg and breadcrumbs
  covering with pastry

Reheating methods

Frying Meat or fish rissoles and croquettes, fritters, burgers, bubble and squeak (fried vegetables).
Baking Meat pies, fish pies, pastry-covered dishes.
Sauces Fish in cheese sauce, curry sauce, savoury mince sauce.

Suggested uses for different foods

Fish Fish in a sauce, Russian fish pie (in flaky pastry), fish cakes, kedgeree, fish pasties, fish mousse.
Meat Curry, shepherd's pie, rissoles, burgers, fritters, croquettes, pasties, meat loaves.
Bread Bread pudding, queen of puddings, raspings, bread sauce.
Vegetables Bubble and squeak, omelettes, salads, pasties with cheese pastry, croquettes, scones (potato), potato cakes, toppings for shepherd's pie, etc.
Stale cake can be used in puddings or for trifle.

Revision questions

1 Why should left-over foods be used up within 24 hours and only be reheated once?
2 Give five rules for the preparation of réchauffé dishes?
3 Why is it important not to recook the left-over food?
4 Suggest a dish that can be made from each of the following:
    a   225 g cooked lamb (cold)
    b   left-over apple purée
    c   stale bread

Raising agents

In order to make flour mixtures (e.g. cakes, bread, batters, pastries) rise and have a light, pleasant texture, a gas must be introduced before baking.

Gases **expand** when heated, and can raise a mixture in the process. **Raising agents** are used to introduce a gas into a mixture.

As a mixture rises, the protein in it coagulates (sets), thus forming with the rest of the ingredients a firm structure containing a **network** of many small holes left by the expanded gas. It is important that the mixture is of the correct consistency, otherwise the gas will expand too vigorously and escape before the mixture has set. The gases used for this purpose are:
  carbon dioxide (CO_2)
  air (a mixture of gases)
  steam (water in a gaseous state)

Raising agents fall into two main categories:
mechanical raising agents
chemical raising agents

Mechanical raising agents

Air is incorporated into mixtures by various mechanical methods:

Sieving

When flour is sieved, air becomes trapped between its many fine particles.

Creaming

When fat and sugar are creamed together, air becomes trapped in the form of tiny bubbles, which make the mixture appear lighter.

Whisking

Egg white can hold up to seven times its own volume of air, because the protein **ovalbumin** can stretch. If beaten too much, the ovalbumin will overstretch and break, releasing air and becoming liquid.

Whole egg and sugar, if whisked together, will trap a large volume of air. This is the main raising agent for sponges.

Folding and rolling

This is used for flaky pastry. Air is trapped between the layers, and is sealed in. During baking, it expands and the fat melts, leaving a space which is filled with steam and raises the pastry.

Rubbing-in

Some air is trapped as the fat is rubbed into the flour.

Chemical raising agents

Carbon dioxide is incorporated into mixtures by the use of:
bicarbonate of soda alone
bicarbonate of soda plus an acid
baking powder (contains bicarbonate of soda and acid)
yeast (not strictly a chemical method as yeast is a living organism)

Bicarbonate of soda (an alkali)

Chemical formula: $NaHCO_3$
When heated, the following reaction occurs:

$$2NaHCO_3 \xrightarrow{heat} Na_2CO_3 + H_2O + CO_2$$

washing soda   water   gas

This results in the production of an unpleasant soda taste and a yellow discoloration, both of which are undesirable for most mixtures. Bicarbonate of soda is therefore only used on its own for strong-flavoured mixtures such as gingerbread and parkin.

Bicarbonate of soda plus an acid

To prevent the formation of washing soda, with its unpleasant taste and colour, a weak acid is usually used with bicarbonate of soda. Carbon dioxide still forms, so the mixture still rises. A variety of acids can be used.

Cream of tartar (potassium hydrogen tartrate)

This is often used and it produces a residue which is colourless and almost tasteless.

$$KHC_4H_4O_6 + NaHCO_3 \xrightarrow{heat} NaKC_4H_4O_6 + H_2O + CO_2$$

cream of tartar

sodium potassium tartrate

Tartaric acid

This is less often used, but is effective as it produces 25 times its own volume of gas if used with bicarbonate of soda in equal quantities. The resulting residue is slightly bitter.

Lactic acid (in sour milk)

This is produced by lactic acid bacteria, but its use is not very accurate as it is impossible to gauge the amount present in milk. It is often used in scone making.

Citric acid (lemon juice) or ethanoic acid (vinegar)

These are not very accurate as it is difficult to gauge the strength of the acid.

Baking powder

This is produced commercially and usually consists of:

- bicarbonate of soda
- acid sodium pyrophosphate
- acid calcium phosphate
- starch, e.g. rice flour

Rice flour or other starch is added to absorb any moisture from the atmosphere, which would otherwise cause the bicarbonate of soda to react with the acid, releasing CO_2. This would make the baking powder ineffective.

The quality of baking powder is controlled by law. It can be added to plain flour, which is used instead of self-raising flour.

Self-raising flour is prepared from soft cake flour (see pp. 86–8) and a standard strength raising agent: it is useful for plain cake mixtures. It is *not* suitable for:

- scones – too weak on its own
- rich cakes – too much raising agent
- bread, pastries, biscuits – chemical raising agent not required

Yeast

Yeast is a microscopic living fungus (see p. 158) which is found naturally on the skins of some fruits and in the air. It is produced commercially on a large scale for the brewing and baking industries.

Yeast can be obtained for baking in both dried and fresh forms.

Dried yeast, fast action yeast, and fresh yeast can all be used for home baking.

Dried yeast consists of tiny pellets or fine granules of yeast, which are pale brown. It will keep for a few months in a cool dry place, but will gradually lose its effectiveness. When added to a liquid, it should be allowed to dissolve for a few seconds before being stirred. Sugar should then be added. Dried yeast is more concentrated than fresh, being approximately twice the strength.

Fast action yeast is added directly to the flour, before the liquid is added.

Fresh yeast is available from some bakers' shops. It should be pale brown in colour, with a slight smell and a crumbly texture. It is compacted into blocks. It must be stored in a cold place, well covered to prevent drying. It can be frozen in small pieces and used from frozen if dissolved in warm water. However, fresh yeast becomes less effective if frozen for more than three months.

Fresh yeast is more sensitive than dried yeast to the effects of osmosis (see p. 165), brought about by mixing it with sugar. It is therefore inadvisable to mix it directly with sugar as suggested in some recipes.

Yeast as a raising agent

Under the right conditions, yeast will produce CO_2 gas and alcohol in a series of chemical reactions known as fermentation. It is the CO_2 gas which is of importance to the baker.

The correct conditions for fermentation are:

1. A source of food (sugar or flour).
2. The correct temperature. It works best at 25–29°C, and as the temperature increases, the yeast is gradually destroyed. At lower temperatures, yeast activity slows down, until at freezing point it is still alive, but dormant.
3. Moisture.
4. The presence of enzymes in the yeast, including:
   maltase – converts maltose to glucose
   invertase – converts sucrose to fructose and glucose
   zymase group – convert glucose and fructose to CO_2 and ethanol (alcohol).

In bread making, fermentation takes place during the time the dough is allowed to rise or prove. The fermentation process produces carbon dioxide gas, which raises the dough (see p. 213).

Steam

Steam is produced during baking from the liquid present in a mixture. This happens slowly, so steam is only suitable as a raising agent for mixtures that contain a lot of liquid, e.g. batters, choux pastry, flaky pastry. The oven temperature must be high to raise the liquid rapidly to boiling point.

Water vapour expands to 1,600 times its original volume, and so is an effective raising agent.

Stretching capacity of mixtures

In order for a mixture to rise, it must have the ability to stretch and hold its shape once risen.

In wheat flour, gluten is formed from the proteins present when water is added. When kneaded, gluten becomes 'elastic', giving flour mixtures the ability to stretch.

Different types of wheat flours produce different amounts of gluten when water is added, so not all flours are suitable for all types of mixture (see p. 86-8).

Using raising agents

1   Store in a cool, dry place.
2   Use only amounts stated in recipes.

Baking powder

Scones:	4-5 tsp to 450 g flour
Suet pastry:	4-5 tsp to 450 g flour
Cakes:	
$^1/_2$ fat to flour	4 tsp to 450 g flour
$^3/_4$ fat to flour	3 tsp to 450 g flour
=fat to flour	2 tsp to 450 g flour

(tsp means *level* teaspoon)

Bicarbonate of soda

Scones: 1 tsp+2 tsp cream of tartar
                   to 225 g flour

3   Once the mixture is ready, bake immediately as the reaction will start as soon as moisture comes into contact with the raising agent.
4   Pre-heat the oven to ensure prompt expansion of the gas and setting of the mixture.
5   Sieve the raising agent with the flour to ensure even distribution.

Experiments with raising agents

Mechanical raising agents

1 Air trapped in flour

Fill two equal-sized glasses with flour and knock them gently so the flour settles. Sieve the contents of one glass twice on to paper and carefully tip back into the glass. What happens?

You will see that the volume of the sieved flour has increased, because it has air trapped in it.

2 Air trapped by egg white

Place one egg white into a grease-free measuring jug. Measure the volume of the egg white. Whisk it until it is foamy and standing in soft peaks. Measure the volume again.

You will see that the volume has increased substantially because of the trapped air.

3 Air trapped by whole egg and sugar

Repeat the above experiment using 25 g caster sugar and one egg, and whisk until thick and creamy.

4 Expansion of air

Partially blow up a balloon and tie the end securely. Place the balloon in a warming cabinet, and leave for 10–15 minutes.

You will see that the balloon has enlarged because the heat has caused the air inside it to expand.

Chemical raising agents

1 Acidity and alkalinity

   a Dissolve a little bicarbonate of soda in water and test with red litmus paper.
   b Dissolve a little cream of tartar in the water and test with blue litmus paper.
   c Dissolve two parts cream of tartar and one part bicarbonate of soda in water and test with pH indicator paper.
   d Test some sour milk with pH indicator paper.

The reactions will indicate the following:

   a Bicarbonate of soda is an alkali.
   b Cream of tartar is an acid.
   c Bicarbonate of soda and cream of tartar neutralize each other.
   d Sour milk contains acid.

2 Evolution of CO_2 gas

   a Place $^1/_2$ tsp bicarbonate of soda in a test tube, add hot water and note the length of the reaction.

b Repeat the above using cold water.

c Repeat using baking powder.

d Repeat using bicarbonate of soda with cream of tartar.

Compare the results and relate to the reaction which occurs in the oven.

3 **Gas production from yeast**

Dissolve 25 g fresh yeast in 150 ml tepid water. Divide between five test tubes and have five balloons ready.

Test tube 1: add ¼ tsp sugar, place balloon over top and stand in warm place.

Test tube 2: place balloon on top and stand in warm place.

Test tube 3: add ¼ tsp salt, place balloon over top and stand in warm place.

Test tube 4: add ¼ tsp sugar, place balloon over top and stand in pan of boiling water.

Test tube 5: add ¼ tsp sugar, place balloon over top and stand in refrigerator.

Leave the tubes for 15 minutes. Observe the results and compare gas production.

Expected results:

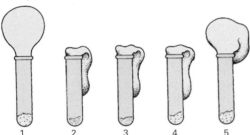

4 **Elasticity of gluten**

Prepare gluten balls from 50 g of:

a strong plain flour

b ordinary plain flour

c self-raising flour

as described in experiment 1 on p. 91. Note the size of the gluten balls. Place on a greased baking tray and bake at Gas 7, 220°C (425°F) for 15 minutes. Observe changes in size and note the colour, structure, smell, and taste of the three samples.

5 **Use of steam**

Prepare two identical Yorkshire pudding batters. Bake one in a cool oven, starting from cold, and the other in a hot oven which has been pre-heated. Compare your results.

Revision questions

1 What is a raising agent?

2 What is the principle behind the use of raising agents?

3 Why is the consistency of a flour mixture important for particular items?

4 What mechanical methods can be used for raising mixtures?

5 What are the gases used as raising agents?

6 What is bicarbonate of soda, and how does it work?

7 What is baking powder?

8 What is the best raising agent for each of the following?

a scones

b gingerbread

c bread

9 Why must chemical raising agents be sieved with the flour?

10 How should chemical raising agents be stored and used?

11 What is the importance of:

a temperature, moisture, and sugar to yeast?

b creaming fat and sugar, sieving flour, beating eggs, and folding in flour in the preparation of a Victoria sandwich?

12 Why should choux pastry and flaky pastry be cooked at a high temperature?

Cakes

Choice and functions of ingredients

Flour

Weak or **soft flour** (see pp. 86–8) is best for cakes as it contains a relatively small amount of gluten-forming proteins. When cakes are baked, the gluten coagulates. This helps to form the structure of the cake, and the lower protein content of weak flours gives the fine, even texture typical of most cakes.

Self-raising flour can be used for plain cakes with the proportion of fat to flour being no more than half. For richer cakes, the amount of baking powder in self-raising flour is too high, so **plain flour** with various amounts of baking powder should be used.

80% extraction flour (see p. 87) can be used, and provides extra fibre (NSP), nutrients, colour, and flavour. It is possible to buy self-raising flour of this extraction, although cakes made with it may have slightly less volume than those made with white flour, because of the extra fibre (NSP).

The starch in flour becomes trapped within the framework produced by the expansion of gas bubbles and gluten during baking, and contributes to the lightness of the cake.

Fat

Fats are added to cake mixtures:

1 To trap air with sugar during creaming, so that the cake will rise.

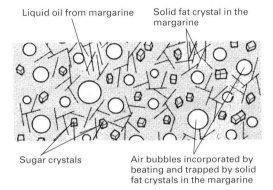

Liquid oil from margarine

Solid fat crystal in the margarine

Sugar crystals

Air bubbles incorporated by beating and trapped by solid fat crystals in the margarine

Air bubbles become trapped when fat and sugar are creamed together.

2 To provide 'shortness' to the cake mixture. As fat is insoluble in water, it prevents gluten strands from adhering to each other, thus shortening them. If this did not happen, the baked mixture would be solid and tough.

3 To add colour and flavour to the mixture.

Margarine is economical and provides colour and flavour. 'Soft' margarine (see p. 95) is specially produced for creaming, but is not very suitable for rubbed–in mixtures as it is too oily.

Butter provides good flavour and colour. For economy, it can be mixed with margarine or another fat.

White cooking fats (vegetable) do not contribute towards the flavour or colour of the cake mixture, but can be creamed with sugar quite well. They can therefore be used in strongly flavoured mixtures.

Lard is unsuitable for most cake mixtures as it does not cream well and has a distinctive flavour which is not good for cakes.

Oil can be used for some mixtures where there is an additional raising agent, but it is not possible to trap air during creaming if oil alone is used.

Sugar

Sugar is added to cake mixtures:

1 To add flavour.

2 To help trap air with fat during creaming so that the cake rises.

3 To contribute to the texture of the cake by dissolving into a syrup and softening the gluten in flour during baking. If too much sugar is added, the gluten is softened too much and the structure of the cake collapses during baking.

4 To contribute to the colour of the cake by caramelizing on exposure to the dry heat of the oven (the crust).

Caster sugar is most suitable as it has small crystals which dissolve easily and give a smooth texture to the cake.

Granulated sugar has coarser crystals and therefore has to be creamed more thoroughly to break these down. It can be used for recipes where the sugar is melted with the fat first.

Soft brown sugar can be used for dark-coloured or fruit cakes, and contributes more flavour.

Syrup or treacle can be used with sugar and contribute towards the texture and moistness of the cake.

Eggs

Eggs are added to most cake mixtures:

1 To trap air during whisking with sugar in sponges or beating into creamed mixtures. Eggs can hold large volumes of air (see p. 205).

2 To help to set the cake once it has risen during baking, by coagulation of the protein.

3 To add colour and nutritional value.

4 To **emulsify** the fat in creamed mixtures; the lecithin in egg yolk is responsible for this (see pp. 115 and 217).

When added to creamed mixtures, eggs should be at room temperature. If they are too cold, the

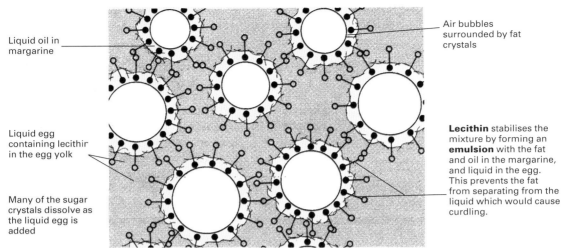

Liquid oil in margarine

Liquid egg containing lecithin in the egg yolk

Many of the sugar crystals dissolve as the liquid egg is added

Air bubbles surrounded by fat crystals

Lecithin stabilises the mixture by forming an **emulsion** with the fat and oil in the margarine, and liquid in the egg. This prevents the fat from separating from the liquid which would cause curdling.

Addition of egg to creamed fat and sugar.

mixture may **curdle**. This means that the fat separates from the sugar and eggs when the eggs are added.

Eggs should be fresh. They should be opened into a separate bowl first, to avoid the possibility of spoiling the cake mixture by adding a bad egg to it.

Dry ingredients

Dry ingredients apart from flour, (e.g. baking powder, spices, salt) should be sieved into the cake mixture with the flour to ensure even distribution.

Liquid

Liquids apart from egg (e.g. milk, lemon juice, or water) help to raise the cake mixture by producing steam during baking, but they may also toughen the gluten (see p. 4) and therefore produce a harder texture in the cake.

Flavourings

Some flavourings, such as citrus fruit rind or dried fruit, contribute to the keeping qualities of a cake, by the presence of oil in the former and moisture in the latter.

Dried fruits should be well washed and dried, and large pieces should be chopped to a uniform size. The fruit can be coated with some of the flour to keep the pieces separate and to help prevent it sinking in the mixture.

Flavourings such as coffee powder should be dissolved in water first, to prevent the cake having a speckled appearance.

A perfect Victoria sponge

Faults in cake making

Curdling of uncooked cake mixture

Cause

If the egg is very cold, it cools the fat. Fat globules become surrounded by water from the egg, so it is difficult for the egg yolk to emulsify the fat. The mixture will hold less air, and the cake will be very close-textured. A mixture may also curdle if too much egg is added at once.

Remedy

Adding a little flour from the mixture may help to absorb some of the water from the egg so that an emulsion can form.

Cake has sunk in the middle

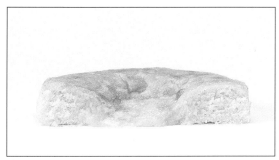

Causes

1 Too much sugar or syrup, causing the gluten to be over-softened so that it collapses.
2 Too much raising agent, causing the gluten to overstretch and collapse.
3 Undercooking, caused by the wrong temperature or cooking time.
4 Opening the oven door before the gluten has set, so that the heavy cold air makes it sink.

Cake has risen to a peak and is cracked

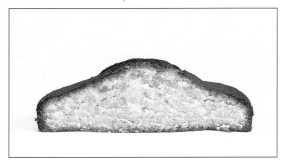

Causes

1 The oven temperature is too high, causing the mixture to rise rapidly, then overcook.
2 Too much mixture for the size of tin.
3 Placing the cake too high in the oven.

Cake has a heavy texture

Causes

1 Too much liquid in the mixture.
2 Too little raising agent used, or incorporated during creaming or whisking.
3 The mixture has curdled and does not hold sufficient air.
4 The oven temperature is too low, or the cake has not been cooked for long enough.
5 Overbeating when adding flour, causing loss of air.
6 Overbeating after adding a liquid.

Cake has a coarse, open texture

Causes

1 Too much raising agent has been used, causing large pockets of gas to be produced.
2 The flour has not been mixed sufficiently.

Cake has risen unevenly

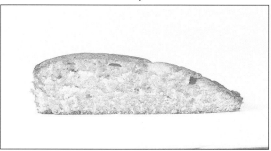

Causes

1 The oven shelf is not level, which may be due to the floor on which it stands.
2 The cake mixture was placed too near the source of heat, which has caused it to rise quickly on one side.

Cake has a hard, sugary crust

Causes

1 The sugar is too coarse for the mixture and does not dissolve in time.
2 Too much sugar has been used.

Cake is badly shaped

Causes

1 The tin has been badly lined or filled with the mixture.
2 The mixture is too stiff and does not even out when baked, or is too wet and has spread out too much.

Cake is dry

Causes

1 Too much chemical raising agent has been used.
2 Too little liquid has been used.
3 Cake has been overcooked.

Fruit has sunk in fruit cake

Causes

1 The mixture is too wet and the heavy fruit cannot be held evenly throughout.
2 The fruit is wet and therefore adds too much liquid to the cake.
3 Too much sugar or raising agent has been used, causing the structure to collapse and the fruit to sink.

Yeast mixtures

Choice and functions of ingredients

Flour

Strong, plain flour from spring wheat, e.g. Canadian wheat, which has a high gluten content (see p. 86), is most suitable for yeast mixtures as it produces a strong, elastic dough. The elasticity of the gluten enables yeast doughs to stretch and hold CO_2 gas in small pockets, as it is produced by the yeast during fermentation (see p. 213).

During fermentation, sugars naturally present in the flour (including maltose which is produced when amylase enzymes in the flour break down the starch) are converted to glucose, and this is fermented by the yeast to CO_2 gas and alcohol.

During baking, the gluten coagulates and the starch gelatinizes with the water. Together these result in a rigid loaf, containing a network of gas pockets. The starch on the outside is changed to dextrin (see p. 11) and the sugars in the flour caramelize, making the crust brown.

Wholemeal flour is suitable for bread making, and provides extra dietary fibre (NSP), B vitamins, and flavour.

Self-raising flour is not suitable because it contains baking powder, and has a low gluten content.

Yeast

The choice, use, and function of yeast in baking are discussed on p. 206). Yeast should be fresh and in good condition, so that its activity is sufficient to raise the dough.

Liquid

The liquid should be measured accurately and should be at blood heat (i.e. warm to the touch) to activate the yeast. Hot water will destroy the yeast, and cold water will slow its activity.

Salt

Salt is added to influence the rate of fermentation, strengthen the gluten, and improve the flavour of bread.

Fat

Fat may be added to improve the keeping qualities of the dough and add colour and flavour.

Bread mixture

450 g strong plain flour
12$^1/_2$ g fresh yeast
or 1 rounded tsp dried yeast
2 tsp salt
1 tsp sugar
275 ml warm water

Oven temperature and cooking time

For a loaf: Gas 8, 230°C (450°F) for 20 minutes, then reduce temperature to Gas 5, 190°C (375°F) and bake for a further 20 minutes.

Variations

Wholemeal bread: use 100% extraction flour.

Brown bread: use wheatmeal flour or 50% wholemeal and 50% white flour.

Milk bread: add 25 g fat, and use milk instead of water.

Bread making (traditional method)

All ingredients and utensils should be warm to assist the fermentation.

1 Dissolve the yeast in some of the liquid and add 1tsp sugar. Leave it to stand in a warm place for ten minutes. This activates the yeast and starts the fermentation process.

2 Sieve the flour and salt. Rub in the fat if used.

3 Add the yeast liquid and the rest of the liquid all at once.

4 Mix quickly to a soft dough, which is elastic and pliable.

5 Knead the dough vigorously either by hand or in an electric mixer using a dough hook. Kneading ensures thorough distribution of the yeast in the dough so that it is in contact with the natural sugars in the flour. It also helps to develop the gluten so that it can stretch during fermentation.

6 Cover the dough with a damp cloth to prevent the formation of a skin, and leave it to rise or 'prove' in a warm place for one to two hours. During this time the process of fermentation takes place, and the reactions involved are summarized below:

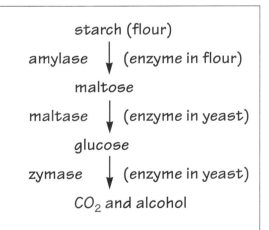

starch (flour)

amylase ↓ (enzyme in flour)

maltose

maltase ↓ (enzyme in yeast)

glucose

zymase ↓ (enzyme in yeast)

CO_2 and alcohol

The temperature inside the dough should be about 25°C for this to work efficiently.

7 'Knock back' the dough by kneading it again, to bring the yeast into contact with more of the flour.

8 Shape the dough into a loaf. Place in greased tin and leave to rise again for 40 minutes so that more CO_2 gas is produced.

9 Bake according to directions, until risen, set, golden brown in colour, and hollow sounding when tapped with the finger.

Bread making (quicker method)

It is possible to shorten the time required for making bread by the traditional method, by subjecting the dough to a longer period of very intensive kneading in the first stage, shaping it into rolls or loaves, and then allowing it to rise for half an hour before baking. This method is often used in bakeries where large mixers are used for the thorough kneading.

The Chorleywood process

This quicker method of bread making was developed at the British Baking Industries Research Association at Chorleywood, and became known as the Chorleywood process. In this method, extra yeast and water are used, and ascorbic acid (vitamin C) is added as a dough improver. Fat is also added.

Almost any type of flour can be used and even weak flour will produce good bread, as the shorter fermentation time results in a smaller loss of protein than in the traditional method. Strict temperature control is also less critical as the rapid fermentation reactions cause the dough temperature to rise.

Bakeries use large mixers for kneading dough.

The bread can be made and baked within two hours. This is a time saving of 60% compared with the traditional method, and so is useful to large bakeries. Bread made by this method also has better keeping qualities.

For making bread at home, vitamin C tablets (obtainable from chemists) can be added to the yeast liquid before it is added to the flour. The dough should be kneaded for five minutes, then shaped and left to rise before baking.

Changes during the baking of bread

1 The dough first rises quickly, as the CO_2 gas expands in the heat.
2 Yeast activity increases at first, but gradually decreases as the dough temperature rises.
3 At 55°C the yeast is killed and fermentation stops.
4 The water is absorbed by the starch granules in the flour. They swell and gelatinize, and support the structure of the loaf.
5 The gluten starts to coagulate at 70°C, and continues to do so until baking is complete.
6 Water, carbon dioxide, and alcohol escape from the dough during baking.
7 Dextrin forms on the outside of the loaf as the starch reacts with the heat. The sugars are converted to caramel which gives a brown colour to the crust.

A perfect loaf

Faults in breadmaking

Loaf is small and dense

Causes
1 Insufficient fermentation and proving.
2 Insufficient liquid resulting in a dough which is too stiff to allow expansion.
3 Inactive yeast, which has not produced enough CO_2 gas.

Loaf has not risen well, and is hard and coarse in texture

Causes
1 The dough has been overfermented. Too much pressure from the CO_2 gas causes gas pockets to break down which leaves large, uneven holes in the baked dough.
2 Yeast was killed before the loaf was baked.

Batters

Batters are a mixture of flour (usually plain), liquid (milk or water), and egg.

They vary in consistency according to their use in a recipe.

Thin batter

100 g plain flour
$^1/_2$ tsp salt
275 ml liquid
1 egg

Uses

Toad-in-the-hole
Yorkshire pudding
Pancakes

Coating batter

100 g plain flour
$^1/_2$ tsp salt
150 ml liquid
1 egg

Uses

Deep fried fish
Poultry joints

Fritter batter

50 g plain flour
pinch of salt
3 tbsp water
1 egg white
2 tsp vegetable oil

Uses

Banana, apple, pineapple fritters
Corned beef, sausage fritters

Method

1 Sieve the flour and salt. Make a well in the centre.

2 Add the egg and a little liquid and gradually work in the flour.

3 Add more liquid and mix to a smooth batter. Add the rest of the liquid and beat for five minutes.

4 During beating, some air is incorporated into the mixture, but this has a limited action as a raising agent during cooking. The main raising agent is steam, which is produced during cooking from the large volume of water in the mixture. In order for this to be effective the cooking temperature must be high so that the water vaporizes rapidly.

5 Use the mixture according to the recipe. Some recipes suggest leaving the mixture to stand for a while, but this is not essential.

6 If food is to be coated with the batter, it must be dry to ensure good adhesion when the batter is applied.

7 If the coated food is to be deep fried, the fat should be at the right temperature. If it is too hot, the batter will cook rapidly, leaving the inside partly cooked or raw. If the fat is too cool, the starch will absorb it, and the food will be heavy and oily.

Note: Batters can be made quickly and successfully in a food processor.

A thin batter mixture can be used to make pancakes.

Sauces

A sauce is a thickened, flavoured liquid which can be added to a food or dish:

1 To enhance the flavour of the food which it accompanies.
2 To provide a contrasting flavour to an otherwise mildly flavoured food, e.g. cheese sauce with cauliflower.
3 To provide a contrasting texture to solid foods, e.g. poultry or fish.
4 To bind ingredients together for dishes such as fish cakes or croquettes.
5 To add colour to a dish, e.g. jam sauce with a steamed sponge pudding.
6 To contribute to the nutritional value of a dish.
7 To reduce the richness of some foods, e.g. orange sauce with roast duck, apple sauce with roast pork.
8 To add interest and variety to a meal.

Sauces should be carefully flavoured and should be tasted before serving, so that adjustments can be made.

A sauce can be served as:

A **coating** for vegetables, meat, or fish.

Part of a meal, e.g. a casserole of meat.

An **accompaniment** to a meal, e.g. cranberry sauce with roast turkey, mint sauce with roast lamb.

Consistencies of sauces

The consistency of a sauce will vary according to how it will be served with the food (see above). Sauces can be classified into three main consistencies:

pouring
coating
binding (panada)

A **pouring** sauce, at boiling point, should just glaze the back of a wooden or plastic spoon, and should flow freely when poured.

A **coating** sauce, at boiling point, should coat the back of a wooden or plastic spoon, and should be used as soon as it is ready, to ensure even coating over the food.

A **binding** sauce or **panada** should be thick enough to bind dry ingredients together, so that

they can be handled easily to be formed into rissoles, cakes, etc.

All sauces should be free from lumps and should not be overcooked, as this may spoil their flavour.

Thickenings

Sauces may be thickened by:

starch, in flour, cornflour, arrowroot, etc.
protein, from eggs
emulsification of oil and water
puréed vegetables or fruits

Sauces thickened by starch

Starch is the main polysaccharide produced by plants (see pp. 9–10), and is present in plant foods in the form of tiny granules. The size and shape of these are peculiar to the species of plant from which they come.

If starch is mixed with cold water, it will not dissolve. However, on heating to 60°C, the granules absorb water and begin to swell. As the temperature increases, so does the swelling, until at 85°C the granules will have swollen to five times their original size, and the liquid will be thickened. If heating continues, some of the granules will rupture, releasing starch which will form a **gel** with the water. On cooling, the gel will set, and the sauce will become solid.

When preparing sauces of this type, it is important to blend the liquid with the starch component before cooking. Otherwise, lumps of starch granules will form, which will not cook properly and will give the sauce an uneven texture. During cooking the sauce should be stirred continually so that it is evenly heated. If it is not stirred, it will cook only at the bottom and the finished result will be lumpy. This is because the convection currents will not be sufficient to circulate the thick mixture.

Examples of sauces thickened by starch include roux sauces, cornflour sauces, and arrowroot sauces.

Roux sauces
Plain white sauce (coating consistency)

> 25 g flour
> 25 g fat
> 275 ml liquid (milk, stock, or vegetable liquor)

Traditional method

1   Melt the fat in a pan and add the flour. Stir until well mixed and heat gently for one minute. During this time, the starch granules will begin to soften and the starch will start to cook. The fat and flour mixture form the 'roux'.

2   Remove from the heat. Gradually add the liquid, stirring well at each addition, to form a smooth paste. If the liquid is added too quickly, lumps will form which will be difficult to remove.

3   When all the liquid has been added, return to the heat, and, stirring all the time, bring to the boil and cook for two minutes. The sauce must be stirred to prevent the formation of lumps.

4   Remove from the heat and add the seasoning and other ingredients. If cheese is used, add it as soon as the sauce is cooked so that it melts. Do not return it to the heat as the protein in the cheese may overcook and become stringy in texture.

All-in-one method

1   Place all ingredients in a saucepan.
2   Heat gently, stirring all the time until the mixture boils.
3   Continue cooking for three minutes until thick and glossy.

This method is quicker than the traditional one, and avoids the risk of overheating the fat and flour at the roux stage.

Sauces thickened by the coagulation of protein

The coagulation of protein by heat is discussed on p. 4. Eggs are normally used to thicken sauces in this way, and as egg white coagulates at a lower temperature than the yolk, it is better to use the yolk alone to prevent spoiling the sauce by overcooking the white.

If the yolk is used as an additional thickener for sauces that contain starch, it should be added after the other ingredients have been cooked and cooled to below boiling point, but not less than the coagulation temperature of the yolk (70°C).

If the temperature is too high, the protein will coagulate rapidly and cause it to harden and spoil the texture of the sauce.

If the yolk or whole egg is used as the only thickener, as in egg custard, it should be well mixed with the liquid, cooked gently (e.g. over a pan of boiling water) to prevent overcooking, and cooled rapidly as soon as it has thickened to stop the coagulation.

Egg custard sauce

275 ml milk
1 whole egg or 2 egg yolks
1 tbsp sugar
few drops vanilla essence

Method

1   Thoroughly mix the egg and milk.
2   Add the sugar.
3   Pour into a double saucepan or mixing bowl over a pan of boiling water.
4   Cook, stirring all the time, until the egg coagulates and the sauce coats the back of the spoon.
5   Remove from the heat, stir in the vanilla essence, and cool quickly to stop the coagulation. Serve immediately.

Sauces thickened by the emulsification of fat

If oil and water are thoroughly mixed, they become dispersed in each other and form an **emulsion**. After standing for a while, the emulsion will separate and the oil will float on top of the water. In order to prevent this separation, the emulsion must be stabilized by the addition of an **emulsifier**. Egg yolk contains a substance called lecithin (see p. 115) which acts as an emulsifier, and is added to mayonnaise to prevent the separation of the oil and water (in the vinegar).

When the emulsion is stabilized by the lecithin, it thickens. The thickness can be adjusted by the amount of vinegar added to the mayonnaise. The oil must be added slowly and thoroughly mixed with the egg yolk to prevent it from separating out.

Mayonnaise

150 ml oil
2 tbsp vinegar or lemon juice
1 egg yolk
3 tsp dry mustard
3 tsp salt
1 tsp caster sugar
pepper

Method

1 Beat the dry ingredients into the egg yolk in a small basin, to help the lecithin to stabilize the emulsion.
2 Add the oil drop by drop, beating thoroughly in between.
3 Continue adding the oil until the mixture starts to thicken, then add the vinegar, drop by drop.
4 Add the oil and vinegar until the mayonnaise is the consistency of lightly whipped double cream.
5 Adjust the seasoning.

It is possible to make mayonnaise in the liquidizer of an electric mixer, and the oil can be added in a slow trickle while the machine is running.

Sauces thickened by a purée

Cooked or raw fruit or vegetables can be puréed to produce a smooth sauce, by rubbing them through a nylon sieve or processing them in a liquidizer.

Fruit which is subject to enzymatic browning (see p. 154) should first be cooked or mixed with an acid (e.g. lemon juice), to inactivate the oxidase enzymes that cause the browning when the fruit is cut.

Apple sauce

450 g cooking apples
2 tbsp water
25 g butter
sugar to taste

Method

1 Peel, core, and slice the apples.
2 Stew the apples in the water and butter until soft.
3 Purée and add sugar to taste.
4 Serve with roast pork.

Salads

A salad is usually a mixture of raw vegetables and fruits, but cooked and pickled foods (e.g. rice, pasta) can also be included.

Salads can be served as:

1 A starter to a meal.
2 An accompaniment to a main course of meat, poultry, fish, etc.
3 A complete main course, including meat, fish, poultry, cheese, egg, or pulses and nuts for protein.
4 A filling for sandwiches and rolls in packed meals.

Salads are nutritionally important because:

1 Vitamins and minerals which are easily lost in cooking are preserved.
2 Fibre (NSP) is provided by many raw fruits and vegetables, and also by pulses if used.
3 Salads provide bulk to the diet and are useful in energy-reduced diets, as most raw fruits and vegetables have low energy values.
4 Water is provided by raw fruits and vegetables.

Points to remember when preparing salads

1 Ingredients used should be crisp, fresh, well cleaned, and refreshing.
2 The ingredients should be prepared just before consumption to preserve their freshness, crispness, and nutritive value.
3 A variety of colours, flavours, and textures should be included to make the salad interesting to eat.
4 The ingredients should be attractively and neatly served with the minimum of handling.
5 The salad should be easy to serve and eat.

Suitable salad ingredients: preparation

Raw vegetables

Lettuce	Discard outer, damaged leaves. Wash well, dry. Shred or tear leaves or leave whole.
Watercress	Discard damaged leaves and thick stalks. Wash well and inspect thoroughly for insects.
Mustard and cress	Wash while still in punnet. Cut in bunches, using the stalks.
Cucumber	Wash the skin if it is to be left on. Slice thinly.
Spring onion	Remove roots and outer skin. Wash well. Cut tops off.
Tomato	Choose firm tomatoes. Wash well. Slice or segment the tomato.
Radish	Remove stalks and roots and wash well.
Celery	Trim off leaves and root ends. Scrub each stalk well and slice.
Pepper (capsicum)	Wash well. Cut in half lengthways, and remove core, seeds, and pith. Slice or dice.
Chicory	Discard damaged leaves. Wash, halve lengthways or slice.
Carrot	Use young carrots. Wash well, serve whole if small or grate.
Cabbage	Use firm white cabbage. Shred finely and wash well.
Cauliflower	Use the head, broken into very small florets.
Mushrooms	Wash, peel if necessary, and slice thinly.

Cooked vegetables

Beetroot	Wash well, boil until soft with skin on, cool. Remove skin, slice or dice, and serve in vinegar or on its own.
Potato	Diced in potato salad or hot, new potatoes with mint and butter.
Carrots	Diced in potato salad.

Beans

Red kidney beans	Soak dried beans overnight in cold water, then boil for at least 20 minutes until soft.
Haricot beans	As above.
Butter beans	As above.
Broad beans	Wash and boil gently for 15 minutes until soft.
French beans	Boil until soft and serve with
Runner beans	a dressing.

Herbs

Fresh herbs can be sprinkled over salads or mixed into dressings to give extra flavour and interest.

Fresh fruits

Apple	Leave skin on. Slice and core, sprinkle with lemon juice to prevent browning.
Banana	Sprinkle with lemon juice.
Grapes	De-seed.
Citrus fruits	Remove segments, discarding pips and pith.
Pineapple	Remove hard core.

Nuts

Almonds
Walnuts
Peanuts
Cashew nuts
Hazel nuts
Brazil nuts
Use blanched, flaked or toasted almonds.

Pickles

Olives	Capers
Walnuts	Onions
Gherkins	Chutneys

Garnishes for salads

Sieved hard-boiled egg yolk
Grated cheese
Nuts
Chopped, fresh herbs

Salad dressings

Salad dressings can be served separately, or combined with the salad ingredients.
They are added to salads to:
1   Provide extra flavour.
2   Moisten the salad.
3   Aid chewing and swallowing the salad vegetables.
4   Prevent browning of fruit or vegetables.
5   Prevent loss of vitamin C by oxidation.
If the dressing is to be combined with the salad ingredients, it should be added just before serving, as soaking the ingredients will soften the leaves of salad vegetables and the vinegar acid will cause staining.

Soups and stocks

Soups

Soups are included in meals for the following reasons:
1   As appetizers.
2   To provide hot food in cold weather.
3   To provide flavour and energy.

Types of soup

Soups are normally based on one main ingredient, e.g. a vegetable, meat, or pulses, and can vary in consistency as follows.

Thick soups

These can be either puréed, or thickened by starch or egg protein.
Puréed These are usually sieved or liquidized and may be further thickened by starch.
Thickened by starch or protein These may have small solid ingredients in them, e.g. vegetable pieces.

Both types of thick soups can have cream added, and are normally served in cold weather as a substantial part of a meal.

Clear soups

These usually consist of a well-flavoured clear stock, served with a garnish, such as thin strips of carrot.
Broths are a variation of clear soups and usually contain small pieces of meat or poultry, with rice, pasta, or oats.

Mixed soups

These usually contain a mixture of ingredients, e.g. meat and vegetables, with perhaps pasta or rice included as well.

Preparing soups

A well-prepared soup should have the following qualities:
  a good flavour and colour
  non-greasy
  well seasoned
  finely chopped ingredients that are easy to fit on to a spoon
  no lumps, if it is a smooth soup
For each 575 ml of water or stock, a soup should have:
  450 g vegetables
  or 225 g meat or poultry
  or 100 g pulses (soaked)
It is important not to overcook the soup as this may spoil its flavour. If stock is used as the liquid, it should be fresh and well flavoured.

Serving soups

Soups can be served with:

    croutons of toast or fried bread

    bread rolls or sticks

    grated cheese

    slices of bread with grilled cheese on top

    chopped fresh parsley

    strips of carrot or celery

All of these will increase the nutrient value of the dish. Usually 150 ml of soup per person is enough.

Stocks

A stock is a well-flavoured liquid which is obtained by simmering a food in water for some time in order to extract flavour from it. Stocks have little food value on their own, and are mainly used as the bases of soups, sauces, and gravies.

Types of food suitable for stock making

1 Vegetables and vegetable liquid, except for green vegetables which can be bitter.
2 Bones from meat, fish, and poultry.
3 Meat, poultry, and giblets.
4 Bones and scraps of white fish.

Rules for making stock

1 The ingredients must be fresh and clean.
2 Cut up the ingredients so that all the flavour can be extracted, and remove fat.
3 Cover the ingredients with cold water, bring slowly to the boil, and simmer for 2–3 hours. To concentrate the flavour, remove the lid.
4 Skim the stock to remove fat and other ingredients that produce a foam on the surface.
5 Strain the stock as soon as it is ready, cool quickly, and store in a cold place.
6 Use the stock as soon as possible. It will keep for up to three days if stored in a cool place.
7 Do not use the stock more than once. Warm stock is an ideal breeding ground for bacteria.

Stock which is made from bones usually sets to a jelly due to the conversion of collagen to gelatine (see p. 117), but it has little food value as there is only a small amount of protein present.

Stock cubes or powders can be used in place of home-made stock and are quick and convenient.

Summary of changes in foods during preparation

What happens	Reasons
Food changes colour	
Red meat turns brown when stored	**Oxymyoglobin** in meat makes it red. It changes to **metmyoglobin** if stored in a place with little oxygen available.
Some cut fruits, e.g. apples, bananas, go brown	**Enzymes** in the fruit react with oxygen in the air, and the surface goes brown. This process is called **oxidation**.
Food loses some of its nutritional value	
Vitamin C (ascorbic acid)	**Oxidized** by exposure to air. This changes its chemical structure so that it cannot be used by the body. It is also dissolved by water.
Vitamin A (retinol)	Destroyed by exposure to light.
Vitamin B_2 (riboflavin)	Destroyed by exposure to light.

What happens	Reasons
Food (e.g. meat) is partially tenderized by	
Pounding and scoring	This reduces the length of the muscle fibres.
Using meat tenderizer powder	Tenderizing powder contains **enzymes** which partially digest the meat protein.
Marinading in vinegar or alcohol	This partially coagulates the meat proteins.
Food increases in size	
Dried fruit or pulses soaked in water	Water passes into the fruit or pulse as a result of osmosis. The water causes the cells inside to swell, thus making the fruit or pulse larger.
Bread dough	Yeast in the dough produces CO_2 gas, which makes the dough rise.
Whipped egg white	The protein **albumin** can stretch and hold up to 7 times its own volume of air.
Food becomes thicker	
Mayonnaise	Egg yolk contains **lecithin** which emulsifies the oil and vinegar and prevents them from separating out. The mixture becomes thickened as the lecithin starts to work.
Whipped cream	As cream is whipped, the fat globules it contains start to **coalesce** (stick together), until the cream becomes thick.
Food curdles	
Cake mixture	If egg is added too quickly, the lecithin in the yolk does not have time to stabilize the fat and sugar, so the fat curdles (separates).
Milk	The protein **caseinogen** will coagulate and curdle if acid is added.
Food absorbs other substances	
Odours	Odours are absorbed by eggs through their porous shells and by fat-containing foods, e.g. butter.
Water	Water is absorbed by some dried foods, e.g. coffee, because they are **hygroscopic** (attract water from the atmosphere).

Summary of changes in foods during cooking

What happens	Reasons
Mixture enlarges (rises) Bread, cakes, scones	Air is trapped during mixing, or gas is produced by chemical raising agents, or steam is produced from water in the mixture. Air, gas, and steam all expand with heat and push up the mixture during cooking.
Food shrinks or loses bulk Meat	Heat makes the protein molecules in meat alter their structure so that they become shorter. The connective tissue becomes shorter and thicker so that the meat shrinks.
Leafy vegetables	Boiling breaks down the cell structure in the leaves, so that they become less bulky.
Food increases in size Pasta, rice	These foods contain tiny granules of **starch**. As they are heated in water, the granules absorb water and swell. Some of them release their starch as heating increases.
Food becomes firmer (sets) Egg protein	Protein molecules in the white and yolk start to coagulate (become firmer) at about 60°C and 70°C respectively. As cooking continues, the whole egg sets.
Gelatine	Gelatine absorbs water and swells. When heated, the gelatine dissolves to form a clear liquid which sets when cooled.
Food changes colour Meat goes brown	**Oxymyoglobin** in uncooked meat makes it red. During cooking it changes to **haemochrome** which is brown.
Green vegetables	**Chlorophyll** in green vegetables becomes bright green when the vegetable is first cooked. If overcooked, it changes to olive green/brown.
Red/blue fruits and vegetables	Anthocyanins in red/blue fruits are purple at pH 7 (neutral), red at less than pH 7 (acid), and blue at more than pH 7 (alkali). They are very water soluble.
Sugar	Sugar crystals are white, but on exposure to heat, they gradually become golden brown due to a change in the sugar molecules, called **caramelization**.

What happens	Reasons
Food loses some of its nutritional value	
Vitamin C (ascorbic acid)	Vitamin C is destroyed by heat. The longer the exposure to heat, the greater the destruction.
Vitamin B_1 (thiamin) Vitamin B_2 (riboflavin)	These are both destroyed by exposure to heat.
Food becomes tender when cooked	
Meat	Connective tissue becomes shorter and thicker. **Collagen** is converted to gelatine in the presence of moisture.
Rice, pulses, pasta, vegetables, fruit	Water is absorbed into the starch granules, which soften and swell. Some starch escapes from ruptured granules and dissolves.
Food becomes thicker	
Cornflour and roux sauces	Both contain starch granules. These soften and swell as they absorb water. Some starch escapes from ruptured granules and dissolves.

Food presentation

In order for food to be appreciated and enjoyed, the **appetite** must be stimulated before a meal. When this occurs, digestive juices are produced so that the body is ready to receive the food when it is eaten.

Appetite stimulation is influenced by the body senses:

sight
smell
touch
taste

Food preparation should take account of these senses, and food should be attractive, well cooked, appetizing, and well presented.

The appearance of food

The first visual impressions of a meal are important factors in the success and enjoyment of the food. These visual impressions include not only the food itself, but also the way in which it is served and the surroundings in which it is eaten. Colour, design, and decoration are important considerations.

Colour

Food colours

There is a wide variety of natural colours in different foods, and a meal should contain as many variations as possible to make it attractive and interesting. The desire to eat is greatly influenced by colour, and if a food is coloured in an unusual way (e.g. if mashed potato is coloured blue), it will affect the enjoyment of it, even if the taste is the same.

The colours of food can be enhanced by the use of decorations and garnishes. Liquid food colourings should be used in moderation to improve a natural colour rather than hide it.

Colour of surroundings

When planning and serving a meal, it is important to take account of the surroundings in which the meal will be eaten. It is useful to select a colour theme for the table and decorations, and to use serving dishes, serviettes, and other items which blend in with this. The surroundings and environment also need to be comfortable, warm, conducive to holding a conversation while eating, and suitably lit.

Design and decoration
The table should be neatly arranged, with appropriate cutlery and decorations.

1   The tablecloth, serviettes, etc., should be well laundered and neatly pressed.
2   The cutlery should be clean, and carefully arranged, so that each course is catered for. Cutlery for the first course should be placed furthest from the serving mat (knives usually on the right), with the cutlery for successive courses placed in order, towards the mat. Cutlery for sweet courses should be placed above the serving mat.
3   Serviettes should be neatly folded, and placed either on a small plate next to the cutlery, or in a wine glass.

4   Centre table mats for hot serving dishes should be neatly arranged, with the cruet (salt, pepper, mustard, oil, vinegar), and any sauces or relishes that are to be served as accompaniments to the meal.

5   Glasses for wine and water should be placed to the top right hand side of the table mat. A jug of water (with ice) should be provided to drink with the meal.
6   Serving spoons and tongs should be neatly arranged in the centre of the table.
7   Table decorations (e.g. flowers, candles, dried grasses, leaves) make the table look attractive, but they should not dominate the table, or be so large that they obscure the vision of the people around the table.

Garnishes and decorations for food

Finishing-off a dish by garnishing (usually applies to savoury foods) or decoration (usually applies to sweet foods) adds to the visual impact and attractiveness of a meal.

1   Neatness and symmetry are important factors in the overall effect.
2   The garnish or decoration should add colour, flavour, and texture to the dish, and should be edible.
3   The garnish or decoration should enhance the dish, not dominate it.
4   It is usual to serve cooked garnishes with hot foods (but parsley and lemon are also served with hot foods).

Suitable garnishes and their preparation
Tomatoes

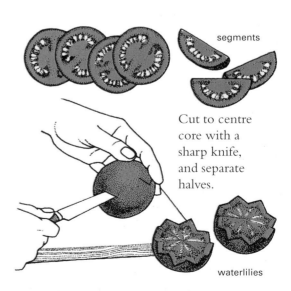

segments

Cut to centre core with a sharp knife, and separate halves.

waterlilies

Cucumber

Peel cucumber,
score flesh with fork,
and slice thinly.

Cut a thin slice almost
halfway and twist.

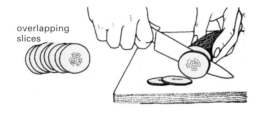

overlapping
slices

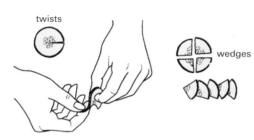

twists

wedges

Cut slices into four
and use wedges.

The skin can be removed or left on for extra
colour.

Parsley

Use chopped, or in sprigs.

Watercress, cress

Lettuce

Use as whole leaves or shredded.

Vegetables

Serve diced, grated, (e.g. carrots, mushrooms,
beetroot, peppers, celery) in strips, or in balls.

Radishes

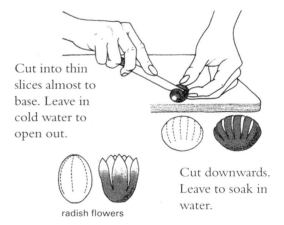

Cut into thin
slices almost to
base. Leave in
cold water to
open out.

radish flowers

Cut downwards.
Leave to soak in
water.

Olives, stuffed olives, gherkins, small onions

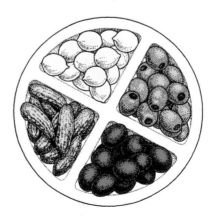

Boiled egg

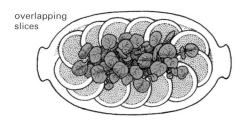

overlapping slices

The white (chopped) and yolk (sieved) can also be used separately.

Bread
Use fried or toasted, and cut into various shapes.

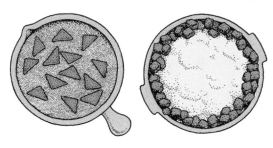

Lemon
Wedges and twists can be prepared in the same way as cucumber.

Cheese
Grate.

Bacon
Roll rashers and grill them.

Puff pastry
Cut into triangles. Roll downwards, shape into crescents, and bake.

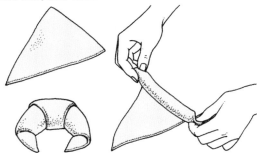

Meat frills

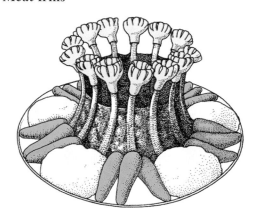

Suitable decorations
Chocolate
Grate, flake, melt and cut into shapes when cold, or caraque (spread a thin layer of melted chocolate on a flat surface; allow to set; draw a long bladed knife across it at an angle, to shave off long, thin scrolls of chocolate).

Icings
Glacé, royal, butter, fondant, etc. Can be piped in various designs.

Marzipan

Add colour and make into different shapes, e.g. fruit, flowers, animals.

Fruits

Use fresh, dried, or crystallized.

Jelly

Chop or use as a glaze.

Nuts

Use chopped, chopped and coloured, flaked, toasted, halved, or whole.

Sugar

Dredge in icing or caster sugar, or use sugar strands, coloured sugar crystals, or crushed caramel.

Cream

Use double or whipping cream, whipped and piped.

Flavour

When food is prepared, its flavour should be checked and adjusted before serving.

Flavours should be subtle, not overpowering, as they can spoil the enjoyment of the meal. Particularly strong flavours such as garlic or curry spices should be carefully used, as guests may find them too strong.

Flavours can be combined to give contrast to the meal, and garnishes or decorations can add flavour to a finished dish as well as making it look attractive.

See pp. 140-1 for further details of the use of herbs and spices.

Serving dishes

The dishes in which food is served should be attractive, clean, and hot if they are to contain hot food. If food has splashed on the sides or the lid of the dish, it should be wiped over. Plates should also be clean and, if necessary, hot.

Serve sauces in a jug or sauce boat with a saucer underneath, or poured over the food.

Bread and bread rolls can be served in a wicker basket, butter in small 'pats' or curls in a cold dish, and cheese on a cheese board.

Butter used to make pats and curls must be hard. Pats can be stored in cold water until serving.

Texture

The texture of food is an important factor in the enjoyment of a meal. Textures should be varied to avoid monotony, e.g. a meat casserole should have crisp vegetables as accompaniments, with a crunchy sweet to follow.

Heavy, 'stodgy' foods, such as suet puddings, should be served in moderation as they can be rather indigestible in large amounts.

Revision questions

1 How is the appetite affected by the appearance of food?
2 What preparations should be made for the serving of a meal?
3 What points should be remembered when garnishing or decorating food?
4 Give examples of garnishes and decorations for savoury and sweet foods.
5 How should serving dishes and plates be prepared for serving a meal?
6 Why is it important to vary the texture and flavour of a meal?
7 Give an example of a meal which is well balanced in colour, flavour, and texture.

Food preparation for assignments, investigations, and examinations

When carrying out an assignment, investigation, or practical food examination, a candidate should show:

1 Knowledge of and confidence in the properties, use, and preparation of different foods for a variety of occasions.
2 Skilful preparation of food using different methods of cooking.
3 Knowledge of the nutritional value of foods and the needs and dietary requirements of different people.
4 Knowledge of how to preserve the nutritional value of food.
5 Awareness of cost and economy and the best use of food for various occasions.
6 Knowledge of and confidence in the use of as many different pieces of kitchen equipment as possible.
7 Hygienic practices in the handling and preparation of food.
8 Ability to present meals of suitable portions in appetizing and attractive ways.

Types of assignment

Practical assignments can include work under these headings:

Individual requirements

e.g. convalescent   pregnant woman
     vegetarian   manual worker
     child   anaemic adolescent

Special occasion

e.g. Christmas   anniversary buffet
     teenage party   picnic
     Divali   child's birthday
     wedding reception   dinner party

Specific foods

e.g. alternatives to meat
     convenience foods
     economical meals
     foods made using a mixer or blender
     eating more fruit and vegetables

Choice of practical work

The choice of practical work should be relevant to the assignment and should demonstrate the candidate's abilities. Candidates are often asked to justify their choice of work, and the reasons given should be applicable to the particular situation being catered for.

Occasion	Reasons for choice in order of priority
Convalescent meal	Nutritional considerations. Portion size in relation to appetite. Stimulating poor appetite. Digestibility and ease of eating meal.
Wedding buffet	Attractiveness, colour, and variety of food. Catering for different tastes. Ease of eating and serving.
Child's lunch	Nutritional considerations and appeal to child. Portion size in relation to age and appetite. Ease of eating.
Anniversary meal	Attractiveness, colour, texture, and complementary flavours. Catering for different tastes. Nutritional balance.
Packed lunch	Nutritional value. Ease of packing to avoid damage to food. Satiety value. Suitability for storage without refrigeration. Ease of eating with minimum of cutlery.

Methods of cooking

The use of a variety of cooking methods will demonstrate the candidate's knowledge of the use of the cooker and the reactions of different foods under various conditions, and will also add variety to the finished result.

Skills

The use of a variety of skills will demonstrate the candidate's abilities and confidence.

These skills include:

adapting and varying recipes

saving time, e.g. by using food processor or all-in-one recipes

pastry making

cake making

meat jointing and preparation

food decoration

yeast cookery

fish preparation

sauce making

garnishing

salad and vegetable preparation

preparation of beverages

Skill in food presentation is also important (see pp. 224-8).

Sensible use of food and economy

Awareness of the cost of food and how to economize are important considerations in food preparation. Skilful cookery does not necessarily require the use of the most expensive foods.

This can be demonstrated by:

1   Using cheaper cuts of meat, e.g. breast of lamb, belly of pork.
2   Economizing on fuel, e.g. batch baking, or using only the oven or only the top of the cooker, or the microwave oven where appropriate.
3   Pressure cooking.
4   Using yogurt instead of cream if possible.
5   Keeping wastage to a minimum.
6   Using up scraps of pastry, etc.
7   Using fruit and vegetables in season.
8   Adding vegetables, pulses, etc. to extend a meat dish.

Preparation of food

The following are important whatever the assignment:

1   Tidy, methodical working.
2   Regular clearing of work surface.
3   A high standard of personal hygiene.
4   Hygienic handling of food.
5   Accuracy in weighing and measuring food.
6   Efficiency in the use of time, equipment, etc.
7   Correct use of tools and cooking method.

Sources of information for investigations

Candidates required to make a written report about their investigation, can obtain information from:

food labels

information leaflets from shops and food companies

food and health magazines and journals

home economics journals

surveys

Government statistical information (in reference section of library)

consumer 'watchdog' reports and journals, e.g. '*Which?*'

computer databases

people, e.g. friends, relations

interviews, questionnaires

Points to note when using information

1   Write out a list of questions to which you need answers.
2   Read through the information, and answer each of your questions. Discard irrelevant information.
3   Write out the information in your own words, keeping as close to the subject as possible.
4   Link the information to any surveys, practical work, or experiments you have carried out.
5   Use charts, graphs, pictures, and diagrams, stating where they came from, and link them to your investigation.
6   Do not copy out chunks of information and paste on lots of pictures to fill out the investigation – be clear, brief, and to the point, and give your own comments.

Example investigation

New reduced-fat spreads are produced every year. Find out whether they are suitable for making cakes and biscuits.

Questions to answer concisely

1   What are reduced-fat spreads? Give some examples.
2   Why do people want reduced-fat spreads?
3   Why are they not called margarines or butter?
4   How are they made? What do they cost?
5   What are the ingredients and nutritional and energy value of these spreads?
6   Are recipes or advice for making cakes and biscuits given on the packaging?
7   Try making cakes and biscuits using reduced-fat spreads, margarine, and butter. How do the results compare? Try various methods, e.g. creaming, rubbed-in, and melting. Note how the reduced-fat spread reacts to mixing with sugar and eggs, handling, and melting. Hold a tasting panel and record the results and comments. Evaluate appearance, flavour, colour, and texture.
8   Conclusion
    a   Are reduced fat spreads easy to use?
    b   Are they economical?
    c   Is there an advantage in using these products?
    d   Can they be used in other methods of cooking?

Plan of work

A timetable or time plan of the work to be carried out during a practical examination or assignment is useful because it shows a candidate's ability to prepare food in a logical order, using time efficiently. Although it may not be a requirement of the assignment or examination, a time plan helps to guide the candidate and to prevent any mistakes.

An example of a practical assignment, similar to those given in examinations, is set out below. It is intended only as a guide to the requirements of a practical examination.

Sample assignment

Current dietary guidelines advise us to eat 5 portions of fruit and vegetables each day. Show how this could be achieved in a variety of dishes for a family of four. Time allowed: 1 hour.

Chosen dishes
    vegetable and cheese crumble
    golden vegetable soup
    crunchy apple layer

Reasons for choice
1   Several different vegetables used and one type of fruit.
2   Vegetables chosen (see recipe below) are colourful and easy to obtain.
3   Dishes use vegetables and fruit in season so are economical.
4   All recipes are suitable for a lacto-ovo vegetarian. Cubes of cooked meat, e.g. ham, chicken, pork, kabanos, or other savoury sausage could be added to the crumble.
5   Fat-reduced cheese, milk, and margarine could be used to keep in line with dietary goals.
6   Dishes have a good supply of NSP (dietary fibre), in line with dietary goals.
7   Cheese provides HBV protein and calcium.
8   Wholemeal flour provides good source of NSP.
9   Semi-skimmed milk reduces the fat content.
10 Yogurt or fromage frais provide good source of protein and calcium.

Recipes
Vegetable and cheese crumble
200 g wholemeal plain flour
100 g margarine
100 g mature cheddar cheese, grated
seasoning
2 tbsps sesame seeds (optional)
1 medium onion
50 g frozen sweetcorn
50 g frozen peas
50 g mushrooms
a few florets of broccoli and cauliflower
50 g broad beans
(or any combination of colourful vegetables)

All-in-one roux sauce:
275 ml semi-skimmed milk
25 g margarine
25 g plain flour
salt and pepper

Golden vegetable soup

2 large carrots
2 medium onions
1 medium potato
1 parsnip (optional)
2 sticks celery (or a celery heart including the leaves)
50 g red lentils
1 vegetable stock cube
750 ml water
seasoning
2 tbsps olive oil or other oil

Crunchy apple layer

450 g cooking apples
6 medium-cut slices wholemeal bread
50 g margarine
50 g demerera sugar
1 tsp mixed spice (optional)
350 g plain Greek yogurt or fromage frais
25 g plain chocolate

Time plan	Order of work
9.30	Light oven: Gas 6, 200°C (400°F). Peel, core, and slice apples and place in pan with 4 tbsps water. Put lid on. Heat gently, and leave to stew until soft, stirring occasionally.
9.40	Place bread in food processor and process until fine crumbs. Heat 50 g margarine in frying pan and fry breadcrumbs on a low heat, turning them frequently.
9.45	Peel and chop vegetables for soup, and place in large pan with oil, and season. Sauté gently with lid on for 5 minutes.
9.55	Wash up. Leave apples to cool.
10.00	Add water, stock cube, and lentils to soup, and simmer for 15 minutes.
	Add demerera sugar and spice to breadcrumbs and leave to cool.
10.03	Peel and chop vegetables into small pieces for crumble, place in pan with water just to cover them, and bring to boil. Simmer for 10 minutes. Add frozen vegetables 5 minutes before end of cooking time. Make crumble by rubbing margarine into flour, and stirring in cheese, sesame seeds, and seasoning.
10.13	Place roux sauce ingredients in pan, and heat, stirring all the time until thickened. Season.
10.18	Drain vegetables for crumble, place in ovenproof dish and pour over sauce. Spread crumble on top and bake in oven for 10 minutes, until golden brown.
10.20	Place layers of apple, breadcrumbs, and yogurt/fromage frais (ending with yogurt/fromage frais) in glass serving dish. Grate some chocolate on top. Serve.
10.25	Liquidize soup and serve.
10.30	Serve crumble. Wash up and clear away.

Commercial restaurants

Commercial restaurants need to provide a good service to customers as well as make a profit, if they are to stay in business. When planning and pricing the menus in a restaurant, the following costs have to be taken into account.

Capital costs include a mortgage for the building, income tax, VAT, licence to sell alcohol, insurance, and business tax.

Running costs include gas, electricity, refuse collection, water metering, sewage disposal, cleaning and maintenance.

Staffing costs include chefs, waiters, accountant, manager, cleaners, bar staff.

Food costs include all ingredients used, storage, transport to restaurant, wastage due to unsold items, disposal of food waste.

Once these are accounted for, a profit margin is added to each dish in a menu. Each dish has to be carefully portioned, so that customers receive equal amounts, and profit is not lost by giving too much. Standard-sized spoons, ladles, slices, and serving dishes help to control this.

Some restaurants may promote 'loss leaders' which are inexpensively priced items which do not make a profit, but encourage customers to come and buy other menu items as well.

Questions and activities

1   Food hygiene is very important. Find out why the following are used or carried out in the food industry:
    a   blue-coloured sticking plasters for cuts
    b   refrigerator and freezer thermometers
    c   'use by' dates on foods
    d   special hats and hair coverage
    e   regular throat and nose checks for staff
    f   regular inspections of food premises
    g   regular veterinary inspection and testing of livestock

2   Study the chart below which shows the features of a range of microwave ovens.
    a   Which models do not have a weight sensor?
    b   Which models have a clear view door?
    c   Which models have the highest power output?
    d   Which models do not have a grill?
    e   Which model has the lowest grill output?
    f   Which models are 'user friendly'? Why?
    g   Which models are likely to be the cheapest to buy? Why?
    h   Which model would you choose for the following people/situations? Give reasons for your choice.
    –   a single person who wants to be able to heat up and defrost food in the microwave
    –   a small takeaway restaurant, which sells pasties, pies, curries, and soups
    –   a public house which sells bar meals e.g. lasagne, mixed grills, quiches, pizzas
    –   a family of four with teenage children who all come home at different times in the evening
    –   an elderly person with failing sight, who often buys frozen meals for one

Model features	A	B	C	D	E	F	G
Auto guide (helps you programme the oven)	*	*	*		*		
Auto defrost	*	*	*	*	*		
Child lock	*	*	*	*	*	*	*
Clear view door	*	*	*		*		
Auto sensor	*	*	*	*	*		
Weight sensor	*	*	*	*	*		
Grill	1.7 kW	1.7 kW	1.3 kW	1.3 kW		1.1 kW	
Microwave power output	800 W	800 W	750 W	750 W	650 W	600 W	600 W
Oven interior	stainless steel	stainless steel	stainless steel	stainless steel	stainless steel	acrylic	acrylic

3 How could you adapt the following recipes to suit: **a** a low-fat diet, **b** a low-salt diet, **c** a low-sugar diet; **d** a high-NSP diet?

meat curry and rice   rice pudding
chilli con carne   apple pie
stew with dumplings   pancakes
spaghetti bolognese   cheesecake (cold)
macaroni cheese   chocolate gateau

4 Study the graphs below which show the number of reported cases of food poisoning for four types of bacteria.

a Which bacteria was most reported as causing food poisoning?

b Which bacteria was least reported as causing food poisoning?

c Which year were there most cases reported for *Listeria*?

d Which year were there least cases reported for VTEC?

e Why have the numbers increased for *Campylobacter*, *Salmonella*, and VTEC since 1985?

f Why have the numbers decreased for *Listeria* since 1988?

g Why is it important to collect information about food poisoning?

h Who needs to have this information?

i What problems are met when trying to collect food-poisoning statistics?

5 You are considering starting a home made cakes business from home.

a How can you find out if there is a need for this type of business in your area?

b Make a list of products you would like to sell, how much they would cost to make and buy, and how you would package and present them.

c Where would you buy your ingredients?

d Which types of outlets could you supply and cater for?

e How will you find out if your premises are suitable for this type of business?

f Which laws and regulations will you have to comply with?

g What skills, apart from cooking, will you need to run such a business successfully?

h Prepare, cook, and serve 3 of your chosen products, and conduct a survey to research the following features of them:

     appearance
     flavour and texture
     presentation and packaging
     price and value for money

In your evaluation, suggest any improvements that you can make, or that the shop/restaurant you supply, may require.

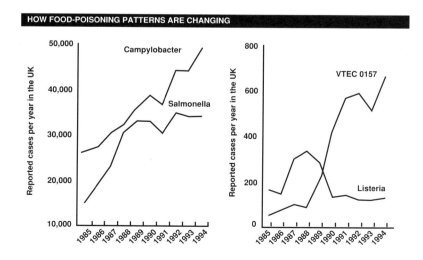

HOW FOOD-POISONING PATTERNS ARE CHANGING

(Source: *Which?* September 1995)

⑤ The kitchen

Kitchen planning

The kitchen is a working room and, in order for it to be easy and efficient to work in, it must be well planned. Modern houses tend to have smaller kitchens than older houses do, yet today more labour-saving equipment is available to put into them. Besides its main function as a place where food is stored and prepared for meals, the kitchen may be used for laundering and cleaning, hobbies, and often eating in and entertaining.

The equipment and kitchen units should be positioned in a logical order so that they form a continuous working area to suit the sequence and stages of the main activities carried out in the kitchen. For meal preparation, this sequence would be:

food storage → preparation → cooking → serving → clearing up

The kitchen should be designed so that time and energy are not wasted by moving from one area to another, and that excessive bending and stretching in order to use equipment are avoided.

Kitchens often contain a dining area, and some have a separate utility room for laundering.

The following kitchen plans are examples of different working layouts. The most efficient layouts are based on a U, L, or parallel lines plan.

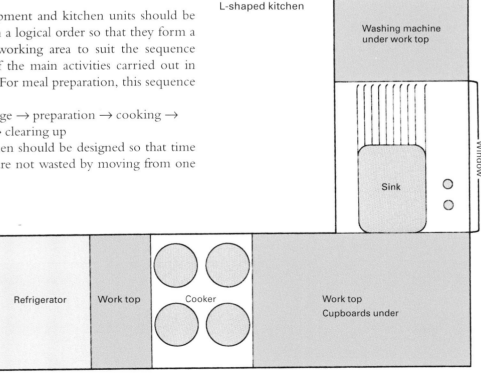

L-shaped kitchen

U-shaped kitchen

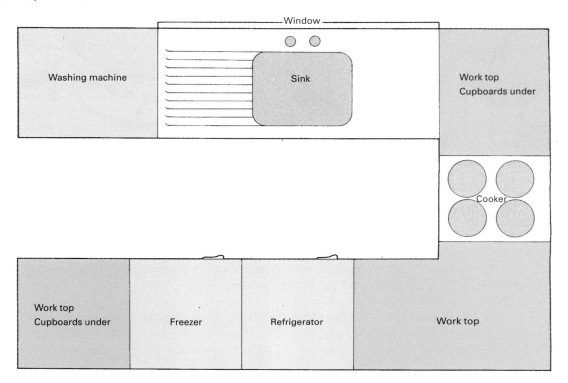

Parallel lines kitchen

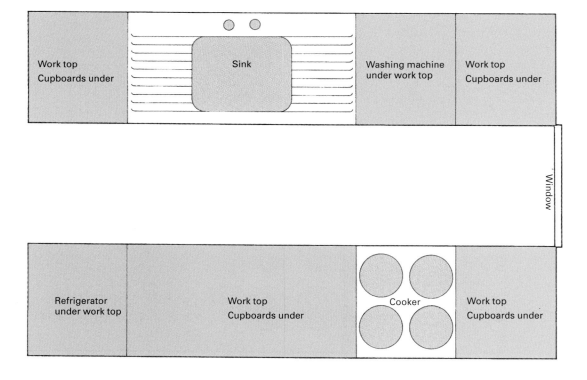

Kitchen units

A wide range of self-assembly and ready-made kitchen units can be purchased, in a variety of styles, materials, and colours. They may be made from:

solid wood, e.g. pine, oak, beech

plastic-veneered (outer covering) chipboard

Usually the interior and shelves are made of plastic-veneered chipboard which is easy to clean and reduces the price of the complete unit.

Types of kitchen unit

Base units are fixed to the walls and floor, and usually have a work top fitted on them. They include drawer units as well as cupboards. Some have retractable work tops to provide an extra work area. Wire baskets can be fitted into cupboards on hinges so that extra storage space is available. Waste bins can be fitted to a cupboard door so that they open when the door is opened and can be shut away when not in use.

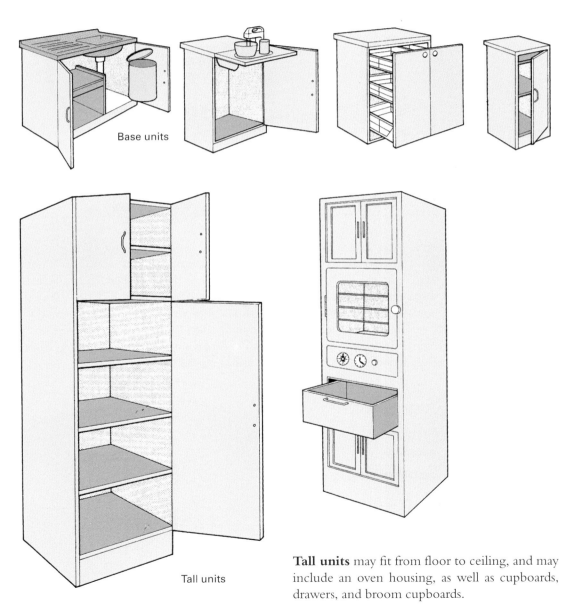

Base units

Tall units

Tall units may fit from floor to ceiling, and may include an oven housing, as well as cupboards, drawers, and broom cupboards.

Peninsular units are base units that do not adjoin a wall, but jut out into the kitchen. They are often used to form a barrier between the kitchen and dining area, and have cupboards on both sides.

Island units are separate base units, which usually stand in the centre of a large kitchen, with a hob or sink unit in the work top. They may house cupboards all the way round or have shelves at either end.

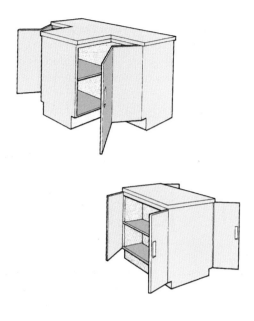

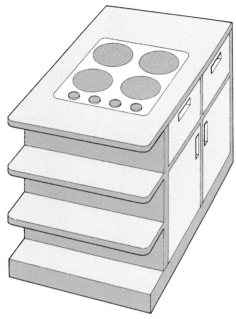

Wall units provide useful extra space, and can be fitted along the walls and into the corners. They should be of a suitable height for the user to reach comfortably into them without danger of pulling something down on to themself. The cupboard doors should not be too wide or they might obstruct the worktop when opened. Some cupboards have sliding doors.

Work tops are usually made of plastic (either melamine or formica sheet) covering chipboard. They often have a rolled edge, which is comfortable to work against. Cooker hobs can be fitted into the worktop. as can sink units, chopping boards, heat-resistant sections for standing pans on, and special shallow sinks for washing vegetables.

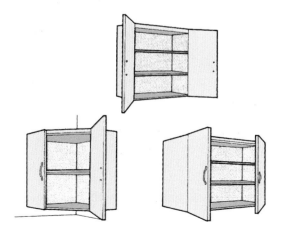

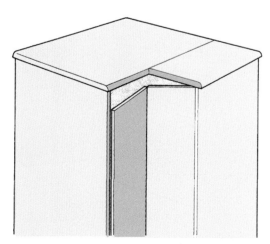

Storage space

Storage space is needed in the kitchen for food, utensils, serving dishes, small equipment, and large equipment. Ideally the units should be laid out to give storage space for each item in the area of the kitchen where it is most used.

Food storage

Food can be divided into four main groups according to how it should be stored.

Dry foods

(flour, sugar, coffee, tea, rice, biscuits, canned foods)

These should be stored in a dry cupboard, at 12°C or above. Dampness due to condensation or leakage will encourage mould growth and rancidity and will reduce the shelf-life of such foods considerably.

A cupboard above the refrigerator (which gives out heat) or with a hot water pipe running through it will provide a suitably dry atmosphere. Wall units are often suitable for this purpose and can be fitted with adjustable shelves and racks for holding small packets and jars.

Semi-perishable foods

(bread, vegetables, fruit)

These require storage at 6–12°C, in a well-ventilated cupboard that has a relatively high humidity (moisture content in the air). This helps prevent vegetables from wilting and deteriorating. However, the humidity must be controlled by good ventilation to discourage mould growth.

Traditionally, walk-in larders or pantries were used for such storage, but today these are rare. Many kitchen units have ventilation grids, or a backless cupboard that can be placed against an air brick on the external wall of the house. Such cupboards are best positioned on a north-facing wall of the house which will be cooler.

Perishable foods

(eggs, cheese, milk, meat, fish)

These should be kept at temperatures below 5°C, i.e. in the refrigerator.

Ready-frozen foods

These should be kept in either the ice box of a refrigerator or a domestic freezer.

The sink area

Much of the work in the kitchen is done in the sink area, and a variety of items can be stored here, including:

  cleaning materials
  household chemicals
  kitchen linen (tea-towels, cloths, etc.)
  pans
  cutlery
  vegetable racks
  waste bin

Cleaning materials and household chemicals should be stored in a high cupboard if there are young children in the home as they are a potential danger if stored in a cupboard under the sink (see p. 268).

Cutlery is best stored in a drawer, and sectioned cutlery trays help to keep it neat. Sharp-bladed knives should be stored with the blade pointing downwards, or in a special knife rack.

Pans can be stored in cupboards, on racks, or on shelves, but they should not be placed too high as they could fall on to the person trying to reach them. The same applies to other heavy equipment and glass articles such as mixing bowls.

The **waste bin** can be fitted to the inside of the sink cupboard door so that it opens when the door is opened. It is best to have the waste bin in the sink area for easy disposal of rubbish. Bin liners help to keep the bin clean and make it easier to dispose of rubbish. Large waste bins are not advisable in the kitchen as they tend not to be emptied until they are full. By this time the waste at the bottom will have started to harbour bacteria and this is unhygienic.

The **washing machine** is often placed in the sink area so that it can be plumbed in to the sink pipes and the waste water can escape through the sink drainage.

Electrical items, e.g. mixers, should be kept in a dry place, and are usually more accessible if kept covered on a work top.

Large equipment

Refrigerators and freezers can be put under work surfaces, or on top of one another if the freezer is an upright type. They must, however, have some ventilation around them to allow heat from the motors to escape.

Washing machines Front-loading automatic washing machines can be kept under a work top and plumbed in to the water supply, to avoid having to move them. Twin-tub machines can also be kept underneath work tops. Top-loading automatic machines require easy access and therefore need to stand under a removable work top or on their own. Automatic machines must be near to drainage.

Tumble driers can be placed on top of certain washing machines, and need some form of vent at the back to allow the moist air to escape.

Cookers can either be free standing, or can be fitted into kitchen units with the hob in the work surface and the oven in the wall or a special unit. If the hob and oven are separate there are often problems with removing them if the owner moves house. If the cooker has an extractor hood fitted above, it should be placed near to an outside wall to allow extracted air to be ducted out. There should be a work top either side of the cooker to form a continuous sequence in the food preparation area.

Ventilation

Ventilation is necessary in a kitchen to extract steam, odours, and grease from the air. These would otherwise spoil decorations and travel to other parts of the house.

Open windows are the simplest form of ventilation, but they cause draughts and a loss of heat. A variety of air extractors and ventilators are available for use all over the house, but for the kitchen, a cooker hood and/or window or wall extractor fan are the most suitable.

Cooker hoods

Cooker hoods either extract or recirculate air, and must have an external outlet if the air is to be completely removed. Some hoods filter the air, remove the odours, then recirculate it. They are normally placed directly above the cooker.

The hood works by drawing air in with a fan and passing it through a filter. Air from the cooker enters a grid underneath the hood and grease particles are trapped by a washable aluminium mesh panel. Hoods that recirculate the air have a carbon or charcoal filter to absorb odours, and this has to be replaced every year or 18 months according to use.

Extractor fans

Extractor fans are usually fitted in windows or outside walls, with suitable ducting to the outside.

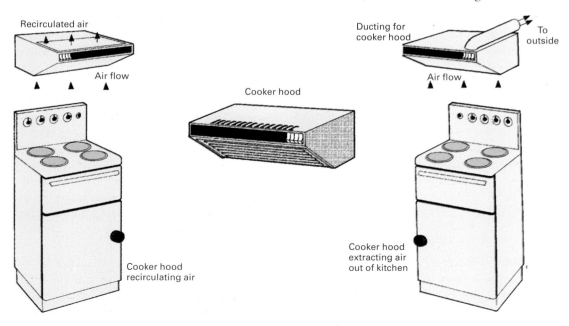

Recirculated air

Air flow

Cooker hood

Cooker hood recirculating air

Ducting for cooker hood

To outside

Air flow

Cooker hood extracting air out of kitchen

An electric motor powers the fan, which draws in air and takes it to the outside. Some types can be reversed to blow fresh air into the room. On the outside, a shutter is fitted to prevent draughts from entering the room when the fan is not in use.

The fan should be placed near the ceiling, but away from hobs and cookers, as it may affect gas burners. The fan unit should be cleaned periodically to remove any fluff or grease that collects in it.

Window extractor fan   Louvre windows

Windows

Louvre windows provide good ventilation as an alternative to ordinary windows, and can be opened at various angles without creating excessive draughts.

Lighting

It is important that a kitchen has sufficient light to make working in it safe and comfortable. Windows should be well placed and large enough to provide adequate daylight, as well as ventilation.

Fluorescent lighting is bright and direct. The bulbs are often in the form of tubes which are fitted close to the ceiling. Low energy fluorescent light bulbs, which fit into standard light fittings, can also be bought.

Ordinary light bulbs should be of at least 100 watts and can be fitted with a glass globe cover that does not shade any of the light. Small strip lights can be fitted under wall cupboards to shine directly on to work surfaces, providing light where it is most needed.

Decoration

A wide range of wall coverings, paints, and materials are suitable for use in the kitchen. Colour is, of course, a matter of personal choice, but colours that create an impression of coolness, e.g. cream, pale blue, green, yellow, and white, are often used as the kitchen is inclined to become hot.

Ideally, decorations used in a kitchen should be easy to clean and should not absorb grease or odours which would spoil their appearance.

Suitable wall coverings include:
vinyl (plastic) coated wallpapers
ceramic glazed tiles
washable vinyl emulsion paint

Flooring

Kitchen floors should have the following characteristics:
easy to clean
non-slip
no loose parts or edges that someone
    could trip over
relatively warm to the feet
non-absorbent to grease and liquids.

Loose mats and highly polished finishes should be avoided as they may easily result in falls. The flooring should be well fitted and firmly held down.

Suitable flooring materials include:
vinyl tiles or sheet flooring
ceramic tiles
quarry tiles

Vinyl flooring is probably best as it is relatively warm to the feet, is easy to fit, and is not as hard as quarry or ceramic tiles. It comes in a wide variety of colours and designs, and the more expensive brands are usually shrink-resistant and last for many years.

Carpet is not advisable in a kitchen as it is difficult to keep clean, and absorbs stains easily. Carpet tiles and industrial hardwearing carpeting can be used, but may still become stained.

Curtains

Curtains around a kitchen window tend to absorb odours and grease and so must be washed regularly. They should not hang over the cooker as this is a fire hazard, or into the sink area where they will get wet.

Roller blinds are a suitable alternative to curtains as they can be kept out of the way during the day. They can be made of either plastic material or specially stiffened fabric.

Their main disadvantage is that mould may grow on them if they become damp as they roll up tightly with little air space around them.

Venetian blinds can be used but they tend to become greasy and dusty and are laborious to clean.

Electric sockets

Electric sockets are normally placed on the wall above work tops in a kitchen. As so many labour-saving devices for the kitchen are electrical, it is best to have at least five sockets in different places in the kitchen.

Cleaning the kitchen

As the main function of the kitchen is food preparation, it is important that it is kept clean and hygienic. Most of the modern materials used in a kitchen are easy to clean and there are many products available to make cleaning easy. It is a good idea to get into a routine, so that there is never a build-up of dirt which would be difficult to remove.

Every day
1 Wipe over work surfaces and cooker hob after use.
2 Sweep up any dry crumbs, dust, etc., from the floor.
3 Wipe up any spillages.
4 Wipe down the sink and draining-board.
5 Empty the waste bin and rinse it out.

Every week
1 Sweep and wash floor.
2 Wipe top and fronts of units.
3 Wash all surfaces.
4 Clean oven if required.

Every few weeks
1 Wipe out and tidy cupboards and drawers.
2 Move oven and other large equipment and clean behind them.
3 Defrost the fridge (see pp. 253-4).
4 Wash walls thoroughly.

Commercial kitchens

The 'Food Safety (General Food Hygiene) Regulations 1995 - Catering Guide' covers premises used to prepare and sell food. Commercial kitchens must meet these requirements, including:

General requirements
1 Premises must be kept clean and in good repair.
2 There must be enough washbasins, toilets, hot and cold water taps, ventilation, drainage, changing facilities, and waste disposal. They must be easy to use and clean, and must not allow food to be exposed to contamination:
  toilets must not open directly into a food room,
  separate sinks must be provided for handwashing,
  outdoor waste storage areas should be sited away from food delivery and preparation rooms,
  pests and vermin must be kept out of the premises.

Floors and walls
1 Must be made from washable, non-absorbent, non-toxic, non-porous materials, e.g. for floors, tiles (quarry, ceramic, or vinyl), terrazzo, resin, or vinyl; and for walls, painted plaster, epoxy resin, ceramic tiles, stainless steel sheeting, or PVC.
2 Floors must not allow water to collect in pools and must have drains if water has to be spilled during food preparation.
3 Walls must be smooth and cleanable up to a height where food is likely to splash during preparation (usually 1.80 m).

Ceilings
1 Can be smooth, washable, painted plaster, or direct-fixed or suspended ceiling tiles (not polystyrene or fibre).
2 Must not allow the accumulation of dirt, condensation, or moulds, and must not shed particles.

Windows
1 Must be fitted with insect screens if they open directly into food rooms.
2 Must not be opened during preparation if contamination by fumes, dust, and insects will occur.
3 Should have sloping sills to prevent accumulation of dirt.

Doors

1 Should be swing doors with kick plates so staff do not have to touch handles.
2 Should be smooth, non-porous, and washable.

Work surfaces

1 Must be made of smooth, washable, non-toxic, non-absorbent materials, e.g. stainless steel, ceramics, food-grade plastics.
2 Continuous surfaces without joints will prevent accumulation of dirt.

Commercial kitchens must be kept clean at all times.

Cleaning tools and equipment

1 Facilities for cleaning, draining, and drying should be easy to reach and use, and sufficient for the size and use of the premises.
2 These include: large sinks, sterilizing sinks, dishwashers, hoses, and space for air drying (so that cloths are not used to dry dishes).
3 Facilities must be hard-wearing and resistant to corrosion by cleaning chemicals.

Washing food

1 Separate sinks for washing food and equipment should be provided if possible; if not, clean the sink thoroughly between each process.
2 Hot, and drinkable cold water must be provided.
3 Signs may be placed above sinks to indicate their use.

Revision questions

1 What are the main functions of a kitchen?
2 Describe the sequence of work involved in preparing food.
3 Why is it important that a kitchen layout should be well planned?
4 What fittings are usually included in:
   a   base units
   b   tall units
   c   island units?
5 How should the following be stored?
   a   dry foods
   b   semi-perishable foods
   c   perishable foods
   d   frozen foods
6 How should the following be stored?
   a   cleaning materials
   b   cutlery
   c   sharp knives
   d   waste bins
   e   pans
   f   refrigerators and freezers
   g   washing machines
   h   tumble driers
7 Why is it necessary to ventilate a kitchen?
8 Describe how cooker hoods and extractor fans work.
9 What are louvre windows?
10 Why is good lighting important in a kitchen?
11 What colours are particularly suitable for a kitchen and why?
12 Suggest two wall coverings suitable for a kitchen.
13 What features should a kitchen floor have?
14 Which type of flooring is most suitable for a kitchen?
15 What are the disadvantages of having curtains or a roller blind at a kitchen window?
16 How many electric sockets should a kitchen have and where should they be placed?
17 What cleaning processes should be carried out in a kitchen on a daily and weekly basis?
18 How are consumers protected by the Food Safety Regulations?
19 What are the requirements of commercial kitchens with respect to food safety?

Materials used in the home

Kitchen equipment and other household items are made from a variety of materials, including:

plastics
glass
wood
ceramics
metals

Plastics

Plastics were invented at the end of the 19th century. Their production was rapidly developed in the 1920s, and now many different types of plastic are made for a wide variety of purposes. All plastics are made from three raw materials:

oil
coal
cellulose

The amounts used, and the addition of other ingredients, account for the differences between the various plastics.

General properties of plastics

1   Generally strong, particularly nylon. Many stretch, and some will split.
2   Good electrical insulators.
3   Do not corrode or decay.
4   Have good resistance to most chemicals.
5   Waterproof and generally greaseproof.
6   Most expand with heat and eventually melt.
7   Some are very hard and will withstand scratching.
8   Some are good heat insulators.
9   Can be moulded into shapes and made into sheets and films.
10 Relatively cheap to produce in large quantities.

There are two main groups of plastics:
thermoplastics, which soften on heating, and harden again when they cool;
thermosetting plastics, which are hardened by heat treatment, and cannot be softened by further heat.

Name	Examples of use
Thermoplastics	
High-density polyethylene	Bottles, crates, bottle caps, carton closures
Low-density polyethylene	Packaging film, bags, bin liners
Polypropylene	Bottle caps and closures, salad and margarine tubs, biscuit and sweet wrappings, trays for microwave meals, pipes, bottles
Polyethylene terephthalate (PET)	Meal trays, carbonated drinks bottles
Polyvinyl chloride (PVC)	Aprons, rainwear, household chemical bottles, cakes and sandwich packs, oil and squash bottles, cling film
Polystyrene	Clear egg boxes, yoghurt pots, lids, bottle caps and closures, disposable cups
Expanded polystyrene	Food trays, take-away food cartons, egg boxes, disposable cups
Acrylonitrile butadiene styrene (ABS)	Salad and margarine tubs and lids
Polyamide (nylon)	Fabrics, machine parts, ropes
Polytetra-fluoroethylene	Non-stick coating for pans and bakeware (PTFE, Teflon)
Thermosetting plastics	
Melamine formaldehyde (melamine)	Cups, beakers, plates, dishes
Phenol formaldehyde (formica)	Saucepan handles, electrical switches, work tops
Polyester	Fabrics, threads, chairs, sinks
Polyurethane	Floors, sponges, paints

Many kitchen items are made of plastic.

Problems with plastics

1   They contribute to pollution. Most plastic items are difficult to dispose of. They do not rot, and they give off toxic fumes when burned. Some are biodegradable (break down naturally) but the process is very slow.
2   The chemical building blocks of plastics (monomers) and some of the additives put into plastics (e.g. plasticizers, stabilizers, colorants) may migrate into foods from plastic packaging. This depends on the temperature, type of food, and type of packaging. For example, fatty foods seem to attract these substances from cling films. There is evidence that some of these substances may present a health risk, so manufacturers have developed new, safer films. Research continues into this problem.
3   Polystyrene containers should never be used in microwave ovens as a toxic substance – styrene – would be released.

Glass

Glass has a wide variety of uses, both decorative and functional. The raw material used to make it is **silicon dioxide** (silica) which is found in sand and naturally as quartz. Some types of glass also have lime, or metals such as lead, added.

General properties of glass

1   Hard, but brittle, and will crack and break under stress.
2   Transparent, so useful for storage.
3   Poor conductor of heat.
4   Good electrical insulator.
5   Non-toxic.

Glass with special properties:

Heat-resistant glass is mainly used for cooking utensils. It withstands heat from liquids or ovens. Some types can withstand direct heat from a flame or electric hotplate.

Toughened glass can withstand quite severe shocks and impacts without breaking, and will only break into small pieces. Can be used for interior glass doors, glass oven doors, and chopping boards.

Uses

Lead crystal glass Glasses, vases, ornaments, decanters.

Soda lime glass Most other purposes, including vacuum flasks, bottles, bowls, windows, light bulbs, cooker doors and panels, mirrors, glasses.

Wood

General properties of wood

1   Good heat insulator.
2   Resists most chemicals.
3   Strong.
4   Shrinks as it dries out.
5   Attacked by insects, bacteria, and fungi unless specially treated.
6   May absorb strong flavours and odours.
7   May stain.

Uses

chopping and bread boards
pot stands
spoons, spatulas
kitchen units
salad and serving bowls
packing crates for foods

Ceramics

These include china and pottery. They have been used in the home for many years, especially in food preparation.

General properties of ceramics

1   Resistant to most chemicals.
2   Can withstand very high temperatures but may crack if subjected to sudden extremes of temperature.
3   Poor conductors of heat.
4   Washable.
5   Can be formed into a wide variety of shapes.

Uses

crockery – plates, cups, jugs, etc.
casserole dishes
serving dishes
clay bricks for roasting
tiles

Metals

There are many types of metal. Their cost and usage depends on how common they are in the earth and how easily they can be extracted.

Types

platinum		iron
gold	very expensive	zinc
silver		tin
aluminium		copper
lead		brass

Steel and stainless steel

There are different types of **steel**, and they are all **alloys** (i.e. mixtures) of iron and carbon, plus other metals such as manganese, silicon, tungsten, or nickel. The different types have special properties to fit them for particular uses.

Stainless steel is composed of 0.3% carbon, 18% chromium, 8% nickel, and 73.7% iron. It resists stains and corrosion because it has a protective layer of chromium oxide on the surface of the steel.

General properties of metals

1   Can be made into different shapes, some more easily than others.
2   Very good conductors of electricity.
3   Some are very strong.
5   Very good conductors of heat.
6   Can be sharpened to produce a cutting edge.

Uses

Stainless steel Sinks, work surfaces, cutlery, pans, baking tins, bowls, serving dishes, cook's knives, scissors, kettles, taps, screws, parts of cookers, refrigerators, and other large pieces of equipment.
Steel Casings of washing machines, cookers, refrigerators, freezers. Steel can be coated with enamel, PVC, or paint.
Copper Bases of pans, bowls, jelly moulds, kettles, etc. Used less often today because of its cost.
Aluminium Pans, baking tins, cutlery. Light, cheap and abundant.
Cast iron Casseroles, pans. It is very heavy and is usually coated with enamel to prevent rusting.

Chopping boards

Chopping boards can be made from plastic, wood, or toughened glass.

Plastic boards are available in different colours. By using one colour for raw meat, one for cooked meat, one for vegetables, etc. cross-contamination by bacteria can be avoided.

Wooden boards were thought to harbour bacteria in the surface, but research has shown that natural enzymes in the wood prevent bacterial growth and that these boards are safe providing they are thoroughly scrubbed. However, the Food Safety Regulations 1995 (see pp. 159–61) forbid the use of wood for 'high-risk' foods (e.g. meat, fish) in commercial kitchens.

Toughened glass boards are easy to clean and are designed so that the surface does not damage knife blades.

Revision questions

1 What are the raw materials used to make plastics?
2 What are the general properties of plastics?
3 Name the two main groups of plastics and give three examples of each, with their uses.
4 What are the general properties of glass?
5 Why is heat-resistant glass useful in the kitchen?
6 What are the general properties of wood?
7 What are the main uses of wood in the kitchen?
8 What are the general properties of ceramics?
9 Why are ceramics useful in the kitchen?
10 What are the general properties of metals?
11 What are the following used for in the kitchen?
   a stainless steel
   b aluminium
   c cast iron
12 How many different uses for metals can you see in the picture opposite? List them.

Cookers

The cooker is one of the most important pieces of equipment in the kitchen. There are many types to choose from, with a range of features.

The most popular fuels for cookers are gas and electricity. Solid fuel cookers or ranges are still used in many homes and microwave ovens (see pp. 190-4) are also popular.

Cookers are a combination of three units:
the hob
the grill
the oven
These are available either as one complete, free-standing unit or as separate units which can be housed in work tops and kitchen walls.

Cookers may also have one or more of the following features:
spit-roaster
griddle
automatic timer
self-cleaning oven lining
time clock and oven timer
glass window in oven door
storage space for baking tins
oven light
double oven
warming drawer for plates
Cookers are generally made of steel with a vitreous enamel finish, which is available in a variety of colours.

Some manufacturers have introduced triple-glazed glass windows and insulated doors. This means that the outside of the door does not get too hot, so there is much less danger of being burnt by touching it.

The hob

Most hobs have four hotplates or burners. The hob is the most frequently used part of the cooker.

Electric hobs

The hotplates are usually 17.5 cm in diameter. The most familiar type is the **radiant ring**, which is an electrical element enclosed in a spiral tube which glows red when heated.

Some have a dual circuit so that just the centre can be heated when small pans are used, to conserve energy.

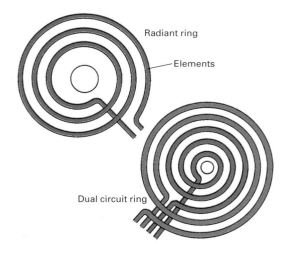

Some hobs have **disc rings** which are flat discs with an indentation in the centre. The element is housed under the disc. The discs do not glow red when heated, and are easier to clean than radiant rings.

Disc ring

Ceramic hobs have the elements housed underneath a flat, ceramic top in insulated bowls. The heated areas are marked on the surface, and can be easily cleaned after use with a special non-abrasive cream.

A ceramic hob

Electric hobs are controlled by separate dials on a panel and food can be simmered by turning the dial to its lowest setting. However, the temperature does not fall instantly as the plate has to cool down first. Heat will be wasted when the plate is switched off, as it takes time to cool down, but careful use can limit this wastage.

Some cooker manufacturers have added a 'hob-hot' warning light for each hotplate, which stays on until the hotplate has reached a safe temperature. This should reduce the chance of someone being burned.

Halogen heat ceramic hobs house special tungsten halogen light filaments. These emit heat which is directed upwards by a special insulated reflector placed beneath each filament. 80% of the heat passes through the ceramic surface, but the area around each set of filaments stays relatively cool. There are up to six power settings, to enable food to be cooked slowly or rapidly. The heat control is similar to gas, and is almost instant. This saves energy and helps to prevent spillages. Halogen hobs are available as separate units or as part of a free-standing cooker.

Gas hobs

Gas burners produce direct heat which is instantly controlled and can be seen. Some cookers have burners of different sizes for large pans or for simmering. Most gas cookers are now lit by electric spark ignition, either from an ordinary electrical plug socket or battery, or by a spark from a piezoelectric system that contains a crystal. The spark can be produced at the touch of a button, or automatically when the burner is switched on. Some burners have a re-ignition device fitted which will ignite the gas automatically if the flame goes out.

Cleaning

Most gas and electric hobs are fitted with trays to catch any spillages and make them easy to clean. On electric cookers, it may be possible to lift up the whole hob, and on gas cookers, removable spill trays around each burner are often fitted.

The grill

Electric grills

Most electric cookers have grills under the hob, and some have eye-level grills. The grill usually extends to the width of the cooker so that it can cook several pieces of food at one time. The grill pan can be placed at different distances from the elements and often has a food grid which can be reversed to give different heights within the grill pan itself. Many cookers have additional elements in the grill section, so that it can be used as a separate oven if required.

It is possible in some grills to use only half the element for grilling small items, to save energy.

Some grills have a fan, which circulates hot air around the food. This speeds up cooking and gives a 'spit-roasting' effect.

Gas grills

Gas grills are often at eye level but some are under the hob. The grill may be one of two types.

Conventional, where the burners heat one or two grill frets, which then glow and radiate heat on to the food below.

Surface combustion Instead of grill frets, this type has a gauze or plate, and the gas burns over the whole surface, ensuring a very even heat even at low settings.

On both gas and electric grills, the grill pan is usually self supporting, so that when it is pulled out, it will stay level and both hands are left free to attend to the food being grilled. Some cookers

have a roasting spit and kebab attachments which give a wider scope for cooking.

The oven

Ovens are heated chambers, made of steel and insulated on the outside with glass fibre and an outer casing of steel. The lining of the oven is coated either with enamel or with a self-cleaning layer which vaporizes splashes of grease as they fall on to it. Usually the door and floor lining are not lined with self-cleaning material.

Electric ovens

Electric ovens do not need vents for the escape of fumes. There is just a small vent to allow steam to escape. This means that the oven is virtually enclosed and therefore heats up quickly and efficiently, maintaining a steady temperature.

There are three main types of electric oven:
convection oven
radiant/convection oven
fan oven

Convection ovens have the heating elements on both sides behind removable side panels.

Radiant/convection ovens have uncovered elements in the top and/or bottom.

Fan ovens (see p. 151) have a fan at the back which circulates the heat and results in more even cooking on all shelves.

Electric ovens are designed to heat from 100–270°C (200-525°F). Most models have a light on the control panel which goes out when the required temperature has been reached.

There is often an interior glass door so that items being cooked can be observed without letting out heat and spoiling the results.

Gas ovens

Gas ovens made in the UK are heated directly by a burner at the back of the oven. The heat rises and circulates, creating zones of heat (see p. 151). These can be used to advantage by cooking foods requiring slightly different oven temperatures on different shelves at the same time, thus saving fuel.

Continental gas ovens are often heated indirectly by flames below the base of the oven, the heat entering the oven at various points. The heat is therefore even, and food can be cooked on any shelf with similar results.

Most modern gas ovens are lit by electric ignition, and they all have a **flame failure device** to stop the flow of gas if the flames go out. A vent is required so that products of combustion can escape.

Temperature control

The temperature in gas and electric ovens is controlled by a device called a **thermostat**. Electric ovens (and hot plates of cookers, irons, washing machine heaters, boilers, etc.) have a bi-metal strip thermostat.

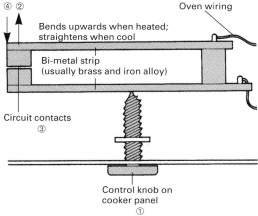

Electric oven thermostat

The control knob ① on the cooker panel sets the temperature, by adjusting the point where the circuit is broken. The metal strip bends upwards when heated ②. This breaks the circuit ③ and cuts the electricity supply to the oven. As the oven cools, the metal strip straightens ④, reconnecting the circuit and heating the oven again.

Modern gas cookers have a liquid expansion thermostat.

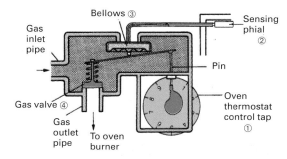

Gas oven thermostat

The temperature is set at the control tap ①. The sensing phial ② contains an oil-based liquid which expands when heated. The bellows ③ open as the liquid expands. As the bellows open, the valve moves down ④ and gradually reduces the flow of gas into the oven burner so the temperature does not rise any further. If the temperature falls, the bellows close, the valve moves up and more gas reaches the burner.

Automatic cooking

Most modern cookers (both gas and electric) are fitted with controls which enable the cooker to be switched on and off automatically. The most obvious advantage of this is that meals can be prepared and then left to cook without the oven having to be switched on manually. A person who is out all day can therefore leave a meal to cook on its own.

Automatic cooking is no different from the ordinary use of the oven except that food is cooked from a cold start, instead of being placed in a pre-heated oven. Most foods cook well in this way. Whole meals can be cooked in ovens where the heat is zoned (see p. 183), e.g.:

top shelf	– meat joint, jacket potatoes
middle shelf	– braised carrots, braised celery
bottom shelf	– egg custard, stewed rhubarb

Gas cookers normally have a safety device which cuts off the gas supply if the oven fails to light at the predetermined time.

There are a few basic rules for using an automatic oven:

1 Usually the cooker is designed to heat up quickly, so there is no need to allow extra cooking time, except for dishes that normally need less than 30 minutes.
2 Always set the timer to turn off the oven when the cooking is completed, to avoid overcooking the food.
3 If a complete meal is being cooked, the total cooking time should be that required by the slowest cooking dish. It is possible to extend the cooking time of certain dishes to fit in with slow cooking ones, e.g. by baking a large pie with a joint of meat or leaving

potatoes large if they are to be roasted with a large joint of meat.

4   Avoid using foods which would separate on standing before cooking, e.g. meringue or egg mixtures.

5   Vegetables, e.g. potatoes, which discolour when exposed to air should be parboiled, basted in fat, or cooked in their skins.

6   Cover all foods which are cooked in liquids with a lid or aluminium foil, to prevent them drying out.

7   Avoid overfilling dishes as they may boil over and spoil others beneath.

8   Cover strong-smelling foods.

9   Set the oven temperature to that required by the main dish, and arrange the others accordingly.

10 Foods that are prone to contamination by bacteria, e.g. poultry, meat, fish, and milk, should not be left in the oven for too long before cooking as the oven will be at room temperature and may encourage bacterial growth. A maximum of 1½ hours in hot weather is advisable. For the same reason, food should not be placed in a warm oven. It is best to chill the foods in a refrigerator before placing them in the oven to reduce the risk of food spoilage.

Solid fuel cookers

Solid fuel cookers or ranges may use coal, coke, or wood as fuel.

Some models have a thermostatic control, but using these ovens requires practice as it is more difficult to control the temperature than with gas or electric ovens. Gas and oil-fired versions of solid fuel cookers are available. They are more convenient as there is no need to clean or fill a hopper.

Solid fuel cookers often heat the domestic water supply as well, and may need to be kept alight all the time. This means that the cooker will need regular refuelling, but the kitchen will always be warm.

Food cooked in a solid fuel cooker does not usually shrink or dry out as much as in gas or electric cookers.

Combination cookers

Some cookers combine two or more different ways of heating food. For example, the combination of normal convection (see p. 151) and **fan-assisted** heating enables food to be cooked more efficiently. Energy is saved as lower temperatures are used, but it does mean that a different temperature chart for cooking foods has to be used to achieve satisfactory results.

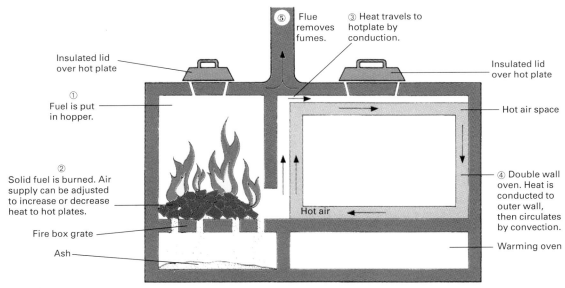

⑤ Flue removes fumes.

③ Heat travels to hotplate by conduction.

Insulated lid over hot plate

Insulated lid over hot plate

① Fuel is put in hopper.

Hot air space

② Solid fuel is burned. Air supply can be adjusted to increase or decrease heat to hot plates.

④ Double wall oven. Heat is conducted to outer wall, then circulates by convection.

Fire box grate

Hot air

Ash

Warming oven

Solid fuel cooker

There are also cookers which combine conventional oven heating with microwave cooking. Such cookers can be used to heat foods quickly using the microwave, and allowing the conventional oven to complete the browning, tenderizing, or setting of the food.

Many modern cookers have a gas hob and electric oven.

Choosing a cooker

Cookers are relatively expensive and before buying one, several factors should be considered:
1. The size in relation to the family's needs and space in the kitchen.
2. The cost in relation to the budget and usage of the cooker.
3. Features that are required, e.g. automatic timing, self-cleaning oven lining.
4. Type of fuel required and facilities available in the home for it.
5. Good design features, e.g. for easy cleaning, operation, and support of pans on the hob.

Cookers should be connected by an expert. Electric cookers must be connected to a 30 amp electricity supply as they draw a heavy current from the mains. Gas cookers must be fitted well to prevent leaks, and can be fitted with an extension pipe to enable them to be moved for cleaning.

It is sensible to have work tops on both sides of the cooker to enable pans and serving dishes to be placed nearby when cooking.

Cleaning the cooker

The cooker hob should always be wiped over after it has been used, and the oven cleaned every week or so, depending on its usage. The hob should be cleaned with a non–abrasive cleaner, to avoid scratching the enamelled surface.

The oven can be cleaned with a special caustic foam or cream, but care should be taken as this may burn the skin and affect metal and plastic surfaces. Self-cleaning oven linings should only be wiped with a damp cloth to remove the ash left from food which has been burnt off them.

The grill can be dismantled on most cookers to remove grease which has splashed on to it.

Many cookers have glass panels which should be carefully cleaned to prevent scratching. Ceramic hobs must be cleaned with a special powder or cream designed to clean and condition the surface.

Revision questions

1. What are the three main parts of a cooker and what are their features?
2. What additional features can a cooker have, and what are their advantages?
3. What is
   a. a radiant ring
   b. a dual circuit ring
   c. a halogen ring?
4. What are the advantages of a ceramic hob?
5. What are the two main types of gas grill?
6. What are:
   a. convection ovens
   b. radiant and convection ovens
   c. fan ovens?
7. How can the zones of heat in an oven be used to advantage?
8. Why is a vent necessary in a gas oven?
9. What is a thermostat, and how does it work in **a** a gas oven and **b** an electric oven?
10. What are the advantages of automatic cooking?
11. What are the general rules that should be followed when using an automatic cooker?
12. How does a solid fuel oven differ from electric and gas ovens?
13. What factors should influence the choice of cooker?
14. How should **a** the oven and **b** the hob be cleaned?

Refrigerators

Refrigeration is important in food storage and in the prevention of food poisoning (see pp. 166-7).

Liquids called **refrigerants** are used to remove heat from the inside of the refrigerator. They are contained in tubes at the back of the unit.

There is growing concern about the effect of refrigerants on the environment. CFCs (chlorofluorocarbons) have traditionally been used as refrigerants, but they are now known to damage the protective ozone layer above the earth and so are being withdrawn. Research into suitable environmentally friendly refrigerants continues.

Temperature distribution

Domestic refrigerators are designed to keep the temperature inside below 7°C, although it varies in different areas of the cabinet. Some fridges have an ice box which is normally marked with a star rating (see p. 167) to indicate the length of time that frozen food may be stored in it. It is *not* designed to freeze food, only to store it once frozen.

The door shelves are the warmest part of the cabinet. The diagram below shows the types of food that should be stored in each part of a refrigerator.

Choosing a refrigerator

When deciding on which type and size of refrigerator to buy, the following points should be considered.

1   Size and capacity required.
2   Storage arrangements inside the refrigerator.
3   Space available in the kitchen.
4   Star rating for frozen food compartment.
5   Workmanship on the refrigerator and its finish.
6   Additional features, e.g. automatic defrosting, digital temperature display.
7   Amount of money available.

Many people find that a fridge/freezer (see p. 197) suits their requirements for cold storage without taking up too much space in the kitchen.

Care of a refrigerator

Defrosting

Moisture is drawn from the air and food inside a refrigerator, and it freezes on the surface of the ice box or heat-exchange panel. If this layer of ice becomes more than 6 mm thick, it will lower

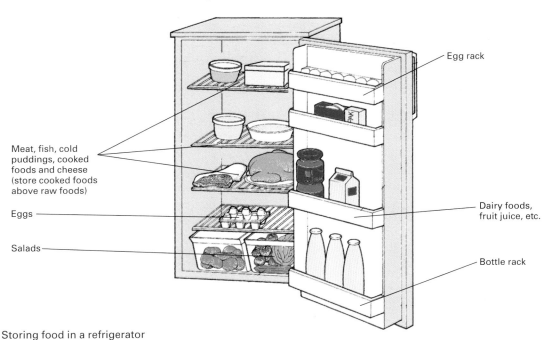

Meat, fish, cold puddings, cooked foods and cheese (store cooked foods above raw foods)

Eggs

Salads

Egg rack

Dairy foods, fruit juice, etc.

Bottle rack

Storing food in a refrigerator

the efficiency of the refrigerator and should be removed by defrosting. Refrigerators can be defrosted in one of three ways.

Manual defrosting

The refrigerator should be switched off, and the food removed and kept in a cool place. The water collected from the melting ice is collected in a tray underneath the ice box, and removed. Once all the ice has gone, the cabinet should be washed out with a solution of bicarbonate of soda in water (1 tablespoon to 575 ml), which will not leave a smell. Once dry, the refrigerator can be refilled and reconnected.

Push-button defrosting

Some models have a button which when pressed stops the refrigeration process and allows the ice to melt. When this has occurred, the refrigeration process starts up again.

Automatic defrosting

Other models defrost automatically when the ice reaches a certain thickness, so that there is no need to check this, and food need not be removed.

It is important that the refrigerator should be kept clean and hygienic inside at all times.

Storing food in a refrigerator

It is advisable to wrap food before placing it in the refrigerator, because:

1 Food loses moisture as it cools down, so unwrapped food will dry out.
2 Some foods absorb odours while others give off odours, and this can spoil the flavour of the food.

Some foods, e.g. meat and fish, should not be wrapped in plastic in the refrigerator as they tend to discolour and develop off flavours and odours without a layer of air surrounding them. Such foods should be stored in a glass or ceramic dish.

Freezers and fridge-freezers

The choice, care, and use of freezers are discussed on pp. 195–203. All fridge-freezers are required by law to have a label to indicate how much energy they use.

Energy

Manufacturer
Model *Hotpoint*
RF30

More efficient

A
B
C
D
E
F
G

Less efficient

Energy consumption kWh/year (based on standard test results for 24 h)	**565**
Actual consumption will depend on how the appliance is used and where it is located	
Fresh food volume l Frozen food volume l	166 Litres 67 Litres

Noise
(dB(A) re 1 pW)

Further information is contained in product brochures

Norm EN 153 May 1990
Refrigerator Label Directive 84/2/EC

Energy label from a fridge-freezer

Revision questions

1 What is the principle on which refrigerators work?
2 What is the significance of:
 *
 **
 ***
 on a refrigerator?
3 How and where should different foods be stored in the refrigerator?
4 What factors should influence the choice of refrigerator?
5 Why is it necessary to defrost a refrigerator?
6 How should a refrigerator be defrosted?

Kitchen equipment

Mixers and blenders (liquidizers)

A blender

Food mixers and blenders have become common in the kitchen. Their main value is that they use electrical energy rather than human energy, and the machine does the job more quickly and often more efficiently. The fact that many people have less time to spend in preparing food than they did in the past has increased the demand for these types of appliance.

A machine should have the following features:

1 It should have the power and capacity to do a range of jobs, e.g. a blender should be able to make a small quantity of mayonnaise as well as blend a large portion of soup; a mincer should be able to mince raw meat as well as cooked meat.

2 It should be easy to keep clean. This is particularly true of mincers and blenders which often take far longer to clean than to use.

3 It should be made of a suitable and durable material.

4 It should be easy to fit attachments and to use.

Choice of mixers and blenders should also be based on how much use the machine will have, its cost, and the amounts of food it will be expected to cope with each time.

Mixers

Mixers are available as small, hand-held models which can be attached to a stand or large, free-standing models which are fitted with a bowl and stand.

Uses

A mixer

Hand-held models These are very useful for whisking mixtures over the heat, creaming and mashing vegetables in a pan, and whisking and beating ingredients in different containers. They can be moved easily to any part of the kitchen.

Many can have a small blender attached to them, and some fit on to a stand with a bowl so that they can operate without being held. A well-designed hand mixer should be relatively light and comfortable to hold, and the switches should be easy to use. Hand-held mixers often have a wall mounting to keep them tidy when not in use.

Free-standing models These are powerful, large-capacity mixers, which operate by the rotation of the beaters on a disc which also rotates. This mixes the ingredients in the bowl thoroughly.

Such mixers can have a variety of attachments, including:

1 **Dough hook**, to mix bread doughs and develop the gluten in the flour in a short time.

2 **Blender** (see p. 256).

3 **Electric can-opener**, which opens cans of any shape without leaving a jagged edge.

4 **Mincer**, for mincing raw and cooked meats, vegetables for chutney making, cheese, nuts, etc.

5 **Sausage maker**, which is attached to the mincer to produce sausages from meat and other ingredients.

6 **Coffee grinder**, for grinding roasted coffee beans.

7 **Potato peeler**, for fast peeling of up to 1.5 kg of potatoes.

8 **Juice extractor**, for citrus fruits.

9 **Slicer and shredder**, for use with carrots, cabbage, onions, beetroot, cucumber, cheese, chocolate, apples, potatoes, etc.

10 **Cream maker** Home-made cream can be made from unsalted butter and milk. It becomes thick when processed through the machine.

11 **Bean slicer**, which slices beans finely and can also be used to shred citrus peel for marmalade making.

12 **Sieve**, to remove the stones from fruit for jam making and to purée fruits and vegetables.

Attachments are usually expensive, so they should only be bought if they are needed and will be used regularly. The bowl of the mixer should be deep enough so that the ingredients will not be thrown out during mixing.

Blenders (liquidizers)

A well-designed blender should have the following features:

    handle

    pouring lip for liquids

    base which is easy to fix and remove

    strong but transparent goblet that will withstand heat from liquids

    capacity to blend dry as well as liquid ingredients

Glass goblets are preferable as plastic ones tend to become scratched and unhygienic after they have been used several times.

Blenders have a variety of uses, including:

    soup making

    puréeing fruit and vegetables

    mixing batters

    baby food preparation

    chopping nuts, herbs, breadcrumbs

    grinding sugar into caster or icing sugar

    fruit and milk drinks

    mayonnaise and salad dressings

When using a blender for hot liquids, take care not to overfill the goblet. The liquid rises up rapidly when the blades start to rotate and, if overfull, some of it could come out at the top and cause scalding.

General care of mixers and blenders

1 Do not run the machine for longer than necessary as this may overheat the motor.

2 Do not exceed the recommended capacity of the machine.

3 Clean thoroughly after use, taking care when dealing with sharp blades, wires, and the motor.

4 When not in use, store in a dry place, covered to keep dust off.

Food processors

Food processors carry out a wide range of jobs, rapidly and using only one piece of equipment. These jobs include:

    finely chopping vegetables and herbs

    chipping potatoes

    finely slicing vegetables and fruit

    finely chopping meat, cheese, boiled eggs

    chopping fat into flour for pastry

    making breadcrumbs

    grinding whole wheat

    shredding vegetables

    peeling vegetables

    grating vegetables and cheese

    puréeing food

A food processor with blender attachment

When choosing a food processor, look for the following features:

1 Ease of cleaning.
2 Safety features, e.g. no blade movement until the lid is on.
3 Capacity.
4 Durability.

It is important to assess just how much the machine will be used as they are expensive, but they do save time and labour and often produce a better result than could be achieved by hand.

Dishwashers

Automatic dishwashers save time and energy. The dishes and other items have to be stacked into the machine. They are then thoroughly washed, rinsed, and dried automatically. Instead of three or four washing-up sessions a day, the entire day's load can be washed in one go at night. The wash is hygienic as high water temperatures are used (60-65°C) and the special detergent contains a germicide. The drying temperature is usually about 74°C, which also makes the process hygienic.

Dishwashers work on the following general programme:

1 **Pre-wash** in cold water to remove large food residues.
2 **Main wash** The water is gradually heated to avoid putting stress on delicate items such as glass. It is agitated around the items while the detergent is added, automatically.
3 **Two short rinses**, which remove food residues and detergent.
4 **Final hot rinse** with a liquid rinse aid to break down the surface tension of the water, to leave the items very clean.
5 **Drying** This is done either by an electric heater or simply by heat from the other processes.

Depending on the type of machine, the whole cycle takes from 20 to 90 minutes. Usually the machines are plumbed in to separate taps. Alternatively, they can be fitted to the sink taps each time, but this is less convenient. Models which have a hot water intake (so that the water does not have to be heated first) save heating bills and time.

The sizes range from a four-place setting capacity to a fourteen-place setting capacity for the needs of a large family. Most models are free standing, but some smaller ones can be fitted to a wall.

The detergents used often have a water softener added and some contain enzymes to break down protein and starch stains.

Most items can be washed, except:

hand-painted porcelain
lead crystal glassware
old cutlery with handles fixed by glue that is not heat-resistant
narrow-necked vessels
some plastic items, e.g. pan handles, childrens' decorated beakers and plates, melamine items

Sink units

Types

Most modern sinks are made from stainless steel which is easy to keep clean, and is strong and hygienic.

Sinks may also be made from fibreglass, fireclay, enamel, or plastic. The draining-board may be separate or may form a single unit with the sink. Separate draining-boards are less hygienic as they may harbour bacteria in the joins between them and the sink.

Sinks are often positioned by a window, which provides a source of fresh air and an outlet for steam.

The sink should be kept clean and grease-free by the regular use of a non-scratch cleaning fluid.

Care of the sink

Avoid putting scraps of food, hot fat, or tea leaves down the sink as these may cause a blockage. If a blockage does occur, the following procedure should be followed:

1 Pour boiling water and, if the source of the problem is fat, washing soda, into the sink.
2 Gently put a soft wire down the plug hole to try to remove the blockage.
3 Use a special suction tool to try to shift the blockage.

4   Place a bucket underneath the U-bend under the sink. Undo the inspection screw and examine carefully.

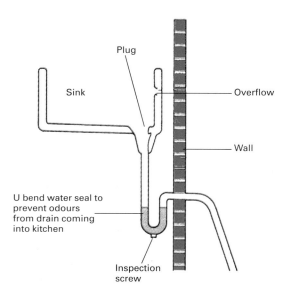

Plug

Sink

Overflow

Wall

U bend water seal to prevent odours from drain coming into kitchen

Inspection screw

If this fails to remove the blockage, it is best to seek the advice of a plumber.

Once the sink has been unblocked, hot water should be flushed down to remove any debris. It is good practice to pour bleach or disinfectant down the sink regularly, to destroy bacteria which may be harboured in the waste pipe.

Waste-disposal units

These can be fitted to the sink and work by grinding up food waste so that it can be washed down the drain. They are operated by an electric motor. Care should be taken to avoid dropping small items of cutlery into the unit as these may damage the blades.

Heated food trays and servers

Occasionally it is necessary to keep food hot for someone who is going to be late for a meal, or to keep part of a meal hot for second helpings. Although nutritionally this may not be the best idea, it avoids the need to cook an extra meal.

Heated food trays and servers can be used for this purpose. They are usually electrical.

Heated food trays have tops made of metal, toughened glass, or a ceramic finish. The base and feet are insulated so that the tray can be put on to the table. The tray has a tubular element beneath the top which heats it to 80-85°C on some models, and 110-140°C on others.

Food servers range from specially heated dishes and portable table cabinets to free-standing cabinets and trolleys. The top may either be a flat surface or have fitted food containers with lids. Some have an unheated cabinet below the heated top for storing plates and cutlery.

Both types of appliance operate from an ordinary socket, which should be disconnected before cleaning.

As with all electrical appliances, when purchasing, check that it carries a BEAB label (see p. 269).

Pans

Pans are relatively expensive but necessary items in a kitchen. It is advisable to buy the best that you can afford as they will last for many years.

Types

The following types of pan are a suitable range for use in the kitchen:

milk saucepan, with a lip for easy pouring
frying pan
wok
vegetable saucepans –three sizes
egg poacher
tiered steamer/casserole pan
pressure cooker
skillet (shallow pan with lid)

Pans can be made from the following metals:

stainless steel
aluminium
enamelled iron or steel

They can also be made from special heat-tolerant glass.

Stainless steel will not chip or flake. It is strong, durable, resistant to rust, little affected by chemical reactions so that it does not stain, and it does not impart a metallic taste to food. It is not a very efficient conductor of heat, so pans usually have a base composed of three layers (tri-core bases). The outer and inner layers are stainless steel and the middle layer is a highly conductive metal (e.g. aluminium) to speed up the heating

These pans are made of stainless steel.

process. Metals such as copper can be welded on to the base of the pan as an alternative to help it heat quickly, but this increases the price.

Once stainless steel heats up, it holds the heat well, the hob burner or hot-plate can be turned down to keep the contents cooking evenly without wasting fuel.

Aluminium is cheaper to produce than stainless steel, and lighter. However, it is not as strong and is discoloured by certain foods.

Enamelled steel or iron can be made into attractive coloured pans. They conduct heat quite rapidly, but are inclined to discolour and chip after a while.

Aluminium and stainless steel pans can be lined with a non-stick coating of polytetrafluoroethylene (PTFE), which is a plastic that resists food deposits sticking to the surface. PTFE melts at a very high temperature, and is not damaged by the heat of cooking. The surface can be damaged by scratching, however, so only wooden or plastic (not metal) spoons should be used. The pans should be washed in hot water with detergents. Scouring pads and cleansers should not be used.

All pans should have the following features:

1   A relatively thick base and sides for strength and durability.
2   A stable design that will not tip over easily.
3   Handles made of an insulating material.
4   A lid that fits well and is easy to remove.
5   A flat base that has good contact with the hot plate.
6   Well-fitting handles that do not become loose.

Electric kettles

Many homes use an electric kettle for boiling water. Non-electric kettles are also available for use on gas or electric hobs.

When buying an electric kettle, look for the following features.

1   **Automatic switch-off button** This prevents the water from boiling away if you forget to turn the kettle off. It saves wear on the element, prevents the kitchen from filling with steam, and saves electricity.
2   **Safety cut-out device** If the kettle is not automatic, it may have a device to turn off the electricity if the water boils away.
3   The **flex connector** should hold the flex firmly and securely. A frayed flex is very dangerous.
4   The **handle** should be easy to grip, comfortable to hold, and well balanced when the kettle is full. It should not become hot and must be securely fixed.
5   The **lid** should fit well and securely, and be easy to remove and put on, without falling out when the kettle is tipped.
6   The **base** must be firm and steady on the work surface.
7   The **spout** should pour well and the steam should be directed away from the hand of the pourer.
8   **Water level indicator** This indicates maximum and minimum water levels for safety, and the number of cups each level will fill.

Jug kettles

Various brands of jug kettle are available. They are made of a special heat-resistant plastic, and can boil as little as a cupful of water or up to 1.5 litres, because of their tall shape. This saves energy and is useful for single people. When buying a jug kettle, look for the same features as for an ordinary kettle.

Cordless kettles

These have a base (often secured to the work surface by a suction pad for safety), connected by a cord to the electricity supply. The kettle is placed on the base for heating. As it has no cord it is safer and easier to use and carry around.

Capacity

Various sizes of kettle can be purchased, and the electrical rating will affect the amount of water it will boil in a certain time. As a guide:

a 2.4 kW kettle boils 1.5 litres of water in 4–4.5 minutes

a 3 kW kettle boils the same amount in 3–3.5 minutes.

Use

The water must cover the element otherwise it will be damaged. The electric plug must be switched off before the kettle is disconnected. It should be placed out of the reach of children.

Removing mineral residues

In hard water areas, the inside of a kettle becomes coated with insoluble mineral deposits or 'scale'. This reduces the efficiency of the element to heat the water, and particles of minerals come off into the water. Minerals can be removed by dissolving with a special kettle descaling liquid. Manufacturers' instructions should be carefully followed.

Kitchen scales

Accuracy in weighing out ingredients is fundamental to good results in food preparation. A variety of scales are available and it is worth buying a good brand to be sure of accuracy and durability.

Look for the following features when buying scales:

1 Easy-to-read dial in metric, and possibly imperial, measurements.
2 Scale pan big enough to take joints of meat and vegetables, as well as dry ingredients.
3 Scale pan which is easy to clean and remove.
4 Compact shape that is easy to store.
5 Hard-wearing and sturdy case.
6 Accurate measuring that can be adjusted if necessary.

Types of scale

The three main types of scale are shown below:
balance scales (top)
spring balance scales (middle)
electronic scales (bottom)

Balance scales have a pan at one end to which ingredients are added and a platform at the other to which weights are added until the two balance and are level. They are usually very accurate.

Spring balance scales are less accurate and are prone to becoming faulty. The scale holds a spring and as ingredients are put into the pan the spring depresses, indicating the weight by revolving a needle on the dial at the front of the scale. Some types have the useful feature of allowing the scale to be reset to zero after each ingredient is added. Some scales can be stored on the wall.

Diet scales are a special type of spring balance scale. They are useful for weighing small quantities (such as 5 g). There is more room on the dial to show the markings, so it is easier to weigh accurately.

Electronic scales with a visual display are accurate and easy to use. They may be battery or mains operated.

Use and care of scales

1 Never drop food into them, especially spring balance scales.
2 Never store spring balance scales with a weight in the pan as this will strain the spring.
3 Clean carefully after use.
4 Use on a flat, firm surface.
5 Do not immerse in water.

Cutlery

Many homes have two sets of cutlery, one for everyday use and another for special meals. In both cases, the following features of good design should be looked for:

1 Strong handles.
2 Well-balanced handles for ease of holding and using.
3 A good cutting edge on knives.
4 A good standard of finish.
5 Well-proportioned prongs on forks and bowls of spoons.
6 Easy-care design that can be cleaned without difficulty and will not retain food deposits in the pattern of the metal.

Cutlery is usually made from either stainless steel or electroplated nickel silver (EPNS). It is also possible to buy solid silver and bronze-plated cutlery but these are very expensive.

Stainless steel cutlery is durable and strong and will not discolour. It can be made into a variety of designs to suit most tastes, for everyday use or special meals.

EPNS This type of cutlery is normally kept for special meals, and after continual use the silver plating may wear off. The silver tends to discolour as it reacts with some foods, but this can be removed by using a special silver cleaner. EPNS cutlery should be treated with care to avoid damaging the silver plating and is best

stored neatly in a special cutlery canteen.

Range of cutlery normally purchased

table knives
knives for side plates (smaller)
table forks
fish knives (look for a design that can be used by both right- and left-handed people)
fish forks
table spoons (for serving)
dessert spoons
soup spoons
teaspoons
coffee spoons
dessert forks

Kitchen knives

A variety of kitchen knives are needed for different purposes, and it is best to buy a good brand with the following features:

1 A strong, easy-to-grip handle.
2 A well-made blade that can be resharpened and retains its sharpness well.
3 A rigid blade that does not bend when cutting (except palette knives which should be flexible).

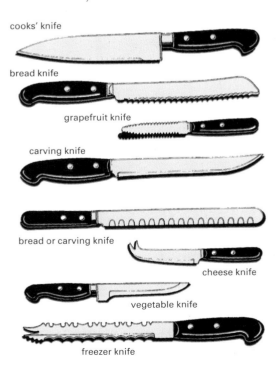

cooks' knife

bread knife

grapefruit knife

carving knife

bread or carving knife

cheese knife

vegetable knife

freezer knife

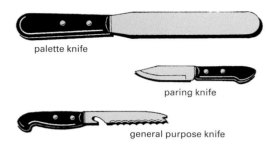

palette knife

paring knife

general purpose knife

Serrated knives have fine sharp points running along the blade. They remain sharp for a long time and are useful for slicing fruit and vegetables finely.

All sharp knives should be stored with the blades pointing downwards in a drawer or in a special rack. They should be used on a chopping board, cutting away from the body.

Equipment in commercial kitchens

The 'Food Safety (General Food Hygiene) Regulations 1995 – Catering Guide' lists the requirements for the construction and hygienic use of commercial equipment, including:

1 Any item that comes into contact with food must be kept clean and in good repair to minimize the risk of contamination of the food.
2 Cleaning must include disinfection if a high-risk food is prepared (e.g. meat, fish, dairy products)
3 Equipment must be made of hard-wearing, non-toxic materials, such as stainless steel, food-grade plastics, glass, ceramics, aluminium, tinned copper.
4 Equipment must be designed to allow easy dismantling and cleaning.

Food wrappings and kitchen papers

In addition to the wrapping materials that are used for freezing foods (see pp. 198-9), the following are commonly used in the kitchen.

Greaseproof paper

This is resistant to grease and is used for:
    lining cake tins
    wrapping foods for packed lunches

    covering puddings that are to be steamed
    covering meat joints in the oven
    tracing decorations on to cakes
It is available in sheets, bags, or rolls.

Baking parchment

This is specially made with a non-stick surface and can be used for:
    piping bags
    baking meringues
    separating meat joints for freezing

Waxed paper

This has a layer of wax on both sides and can be used for:
    separating meat joints in the freezer
    wrapping packed lunches
    sealing home-made jam

Rice paper

This is an edible paper which can be used to bake items such as macaroons that stick to a baking sheet and cannot be removed easily. The rice paper can be eaten with the macaroon.

Plastic cling film

This is a useful wrapping as it clings easily to itself and most other surfaces forming a seal over food. It is particularly useful for storing left-over foods in the refrigerator so that they do not dry out, and can also be used to wrap packed lunches. It is not suitable for use on its own in the freezer as it is easily torn and may not form a completely protective layer over the food. See p. 245 for problems with clingfilm.

Aluminium foil

In addition to its use in freezing, aluminium foil may be used for:
    covering casseroles or roasting meat
    lining casseroles containing food to be frozen
    wrapping foods (e.g. corn on the cob, potatoes) to be baked in the oven or on a barbecue
    covering foods that are to be steamed
    wrapping foods for refrigerator storage
It is a good conductor of heat, and is light, strong, and easy to wrap around dishes.

Textiles in the kitchen

Cotton and linen are traditionally used for making teatowels, dishcloths, tablecloths, and serviettes, because they are:

strong and hard-wearing

absorbent

easily dyed

washable at high temperatures

Man-made textiles are cheaper but less suitable for teatowels and dishcloths.

Oven gloves can be made from cotton or linen, or a mixture of these and man-made textiles, but they must have several layers of padding to insulate the hands from heat.

The care labels for cotton and linen are as follows:

Cotton
hot wash (60°C); do not bleach; hot iron; may be dry cleaned; tumble dry

Linen
hot wash (95°C); chlorine bleach may be used; hot iron; do not dry clean; do not tumble dry

Revision questions

1. What is the main advantage of owning an electric mixer, or food processor?
2. What are the features of a well-designed and efficient mixer, blender, and food processor?
3. What are the uses of hand-held mixers?
4. What attachments can be obtained for free-standing mixers and what are their advantages?
5. How should mixers, blenders, and food processors be looked after?
6. What are blenders used for?
7. What are food processors and what are they used for?
8. What is the main advantage of owning a dishwasher?
9. How do dishwashers clean items and why is the whole process hygienic?
10. What items should not be placed in a dish-washer?
11. Why are heated food trays useful?
12. What types of pans are most useful in the kitchen?
13. What metals are used for pans and why?
14. What are the features of a well-designed pan?
15. What are the features of a well-designed electric kettle?
16. How should an electric kettle be used so that it is safe and lasts a long time?
17. What are the three main types of kitchen scales and how do they work?
18. How should scales be used so that they remain accurate?
19. What are the features of well-designed cutlery?
20. What are the features of good kitchen knives?
21. List three kitchen wrapping materials and say what they are used for.

Consumer protection

A wide variety of goods and services are available to consumers today, and in order to protect them from unfair trading, poor service, bad workmanship, and unsafe goods, a number of Acts of Parliament and Codes of Practice have been established to cover most aspects of trade and business.

Consumers need to be aware of their rights under the law, and should find out how they can seek compensation or advice when necessary. To get the best value for money when buying goods or services, follow these guidelines.

1. Find out about the goods or service in detail before buying, and compare different types and makes for quality, value, design, after-sales service, and suitability.
2. Ask for a demonstration of use for large pieces of equipment.
3. Read instructions and information leaflets carefully and thoroughly, particularly guarantees and servicing details.
4. Ask the opinions of people who have bought a similar item or service.
5. Consult consumer magazines such as *Which?*

6 Keep all receipts and sales agreements for large pieces of equipment and services.

7 Do not let yourself be pressurized into buying goods or paying for a service that you have not had time to consider.

Whenever a person buys goods or a service, they enter into a contract with the seller. The contract gives both parties rights and obligations, which are covered by law and by codes of practice, which are followed by many trade associations. Several consumers' associations also exist to monitor the interests of consumers and to deal with complaints.

In the UK people are protected by two types of law:

criminal law

civil law

Criminal law aims to prevent behaviour that would be harmful to the community as a whole, e.g. fraud or dangerous acts such as selling unfit food or unsafe appliances. People who break the law in this way are prosecuted and can be fined or imprisoned.

Civil law is mainly concerned with people's obligations to one another, as in a contract between a customer and a shopkeeper. If a consumer feels he or she has been wrongly treated, then they may enforce their rights under the law and take the matter to court.

Both criminal and civil law can be statutory, i.e. contained in Acts of Parliament. The following Acts (listed alphabetically) are some of the many that exist to help the consumer. They must be upheld by manufacturers, shops, services, and other bodies that sell to the public. They are all carefully worded in legal terms and regularly updated.

Consumer Credit Act 1974

Covers control of consumer credit.

Requires credit traders to be licensed.

Controls credit advertising, wording on documents, credit charges, credit reference agencies, and debt collecting.

Consumer Protection Act 1987

Protects consumers by regulating the goods and services they buy.

Prohibits supply of unsafe goods, and requires unsafe goods to be removed from sale immediately.

Sets safety standards for manufacturers and organizations to follow.

Requires manufacturers and retailers to inform consumers when unsafe goods have been on sale, so that they can return them.

Prohibits misleading information about prices.

European Communities Act 1972

Prohibits supply of goods that are not of a specified standard or composition.

Requires safety controls on certain goods.

Fair Trading Act 1973

Promotes the fair trading of goods and services.

Controls restrictive practices so that traders and consumers are fairly treated.

Food Safety Act 1990

See pp. 159–61 for details.

Food and Environment Protection Act 1985

Protects public from food made unsafe because of substances in the environment, e.g. misused pesticides, fish from polluted waters.

Prices Acts 1974 and 1975

Encourages fair trading, protection, and price information for consumers.

Controls how prices and sale prices of goods are displayed and indicated.

Sale of Goods Act 1979

Goods must be of merchantable quality, i.e. fit for the purpose for which they were intended; must perform in the way that the seller has told the consumer they will; and must match the description given.

Consumers are entitled to a refund or compensation if any of the above requirements are broken, except where the consumer is aware of faults, damage, or 'second' quality before purchase.

The Act covers second-hand, reduced-price, and sale goods, sold by manufacturers, mail-order firms, and market traders.

Traders are not obliged to give receipts and are not allowed to refuse refunds on faulty goods without a receipt (but it is best to keep receipts to avoid problems if a fault occurs).

Trade Descriptions Act 1968
Prohibits false or misleading descriptions of goods.
Prohibits false claims about goods and services.

Weights and Measures Act 1985
Controls weighing and measuring equipment used by manufacturers, retailers, and suppliers of services.
Advises on and regulates quality-control systems in manufacturing and packaging establishments.
Requires quantities of goods to be displayed on the package.

In addition, many retailers and manufacturers give quality-assurance guarantees. If a product is found to be faulty, consumers are invited to return it, and will receive a replacement or a refund of money. Manufacturers like to know how, where, and when the fault occurred, so that they can put it right and prevent it from being repeated.

How to complain
If a consumer feels that a trader has broken any of these Acts, or if goods have to be returned to the trader for any reason, they need to be aware of their rights under the law. Several organizations exist to help the consumer if complaining to a trader proves unsuccessful. These include:
Citizens' Advice Bureaux
local council consumer advice centres
local trading standards departments (sometimes called consumer protection or weights and measures departments)
local council environmental health departments
On a national scale there are the following:
Department of Trade and Industry
Ministry of Agriculture, Fisheries, and Food
Department of Social Security
Lord Chancellor's Office
However, these would only be called in to help if the local authorities were unable to obtain a satisfactory settlement or if the case was serious.

The Office of Fair Trading, which was set up under the 1973 Fair Trading Act, protects consumers' and traders' interests by:
1 Publishing information to help people to know their rights.
2 Encouraging trade organizations to issue codes of practice to raise standards of service and deal with complaints.
3 Monitoring traders and checking up on those who break the law.
4 Controlling practices that are not in the interests of consumers or other traders, e.g. monopolies (where one trader supplies and controls a product or service so that no one else can compete with it).
5 Licensing firms that give credit or hire out goods to consumers.
The Office does not deal with individual cases of consumer complaints, or disputes with traders.

There are also public consumer 'watchdog' and consultative councils, some of which deal with goods and services. These include:
Oftel – telecommunications
Ofgas – gas supply
Ofwat – water supply
Consumers' Association (produces magazines and reports on a variety of goods and services)
National Consumer Council
National Federation of Consumer Goods
Parents for Safe Food
Food Commission

Paying for goods and services
The development of computer technology has enabled traders and customers to choose a method of payment that best suits their needs.

Cash is convenient for small items but there is a risk of theft and loss if large amounts are carried. Cash-dispensing machines with a direct computer link to a bank or building society account are found in most high streets and shopping centres.

Credit cards (e.g. Access, Visa) enable customers to buy goods up to a certain value (the credit limit), then pay the credit company later, either in small monthly payments, or in a lump sum. The credit company charges interest if the sum is paid off over several months, which

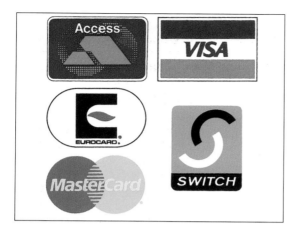

them to pay for goods, e.g. at Christmas. This helps spread the cost, and is especially useful to low income families.

can be expensive. It is easy to get into debt, and consumers must be sure that they can pay off the credit without running short of money.

Bank link cards (e.g. Switch, Delta) enable customers to pay for goods by a computer link between the trader and bank. As long as the account has enough money in it, the trader can transfer the customer's money to pay for the goods. Many supermarkets offer a 'cash back' facility, which enables customers to use a bank card to obtain cash after buying goods. The shop links their computer with the customer's bank account, gives out the required sum, and the account is debited accordingly.

Credit accounts (e.g. storecards and chargecards), enable customers to buy goods from a particular trader and pay over an agreed period of time. Some traders charge interest for this facility, in which case the customer may end up paying a lot more for the goods than the original price. There is a risk to the trader that the customer may not keep up payments.

Direct debit and standing order schemes enable customers to have their bills paid at an agreed time (e.g. every month) by direct computer link between the bank and trader. This ensures that bills are paid on time and may help to spread the cost.

Many supermarkets and petrol companies offer a **points scheme**. Customers earn points every time they buy goods, and in return receive vouchers, savings coupons, goods, or cash when they reach a specified number of points.

Some supermarkets offers **savings schemes** in which where customers buy stamps and use

Revision questions

1 What guidelines should consumers follow in order to get the best value for money from goods and services?
2 What is the difference between civil and criminal law?
3 What are the three main principles of the Sale of Goods Act?
4 If a consumer takes back faulty goods under this law, what is the trader obliged to do for the customer?
5 What is the Consumer Protection Act and why is it enforced?
6 What does the Prices Act enforce?
7 What does the Trade Descriptions Act enforce?
8 How does the Weights and Measures Act affect the retail of food?
9 Which local organizations exist to help consumers with individual problems?
10 Which national organizations exist to protect and help all consumers and traders?
11 What are codes of practice?
12 Name three methods of obtaining credit. Give the advantages and disadvantages of each.
13 What is meant by the credit limit on a credit card?

Kitchen safety

Every year, thousands of accidents occur in the home, and the kitchen is one of the main areas of potential danger. Many accidents can be prevented and only happen because insufficient attention is paid to safety precautions. This does not mean that people should be constantly on guard, but that living safely should become a habit.

The following lists of dangers and safety precautions are grouped according to areas in the kitchen. Many of them are a matter of common sense.

Danger	Precaution
Food preparation	
Knives	Keep sharp. Use on a chopping board, cutting away from the body. Store away from the reach of children, with sharp blades pointing downwards.
Cooker	Fit a pan guard around the hob to stop children pulling pans down. Always use oven gloves to remove items from the oven. Turn off hotplates and burners after use.
Frying	Never overfill pan with fat. Never leave pan unguarded. Heat to required temperature and no higher. Keep pan handle turned inwards. Keep a lid nearby in case fat ignites. Turn off the heat after use.
Steaming	Keep face away from pan when removing lid. Do not allow pan to boil dry.
Clothing	Keep sleeves rolled up, scarves, ties, etc. tucked in, tie hair back out of the way of flames or electric mixers. Avoid wearing high-heeled or loosely fitting shoes which may cause a fall.

Danger	Precaution
Floor	
Spillages	Wipe up immediately.
Surface	Do not polish the surface too highly or put loose mats on a polished surface. Keep the floor clear of obstructions. Ensure that there are no curled edges or broken tiles which could be tripped over.

Danger	Precaution
Electrical equipment	
Wiring	Check that plugs are wired correctly, that there are no bare wires exposed anywhere along the length of flex, and that the flex is not frayed. Check that there is no undue strain on the wire. Keep wires well out of the reach of children, and where they will not be tripped over.
Plugs	Check that these are not broken and do not have screws missing. Do not touch with wet hands. Switch off socket before removing plug to avoid getting a shock from the pins as they are pulled out.

EARTH WIRE
Yellow and green

FUSE, a safety device which stops the current if the circuit is overloaded, e.g. if an appliance is faulty

LIVE WIRE
Brown

NEUTRAL WIRE
Blue

Clamp for wires
Ensure that wire sheath is securely held to avoid pulling the wires from their contacts

Wiring a plug

Danger	Precaution
Sockets	Cover when not in use to prevent children from putting items into the pin holes. Do not overload by running several items from an adapter plug.

Danger	Precaution
Electrical equipment (continued)	
Equipment	Buy reliable makes that are covered by a British Standard or other safety check (see below). Use according to instructions. Have equipment serviced regularly. Store in a dry place with the wiring neatly placed to avoid bending it.
Fuses	Use the correct fuse for the appliance, i.e. 3 amps for appliances up to 700 W 5 amps for appliances up to 1200 W 13 amps for appliances up to 3000 W.

Danger	Precaution
Cleaning materials	Store out of reach of children. Do not put into empty soft drinks bottles, because they may be drunk by mistake. Never mix lavatory powder cleaners with bleach as this causes a dangerous reaction. Wear rubber gloves when using caustic solutions.
Fires	Put a guard around all fires, especially where there are children around. Do not dry clothes around fires.
Table cloths	Avoid using where there are toddlers who may pull on them, making items on the table fall off.

Other equipment

Danger	Precaution
Storage	Avoid storing heavy items in high cupboards or on high shelves where they may be difficult to retrieve. Avoid stacking equipment where it may fall down. Check that cupboards are securely fixed to the walls. Store sharp or bladed equipment safely. Stand on a specially designed kitchen stool or other stable chair to remove items from high cupboards.

Miscellaneous

Danger	Precaution
Tea towels	Do not hang over cooker to dry.
Curtains	Keep away from flames.
Movement	Never run in a kitchen. Avoid walking around with heavy, hot, or sharp items. Avoid reaching over cooker, and keep face away from steam and hot air from the oven.

Safety symbols

Various boards and councils have been established to set and maintain standards of safety to protect consumers from unsafe goods. In many cases, manufacturers have to submit their products for testing if they are to be allowed to sell them to the public. Goods that meet such requirements bear a symbol of approval from the board that governs those particular goods. These symbols include:

The Kitemark This appears on many items that comply with the BSI (British Standards Institution) codes of practice.

The Safety Mark This appears only on goods that comply with the British Standards for safety, e.g. gas appliances, light fittings.

BSI SAFETY MARK

The British Electrotechnical Approvals Board sign appears on most domestic electrical appliances, and it is an assurance that the product is safe.

Furniture Safety
Under the Consumer Safety Act, this symbol must appear on new furniture (upholstered) if it is not resistant to lighted cigarettes, matches, or both. The label must be permanent.

National Inspection Council for Electrical Installation Contracting
Reliable electrical contractors may display this label and they are regularly inspected to protect the consumer against faulty, unsafe, or defective workmanship.

British Gas This appears on products that have passed British Gas standards for performance, reliability, and fitness for purpose.

Many homes now have domestic fire extinguishers, fire blankets, or smoke detectors, which are simple to operate and effective in use. They should comply with British Standards and be regularly checked. It is important to follow the manufacturer's instructions for using extinguishers, and to remember that water-operated ones must not be used on electrical or chemical fires.

A fire extinguisher can be kept in the kitchen.

First aid

If an accident occurs, in the home or anywhere else, it is important to know how to treat the injured person before expert medical help arrives. The following instructions cover the most common causes of injury. It is very useful for anyone to follow a first aid course, such as those run by the St. John's Ambulance Brigade.

Heavy bleeding

1. Lie patient down and raise injured part to reduce blood flow.
2. Press a clean pad on to wound and maintain pressure for 10 minutes, until clot forms.
3. Remove loose dirt but do not probe wound.
4. Apply a clean dressing firmly to wound. If anything is lodged in it, put a dressing around it.

Broken bones

These are of three types:

a Open fracture (bone is protruding through skin).

b Closed fracture (no open wound; may be internal damage to organs).

c Dislocation (one or more bones pulled out of a joint).

1 Do not move the patient.
2 Make them comfortable.
3 Cover open wounds.
4 Immobilize the injured part with a splint.
5 Bandage it for support.
6 If possible, raise the injured part to prevent swelling and pain.
7 Loosen clothing, cover patient with blanket.
8 Do not give patient anything to eat or drink.

Burns and scalds

1 Cool the whole area with cold water for several minutes to kill the pain and reduce risk of blistering.
2 Do not remove clothing that has been burnt.
3 Remove clothing that has been soaked in a corrosive chemical (protect own hands first).
4 Remove jewellery if possible as the area may swell.
5 Cover the area with a clean cloth to reduce the risk of infection.
6 Lie patient down and keep them warm.
7 Badly burned patients may be given sips of water.
8 Protect blisters, do not burst them.
9 If clothing catches fire, throw patient to the floor and smother flames with a rug or blanket.

Choking

1 A series of sharp blows between the shoulder blades may dislodge the obstruction. Try to get the person to bend over so that the head is lower than the chest.
2 If this does not work, try to hook out the obstruction with a finger.
3 Small children should be turned upside down and hit on the back.
4 As a last resort, use the Heimlich manoeuvre. Stand or kneel behind the patient, with one arm around their abdomen. Hold your fist with your other hand. Pull both hands towards you quickly, thrusting your elbows inward and upwards to compress the patient's abdomen. The aim is to push out and dislodge the obstruction. This may cause internal injury to a young child, and should only be used for older children and adults.

Electric shock

1 If possible switch off the power supply. Do not touch the patient until this is done.
2 If this is not possible, push the patient away from the appliance with a wooden handle or stick.
3 Look for signs that the patient is breathing, and if necessary begin resuscitation (see p. 270).

Poisoning

The following can all cause poisoning:

acids	lavatory cleaner
ammonia	metal polish
bleach	oven cleaner
carbolic soap	paint thinner
carpet cleaner	paraffin
caustic soda	petrol
detergents	rust remover
polish	shoe polish
grease remover	washing soda

1 Telephone for ambulance.
2 Do not induce vomiting.
3 Dilute the poison by giving tepid milk or water in sips.
4 Wipe face and lips gently with cloth or sponge.
5 Do not pour water into the mouth of an unconscious patient as this may choke them.

If the patient has swallowed pills, try to make them vomit by putting fingers into their throat. Do not give salt water or anything else to make them vomit.

Shock

Shock is a medical term used to describe the effect on the body of a large loss of blood or other body fluid following severe bleeding, burning, heart failure, persistent vomiting or diarrhoea, or an emergency operation. The symptoms of shock are:

cold, clammy skin, heavy sweating

faintness, blurred vision

nausea, vomiting

confusion, anxiety

thirst

shallow breathing, may be rapid

rapid, weak pulse

This is a serious situation and should be treated immediately.

1 Lie patient down with feet raised and head on one side.
2 Try to stop the loss of blood or fluid.
3 Call for medical help.
4 Loosen tight clothing. Do not move unnecessarily.
5 Cover patient with a blanket.
6 Do not give anything to drink.

In all cases of injury, seek medical advice when first aid has been administered.

Resuscitation

If someone has stopped breathing it is important to start mouth-to-mouth resuscitation before medical help arrives in order to save their life. The brain suffers damage if it is without oxygen for more than three minutes and death will follow soon after.

What to do:

1 Check the patient's breathing. If it has stopped:
2 Clear the mouth by removing false teeth, dirt, or any other objects.
3 Bend the head back with one hand and push the jaw upwards with the other to lift the tongue away from the back of the throat.

4 Squeeze the nostrils together, place your mouth over the patient's mouth, and blow gently. Watch for the chest to rise.

5 Let the chest fall (take your mouth away) then repeat about fifteen times a minute, continuing until the patient starts to breathe again or until help arrives.

6 Place the patient in the recovery position, with the head to one side in case of vomiting, and one arm underneath to prevent the patient rolling on to his or her back.

7 If the heart has stopped, it will need to be massaged. Press on the lower half of the breast bone using the heel of one hand and the other on top. Press about once a second five times, then continue mouth-to-mouth resuscitation. Repeat until the heart starts beating and breathing is continuous.

First aid kit

A first aid kit should always be kept in the home, to treat both minor and more serious injuries. It should contain:

adhesive plasters (various sizes) for minor cuts and grazes

prepared wound dressings

sterilized cotton wool

gauze bandages in a roll

triangular bandages for slings

crepe bandage

safety pins

tweezers

scissors

roll of surgical tape

antiseptic solution to clean wounds

antiseptic cream

Revision questions

1 Study the diagram below and list all the possible dangers in the kitchen:

2 What should you do if:
   a the wires from a plug become frayed?
   b the fuse in a plug 'blows' and the piece of equipment fails to work?

3 What are the wiring colours for
   a the earth wire in a plug
   b the neutral wire in a plug
   c the live wire in a plug?

4 How does the British Standards Institution protect consumers?

5 What first aid should be applied for the following injuries?
   a a deep cut to the arm
   b a suspected broken leg
   c a scalded hand
   d an electric shock
   e poisoning from swallowing bleach
   f swallowing pills

6 What should a first aid kit contain?

Questions and activities

1 Study the chart below which shows facts and figures about some fridge freezers.

a Which is the most expensive model?

b Which freezer holds the most?

c Which fridge holds the least?

d Which model would be the easiest to pull out and clean behind?

e Which models have the freezer at the top?

f Which models are rather noisy?

g Which models have a poor fridge temperature range? What problems might this cause?

h What does 'electrical efficiency' mean? Why is it important?

i What is the purpose of adjustable feet?

j What does 'poor freezer storage flexibility' mean? What problems might this present?

k Which model would you choose for the following situations? Give reasons.
- a single pensioner with a small kitchen
- a family of four
- a married couple who grow their own vegetables and fruit

	Candy Eco System CCM28/12G	Creda Coldstore 86404	Hotpoint Iced Diamond RF60A	Lec T250W	Lec T455 WS	Servis M765	Tricity Bendix FD804W	Zanussi ZFC60/30LE
Specification								
Price (£)	370	320	480	230	300	370	250	490
Country of origin	UK	Italy	UK	UK	UK	Italy	UK	Italy
Annual running cost	35	51	46	35	41	60¹	43	23
Height x width x depth (cm)	162x55x61	135x55x61	167x55x62	120x53x64	149x54x65	168x51x59	139x51x60	166x60x60
Fridge storage volume (litres)	147	99	146	98	85	126	106	147
Freezer storage volume (litres)	75	77	105	62	93	94	65	70
Features								
Fridge temperature indicator								
Freezer temperature indicator								
Adjustable feet	2	2	2	2	2	2	4	2
Bottles fit upright in main comp.				✓	✓			✓
Hidden evaporator	✓					✓		✓
Fridge shelves (inc. half shelves)	4	3	4	3	2	4	3	5
Freezer compartments/drawers	3	3	4	1	3	4	2	3
Freezer on top				✓			✓	
Fridge on top	✓	✓	✓		✓	✓		✓
Performance								
Thermostat setting ①	☆	○	☆	★	☆	○	★	○
Fridge temperature range ②	★	◗	☆	★	★	●	★	◗
Fridge temperature stability ③	☆	★	★	★	★	☆	★	★
Freezer temperature stability ③	○	☆	☆	★	☆	☆	★	★
Defrosting	○	○	●	○	○	○	○	○
Electrical efficiency ④	☆	◗	○	◗	◗	◗¹	◗	★
Noise	◗	○	◗	○	○	◗	○	○
Freezing capacity (kg/24hr) ⑤	5	12	18	7	12	see²	5	10
Drawbacks								
No audible or visible warning	✗	✗		✗			✗	
Reset thermostat after freezing	✗				✗			
No rollers/ castors	✗	✗	✗	✗	✗	✗	✗	
Poor freezer storage flexibility	✗				✗		✗	
No bottle grip/rack divider			✗					
Poor fridge storage flexibility					✗	✗		
Total test score	7	7	7	7	7	5	7	8

Key

★ = best
☆
○
◗
● = worst

✓ = Has this feature
✗ = Has this drawback

Performance:
① How closely it kept to the correct temperatures in normal conditions using the recommended setting.
② Those with a poor rating had a wide temperature range between their coldest and warmest parts.
③ How well it maintained the right temperatures as the room became warmer and colder.

④ This takes capacity into account. The higher the rating the cheaper to run.
⑤ The amount of fresh food that can be frozen in 24 hours. We had problems with some one-control models. Frozen food in the Servis M765 warmed up when we added fresh food to the freezer, and the fridge became too cold.

Total test score
This score, out of ten, takes into account all our test results but gives most weight to the more important tests. These are: Energy efficiency: 25 per cent, Freezer temp stability: 20 per cent, Freezing ability: 15 per cent, Noise: 10 per cent, Defrosting: 7.5 per cent.

(Source: *Which?* August 1995)

2 Study the chart on cook's knives on the right.

   a Which knife costs the most?

   b Which knife has the longest blade?

   c Which knife is the lightest?

   d Why is it important to be able to grip the handle comfortably?

   e Why is an easy-to-control blade important?

   f Which knives stayed sharp? Why is this an advantage?

   g Why is it inadvisable to use a blunt knife?

   h What does 'resistance to corrosion' mean?
   Which knives are likely to corrode?

i Which knife would you choose for the following people? Give reasons.

   a tall, young man, who has just passed exams to qualify him as a chef

   an elderly aunt, who has arthritis in her hands

   three students who are setting up home in a flat and will be sharing the cooking

   a person who is setting up a sandwich-making business from home

3 Study the chart on saucepans on the right.

   a Which is the most expensive pan? Why?

   b Which models are not easy to pour from?

   c What are the advantages of having wooden or plastic handles?

   d Why is handle strength important?

   e What problem might left-handed people experience with pans that have a pouring lip?

   f Which type of pans are easy to clean?

   g Why is the weight of the pan important?

   h What does 'stability on hobs' mean?

   i What test was used to see how evenly the pans heat food?

   j What type of pan did food stick to the most?

k Which pans would you choose for the following situations? Give reasons.

   a person with weak hands and wrists

   a newly married couple, setting up home

   a small restaurant

l How are consumers protected and what should they do, if the following happens?

   a new pan handle becomes dangerously loose after 5 uses

   the handles of a new set of pans become cracked after 3 sessions in a dishwasher

   the base of a pan buckles when heated causing the pan to rock on the hob

	Boots Recycled Cook's Knife	Boots Sabatier Diamond Cook's Knife	Global G-2	Gustav Emil Ern 85P	Ikea Drabant Cook's Knife	J A Henckeis Four Star Chef's Knife	Kitchen Devils French Cook's Knife	Kitchen Devils Professional Cook's Knife	Laser 7 Cook's Knife	Laser Fusion Edge Cook's Knife
Specification										
Price (£) ①	7	15	31	22	11	45	6	15	12	17
Country of origin	Germany	France	Japan	Germany	Japan	Germany	UK	UK	UK	UK
Weight (g)	115	150	155	175	160	210	75	175	160	145
Blade length (cm)	20	20	20	20	19	20	16	21	20	20
Serrated edge									✓	✓
Features										
Comfortable grip	✓		✓	✓				✓	✓	
Easy-to-control blade		✓			✓					✓
Uncomfortable grip						✗				
Handle short for larger hands		✗			✗		✗			
To heavy for some users						✗				
Performance										
Initial sharpness ②	☆	○	☆	☆	☆	★	★	☆	○	☆
Staying sharp ③	○	◗	☆	★	○	☆	★	★	★	★
Resistance to corrosion	☆	☆	★	☆	◗	◗	☆	○	☆	◗
Ease of resharpening ④	☆	○	○	☆	○	☆	☆	☆	◗	◗
Chopping parsley ⑤	☆	★	★	☆	☆	☆	○	○	●	●
Slicing carrots ⑤	☆	★	★	☆	☆	☆	☆	◗	◗	◗
Finely slicing cucumber ⑤	★	★	★	★	★	☆	★	☆	○	○
Total test score	8	7	9	8	6	6	8	7	6	6

Specification

① This is the price you can expect to pay by shopping around. Most of these knives are also sold in sets, which can work out cheaper.

Performance

② Our tests use a special edge-testing machine which measures how far each knife will cut through a swatch of silica coated paper.

③ Using the same machine, we measured how sharp each knife was after 60 cuts.

④ We measured how much the blade increased in sharpness after ten strokes through a knife sharpener.

⑤ Testers from the Consumer Studies Department of the University of North London assessed the knives for a range of cutting tasks: rapid chopping (chopping parsley); cutting through harder vegetables (slicing carrots); and delicate, accurate work (slicing cucumber).

Total test score

This score, out of ten, takes into account all our test results. It ignores price, and gives more weight to the more important tests. These are: Initial sharpness: 15 per cent; Corrosion resistance: 20 per cent; Staying sharp: 20 per cent; User trial: 35 per cent

(Source: *Which?* July 1995)

Key

★ = best
☆
○
◗
● = worst

✓ = Has this feature
✗ = Has this drawback

	Non-stick: aluminium					Stainless steel		Cast iron		Copper
	Debenhams Le Vrai Gourmet	**Morphy Richards** Canterbury	**Prestige** Debut	**Tefal** Classic	**Tefal Resistal**	**Cuisinox** Elysée	**Pretsige** Cuisine	**Le Creuset** Traditional	**Morso**	**Castle**
Specification										
Price per pan (£) ①	44		25	12	21	53	47	38	36	85
Number of pans per set	3 or 5	5	3 or 4			3 or 4	3 or 5	5		
Price per set (£)	115/170	30	68/88			160/220	100/150	179		
Country of origin	Thailand	UK	Spain/UK	France	France	France	UK	France	Denmark	R of Ireland
Handle material ②	Plastic	Plastic	Plastic	Plastic	Aluminium	Steel	Wood	Wood	Wood	Brass
Steam vent on lid ②		✓		✓	✓					
Features										
Dishwasher safe		✓	✓	✓	✓	✓				
Lightweight in use	✓	✓	✓	✓	✓	✗		✗	✗	✗
Comfortable handle	✓		✓	✓	✓	✓				✗
Pan easy to clean	✓	✓	✓	✓	✓	✗	✗	✗	✗	✗
Easy to pour	✓	✓	✓	✓	✓	✓	✓			✓
Performance										
Speed of heating	☆	☆	☆	☆	☆	☆	☆	○	◗	☆
Evenness of heating ③	○	○	☆	◗	○	○	◗	○	◗	◗
Stability on hobs ④	☆	○	☆	☆	☆	☆	◗	☆	☆	☆
Sticking food ⑤	☆	★	★	★	★	◗	◗	●	●	◗
Drop test ⑥	○	○	○	☆	☆	○	○	●	○	★
Handle strength ⑦	○	☆	☆	★	★	★	○	★	★	★

Specification and Convenience

① This is the price for an 18cm (7 inch) pan, or the nearest equivalent.

② See 'Making the right choice', p38.

  ✓ = good for this.

  ✗ = bad for this.

  Pans with no rating were average.

Performance

A team from the Consumer Studies Department of the University of North London assessed each pan for weight, balance, pouring and cleaning by making scrambled eggs, and boiling water and pouring it into different sized containers. They then washed and dried the pans to see which were easiest to clean. An experienced chef and recipe developer made a sauce to assess low temperature performance, too.

③ We assessed evenness of heating by melting sugar crystals over a low heat.

④ See 'Hob types', p38.

⑤ Food burnt on to those pans with a ◗ or ● rating, and was difficult to remove.

⑥ We dropped the pans five times from a height of one metre on to a concrete floor.

  ★ = undamaged

  ☆ = slight damage

  ○ = damaged but usable

  ◗ = barely usable

  ● = unusable

⑦ How well the handle was secured to the pan.

Key

★ = best
☆
○
◗
● = worst

✓ = Has this feature
✗ = Has this drawback

(Source: *Which?* May 1995)

4 Working in a kitchen can present problems and dangers to a disabled person.

   a List some problems and dangers which might be experienced by

       a partially sighted person

       a wheelchair-bound person

       a person with arthritic hands, knees, and hips

   b Find out and list some of the ways in which these problems and dangers can be overcome or avoided for each person.

   c Find out and list any organizations that offer help and advice to disabled people living at home.

5 The following is part of a fictional report from environmental health officers, who have visited the kitchen of a small high street cafe.

'The kitchen failed to meet the required standards for these reasons:

   1 The ceiling is constructed of old fibre tiles, some of which are missing and loose.

   2 Large amounts of spider webs are attached to the ceiling and pipes.

   3 There are cracks in many of the wall tiles, and several are missing.

   4 There is only one china sink and wooden draining board. The sink is badly stained and the draining board split in several places.

   5 The work tops are cluttered with equipment, much of which appears not to have been moved recently.

   6 The staff toilet leads directly into the kitchen by a single door.

   7 There is a large (overflowing) rubbish bin situated near the food storage area.

   8 The windows and back door lead out to a yard containing empty boxes and other accumulated refuse, stacked against the outside wall of the kitchen.'

What alterations and repairs would the owners of this cafe need to make, to satisfy the requirements of the food safety regulations? Give reasons for your answers.

Weights

It is difficult and impractical to convert imperial weights into metric weights exactly, therefore 25 g is used as equivalent to 1 oz (exact conversion: 1 oz = 28.35 g). As this conversion is slightly less than the imperial measurements, it is necessary to adjust the quantities of ingredients used above 100 g, by rounding them up to the nearest 25 g, as shown in the chart below.

| Imperial/oz | Metric/g | |
	practical conversion	exact conversion
1	25	28.35
2	50	56.70
3	75	85.05
4 ($\frac{1}{4}$lb)	100	113.40
5	150	141.75
6	175	170.10
7	200	198.45
8 ($\frac{1}{2}$lb)	225	226.80
9	250	255.15
10	275	283.50
11	300	311.85
12 ($\frac{3}{4}$lb)	350	340.19
13	375	368.54
14	400	396.89
15	425	425.24
16 (1lb)	450	453.59

Liquid measures

As with weights, exact conversions from fluid ounces to millilitres are impractical, therefore the following equivalents are used:

| Imperial/floz | Metric/ml | |
	practical conversion	exact conversion
1	25	28.41
2	50	56.83
3	75	85.24
4	100	113.65
5 ($\frac{1}{4}$ pint)	150	142.07
10 ($\frac{1}{2}$ pint)	275	284.13
15 ($\frac{3}{4}$ pint)	425	426.20
20 (1 pint)	575	568.26

Oven temperatures

	Uses	Gas	°C	°F
very cool	warming plates	$\frac{1}{4}$	110	225
	keeping food hot	$\frac{1}{2}$	120	250
cool	egg custard milk puddings	1	140	275
cool	rich fruit cakes braising	2	150	300
moderate	shortbread meat loaves stews, casseroles	3	160	325
moderate	gingerbread fish	4	180	350
fairly hot	Victoria sandwich rubbed-in cakes	5	190	375
fairly hot	choux pastry Swiss roll baked soufflés	6	200	400
hot	roasting flaky pastry batters	7	220	425
very hot	bread scones	8	230	450
very hot	small puff pastry items browning of foods	9	240	475

For fan ovens, reduce the temperature by 25°C. For example, a fan oven set at 175°C is as hot as a conventional oven set at 200°C. A shorter cooking time may also be needed.

Refer to the manufacturer's instruction booklet for details.

Index

If more then one page number is given, look up the **bold** one first.